GAIA'S GARDEN

GAIA'S GARDEN

A GUIDE TO HOME-SCALE PERMACULTURE

TOBY HEMENWAY

CHELSEA GREEN PUBLISHING COMPANY

White River Junction, Vermont

For Kiel

AND IN LOVING MEMORY OF

MY FATHER, TEE,

AND

MY SISTER LESLIE

Designed by Dede Cummings and Carol Stephens.

Printed in the United States.

11 10 09 08   10 11 12 13

Library of Congress Cataloging-in-Publication Data

Hemenway, Toby, 1952–
Gaia's Garden: a guide to home-scale permaculture / Toby Hemenway
    p. cm.
Includes bibliographical references and index (p.).
ISBN 1-890132-52-7 (alk. paper)
1. Natural landscaping. 2. Organic gardening. 3. Permaculture. 4. Gaia
    hypothesis. I. Title.

SB439 .H44 2001
635'.048—dc21   2001017353

Chelsea Green Publishing Company
P.O. Box 428
White River Junction, VT 05001
(800) 639-4099
www.chelseagreen.com

CONTENTS

PART THREE
ASSEMBLING THE ECOLOGICAL GARDEN

Photos and
Illustrations

Photos and Illustrations, continued

Tables

FOREWORD

by John Todd

As the readers of *Gaia's Garden* will discover, Nature is an extraordinary designer. I teach ecological design to university students and one of my favorite teaching tools is a simple one. My students collect samples from at least three aquatic habitats, such as a wet pool in the woods, an animal wallow on a farm, and a pond or lake, and mix them together in a glass jar. With lids screwed on tightly, the students turn their jars upside down and place them in sunny windows to watch and record the unfolding drama within. I myself have kept such a jar near my desk for several years.

In the presence of sunlight, a microcosm, or miniature world, begins to organize itself. Tiny bubbles of oxygen congregate under small aquatic plants and on the surface film of the water. Within days, an internal physical structure or architecture starts to evolve, complete with biological zones of activity. Life burrows on the bottom in the sediment zone. Aquatic weeds, fragments at first, grow into miniature "forests" that reach up into the water column. The water itself teems with a diversity of microscopic life. With magnifying glasses the students discover creatures reminiscent of shrimp and other minute creatures resembling monsters from one's imagination. The water/air interface is another zone with its own activity, where tiny insects skate across the surface film. The air column above plays its own role, exchanging gases with the water below. At night, when the air column cools, water droplets condense at the top of jar. Tap it with a pencil and it rains inside.

Within the first few weeks an observer can notice grazing and predatory cycles. Swimming animals, called zooplankton, appear seemingly out of nowhere, then disappear to be replaced by other species. Snails lay egg clusters on the walls. The aquatic plants grow into complex shapes to gather light and nutrients. Some plants penetrate the water/air interface and grow up into the air. Algae on the walls create a green carpet that consumes carbon dioxide and saturates the jar with oxygen gas during the day. The snails graze the algal carpets, leaving winding and spiraling paths that let light through to the rooted plants within.

The communities that adapt within are unique, part forest pool, part farm wallow, and part pond. All the life forms in the jars are familiar to biologists, but the combinations of species are unlike anything in the ecosystems from which they have been derived. Ecologically they are new. And each of the students' microcosms develops differently from the others. The water and sediment samples that seed the jars vary for each student and these differences will affect the life within the jar. Even where the jars are placed on the window will determine their fate.

What is perhaps most fascinating and relevant to my tale here is that despite their differences, all the glass jar communities have four basic attributes in common. First, they have the ability to self-organize in the presence of sunlight. (In darkness or dim light, they do not. Waste products accumulate and most of the organisms die.) Sunlight generates nutrient cycling, gas exchanges, growth, grazing, predation, death, and decay: an ecological dance.

Secondly, self-organization leads to self-design. A living "architecture" is formed where light, space, and the limits of the jar interact with all the life within. The jar's inhabitants occupy the space optimally. Self-design leads to a beauty and a deep aesthetic within the jar that an observer immediately senses.

Thirdly, these microcosms can repair themselves. If a window blind is left closed and the sunlight blocked for several days the ecosystem within will collapse. But if the jar is returned to the light soon enough, the living systems will begin to reorganize itself. The self-repair process generates a new system, usually different than the one from which it was derived. The attribute of self-repair is essential to the sustainability of the system. Perturbations, whether they be hurricanes, drought, or toxic assault, happen in all systems, but life-in-concert has the mechanisms to adapt.

A final characteristic of the microcosm is the ability to self-perpetuate. The microbial life within the jar reproduces over time periods measured by minutes for bacteria and hours for algae. Higher forms perpetuate their species in days or weeks. Cycles wax and wane with the season, but with any luck the system will persevere. In the jar on my office desk, a microcosm has been unfolding for years. Over time some of the original life forms have gone extinct, for the small size of the jar tests the limits of life working in concert. Yet as a whole, the system is amazingly persistent. The miniature ecosystem that I am looking into now as I write may well outlive me.

The Lilliputian world within the jar has a real power: it reveals Nature as designer. Ecologists have begun to decode the language of natural systems on a larger scale than in my jar. From the rain forests, coral reefs, mangrove swamps, prairies, deserts, lakes, and northern forests, they are deciphering principles of natural design. This knowledge embodies the genius of evolutionary time and the collective experience of all life as a whole system. Like the title of this book, it is Gaian knowledge.

Seeing the world as an ongoing process of ecological design transforms how one approaches the basic problem of supporting humanity. Ecological knowledge is now being used to develop new living technologies that can repair damaged environments and recycle wastes into beneficial new products. These eco-technologies are beginning to influence the design of infrastructures for human communities. In *Gaia's Garden*, author Toby Hemenway takes this thinking a powerful step forward by bringing living systems' intelligence to the household. The book sets forth the radical notion that ecological design, applied at the level of the home, can utterly transform how landscapes are sustained and humans fed. This book provides a genuine alternative to the contemporary industrial/global machine, which extracts resources and exploits humans and landscapes for its own ends and means. If the ideas presented here are widely adapted, then we have the possibility of forging a culture based upon Earth stewardship. In my opinion, ecological design as developed in *Gaia's Garden* represents the only long-term hope for humanity.

Gaia's Garden owes its heritage to the Permaculture teachings pioneered by Bill Mollison and David Holmgren over the last quarter century. In its quiet and wise way, this book outlines a radical redesign for the future of gardening and agriculture, organized around the basic premise that in the growing of foods and the crafting of landscapes, it is possible to substitute ecological information and human stewardship for today's dependence on capital, hardware, chemicals, machines, genetically engineered organisms, and destructive technologies. Hemenway shows us that the task of restoring the Earth begins in our own gardens.

One of my favorite tales from the book embodies the worldview of the ecological designer in practical ways—through what Hemenway terms "polyculture," and what I shall call "gardening in the image of a meadow." Instead of the often back-breaking labor that goes into tilling, sowing, weeding, and chemically controlling a conventional vegetable garden, Toby Hemenway's meadow-inspired food garden works on totally different principles. It provides its own fertilization, has internal weed suppression and pest-control mechanisms, and manages its internal moisture levels through dry times and wet, functioning as a self-organizing ecology. The cycle begins about one month before the last frost, when the gardener prepares the garden bed with sheet composting or mulching. After the last frost, the gardener broadcasts seeds of radish, dill, parsnip, calendula, and many varieties of lettuce over the garden and spreads one-quarter inch of compost over the seeds. That's it. Then Nature goes to work. After four weeks, the radishes are ready for harvesting. Cabbage seedlings can fill the holes they leave. By week six, the dense lettuce crop begins yielding mesclun, leaving other lettuce varieties to grow to full size over the next several months. When the soil warms up in late spring and early summer, bush beans and buckwheat take the space formerly occupied by the lettuce. Dill and calendula, whose flowers are edible, are harvested next. The cabbage varieties mature over an extended period, and by fall the parsnips are ready to harvest. The gardener pokes garlic cloves and fava beans into these newest openings, to be harvested the following year. The polyculture provides enough botanical diversity to control pests and disease as well as to protect the plants from excess rain and drought.

Variations on this polyculture theme throughout the book expand the meaning of gardening from the traditional battle to control Nature to a conscious and conscientious attempt to imitate and re-create natural systems in the backyard. *Gaia's Garden* shows how ideas and patterns from Nature can be blended and integrated to create larger systems. These larger systems in turn connect with each other to create a self-tending and co-evolving garden landscape.

Ecological design is predicated upon place. Each garden, each valley and each region is different. These differences, in the hands of an Earth steward, can be honored and used toward creative and diverse ends. Each garden is a reflection of the potential of place and the intimacy with which the gardener can connect with the needs and latent forces of the land. Earth wisdom becomes an expanding universe for the seeker, until the garden becomes an Eden where the gardener and garden exist in true harmony. The world we dream of, sustainable and beautiful, takes shape in the ecological garden. *Gaia's Garden* is a fine place to begin.

PREFACE

THIS BOOK BEGAN WHEN I visited a garden that felt unlike any I had seen.

Sometimes in a tropical forest or snorkeling in a coral reef, I have felt an aliveness, a sense of many interlocking pieces clicking together into a living and dynamic whole. These are places that naturally exude abundance. Sadly, this feeling was utterly lacking in any human-made landscape I had experienced. Natural landscapes seem so rich—they seethe with activity, they hum with life in comparison to ours. Why is it that nature can splash riotous abundance across forest or prairie with careless grace, while we humans struggle to grow a few flowers? Why do our gardens offer so little to the rest of life? Our yards seem so one-dimensional, just simple landscapes that offer a few vegetables or flowers, if that much. Yet nature can do a thousand things at once: feed insects and birds, snakes and deer, and offer them shelter; harvest, store, and purify water; renew and enrich the soil; clean the air and scent it with perfume; and on and on.

Then I visited a garden that felt the way nature does, yet hung heavy with fruit and edible greens. Soon I found a few others like it. In these places, using new techniques from permaculture and ecological design, and old ones from indigenous people and organic gardening, a few pioneers have created landscapes that feel like nature but provide a home for people as well. These are true backyard ecosystems that were designed with methods and concepts gleaned from nature, and that feel as alive as any forest. I wanted to know how to create these places,

and I wanted to help others create more. *Gaia's Garden* is the result of that pursuit.

These gardens represent a new type of landscape that provides for people as well as for the rest of nature. You could think of them as "edible landscaping meets wildlife gardening," but they are more than that. These are true backyard ecosystems—not just disconnected fragments—that are as resilient, diverse, productive, and beautiful as those in nature. They are not merely flowery showplaces or ruler-straight arrays of row crops. Yet they also are not the brambly tangles that identify many wildlife gardens. They are places where conscious design has been melded with a respect and understanding of nature's principles. The result is a living and riotously abundant landscape in which all the pieces work together to yield food, flowers, medicinal and edible herbs, even craft supplies and income for the human inhabitants, while providing diverse habitat for helpful insects, birds, and other wildlife. Places where nature does most of the work, but where people are as welcome as the other inhabitants of Earth.

Although this book is about environmentally friendly landscapes, it not an eco-fanatic's manifesto. It's a book on gardening, full of techniques and garden lore. But between the lines on these pages is a plea for less consumption and more self-reliance. Anyone who would pick up this book is probably familiar with the environmental destruction humans have wrought in the past few decades, so I'm not going to assault my readers with grim statistics. Suffice it to say that we have to do better. This book is an attempt to show one way to proceed. Our home landscapes consume immense amounts of resources. Providing for our needs spurs relentless conversion of wild land into factory farms and industrial forests. Yet our yards, city parks, curbsides, even parking lots and office courtyards could be lush, productive, and attractive landscapes that aid nature while yielding much for us as well, instead of being the grassy emptinesses that they are. This book shows how to do this, using techniques and examples devised by the pioneers of the sustainable-landscaping movement.

I assume that most of my readers have done a little gardening. *Gaia's Garden* is not an introductory gardening book, but I do attempt to explain some new techniques and concepts well enough for novice gardeners to implement them. Many of the subjects touched on here are large enough to deserve a book of their own, so lamentably I've had to limit how deeply I plunge into some fascinating topics. This may be frustrating to some readers, but I've included an annotated bibliography and a resources section to allow further pursuit of these subjects.

Most plants mentioned in this book are identified by common name to avoid the Latinate bafflement that botanical nomenclature can inflict on many gardeners. For a few unusual species, I've added the botanical name. The various tables and lists of plants are also alphabetized by common name, but in those I have included the botanical name, as that is the only way to be sure we're all talking about the same species.

With hundreds of thousands of plant species to choose from, these tables cannot hope to be comprehensive lists of all useful plants, but I hope my selections will provide readers with a broad palette from which to choose. To represent the wide variety of geographic regions on this continent, I've also tried to give examples from many areas and for different climates. More Americans now live west of the Mississippi than east of it, and this book reflects that bi-coastal reality.

Most of the ideas in this book aren't mine. Many of the techniques shown here have been practiced by indigenous people for millennia, or worked out by gardeners of all stripes. They have also been compiled in the ever-broadening array of books on ecological design and permaculture. In this book, I've attempted to synthesize these permacultural ideas with ecologists' growing understanding of what makes nature work. I can claim credit for few of the techniques and concepts described here, merely for the way some of them are presented. And of course, any errors are my own.

This book required the collaboration, hard work, and support of numerous people. I visited many gardens while researching these pages (one of the major perks of my subject choice). For letting me visit their sites and for their generosity with time and knowledge I thank—in alphabetical order—Earle Barnhart, Douglas Bullock, Joe Bullock, Sam Bullock, Kevin Burkhart, Doug Clayton, Joel Glanzberg, Ben Haggard, Marvin Hegge, Simon Henderson, Alan Kapuler, Brad Lancaster, Penny Livingston, Art Ludwig, Anne Nelson, Jerome Osentowski, John Patterson, Barbara Rose, Julia Russell, James Stark, Roxanne Swentzell, Tom Ward, and Mary Zemach. For support and fruitful ideas I thank Peter Bane, Bill Burton, Brock Dolman, Ianto Evans, Jude Hobbs, Keith Johnson, Michael Lockman, Bill Mollison, Scott Pittman, Bill Roley, Michael Smith, and Rick Valley. For telling me that books were not as hard to write as I feared, a special thanks to Stuart Cowan. To my agent, Natasha Kern, I owe a huge debt for her perseverance, her ideas, and her confidence. Thanks also to my very skillful editor, Rachael Cohen, who has smoothed the text considerably and tidied up my grammatical excesses. The staff at Chelsea Green have been a pleasure to collaborate with. And for a thousand graces, large and small, while I disappeared into this book, I am grateful to my wife, Carolyn.

Toby Hemenway

PART ONE

The
GARDEN
as
ECOSYSTEM

Chapter 1

Introducing the Ecological Garden

A MOVEMENT IS AFOOT toward more natural landscaping. Many gardeners are turning their backs on the lawn, in particular. People are digging up their resource-guzzling grassy swards and installing native plant gardens, wildlife-attracting thickets, or sun-dappled woodland habitats. It's an encouraging trend, this movement toward more ecologically sound, nature-friendly yards.

Yet not everyone is on board. Some gardeners hesitate to go natural because they can't see where their vegetable garden fits into this new style. What will happen to those luscious beefsteak tomatoes? Or ornamental plants—does natural gardening mean tearing out a treasured cut-flower bed or pulling up grandmother's heirloom roses to make room for a wild-looking landscape?

Nurturing wildlife and preserving native species are admirable goals, but how do *people* fit into these natural landscapes? No gardener wants to feel like a stranger in her own backyard. Gardeners who refuse to be excluded from their own yards, but love nature, have been forced to create fragmented gardens: an orderly vegetable plot here, flower beds there, and a back corner for wildlife or a natural landscape. And each of these fragments has its weaknesses. A vegetable garden doesn't offer habitat to native insects, birds, and other wildlife. Quite the contrary—munching bugs and birds are unwelcome visitors. The flower garden, however much pleasure the blooms provide, can't feed the gardener. And a wildlife garden is often unkempt and provides little for people other than the knowledge that it's good for wild creatures.

This book shows how to integrate these isolated and incomplete pieces into a vigorous, thriving backyard ecosystem that benefits both people and wildlife. These gardens are designed using the same principles that nature uses to create healthy plant communities, so that the different plantings and other elements interconnect and nurture one another. These gardens are more than the sum of their parts. Ecological gardens feel like living beings, each with its unique character and essence. *Gaia's Garden* provides tools to understand, design, and construct a backyard ecosystem that will serve people and the rest of nature.

Ecological gardens meld the best features of wildlife gardens, edible landscapes, and conventional flower and vegetable gardens. They are based on relatively new concepts such as permaculture and ecological design, yet use time-tested techniques honed to perfection by indigenous people, restoration biologists, organic farmers, and cutting-edge landscape designers. These gardens combine low environmental impact, low maintenance once established, and high yields with elegant aesthetics.

Ecological gardens are filled with beautiful plants that have many uses, providing fruit and vegetables, medicinal and culinary herbs, eye-catching arrays of colorful blossoms, soil-building mulch, protection from pests, and habitat for wildlife. With thousands of plant species to choose from, we can find plenty that do several of these jobs at once. Multifunctional plants are a hallmark of gardens based on ecological principles; that's how nature works. We can choose food plants that support insects and other wildlife, herbs that break up hardpan, cover crops that are edible, or trees that add nutrients to the soil.

These gardens can even yield income from edible and medicinal plants, seeds and nursery stock, or dried flowers, and provide construction or craft materials such as lumber, bamboo poles, basket wil-low, and vegetable dyes. Yet in a garden designed along ecological principles, birds and other animals feel just as welcome in these living landscapes as the gardener. With good design, these gardens need only infrequent watering, and the soil renews itself rather than demanding heavy fertilizing. These are living ecosystems, designed using nature's rules, and boasting the lushness and resilience of the natural environment.

GARDENS THAT *REALLY* WORK WITH NATURE

Ecology, Mr. Webster tells us, is "concerned with the interrelationship of organisms and their environments." I call these gardens ecological because they connect one organism—people—to their environment, they link the many pieces of a garden together, and because they can play a role in preserving healthy ecosystems.

Ecological gardens also blend many garden styles together, which gives the gardener enough leeway to emphasize the qualities—food, flowers, herbs, crafts, and so on—he or she likes most.

WHAT IS PERMACULTURE?

I refer often in this book to permaculture and ecological design, two closely related fields upon which many of the ideas in this book are based. Since permaculture may be an unfamiliar word to some readers, I should do some explaining.

Permaculture is a set of techniques and principles for designing sustainable human settlements. The word, a contraction of both "permanent culture" and "permanent agriculture," was coined by Bill Mollison, a charismatic and iconoclastic one-time forester, schoolteacher, trapper, and field naturalist, and one of his students, David Holmgren. Mollison says the original idea for permaculture came to him in 1959 when he was observing marsupials browsing in the forests of Tasmania, and jotted in his diary, "I believe that we could build systems that would function as well as this one does."

In the 1970s, he and Holmgren began to develop a set of techniques for holistic landscape designs that are modeled after nature yet include humans. Permaculture's vision is of people participating in and benefiting from an abundant, nurturing natural world.

Though permaculture practitioners design with plants, animals, buildings, and organizations, they focus less on those objects themselves than on the careful design of relationships among them—interconnections—that will create a healthy, sustainable whole. Interconnections are what turns a collection of unrelated parts into a functioning system, whether it's a community, a family, or an ecosystem.

The aim of permaculture is to create ecologically sound, economically prosperous human communities. It is guided by a set of ethical principles—care for the earth, care for people, and sharing the surplus. From these stem a set of design guidelines. Some of these guidelines are based on our understanding of

Some of ecological gardening finds its roots in edible landscaping, which freed food plants from their vegetable-patch prison and let them mix with the respectable front-yard society of ornamentals. Ecological landscapes also share traits with wildlife gardens, since they provide habitat for the more-than-human world. And since local flora get prominent billing in these gardens, they have much in common with native plant gardens.

But these landscapes aren't just a simple lumping-together of other garden styles. They take their cues from the way nature works. Some gardens look like natural landscapes, but that's as far as the resemblance goes. I've seen native plant gardens that require mountains of fertilizer to survive in unsuitable soil, and buckets of herbicides to quell the vigorous grasses and weeds that happily rampage among the slow-growing natives. That's hardly "natural." An ecological garden both looks and works the way nature does. It does this by building strong connections among the plants, soil life, beneficial insects and other animals, and the gardener, to weave a resilient, natural web. Each organism is tied to many others. It's this interconnectedness that gives nature strength. Think of a net or web: Snip one thread, and the net still functions, because all the other connections are holding it together.

Nothing in nature does just one thing. This multipurposeness—wherein each interconnected piece plays many roles—is another quality that distinguishes an ecologically designed garden from others. In the typical garden, most elements are intended to serve only a single purpose. A tree is chosen for shade, a shrub for its berries, a trellis to restrain that unruly grapevine. But by designing a garden so that each piece can play all the roles it's capable of, not only can the gardener let nature do much of the work, the garden will be prone to fewer problems, and will become a lusher, richer place. That shade tree, for example. Can't it also offer nuts or other food for both people and wildlife, and maybe attract pollinators that will later help fruit trees bear more heavily? Plus, the tree's leaves will harvest rainwater and pull dust out of the air, and build the soil when they fall. That tree is already doing about fifteen different jobs. We just need to connect these "yields" to other parts of the garden

nature, such as, "Each element should perform several functions," and, "Use natural plant succession to create favorable sites and soils." Others are borrowed from stable, long-term societies, such as, "Use renewable resources," and, "Begin the garden at your doorstep." Many of these design guidelines are given in various books about permaculture, listed in the bibliography. Together they combine to create a way to design sustainable gardens, landscapes, towns, and cultures.

From this it is obvious that permaculture is about much more than gardening. But since permaculture emphasizes the role of plants and animals in human life, many people have come to permaculture through their love of gardening and agriculture. What I call ecological gardens draw much from permaculture. This book could easily have been called *The Permaculture Garden*, but that title has already been used by a British author, Graham Bell. Also, I wanted to use a term that was familiar to most people, and permaculture is not yet widely recognized in North America. I hope this book will help remedy that. Most of the gardeners interviewed for this book consider themselves permaculturists, and many of the techniques described here were first assembled in Mollison's books on permaculture.

Gardeners are people who love plants, and by extension, nature itself. For gardeners to be on the forefront of a better relationship between humans and nature seems only natural. It is my hope that the ideas in this book, based on permaculture and other methods of sustainable design, will encourage gardeners to reduce their own ecological impact, and lead the way, through beautiful, lush landscapes, for others to do the same.

that need them. That will mean less work for us and better health for the landscape.

The grape arbor could be shading a too-sunny deck on the hot south side of the house; that means it will cool both deck and building, and offer fruit to the lucky souls lounging beneath it. The pieces are all there, ready and waiting. We just need to link them together, using nature's marvelous interconnectedness as a model.

This connectedness goes two ways. In nature each piece not only plays many roles, each role is supported by many players. For example, each insect pest in a natural landscape is pursued by a hungry army of natural predators. If one predator bug, or even a whole species, falls down on the job, others are there to pick up the slack. This redundancy shrinks the risk of failure. So, looking back at that lone shade tree from this perspective, don't plant just one, plant a cluster of several varieties. If one grows slowly or doesn't leaf out densely, the others are there to fill in. The combination will cast shade over a longer season, too. See the synergy? Continuing in this vein, to the grape arbor we could add a clematis to contribute color, a jasmine for scent, or some beans to boost the harvest.

Here's another example of how connectedness can make gardens more natural and also save work. Deer are a big problem for me, chomping down almost any unprotected plant. They've trampled a well-worn path into my yard from the southwest. So I have placed a curving hedge on that side to deflect them from other tasty plantings. The hedge is partly made up of a few native shrubs already growing there—oceanspray, wild roses, a

lone manzanita. But I chose the other hedge species to do several jobs. I've planted bush cherries, Manchurian apricots, currants, and other wildlife plants, including thorny wild plums and gooseberries to hold back the deer. But on the inside of the hedge—my side—to some of these I've grafted domestic fruit varieties. The wild cherries have a few twigs of sweet cultivars on them, and the shrubby apricots and wild plums are sprouting an assortment of luscious Asian plums. This food-bearing hedge (sometimes called a *fedge*) will feed both the deer and me.

I've connected this hedge to other natural cycles. It's a good distance from our house, and I quickly tired of lugging fertilizer and the hose to

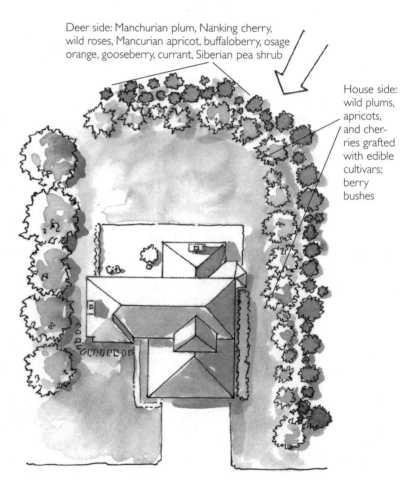

Deer side: Manchurian plum, Nanking cherry, wild roses, Mancurian apricot, buffaloberry, osage orange, gooseberry, currant, Siberian pea shrub

House side: wild plums, apricots, and cherries grafted with edible cultivars; berry bushes

A deer-deflecting food hedge, with wildlife plants on the outside, but human-used varieties on the side toward the house.

it. So I planted some clovers and two shrubs, Siberian pea shrub and buffaloberry, in the hedge, to add nitrogen to the soil. And I seeded-in several deep-rooted species, including chicory, yarrow, and daikon radish, which pull nutrients from the subsoil and deposit them on the surface at leaf fall. These will build up the soil naturally. I wanted to conserve water, so I planted mulch-producing species such as comfrey and cardoon (a thick-leaved artichoke relative). I slash their leaves periodically and leave them on the ground to create a mulch layer that holds moisture in the soil under the hedge. The hedge still needs some irrigation in southern Oregon's ninety-day dry season, but the mulch plants have saved lots of water. And the fruit is looking plump this spring.

Nature has a broad back, and with a little ingenuity and a change in viewpoint, a gardener can shift plenty of labor to this willing partner. Nature can be the gardener's ally. We still hold vestiges of an earlier time's regard for nature as an enemy, or as something to be conquered and restrained. Say the word "insect" to a gardener, and he will nearly always think of some chomping, sucking pest that tatters leaves and ruins fruit. Yet the vast majority—90 percent or more—of all insects are beneficial or harmless. A diverse and balanced ensemble of insects in the landscape means good pollination and fruit set, and quick, nontoxic control of pest outbreaks, held in check by predaceous bugs. We need insects in the garden. Without them, our workload would be crippling—hand pollinating every bloom, grinding fallen leaves into compost by hand.

The same applies for all the other denizens of life's kingdoms. Not only are bugs, birds, mammals, and microbes essential partners in every kind of garden, but with clever design, they can work with us to minimize our labor and maximize the beauty, health, and productivity of our landscapes. Even domestic animals can help with gardening, as I'll explain in chapter 7.

WHY IS GARDENING SO MUCH WORK?

One object of an ecological garden is to restore the natural cycles that have been broken by conventional landscape design and agriculture. Have you ever wondered why a forest or meadow looks perfect and stays nearly disease free with no care at all, while a garden demands arduous hours of labor? In a garden, weeds still pop up like, well, weeds, and every plant seems to be covered in its own set of weird spots and chomping bugs. This happens because most gardens ignore nature's rules.

Look how gardens differ from natural landscapes. Not only does nature never do just one thing, nature abhors bare soil, large blocks of a single plant type, and vegetation that's all the same height and root depth. Nature doesn't till, either—about the only time soil is disturbed in the wild is when a tree topples and its upturned roots churn the earth. Yet our gardens are virtual showcases of all these unnatural methods. Not to mention our broadscale pesticide use and chemical fertilizers.

Each of these unnatural garden techniques was developed for a specific purpose. Tilling, for example, destroys weeds and pumps air to microbes that, metabolically supercharged, release a flood of nutrients for fast crop growth. These are great short-term boons to plant-growers. But we now know that in the long term, tilling depletes fertility (those revved-up microbes will burn up all the nutrients, then die), causes more disease, and ruins the soil structure with compaction to hardpan and massive erosion as the result.

The bare soil in a typical garden, whether in a freshly tilled plot or between neatly spaced plants, is a perfect habitat for weed seeds. Weeds are simply pioneer plants, molded by millions of years of evolution to quickly cover disturbed, open ground. They'll do that relentlessly in the bare ground of a garden. Naked earth also washes away with rain, which means we'll have to do more tilling to fluff the scoured, pounded earth that's left, and add more fertilizer to replace lost nutrients.

Solid blocks of the same plant variety, though easy to seed and harvest, act as an "all you can eat" sign to insect pests and diseases. Harmful bugs will stuff themselves on this unbroken field of abundant food as they make unimpeded hops from plant to plant, and breed to plague proportions.

Each of the conventional techniques cited above arose to solve a specific problem, but like any single-minded approach, they often don't combine well with other one-purpose methods, and they miss the big picture. The big picture here, in the typical garden, is not a happy one. Lots of tedious work, no habitat for native or rare species, struggling plants on intensive care, reliance on resource-gobbling poisonous chemicals, and in general, a decline in the garden's health, yield, and beauty unless we constantly and laboriously intervene. Yet we've come to accept all this as part of gardening.

There is another way to garden. Conventional landscapes have torn the web of nature. Important threads are missing. We can restore many of these broken links, and work with nature to lessen our own load, not to mention the cost to the environment. For example, why till and add trainloads of fertilizer, when worms and other soil life, combined with fertility-building plants, will tailor the finest soil possible, with very little work? That's how nature does it. Then all we need to do is make up for the small amount of nutrients lost to harvest. (Plants are mostly water, plus some carbon from the air. The tiny amounts of minerals they take from the soil can easily be replaced if we use the proper techniques.)

"Let nature do it" also applies to dealing with pests. In a balanced landscape, diseases and insect problems rarely get out of control. That's because in the diverse, many-specied garden that this book tells how to create, each insect, fungus, bacterium, or potentially invasive plant is surrounded by a natural web of checks and balances. If one species becomes too abundant, its sheer availability makes it a tasty, irresistible food source for something else, which will knock it back to manageable lev-

els. That's how nature works, and it's a useful trick for the ecological gardener.

To create a well-balanced garden, we must know something about how nature behaves. Toward that end, this book offers a chapter on ecology for gardeners; many examples of nature's principles at work are woven throughout the other chapters. When we use nature's methods—whether for growing vegetables, flowers, or wildlife plants—the garden becomes less work, less prone to problems, and vastly more like the dynamic, vibrant landscapes found in nature. These backyard ecosystems are deeply welcoming both for the wild world and for people, offering food and other products for self-reliance, as well as beauty and inspiration.

BEYOND—WAY BEYOND—NATURAL GARDENING

Some of what you have read so far may sound familiar. The past twenty years have seen the arrival of native plant gardens and landscapes that mimic natural groupings of vegetation, a style usually called natural gardening. Many of these gardens attempt to re-create native plant communities by assembling plants into backyard prairies, woodlands, wetlands, and other wild habitats. So gardening with nature may not be a new idea to some readers.

Ecological gardens also use principles derived from observing and living in wild land, but toward a different end. Natural gardens consist almost exclusively of native plants, and are intended to create and restore habitat for oft-endangered flora and wildlife. They are often described, as Ken Druse puts it in *The Natural Habitat Garden,* as "essential to the planet's future." I support using native plants in the landscape. But natural gardens, offering little for people, will never have more than a tiny effect on environmental damage. Here's why.

In the United States, all the developed, inhabited land—cities, suburbs, and rural towns, including roads, buildings, yards, and so on—covers only about 6 percent of the nation's area. You could fill every yard and city park with native plants and not even begin to stanch the loss of native species and habitat.

However, even if developed land in cities and suburbs were packed with natives-only gardens, it would never be wild. Divided into tiny fragments by streets, plastered over with houses and highways, all the streams culverted and run underground, filled with predatory cats and dogs, this is land that has been taken over by humans and our allies, removed from larger ecosystems, and it's going to stay that way. I don't deny that if we planted suburbia with natives we might rescue some tiny number of species. But many native species, particularly animals, are incompatible with land occupied by modern people, and require large tracts of unspoiled terrain to survive. Planting suburban yards with natives won't save them.

Also, the real damage to the environment is done not by the cities and suburbs themselves, but by meeting their needs. We, who live in the developed 6 percent of the land, have an insatiable appetite, and use between 40 and 70 percent of America's land area (estimates vary widely) to support us. Monocultured farms and industrial forests, livestock grazing, reservoirs, strip and open pit mines, military reservations, and all the other accoutrements of modern civilization consume a huge amount of space, almost none of it native or healthy habitat. Each non-homegrown meal, each trip to the lumberyard, pharmacy, clothing store, or other shop, commissions the conversion of once-native habitat into industrial desert. Every one thousand square feet of house means that about one acre of clearcut forest has the homeowner's name on it. Certainly, natives should be included wherever they can do the job, but native plant gardens won't reduce our depredations of wild land very much unless we also lessen our resource use. A native plant garden, while much easier on the environment than a lawn, still means that the owner is causing immense habitat loss elsewhere, out of sight.

Every bit of food, every scrap of lumber, each medicinal herb or other human product that comes from an urban yard means that one less chunk of land outside the cities needs to be denuded of natives and developed for human use. Factory farms and industrial forests—pesticide-laced, monocropped, sterilized of everything but a single species—are far more biologically impoverished than any suburban backyard. But farms and tree plantations are the lands that could truly become wilderness again. Cities and suburbs are already out of the natural loop, so we should strive to make them as useful to people as possible, not simply office parks and bedrooms. Urban land can be incredibly productive. In Switzerland, for example, 70 percent of all lumber comes from community woodlots. Our cities could provide for most human needs, and let cropland and tree farms return to nature.

I'm not talking about converting every backyard to row crops. By gardening ecologically, designing multifunctional landscapes that provide food and other goods for ourselves while creating habitat for other species, we can make our cities truly bloom. But a yard full only of native plants, lacking any for human use, simply means that somewhere else, out of sight, there is a non-native–containing farm and a factory forest, with the environmental destruction they bring, providing for that native-loving suburbanite's needs. In contrast, a yard planted with carefully chosen exotics (and sure, natives too) will reduce the ecological damage done by the human occupants far more than a native-plant garden. Taking care of ourselves in our own yards means that factory farms and forests can shrink. Somewhere a farmer won't have to plow quite so close to a creek, saving riparian species that would never live in a suburban lot.

THE NATIVES VERSUS EXOTICS DEBATE

Gardening with native plants has become not merely popular in recent years, it's become a *cause célèbre*. Supporters of natural gardening can become quite exercised when someone recommends non-native plants. Governments, agribusinesses, and conservation groups have spent millions of dollars trying to eradicate exotic invasive species. The arguments for natives have merit—of course we want to preserve our native species and their habitat. But I feel that much of the energy spent on planting natives and yanking exotics is misdirected and futile. Certainly I'd rather see a yard full of natives than a sterile lawn. But I would prefer even more to see a suburban yard full of non-native plants that produce food and other products for the residents than one stocked only with inedible natives.

Without major changes in our land-use practices, the campaign to eradicate exotic plants is futile. A little ecological knowledge shows why. Look at most invasive plants. European bittersweet and Japanese honeysuckle swarm over New England's forest margins. Kudzu chokes the roadsides and forest edges in the South. Purple loosestrife infests the waterways of both coasts and the Midwest, and Russian olive forms small forests in the West. But in nearly every case, these plants are invading disturbed land and disrupted ecosystems, fragmented and degraded by grazing, logging, mining, roadbuilding, and other human activity. Less-disturbed ecosystems are much more resistant to invasion, though exotics do threaten them at roadcuts and logging sites.

One pro-native garden writer describes what he calls "the kudzu phenomenon, where an exotic displaces natives unless we constantly intervene." But our intervention is the problem. We assume

> **Invasive exotics are almost exclusively pioneer species that need sunlight, churned-up ground, and often, poor soil.**

nature is making a mistake when it creates hybrid, fast-healing thickets, so we never allow disturbed habitat to stabilize. We can spray and uproot bittersweet and honeysuckle all we want, but they'll come right back. These are species that love sunlit edges, and we've carved eastern forests into countless tiny pieces that have more edge than interior, creating perfect habitat for these invaders. The same goes for kudzu, loosestrife, and all the rest. In the East, purple loosestrife followed the nineteenth-century canals into wetlands, and in the West, it has barreled down irrigation ditches into marshland and ponds. Humans create the conditions in which exotics thrive.

Invasive exotics crave disturbance and they love edges. Those are two things development spawns in huge quantity. Unless we stop creating edge and disturbance, our eradication efforts will be in vain. The only long-term hope for eliminating invasive exotics lies in avoiding soil disturbance, restoring intact forest, and shading the invaders out with other species. In other words, we need to create landscapes that are more ecologically mature. Invasive exotics are almost exclusively pioneer species that need sunlight, churned-up ground, and often, poor soil (kudzu and Russian olive are nitrogen fixers whose role is to build fertility, so they prosper in farmed-out fields and overgrazed rangeland).

Here's why exotic invasives are so successful. When we clear land, or carve a forest into fragments, we're creating lots of open niches. All that sunny space and bare soil is just crying out to be colonized by light- and fertility-absorbing green matter. Nature will quickly conjure up as much biomass as possible to capture the bounty, by seeding low-growing "weeds" into a clearing, or, better yet, sprouting a tall thicket that reaches into all three dimensions to better absorb light and develop deep roots. That's why forest margins are an impenetrable tangle of shrubs, vines, and small trees: There's plenty of light to harvest.

When humans make a clearing, nature leaps in, working furiously to rebuild an intact humus and fungal layer, harvest energy, and reconstruct all the cycles and connections that have been severed. A thicket of fast-growing pioneer plants, packing a lot of biomass into a small space, is a very effective way to do this. Permaculture's co-originator, David Holmgren, calls these rampantly growing blends of natives and exotics "recombinant ecologies," and believes that they are nature's effective strategy of assembling available plants to heal damaged land. If we clear out the thicket in the misguided belief that meadows should forever remain meadows, or that all forests should have tidy, open understories, we are just setting the recovery process back. Nature will then relentlessly return to work, filling in with pioneer plants again.

The sharply logged edge of a woods abutted by a lawn or field—so common in suburbs—is a perfect home for sun-loving exotics. If we plant low trees and shrubs to soften these margins, thus swallowing up the sunlight that pierces the forest edges, the niche for the invader will disappear. Simply removing the exotic won't do any good; it will come right back into the perfect habitat that waits for it (herbicide manufacturers are helping fund the campaign for native plants, since they know a repeat customer when they see one). Nature abhors a vacuum—create one, and she'll rush in with whatever's handy. To eradicate invasives, the habitat for it must be changed into a more mature, less hospitable landscape. The conditions that support the invader must be eliminated.

Pioneer weedscapes may be nature's way, but most people don't want their yard edges to be a tangled thicket. To avoid this and still stay off the "clear, spray, and curse" treadmill, we can learn from the more mature forest edges near us. What species nestle into the sunny margins of old woods? Perhaps dogwood, cherry, crabapple, or small vari-

eties of maple. The species vary around the country, but edge-loving trees and shrubs are good candidates for jump-starting a yard or woodlot margin toward a more mature ecological phase. Plant them at those overgrown woody edges. You can't fight nature—nature always bats last—but you can sometimes be first to get where it's going.

The nineteenth-century scientist Thomas Henry Huxley likened nature to a brilliant opponent in chess: "We know that his play is always fair, just, and patient. But also we know, to our cost, that he never overlooks a mistake, or makes the smallest allowance for ignorance." Nature has a patience that humans lack. We may uproot some bittersweet or kudzu for a few seasons, but nature will keep reseeding it, year in, year out, waiting until we tire of the battle. Nature takes the long view.

It is only our limited time frame that creates the whole "natives versus exotics" controversy. Wind, animals, sea currents, and continental drift have always dispersed species into new environments. Our jet-age mobility has merely accelerated the trend, albeit to an unnerving and often economically damaging pace. Eventually an invasive species, after a boom-and-bust period, comes into equilibrium with its surroundings. It may take a decade or a century, time spans that seem like an eternity to a homeowner contending with Scotch broom or star thistle, but one day the new species becomes "implicated" into the local ecosystem, developing natural enemies and encountering unwelcome environments that keep it in check.

"Native" is merely a question of perspective: Is a species native to this hillside, or this county, the bioregion, continent, or perhaps just to this planet? Of course I lament the species choked to extinction by purple loosestrife or cheatgrass (though I see a certain irony in immigrant-descended Americans cursing "invasive exotics" that displace native species), and it is foolish to deliberately introduce a species known to be locally invasive. I love native plants and grow them whenever appropriate. But nearly the whole issue—from branding certain fast-spreading, soil-building pioneer plants as evil, to creating the conditions that favor their spread—stems from not understanding nature's ways. When we think ecologically, the problem either evaporates as a misunderstanding, or reveals solutions inherent in the life cycle of the invader. A plant will thrive only if conditions are right for it. Modify those conditions—eliminate edge, stop disturbing soil, cast shade with trees—and that invasive exotic will cease to be a problem.

I'm also uneasy with the adversarial, polarized relationship with plants that an overzealous enthusiasm for natives can foster. It can result in a "natives good, everything else bad" frame of mind that heats the gardener's blood pressure to boiling at the sight of any exotic plant. Rage is not the best emotion to be carrying into the garden. And we're all utterly reliant on non-natives for so many of our needs. Look at our diet. I'd be surprised if the average American regularly consumes a single plant native to his or her state. About the only food crops native to North America are sunflowers, hops, squash, and some nuts and berries. Nearly everything we eat originated in South America, Europe, or Asia. Get rid of exotics, and most of us would be pretty hungry until we learned to prepare local roots, berries, nuts, and greens.

This is why I advocate a sensible balance of native and exotic plants in our landscapes. We may not be able to restore our cities to native wilderness, but our gardens can play an important role in restoring our planet's environment. A major premise of this book is that our own yards can allow us to reduce our incessant pressure on the planet's health. The techniques of permaculture and ecological design allow us to easily, intelligently, and beautifully provide for some of our own needs. We can create landscapes that behave much like those in nature, but tinker with them just a bit

to increase their yield for people while preserving native habitat. And in so doing, we can allow some of those factory farms and industrial forests to revert to wild land.

We have assembled enough knowledge from cultures that live in relative harmony with their environment, and from scientific studies of ecology and agriculture, to create gardens that offer both habitat to wildlife and support for people. They don't look like farms. Instead they have the same feel as the native vegetation, but can be tweaked to provide for the needs and interests of the human residents. Picture your favorite natural landscape, and then imagine plucking fruit from the trees, making a crisp salad from the leaves, clipping a bouquet from the abundant flowers, laying in a supply of garden stakes from a bamboo patch. These gardens tailor a large place for people, yet still behave like ecosystems, recycling nutrients, purifying water and air, offering a home for native and naturalized flora and fauna.

Both natural gardens and ecological gardens emphasize the role of *plant communities,* that is, groupings of trees, shrubs, and nonwoody plants that naturally occur together and seem to be connected into a whole. The difference is that natural gardens attempt to mimic native plant communities, while the gardens in this book combine natives, food plants, medicinal and culinary herbs, insect- and bird-attracting species, plants that build soil, and others into synergistic, mutually beneficial groupings. These "synthetic" plant communities, which permaculture calls *guilds,* form healthy, interacting networks that reduce the gardener's labor, yield abundant gifts for people and wildlife, and help the environment by restoring nature's cycles.

Indigenous people, especially those living in the tropics, have been using guilds for millennia to

Plant communities **are groupings of trees, shrubs, and nonwoody plants that naturallly occur together and seem to be connected as a whole.**

create sustainable landscapes. Only recently have we understood what they were doing and how they do it. Anthropologists mistook the lush and productive home gardens that enfolded tropical houses for wild jungle, so perfectly had the inhabitants mimicked the surrounding forest. From these gardeners, we've learned something about creating landscapes that work just like nature, but offer a role for people.

In temperate climates, the art and science of fashioning communities of useful, attractive plants is a new and vigorous field. Many of the gardeners I spoke to while researching this book are pioneering these techniques. The last few chapters of this book explain how to design and use guilds to create vibrant "food forests" and beautiful habitats for people and wildlife. I hope that some who read this book will add to this burgeoning field.

MAKING THE DESERT BLOOM, SUSTAINABLY

To help readers get a feel for an ecological garden, let me describe one of the finest examples I've seen. North of Santa Fe, New Mexico, sculptor Roxanne Swentzell has created an oasis in the high desert she calls Flowering Tree Permaculture Institute.

When I arrived at Flowering Tree, I stepped out of my car and was blasted by the mid-nineties heat and the searing glare reflected from the bare, eroded hillsides nearby. But before me was a wall of greenery, a lush landscape that I'd spotted from at least a mile away, in soothing contrast to the yellow sand and gravel of the desert.

I entered the yard through a gap between arching trees, and the temperature plummeted. The air here was fresh, cool, and moist, unlike the dusty, sinus-withering stuff I'd been breathing outside. A canopy of walnut trees, piñon pine, and New Mexico black locust sheltered a lush understory of pomegranates, nectarines, jujube trees, and almonds. An edible passionflower swarmed up a rock wall. Grapevines arched over an entry trellis.

Two small ponds sparkled with rainwater caught by the adobe house's roof. Winking brightly from under shrubs and along pathways were endless varieties of flowers, both native and exotic.

Roxanne, an athletic-looking woman with high, solid cheekbones bequeathed by her Santa Clara forebears, greeted me, smiling at my somewhat dazed appearance. She'd seen this before, as visitors gawked at the luxuriant growth so dissimilar to the barrenness outside. "We've got about five hundred species here, on one-eighth acre or so," she told me. "We've tried to make it a self-sufficient place that will take care of us while we take care of it. So we grow whatever we can that will survive in this climate."

In 1986, she moved onto a parcel of bare land on the Santa Clara homelands. She describes the place as "no trees, no plants, no animals, just pounded-down dirt and lots of ants." She and her two young children built a passive-solar adobe house and began planting. But the climate was too harsh. Dry winds swept down from the scoured, overgrazed hills and burned up the seedlings, killing those that hadn't frozen in winter or baked to husks in summer.

Local permaculture designer Joel Glanzberg entered Roxanne's life at about this time, and helped her ferret out techniques for gardening in the desert. They dragged in rocks and logs to shade seedlings, and dug shallow ditches, called swales, to catch precious rainwater and create sheltered, moist microclimates. To cast much-needed shade and generate organic matter, Joel and Roxanne planted just about any useful drought-tolerant plant, native or exotic, that they could find. Thirstier species they placed within reach of the *asequia,* or irrigation ditch, that surged with water once a week by tribal agreement. Without reliable water, the garden would have been impossible to establish in the desert heat.

They hauled in manure and mulch materials to build rich soil that would hold moisture through drought. Once the hardy young trees and shrubs

Designer Joel Glanzberg stands in a barren desert plot in 1989 at Flowering Tree Permaculture Institute in New Mexico.

had taken hold, they set more delicate plants in their shade. They blended berry bushes and small fruit trees into an edible hedge along the north border, to provide the family with food as well as to block the winds that roared down the nearby canyon. All these techniques combined into a many-pronged strategy to build fertile soil, cast shade, damp the wild temperature swings of the desert, and conserve water. Together, these practices created a mild, supportive place to grow a garden. Slowly the barren landscape transformed into a young, multistoried food forest.

Roxanne told me, "The garden was hard to get started, but once the little seedlings took off, then boy, they took off." At my visit, the landscape was eight years old, and trees, where none had been before, were as tall as the two-story house. Blessed, cooling shade, from dense to dappled, halted the searing rays of the sun. Instead of baking the soil, the fierce solar heat was absorbed by the thick leafy canopy and converted into lush greenery, mulch, food, and deep-questing roots that loosened the soil. In the bright gaps, flowers and food plants vied for sunlight. Even in the shade, a many-layered understory of shrubs and small trees divided the yard into a path-laced series of small rooms.

I caught glimpses of birds dancing from twig to twig before they disappeared into the shrubbery. A constant rustling and chirping enveloped us on all sides, and I knew that dozens more birds were hidden in the foliage. Metallic-sheened beneficial wasps dove into the blossoms that surrounded us, and butterflies of all sizes and colors soared and flapped from flower to leaf. Roxanne carried pruning shears with her as she walked, and lopped off the occasional too-exuberant branch from the mulberries, plums, black locusts, and other vigorously growing trees and shrubs that lined the paths. These would feed her turkeys, or become more mulch.

She pointed out a crimson trumpet-blossomed *Penstemon barbatus* (beard-tongue) that looked unhappy in the deep shade. "Things change so fast here," she said. "This was in full sun two years ago. Now it's completely shaded out, and I think it might be rotting from the soil staying too wet. And look at all these peaches. I better get busy harvesting."

The techniques and design strategies (which this book will describe in detail) had transformed the landscape. Roxanne and her helpers had rejuvenated a battered plot of desert, created a thick layer of rich soil, and brought immense biodiversity to a once-impoverished place. Here in the high desert was almost too much water and shade. Food was dropping from the trees faster than they could harvest, and birds that no one had seen for years were making a home in the yard.

Not everyone begins with as difficult a challenge, as devastated a site, as Roxanne. But there's quite a gap between the typical yard and what Roxanne and other similar gardeners have created. The average yard is both an ecological and agricultural desert. The prime offender is short-mown grass, which offers no habitat and nothing for people except a place to sit, yet sucks down far more water and chemicals than a comparable amount of farmland. The common, single-function plantings found in most landscapes also have their share of drawbacks. Highly bred flowers, lacking pollen and nectar, displace bird- and insect-nurturing varieties. Many ornamental plants are no more than pleasant eye candy, and could be replaced by equally attractive species that have uses for people and wildlife.

Typical gardening techniques don't help much, either. A tidy layer of bark mulch, instead of more natural and protective ground plants, robs small animals and insects of their homes. The heavy chemical used in most lawns—needed because natural soil fertility and insect predators are absent—pollutes water, kills wildlife, and is almost certainly linked to many human ailments. And as mentioned, unproductive home landscapes mask and contribute to the immense environmental damage our resource consumption does elsewhere, out of sight.

The ecological garden offers a solution. Our yards could be deeply connected to nature, yet be more than just wildlife or native plant gardens—they could link *us* to nature's abundance as well. The techniques and strategies to do this have been worked out by resourceful and imaginative pioneers. These people have mapped a new terrain and brought back what they've learned. I spoke to many of them and visited their vibrant, naturally productive landscapes while researching *Gaia's Garden*. These pioneers shared their knowledge, which I have done my best to present in the following pages.

Four years later, Joel stands in the same spot. An intelligent permaculture design has created a lush oasis around him.

can apply to make their yards work more like nature. Fear not—this is not a textbook, it's a gardening manual, so I don't go into technical details. I give plenty of practical examples of ecological principles at work. Next, chapter 3 describes the design process and techniques that you can use to create an ecological garden. Most of these ideas will be familiar to those versed in permaculture, but may be new to people from a traditional gardening background.

Moving from theory toward practice, the second part of the book looks at the pieces of the ecological garden. A chapter each delves into soil (chapter 4), water (chapter 5), plants (chapter 6), and animals (chapter 7), but from a different perspective from that of most garden books. Instead of viewing soil, water, plants, and animals as static, as objects to be manipulated into doing what we want, I treat them as dynamic and constantly evolving, as having their own qualities that need to be understood to work with them successfully, and as intricately connected to all the other parts of the garden.

Part 3 shows how to assemble the garden's elements into a backyard ecosystem. Chapter 8 begins with simple interplanting techniques, and

HOW TO USE THIS BOOK

Gaia's Garden is divided into three parts. The rest of part 1 continues this introduction to the idea of the garden as an ecosystem. Chapter 2 offers a simple guide to concepts from ecology that gardeners expands on these to show how to create polycultures (blends of several to many plant species that work together) and human-designed plant communities, or guilds. Chapter 9 offers several methods for designing garden guilds. Building on these two chapters, chapter 10 describes how to assemble plants and guilds into a multistoried food forest or forest garden. The final chapter reveals how these gardens take on a life of their own, and mature into self-sustaining mini-ecosystems that are far more than the sum of their parts. I also give a few tips and techniques for accelerating this process.

The main text of the book explains the ideas behind an ecological garden, and gives examples and descriptions of the ideas in action. Specific garden techniques are usually set off from the text in boxes so they are easy to find. I have also included lists of plants relevant to the ideas in the text (insect-attracting species, drought-tolerant plants, and so forth). The appendix contains a large table of useful, multifunctional plants and their characteristics.

Many of the techniques and ideas in this book can be used by themselves, simply as ways to make a conventional garden more productive or earth-friendly. There's nothing wrong with taking a mix-and-match approach to these ideas, using only the ones that are easy to fit into an existing landscape. But these techniques are also synergistic; the more that you put into practice, the more they work together to create a richly connected and complete landscape that is more than a group of independent parts. These resilient, dynamic backyard ecosystems act like those in nature while providing benefits for us and for wildlife, and reducing our demands on the diminishing resources of this planet.

Chapter 2

A Gardener's Ecology

SOMETHING WAS STEALING the Bullock brothers' food.

Joe, Douglas, and Sam Bullock had moved to Washington's San Juan Islands in the early 1980s, and set to work creating a food forest. They built up their property's soil, and planted fruit trees, nut trees, and hundreds of other species, all calculated to boost the biological diversity and lushness of this once-scrubby, blackberry-entangled parcel. Now, a decade later, walnut trees and bamboo groves shaded the paths. Plums, peaches, cherries, and apples hung in thick festoons from spreading branches, and beneath them, flowers, berries, edible greens, and soil-building plants sprawled over every inch of earth. The Bullocks had created a self-renewing ecosystem that fed them, furnished nursery stock for their landscaping business, and sheltered local wildlife.

One edge of their property bordered a wetland that had been reclaimed from abandoned farmland a few years before. At the marsh's edge, cattails grew in thick stands. Young cattail shoots are a delicious wild food, and for several springs and summers the brothers had harvested the baby shoots, steamed or sautéed them, and added them to meals. But one year the shoots disappeared, leaving only tough mature cattail stalks. Their natural food source had dried up, and the brothers wanted to know why.

A close look at the marsh revealed that some animal was gnawing the tender shoots off at the waterline before the sprouts were big enough for the brothers to see. The thieves were thorough. Nothing remained for the Bullock brothers and their families.

The culprit was quickly obvious. "We'd noticed that as the bog matured and became more productive, the muskrat population was really taking off," Douglas Bullock told me. The brothers had built garden beds that extended into the marsh, copying an idea from the ancient Aztecs. They had created peninsulas by piling straw and branches that reached out like fingers from the shoreline, covered them with rich bog muck, and planted these self-watering garden beds, called chinampas, with food and wildlife plants. The local animals, already enjoying the new wetland, responded to the enhanced habitat of the chinampas with explosive breeding. Ducks, kingfishers, herons, and other water birds now abounded, and so did muskrats. "Suddenly the bog looked like a busy harbor, criss-crossed with muskrat wakes," Douglas said. Whole flotillas of muskrats were tunneling into the rich soil along the marsh edge and nibbling down the cattail shoots. The less agile humans couldn't compete with the industrious rodents.

The brothers lamented the loss of their wild food, yet refused to begin exterminating the culprits. "For one thing, we weren't going to kill off the wildlife that we ourselves had attracted," Douglas explained. "For another, we could have shot muskrats for weeks and they'd just breed right back again. The habitat was too good."

A cattail-less season or two went by. Then, suddenly the tasty shoots were back, and the once-busy "harbor" was more tranquil. The muskrat population had dwindled. What had happened?

"Otters moved in," Douglas said. "The muskrats were a great new food source. We'd never seen otters here before. More than otters showed up, too. We got other predators: bald eagles, hawks, owls. They cleaned up." Instead of futilely trying to trap the fast-breeding muskrats, the Bullocks sat back and let nature do the job. The brothers merely provided a rich, diverse habitat where a vigorous food web—one that included predators—could emerge and right imbalances, such as a horde of ravenous muskrats.

THREE ECOLOGICAL PRINCIPLES

The Bullocks have built a superb example of ecological gardening, where humans and wildlife can reap the abundance and live in harmony. What happened on the brothers' land illustrates several principles of ecology that gardeners can use. The cattail/muskrat/otter progression is a good jumping-off point to look at three important and related concepts: the niche, succession, and biodiversity. I'll begin with those and then, throughout this chapter, give examples of other ecological

ideas that can help create sustainable gardens. The ideas presented on the next few pages lay the foundation for the ecological garden. The examples and techniques given in the rest of this book are grounded in these principles of nature.

Finding a Niche

Decades before the Bullocks arrived, the lowest part of their property had been wetland. An industrious farmer had diked, drained, and dried up the "useless" bog and raised crops there for many years. The ecologically oriented Bullocks understood that wetlands, besides being essential for clean water and wildlife habitat, were some of the most productive ecosystems on the planet, teeming with more plants and animals than any farm. They decided to restore the wetland, and tore out the dikes and drains. Water collected in the low ground, and soon the wetland was back.

While the marsh returned, the Bullocks ferried countless loads of mulch and manure onto their land in their straining pickup truck. The brothers also forked rich muck from the bog onto the shore, building soil with organic matter and nutrients. In a few years, this tremendous increase in fertility paid off multifold. Not only could the Bullocks grow more plant varieties than before, but opportunistic wild species could find homes in the enhanced habitat as well. The combination of water and fertile soil was irresistible.

Some of the earliest new tenants were the cattails. Their seeds may have been brought to the renewed bog by waterfowl, or perhaps had lain dormant in the soil for years, hoping for the return of the wetland. The cattails capitalized on the ripe habitat, busily converting sunlight, water, and bog muck into fast-growing shoots.

Wherever there is tender greenery, there is someone to consume it, a lesson that gardeners quickly learn when rabbits, field mice, porcupines, raccoons, and all the rest descend on their vegetables. You can think of this as some horrible corollary of the "Field of Dreams" effect: If you build it, they will come and eat it; but in ecologist's terms, this exemplifies the *niche,* or role played by each organism. The Bullocks, by creating habitat, opened up an opportunity for life to exploit. As if being asked to audition for a new role in a play, organisms suited to the job showed up to occupy this new niche. Think of a niche as a profession, and habitat as the workspace for performing that job.

As habitat becomes more varied, more niches appear. Often, providing habitat triggers a cascade of niches, which is precisely what we're trying to do in the ecological garden. The Bullocks' place is a good example of a niche cascade. The fertile habitat provided a niche for the cattails, which then furnished a new food supply that was quickly exploited by muskrats, animals that are custom-made for eating tender shoreline plants. The opportunism of the muskrats led to both their rise and fall: They fattened happily on the cattails, but that busy harbor of paddling rodents was a beacon for predators. In the still-wild San Juan Islands, otters sheltered somewhere nearby. Nature's grapevine is fast and effective, and it was only a season or two before the otters caught wind of the potential harvest, and moved in. Just as the cattails had started small, ramped up to thriving numbers, and were chewed down to a vestige, so too did the muskrats appear, burgeon, and crash in a cycle now interlocked with those of the cattails and otters.

Eventually a form of stability descended on the Bullocks' land, but it fluctuates now and then as one species or other briefly gains the upper hand and is then hauled back in line. But, where neither cattail, muskrat, nor predators could survive before, all three now thrive, because the Bullocks provided habitat and soil nutrients. The brothers supplied the beginnings, and nature did the rest. Instead of depleted farmland, the Bullocks and their friends can admire a verdant, multispecied wetland, rustling with cattails, sedges, willows, and wildflowers, ripe with blueberries and other fruit, filled with the music of waterfowl and frogs, and offering a glimpse of otters and eagles.

Gardening in Succession

In less than a decade, the Bullock brothers' property leapt from a brambled, overgrown field to a verdant young food forest. Above the bog, where blackberries once sprawled in impenetrable tangles, branches laden with plums and cherries now cast dappled shade on glowing nasturtium blossoms. Nut trees shelter a bamboo grove, and vegetable beds wind into the woods. The brothers created this rich landscape quickly, by working with nature rather than against her. Some of the many techniques they used will gradually unfold throughout this book, but first we'll examine one of the overarching strategies that guided their work: accelerated succession.

When plants first colonize bare earth—for example, an abandoned farm—a progression begins. Certain types of annual grasses, herbs, and flowers are the first flora to arrive, and because of their penchant for speedy colonization, they are called pioneer plants. They're well adapted to invading naked or disturbed soil and mantling the floral emptiness with green. Pioneer plants fill the vegetal vacuum and restart the cycles of life. We know most of this fast-colonizing horde as weeds: crab grass, dandelion, sheep sorrel, pigweed, plantain, chicory, wild lettuce, and many more. Abandoned fields and fresh earth are their milieu, and they have a job to do: sheltering the bare soil from erosive rains, and ferrying nutrients from deep in the soil to the surface where they can be used. These fast-growing, short-lived pioneers preserve and restore the fertility of disturbed ground.

If these weeds are left alone, in a few seasons the short, early annuals are crowded and shaded out by a taller, mostly perennial crew. In the northern half of the United States, these include asters, fireweed, goldenrod, spurge, perennial grasses, and many others. The dense foliage, branching stems, and many textures of the tall weeds offer more niches for insects and birds to shelter, breed, and feed. The amount of living matter, called biomass, increases as nutrients and sunlight are gathered and transformed into tough stalks, thick greenery, and hardy seeds, which in turn become food for insects and other animals. In this way, life quickly gets a firm toehold on the bare ground. Where before the elements needed for life were confined to a thin band of topsoil, now these nutrients surge in a much thicker layer of vegetation filled with mobile animals. Life is scaffolding its way into new territory.

The progression from bare earth to short annual weeds to tall perennials is called *succession*. If allowed to continue, in five to fifteen years the weedy field will be clothed instead with perennial shrubs. With enough rain and fertility, in two or more decades the shrubs will give way to a young forest.

Though succession is a nearly irresistible process, it isn't smoothly linear. At any stage, fire, wind, lightning, the plow, or other disturbance can set it back to an earlier phase. Most landscapes are a mosaic of many successionary stages, at many scales. After disturbances ranging from a catastrophic forest fire to a single blown-down tree, the earliest pioneers can slip in, resulting in a patchy landscape of varying ages and stages.

How does this relate to gardening? Conventional gardens mimic immature ecosystems. They are usually dominated by early-succession plants. Most grasses, flowers, and especially annual vegetables are pioneers. This means that in our love of lawns and orderly gardens, we're attempting to keep our yards at an early stage of ecological development. The bare earth and disturbed soil of a vegetable garden sing a siren song to weeds, which eagerly cover naked ground, pull nutrients out of underlying rock, and prepare the locale for a more mature ecosystem such as shrubland or forest. A pure expanse of well-watered grass is aching, in nature's scheme, for a blitzkrieg from seedlings and shrubs, or at the very least, a spike in diversity via fast-growing annual weeds.

> **A forest is not a static unchanging place, but has a dynamic and resilient stability.**

A yard is a dynamic system, not an unchanging still life. By viewing our landscapes as dynamic ecosystems, rather than as static collections of inert objects, we can create gardens that inherently grow in healthy patterns and directions. This perspective lets us transfer much of the labor of maintaining our yards to nature.

With this viewpoint in mind, we can ask: What kinds of ecosystems do most yards contain? The answers tell us why yard work is so tedious and never-ending. A lawn of grass edged with flowers is an ecological cousin to prairie. The other major plant arrangement found in suburbia, the archetypal turf dotted with occasional trees and shrubs, mimics a savanna (I wonder at the ancient dreams we're acting out when we create these landscapes, which mimic those of our species' infancy on the plains of Africa).

Prairie and savanna flourish only under certain environmental circumstances. These include low rainfall, heavy animal grazing, and frequent fire. Since few suburbanites encourage parched earth, herds of bison, and wildfire in their yards, conditions in most lawns don't favor savanna and prairie. So, what happens to these unhappy ecosystem fragments? A prairie or savanna kept unburnt, well fertilized, and bathed under the stuttering hiss of sprinklers is being urged to ripen into shrubland and forest. This is ecological succession, omnipresent and relentless.

Weeds in our lawn and maple seedlings in the flower beds are testimony to succession's power. Viewed ecologically, the standard suburban yard just wants to grow up. Understanding this lets us ally ourselves with nature's considerable might, instead of battling her.

An immature ecosystem like a lawn demands that we expend time, energy, and materials to wrench back the hands of the ecological clock, holding the land at prairie phase with mowing and weeding. Yet nature—and our irrigation and fertilizers—will inexorably advance the clock another tick, sprouting seedlings and saplings, inundating us with her fecundity. With sprinkler and fertilizer we're tromping on the accelerator, yet with tiller and pruning saw we're slamming on the brake. No system runs well under that kind of schizophrenic regime.

Typical lawns, and vegetable and flower gardens too, to a great extent, suffer from another ecological fault: They are monocultures. As we saw in the previous chapter, nature relies on multifunctionality and redundancy, neither of which can be found in a trophy lawn of Kentucky bluegrass.

Backyard Biodiversity

Even when we allow succession to occur, not every backyard will attract muskrats and otters like the Bullocks' place, but all gardeners can profit from the same natural cycles at work there. Diverse habitat will shrink pest problems. For example, a garden bed planted all to broccoli or roses is a magnet for pests, which will happily chow down on the abundant food so kindly provided, just as the muskrats did with the cattails. When that happens in the typical garden, out come the sprays and insecticidal soaps, adding unpleasantly to the gardener's labor. But by providing habitat for these pests' natural predators, gardeners can let nature do the bug control. Just as the otters, still abundant in the wild San Juans, came to the rescue, so too will beneficial insects, who will shelter in hedges and nature-scapes, ready to pounce on aphids and Japanese beetles. The key is providing biodiversity in the landscape. *Biodiversity* is the variety of organisms present, considered from many levels: cultivar, species, genus, family, and on up to include all five kingdoms, as well as the diversity of habitats and ecosystems. For our purposes, biodiversity means having a semi-wild but well-designed palette of useful plants that will attract and sustain the helpful insects, birds, and other animals we need.

Garden biodiversity comes in two intersecting forms. One is the diversity that the gardener fashions by planting a broad assortment of flowers, shrubs, and trees, which creates a many-layered habitat. The second is the diversity of life that lingers nearby in still-intact wild places—the birds, bugs, and plants both imported and native that are poised to spread into this welcoming habitat. The two depend on each other.

Most towns have enough vacant lots, neglected corners, parks, and flowery landscaping to nurture a lively community of small wildlife. In any but the most impoverished landscape, even in cities, these wild plants and animals have no trouble zeroing in on good habitat. If I lived inside a biological desert—for example, the pesticide-saturated megafarms that supply conventional supermarkets—I couldn't rely on the ready supply of wildlife, including insects, to find my floral offerings. That's why habitat is important. Every blossom-decked corner is a reservoir for helpful wildlife.

The idea of attracting beneficial insects is not new, but the ecological garden carries the concept a few steps further. Almost everything in such a garden has more than one function. I'll go into this idea in detail in a few pages, but here are some quick examples. To attract helpful insects, we could plant bee balm, which also makes a delicious tea, fills the air with minty fragrance, and offers a colorful pink-to-red flower. Or if we're installing a hedge, we can add a shrub such as wild apricot or Nanking cherry, ornamentals whose fruits are good for both wildlife and jam. Then we could

Biodiversity is the variety of organisms present, considered from many levels: cultivar, species, genus, family, and on up to include all five kingdoms as well as the diversity of habitats and ecosystems.

mix in autumn olive, with flowers and berries for insects and birds, but whose roots bear soil-building nitrogen-fixing microbes. I could continue, but the point should be clear. By filling our garden with multifunctional plants and other elements, we create a dense web full of many niches for wildlife, and a rich place for humans as well: a wealth of food, flowers, medicinal herbs and other products, and a place of beauty. Diversity offers a cascade of benefits.

Our love of tidy but not very diverse yards is imprinted upon us by our culture. The immaculate lawn, under siege from ecological writers everywhere, developed in the mild and evenly moist climate of Britain. Its implications are deeply woven into our psyche. A lawn in preindustrial times trumpeted to all that the owner possessed enough wealth to use some of his land for sheer ornament, instead of planting all of it to food crops. And close-mowed grass proclaimed wealth too: a herd of sheep large enough to crop the lawn uniformly short. These indicators of status whisper to us down the centuries. By consciously recognizing the influence of this history, we can free ourselves of it, and let go of the reflexive impulse to roll sod over the entire landscape.

Our addiction to impeccable lawns and soldier-rows of vegetables and flowers is counter to the tendency of nature and guarantees constant work. But we don't need to wield trowel and herbicide with resentment in an eternal war against the exuberant appetite of chicory and wild lettuce for fresh-bared soil. Instead we can create conditions that encourage the plants we want, and let nature do the work, as I'll show next.

A MATURE GARDEN

Since landscapes have an irresistible tendency to mature, why not hop on board the successionary freight train and take advantage of nature's momentum? This is what the Bullock brothers have done, and so can we. With a nudge here and a

tweak there, we can actually accelerate succession, using nature to help a garden mature much faster than it otherwise would. In the ecological garden, we're creating well-developed, productive, and lush landscapes very quickly by riding the tracks already laid down by nature.

Table 2-1 lists the differences between immature and mature landscapes. We can use this understanding to create mature ecosystems in our yards. Table 2-1 reveals some important trends. As a landscape matures, organic matter builds up, in the form of plants, animals, and rich soil. Fewer imports of nutrients are needed from or lost to the outside, and the cycles and patterns become more complex. To help visualize this evolution, let's compare a young ecosystem—a typical annual vegetable or flower garden that starts from seed every year—to a mature woodland.

In the annual garden, the soil is bare many months of the year. The climate is harsh and varies wildly, as the sun bakes the ground in summer, and freeze-thaw cycles heave the exposed soil in winter. Because the short plants are poor protection, wind blasts the ground and rain pounds the soil, washing away nutrients. Even more fertility is carried off each year as the vegetables are harvested and the bare stalks are yanked up during fall cleanup. Thus the nutrient cycles are open, in straight lines—into the garden and then out—rather than closed with lots of recycling. This means that fertility must be imported to replace all that is lost from leaching, erosion, and the near-total removal of plants. And unless the gardener avidly composts and mulches, there's little soil life that can survive the harsh, erratic conditions and low levels of organic matter.

Here, plant diversity is tightly controlled. In fact, true diversity is unwelcome, since it's defined as weeds, pests, and raiding birds or rodents. Nature's knack for spontaneity often means trouble, rather than enjoyment and improvement.

This garden is a simple place. Plants occur in only one layer, about one to three feet high. The flora is in orderly rows or clumps, in very basic

MATURE ECOSYSTEMS

...re ecosystem	Mature ecosystem
	High
(rocks, rainfall)	Biological (plants, animals, humus)
...ny imports)	Closed (recycling)
	Low
...tant	Important
...sh, shaped by ...ving forces	Many, mild, shaped by plants
	Perennials
	High
...y low	High
	High
of plants, nut...	
Food chains	...t, simple, linear	Complex, weblike
Specialization into niches	Few, wide	Many, narrow
Symbiotic relationships	Few	Many
Average size of organisms	Small	Large
Life cycles	Short, simple	Long, complex
Breeding strategy	Many seeds or young, given little support	Few seeds or young, well supported
Stability (resistance to disturbance, invasive plants)	Low	High
Overall complexity and organization	Low	High

Source: Adapted from W. H. Drury and I. C. T. Nisbet, "Succession," *Journal of the Arnold Arboretum* 54 (1973): 331–68.

patterns. The food chain? Only two links: plants to people, or dismayingly, plants to bugs or birds. There are no symbiotic relationships or partnerships, unless the gardener is clever enough to create them through companion planting or with insect-attracting flowers.

With its plants being uprooted every fall, low diversity, and high susceptibility to weeds, pests, and disease, an annual garden is unstable and easily harmed.

Painting this rather dismal portrait of a place where gardeners derive so much pleasure, I've gotten depressed. Before I cheer myself up by examining a mature woodland, I'll mention that the reason these gardens work at all and engender so much enjoyment, is because of the labor that

humans put into them. Annual gardens need our efforts, because we must replace and reconnect all the missing cycles and effort usually provided free by nature. And we enjoy the creative effort and the therapeutic work that goes into our gardens. But if we share the work with nature, and bring into our gardens the wisdom gained in three billion years of evolution, we can have all that the annual garden offers and vastly more.

Let's look at a well-developed forest and see what lessons we can extract from it for our own yards. First, the soil is covered with a layer of duff and shaded by many layers of plants that remain year-round. The vegetation softens the force of rain, sun, and wind, and creates mellow microclimates where seeds quickly germinate and life nestles in comfort. The permanent presence of roots and constantly building carpet of leaf litter offer a perfect home to worms and other creatures of the soil. The abundant soil life captures nutrients and recycles them to plants before they can be washed away. These nutrients are stored, long- and short-term, in ever-present tree trunks, perennial shrubs and herbs, lichens, fungi, mulch, and soil organisms. The forest builds a tremendous reserve of organic matter and minerals. All this biomass acts as a savings account, holding and recycling the forest's valuables as insurance against drought, infestation, or other stressful times.

Most of the forest spans the seasons and the decades. Each year, only a small proportion of the biomass is replaced, that is, only a few plants and animals die. Think of how most of a massive tree persists from year to year, while just its leaves and a few roots die back. Continuity is the rule, unlike the annual garden. Most of nature remains standing through the changing years.

What does die each year is recycled within the ecosystem, with almost no loss. Nearly all of life's products, from tree trunks and deer bones down to insect wings and bacteria cells, are recyclable. Nature assembles and breaks down, dissolves and renews, using the same molecules over and over. She leaves no landfills and toxic dumps in her wake. In nature, there is no such thing as waste. Everything is food for something else, connected in life and death to many other species.

The forest contains hundreds of species of plants, and thousands of varieties of animals and microbes. Biodiversity in the woodland is immense, which allows countless relationships to form. Tied together in interdependent webs, these creatures use nearly all the available food and habitat in the forest, leaving few, if any, niches open for invaders. This hyper-efficient use of resources also means that no single species is likely to get out of balance. What could a pest eat that wasn't already being eaten by some better-established creature? And since these forest species have evolved together, each has defense

mechanisms—tough waxy coatings, bad-tasting chemicals—to ward off its enemies. Invaders can only take advantage of new openings, such as when a tree falls and opens fresh bare ground. But then the forest quickly closes in, and will smother the invader unless the new species finds an unused, narrow niche and makes its peace within the web of life.

The forest is diverse in patterns and cycles as well. From open sky to earth, the vegetation ranges in many layers: high canopy, low trees, shrubs, tall herbs, ground hugging rosettes and creepers, and vines that span the whole range. Amid all this varied habitat are hundreds of niches for insects, birds, and other creatures. Food webs are complex, with plants, grazers, predators, top carnivores, and decomposers entwined in a varied and many-partnered dance. Relationships among species are equally enmeshed. Trees have symbiotic partnerships with specific fungi and bacteria that bring nutrients from soil to root. Plants extract minerals from deep in the soil for others to use. Birds and mammals ferry seeds to new locales, redistributing fertility in the form of manure along the way. If one thread of this web is broken, thousands of others stand near to hold the forest's fabric intact.

A forest is not a static, unchanging place, but has a dynamic and resilient stability. Compared to a conventional garden, there is little role for pests, disease, invasive plants, and upheaval. Nature has sewn the forest together into a unified tapestry, rather than a collection of disconnected plants and animals.

With the contrasts between the annual garden and the mature forest in mind, we can think about arranging our gardens so they will mimic mature ecosystems, rather than young ones. We don't need to do all the work, either. Just as in the Bullock brothers' landscape, if we lay the groundwork, nature will create many of the connections and fill in the gaps.

Here are the features of natural landscapes that are most important to include in the ecological garden:

- deep soil that is rich in nutrients and organic matter;
- plants that draw fertility from deep in the earth, from the air, and from rainwater;
- many layers of vegetation to create varied niches for other creatures;
- an emphasis on perennial plants;
- mutually helpful relationships among plants, insects, birds, microbes, mammals, and all other inhabitants, including people;
- increasingly closed cycles; that is, over time the garden should require fewer supplies from outside, producing most of its own fertilizer, mulch, seeds, new plants, and so on. Except for the harvest, little from the garden is lost by leaching and erosion—it's all recycled.

In the rest of this chapter, I'll briefly describe how to apply these insights from ecology in the garden. But the rest of the book will go into a great deal more detail.

A FEW OF NATURE'S TRICKS FOR GARDENERS

Along with differing levels of biodiversity, one of the biggest contrasts between most gardens and natural landscapes is that if left untended, a garden falls apart, while nature doesn't. We've all returned from vacation to find our favorite plants eaten, weeds rampant, and the whole garden drooping from that unexpected hot spell. The natural condition of a garden, without the gardener, is dead—or returned to wilderness. The natural condition of a forest is healthy and vigorous. However, with a few lessons from nature, we can design gardens that will inherently become more fertile, healthy, well-watered, and will have the dynamic stability, resilience, and exuberance of natural ecosystems. This section gives a brief overview of how to do this; the rest of the book will go into detail.

Soil Building

How can we apply nature's wisdom to the garden? First, as in any garden, start with the soil. Nature builds soil from the top down and from the bottom up. By "top down" I mean the constant rain of leaf litter from above that decomposes into fluffy earth. Nature doesn't rotary-till, and we don't need to either. To create a mature soil quickly, just pile on the organic matter with deep layers of mulch. The mulch quickly composts in place to create mature soil that is bursting with organic matter, teeming with soil life, ready to nurture healthy plants. Chapter 4 gives detailed techniques for building soil with mulches.

The complement, bottom-up soil building, is done with plants. In nature, fertility comes from the vegetation and soil life, not from a bag of fertilizer. Many plants excel at pulling nutrients from deep in the earth and siphoning them to the surface where other plants can use them. These varieties are discussed in chapter 6 and cited in the appendix. In a vegetable garden, harvesting will constantly remove nutrients, so this withdrawn fertility will have to be replaced with small additions of mulch, compost, or fertilizer. But with nutrient-accumulating plants in the garden, the task of spreading fertilizer will dwindle to almost nothing.

Together, the top-down and bottom-up techniques will quickly generate the finest soil you've ever seen.

Perennials versus Annuals

Next, the ecological garden imitates a mature ecosystem by emphasizing perennials rather than annuals. For ornamental and wildlife gardens, this is easy, as thousands of perennial flowers, shrubs, and trees are available. At first glance, though, perennials seem a tough limitation for vegetable gardens. However, I'm not saying that tomatoes and peppers are taboo. I still grow plenty. But many annuals can be replaced with perennials. Perennial greens abound: Good King Henry, perennial kale and broccoli, French sorrel, and many others, some of which are described in chapter 6. There are perennial onions, root crops, herbs, and of course, vegetables such as asparagus, artichokes, and rhubarb. And don't forget the obvious perennial food plants, such as berries, fruits, and nuts.

The advantages of perennials are legion. They eliminate seed-starting, tilling, and the opportunity for weeds that tilling brings. That makes three chores slashed off the list at one stroke. Perennials also need less water and fertilizer than annuals. Their deep root systems tap into pockets of moisture and nutrients that annuals just can't reach. Because they are year-round plants, perennials also offer dependable habitat to wildlife and beneficial insects.

Multiple Stories

An ecological garden has many layers, from a low herb layer through shrubs and small trees to the large overstory. Each layer can contain ornamental species, varieties for food and other human uses, wildlife plants, and flora for building soil and maintaining a healthy ecosystem. Together the layers provide diverse habitat, many products, and plenty of visual interest. In sunny climes, large trees can be closely spaced to provide shade, while in cooler or grayer zones the trees can be spread out to allow ample light and warmth. Chapter 10 tells how to create these forestlike gardens.

Plant Communities

The plants in an ecological garden, just as in nature, aren't isolated individuals but form communities. Long ago, ecologists (as well as native peoples) recognized that many plants and animals occur in distinct groups. Certain species seem always to show up with the same companions. In the arid West, piñon pine and juniper appear together, and with them frequently are Gambel's oak and mountain mahogany. In the East, a common community is the oak/hickory forest, with mapleleaf viburnum

and dogwoods often filling the understory. There are hundreds of plant communities, and each contains a recognizable array of trees, shrubs, and flowers whose composition varies from one community to the next. These communities can include specific animals, too. Oak/hickory forests are home specifically to blue jays, tanagers, and grosbeaks. Piñon/juniper groves often harbor piñon jays and bushtits. Different environments favor different communities.

In the ecological garden, we steal a page from nature's book and often group plants in communities. Some gardeners have re-created the natural plant communities that occur in their region, while others have tinkered with plant groupings, swapping some plants with human uses or other functions in place of natives. The design of multifunctional plant communities is a new field that's in its infancy, and at the cutting edge of horticulture. Clever garden designers have put together some beautiful, productive, and labor-saving plant combinations. A single garden plant community, besides providing the gardener with eye-catching blossoms and foliage, food, and herbs, might also contain plants to repel pests, generate mulch, accumulate nutrients, attract beneficial insects, and shelter wildlife. Much of this book, in particular chapters 8, 9, and 10, tells how to create harmonious groupings of plants that nurture each other and provide for both the gardener and wildlife.

Stacking Functions

Our discussion of niches, succession, and biodiversity leads to another important principle of the ecological garden: Every part of the garden does more than just one thing. Permaculture designers have a bit of jargon to describe this. They call it "stacking functions." Nothing in nature has only one function; it is furiously efficient in this way. A shrub, for example, doesn't just cast shade. It feeds winter-starved birds with its berries, offers shelter, mulches the soil with its leaves, provides browse for hungry deer and porcupines, blocks the wind,

DO PLANT COMMUNITIES REALLY EXIST?

Ecologists have been arguing for decades about whether plant communities are real. Some say they are merely random assemblies of species that happen to like the same climate, soil, and other environmental conditions. Other ecologists believe communities form in part because of interactions and mutual benefits among the members, and act somewhat like whole organisms. The jury is still out. In support of the random-grouping argument, a little botanizing shows that any two examples of the same community always contain different species and numbers of plants. No two communities are alike. Also, as the climate changes, the species that make up the community change gradually, with one or two species dropping out here, and a couple of new ones moving in there. If communities were tightly bound systems like organisms, they should have distinct boundaries. Thus, you'd expect their makeup to change abruptly, as if you'd traveled from one country into another, rather than gradually.

On the other hand, a plant community has a definite structure. If it lacks certain members, the community as a whole suffers. For example, Douglas fir forests that don't contain a particular fungus—a type of truffle—aren't as healthy as those that do. Without the truffle, the fir forest won't have many red-backed voles, a rodent that feeds on the fungus. Lacking voles to eat, the spotted owl population will diminish. This poverty ripples through many species, and the whole community is diminished. Thus, communities are linked together in an intricate webwork. Also, ecologists have shown that even when there are no environmental gradients—when temperature and nutrient levels remain the same over a large area—organisms still sort themselves into different highly structured groupings that vary from place to place.

I believe that communities are held together by their interactions as well as by their environment. The ecological gardens I've seen seem to bear this out: communities—groups of plants linked in relationships—make for very healthy gardens, as we shall see.

holds the soil with its roots, collects and channels rainwater, and on and on.

Nature always stacks functions, because that shrub, or any living thing, represents a big investment in matter and energy, two things that nature husbands with immense stinginess. She is supreme at getting the most bang for her buck, squeezing every erg of energy out of that shrub, tying it into lots of other cycles to maximize the return. The shrub's berries took energy to grow, so when a bird eats them, the plant trades its effort for seed dispersal, making hard seeds that will pass unharmed through the bird's gut to germinate on new ground. The leaves gather solar energy, but with no extra effort are arranged to channel rainwater to the stems and down to the roots, increasing the shrub's collection area. By making plants perform multiple functions, nature uses her energy investment very efficiently

Most human designs, in contrast, are prodigiously wasteful. We seem to hurry our goods from source to landfill in an arrow-straight stream, while nature would bend and re-bend that stream into a zigzag course, extracting benefit at every turn and recycling what's left. By designing our gardens with the same principles in mind, they become far less wasteful and troublesome, far more productive and bountiful. Stacking functions is a key rule, and one of the most important to follow.

Here's an example of stacking functions in a landscape design. Adjoining my house is a 5,000-gallon water tank that stores rainwater. It's mostly buried, but the ten-by-twelve foot lid projects above the ground, an ugly gray slab of concrete next to the kitchen. To hide the concrete, I nailed a cedar deck over it, but in the blazing summer sun the deck was too hot to enjoy. Then I built an arbor over the deck, and trained two seedless grapes on the arbor. A trellis on the tank's side is entwined by jasmine, wafting perfume over the deck. Now the cistern has become a cool, shady spot beneath the fast-growing grapes, where my wife and I linger while lunching at a small table beneath the green canopy. Our houseplants spend their summer vacation there on one light-dappled corner. In late summer, after we've eaten lunch, we simply reach overhead for a dessert of sweet grapes.

The grape leaves shade our house as well, keeping the kitchen cool in summer, but in autumn the leaves drop, allowing the much-needed sun to stream onto the deck and the kitchen window. The leaves go to the compost pile or straight to a garden bed as mulch. When I prune the vine in winter, I take plenty of cuttings to propagate for friends. Overflow from the cistern irrigates the grapes and other plantings nearby.

By combining the water tank, grapevine, and deck in the right arrangement, I've increased the usefulness of each, and get benefits that none alone would provide. Nearly every element does several jobs.

Gardeners are already good at stacking functions. A simple compost pile is multifunctional: it disposes of waste, creates fertile humus, boosts soil life, and even offers the gardener a little exercise through turning and spreading. Even a one-specied hedge of privet can serve as a windbreak, privacy screen, and bird habitat. By recognizing the advantages of stacking functions, and designing our gardens with this in mind, we can gain wonderful synergies from our own backyards.

The concept of stacking functions has two halves, two rules that reinforce each other. The first is that each element of a design—each plant or structure—should do more than one job. My grape arbor illustrates that rule: The grapevine shades the deck while letting in light in winter, cools the house, provides food, mulch, and propagation stock, and helps beautify an otherwise ugly water tank.

The second principle is the complement of the first. Each job to be done in a design—each system or process—should be performed or supported by more than one element. In other words, always have backups in place. Once again, gardeners already follow this rule more or less unconsciously.

We plant several varieties of vegetables in case one fails, or different fruits or flowers to yield over a long season. And every gardener has an array of sprinklers, drip irrigation gadgets, soaker hoses, special hose nozzles, and watering cans, all for the single purpose of delivering water to our plants. Multiple, layered systems such as these are more effective at doing the total job than any one device would be.

There are many advantages to this sort of redundancy. A quick glance at how nature does it shows some of the benefits. One is disaster protection. Most important functions in organisms and ecosystems have backups, often several layers deep. Look at our sense of balance. We use three independent methods to keep our equilibrium. First, our eyes tell us what position we're in. Second, our ears contain a fluid-filled chamber lined with hairs that are sensitive to orientation. The hairs' position tells our brain which way is up. And third, our muscles and tendons have receptors that telegraph data on our limb movements and positions. By devoting energy and organs to this "tell me three times" strategy, our bodies make a big investment in not falling over. It's worth it, because if we relied only on, say, our eyes, a flash of blinding sunlight on a steep mountain path could drop us off a cliff. Any organism or system with backups survives longer. For example, if the soil is well mulched, then when the irrigation fails during a vacation, the plants may survive the waterless glitch.

Redundancy also boosts yield. Using another example from the human body, think of how the lower digestive tract filters all the nutrition it can from food by making multiple passes on a meal. The small intestine extracts a portion of the nutrient load, then the large intestine absorbs more, and the bacteria in the gut convert yet more to a useful form. This multilayered approach ekes out nearly all available sustenance from food. In the same way, a garden with several layers of water-conserving techniques, frost protection, disease proofing, wind deflection, or soil-building strategies will gain a cumulative benefit from the multiple techniques.

These benefits of redundancy aren't lost on ecological gardeners and permaculturists, who sum up this principle with this guideline: Each function should be served by multiple elements.

The two aspects of function stacking—each element performs multiple functions, and each function is served by multiple elements—can be used throughout the garden, on many levels, to align the landscape with nature's might. The succeeding chapters give plenty of examples.

Since this chapter is about ecology for gardeners, I won't attempt to cover every ecological concept. The ideas covered—the niche, succession, biodiversity, stacking functions, and others—are those that seem to me most important for gardeners to understand so they can create natural landscapes that provide for people's needs. Ecology studies the relationships among living creatures. It is those relationships that transform a collection of inert objects into a living, dynamic landscape. With this in mind, we can now look at some design tools for building just such a landscape.

Chapter 3

Designing the Ecological Garden

GARDENING BOOKS AND magazines are packed with design ideas. They describe how to group plants according to color, or juxtapose shapes and foliage patterns to please the eye. They can teach methods of massing plants to carry the gaze toward a stunning landscape feature. Some will reveal tricks that make a small yard look large or help a large lot feel cozy and intimate. These types of garden design techniques aid in selecting plants that are quite attractive and will make your yard look very pretty.

That's not what this chapter is about.

I'm not knocking the aesthetics of garden design. An ugly landscape cramps the soul, while a beautiful one invites, relaxes, and heals the viewer. Yet a garden that is designed only to look pretty barely skims the surface of what landscapes can offer. A place designed according to principles deeper than those of mere appearance can still be beautiful, but will also shelter wildlife, feed people and animals, purify the air and water, and be an asset to the earth.

No human designed an alpine meadow, or a tropical forest, or a creekside grotto, yet these wild landscapes are never ugly. They follow a larger natural order that seems to ensure beauty. In the previous chapter we began to glimpse a few aspects of nature's order. Now we can use these principles and patterns of nature to design our gardens.

An ecological design recognizes that nothing in nature stands alone and disconnected. Any garden will reflect this connectedness, whether we want it to or not. Plant a big patch of broccoli or roses, for example, and aphids will quickly find it, feasting on the new food source. Presto, our new plant is connected to the rest of nature, even if we'd rather it weren't. Anything we plant will instantly tie to natural cycles, taking in nutrients and water, releasing oxygen and other molecules to the air and soil, converting sunlight to greenery, and being seen as food and habitat by insects, birds, microbes, and the rest of life.

The environmentalists' adage that everything is connected to everything else is true. Any element of a design—a plant, a path, or a greenhouse or other structure—is in relationship with many other elements. How the design's pieces are connected is at least as important as what the pieces are. An ecologically designed garden will do more than just accept this dynamic interconnectedness—it will revel in it and turn it to advantage. For example, if one of our favorite plants is a magnet for aphids, then a good designer will discover and create conditions that discourage aphid infestations. Instead of installing a solid block of roses or broccoli, we can scatter the plants among other species to make them harder for aphids to find. Reducing the amount of nitrogen in the soil will help too, since aphids particularly enjoy succulent, nitrogen-fattened plants. And we can foster habitat for aphid predators such as ladybugs and parasitic wasps, a remedy that will reduce insect pests in general. The best solutions will have benefits that reach far beyond the original problem.

A rosebush, for example, is connected to many other species, including the aphids it so readily attracts. The aphids in turn lure ladybugs, the ladybugs are hungrily devoured by birds, and the birds leave their droppings to feed microbes and fertilize the rose. Each plant or object in a landscape is busy interacting with other elements and being acted upon in turn. Thus, to have a landscape that doesn't just look natural, but acts like a natural ecosystem, we need a way of thinking about the pieces of our design that goes beyond mere appearances. If we fully grasp what each design element is, and how it connects to the other pieces, we can connect the parts in a way that is elegant, efficient, productive, and beautiful.

Remember how self-reliant a natural landscape is. An ecosystem provides for itself. No one brings in truckloads of fertilizer to a forest; no one carries its waste to the dump. The forest takes care of all that internally, producing fertility and recycling litter and debris. In other words, the forest's inputs and outputs are balanced, with little waste. And sunlight powers virtually all the work.

A natural landscape harvests the energy (sun, wind, heat) and the matter (water and nutrients) that flow through it, acting as a net to catch these resources and transform them into more life. Nearly everything that enters a natural landscape is captured and used, absorbed and reincarnated as leaf, bug, flesh, or feather. And anything produced in that landscape, from byproducts such as sugary root secretions to "wastes" such as manure and molted insect casings, is recycled, swallowed up again and reincorporated into new living tissue.

Billions of years of evolution have left few loose ends in nature. One creature's waste is another's food. Nearly every niche is tightly held, every habitat is packed full of interconnected species. Nature's immense creativity ensures that anything faintly resembling a resource will be used as one— if one species can't use it, another will.

It is this interconnectedness—this linking of one species' "outputs" to another's "inputs"—that we seek to re-create in the ecological garden. Unfortunately, we don't have billions of years to wait while our gardens evolve to the immense webbiness of the natural landscape. But we have another tool: our creative minds. We can consciously evaluate the pieces of our landscape, and design the connections. Then our gardens can be almost as interlinked as nature is, producing no waste or pollutants, needing little excess labor, ripe with habitat, yielding abundantly. This chapter offers a set of steps for designing a garden such as this—one that has the feel and dynamics of nature. Then we'll look more closely at nature's patterns and how they can be applied to the garden.

THE ECOLOGICAL DESIGN PROCESS

Briefly, the steps in creating an ecological garden design are:

- **Observation:** Here we ask, What do we have to work with? What are the conditions and constraints of the site?
- **Visioning:** What should the design do? What do we want? What does the site need? How should it feel?
- **Planning:** What do we need to make our ideas happen? How should the pieces be assembled?

- **Development:** What will the final design look like? How will we make it happen?
- **Implementation:** The final step: How to install the garden.

One note before we examine the design process. Every landscape design has two "clients" with their own needs: the people who live there, and the land itself. When people try to force a design upon a place that won't support it—large green lawns in the desert, for example—they're fighting an uphill battle. Only vast amounts of work, energy, resources, and money will keep an unsuitable design functioning. Those kinds of high inputs are contrary to an ecological design—nature doesn't work that way. And if the gardener relaxes for a moment, nature will prove how unsuitable the design is. With a few lengthy dry spells, sweltering summers, hordes of munching insects, or any other of its tricks, nature will outlast the gardener and defeat an impractical design.

We're trying to design places that piggyback onto nature and work with its boundless energy, not fight against it. We can do this by recognizing that the land has its own set of requirements and tendencies just as we do.

Let's go through the design steps in detail.

Observation

Knowing the site is the first step in good design. You can begin the process by making a map of the site. The map doesn't have to be pretty, but it should include buildings, roads, and paths; existing trees and other principal plants; slope and major land features; drainage and watercourses; soil types and conditions (clay or sandy, boggy or dry, and so on); and scales and distances. Almost any good book on conventional landscape design will give details for making a simple map of a property. Several are listed in the bibliography.

Making a map creates more than just a piece of paper. Each time I prepare a map, I become aware of details I would never notice otherwise. Mapmaking

puts me in intimate contact with a place. Slope, view, distance, pockets of coolness and warmth, flickers of sun and shadow, all come into sharp relief as I walk the land. The knowledge deposits itself in my mind and waits for use. The place takes on a wholeness, a fullness that my senses encompass, all symbolized on a simple piece of paper that connects to an image inside me.

Observation goes far beyond simply noting the objects on the site. Observation at its best means being immersed in the place. Who lives there? When do various birds and other animals come and go? What do they eat or otherwise use at the site? What interactions take place among the plant, animal, and human inhabitants? The first step is just to list these observations. Later, you can research your observations in books or flesh them out with further fieldwork.

It's not easy to separate the process of observation from analysis. We almost automatically combine a raw observation, such as "this plant's leaves are turning yellow" with an analysis: "because it needs more nitrogen." But in the early phase of observation, it's important to retain a childlike quality of wonder without moving instantly to analysis. Analysis channels our thinking and reduces our options. When we leap down the path to "nitrogen deficiency" we immediately think of a certain class of solutions: this plant needs fertilizer. But by patiently remaining with the simple observation that "this plant's leaves are turning yellow," we open many options. Later, with other observations to help inform us we can ask: Should we keep this sickly plant? Should we add companion plants to aid it? Is this an appropriate species to have here? What plants will be happier in these conditions? How much soil improvement do we want to engage in? By not moving too quickly to the analysis phase we leave open a wealth of options that goes far beyond a choice of fertilizers. We're not looking for solutions at this point in our design process, but simply an understanding of what we have.

Keep track of these observations. The most

TABLE 3-1.

WHAT TO OBSERVE—A DESIGNER'S CHECKLIST

- Areas of shade and sun
- Wind direction, intensity, and change over the seasons
- Temperature highs and lows, dates of first and last frosts
- Points of sunrise, sunset, winter and summer solar zenith
- Microclimates (cool, hot, wet, or dry spots)
- Rainfall amounts and seasons, snow, hail
- Soil (drainage, heavy or light, sand or clay, rich or depleted, stable or slumping)
- Creeks, gullies, water movement during rain, flooding zones
- Rock outcrops
- Views in various directions
- Activities of neighbors that may affect design (noise, children, pets, visits, etc.)
- Utilities: power, phone, sewer, and gas lines
- Homeowners association and government activities: recycling, yard waste pickup, herbicide spraying, water rationing, zoning and construction restrictions, easements
- Traffic and access roads, frequency of traffic, heavy or light vehicles, pedestrian traffic
- Location and impact of structures: house, garage, fences, walls, etc.
- Vegetation: species present, invasive or noxious plants, rare species, and their state of health
- Animals: native and introduced, pests, "scary" animals (snakes, spiders)
- History of the land (talk to locals, study old books, maps, photos)
- Resources in neighborhood (sources of organic matter, soil, and building materials): sawmills, factories, food processors, stores, landfills, plant and seed sources

common way to do this is with a written list, but not everyone's brain is wired the same way. Some people will find it more useful to make a video or tape recording with commentary, or annotated sketches. Choose a method that works for you.

After making the initial observations, do research via books or the internet to get details or to learn more about characteristics that can't be observed directly.

Visioning

Now that we know what we have at the site, we can dream about what we want, what the place can look and feel like, and what could be happening there. During this phase it helps to have a notebook or tape recorder to preserve our ideas. Long, multiple lists are fine. We're just brainstorming without judgments or practical considerations here. Later we'll winnow the lists.

This phase is a no-holds-barred process, reined in only by ecological and ethical constraints. This simply means that the new landscape should be a net asset; that is, Earth and its inhabitants should be better off, not worse, for the changes to this space. Unfortunately, many conventional landscape designs leave the planet a poorer place. Unlike natural landscapes, they are dependent on massive inputs of fertilizer, pesticides, water, and fossil fuel–driven machinery. They're devoid of habitat and offer little more to the owners than a place to park a lawn chair. It's not difficult to do better.

For a garden to be considered ecological, the new landscape should:

- require few outside inputs, especially once it's mature;
- create rather than destroy wildlife habitat;
- enhance air, water, and soil quality; and
- eventually result in less work instead of more for the human occupants.

Further chapters of this book will detail techniques that easily meet these requirements, but we should hold these principles firmly in mind during the garden design.

Now we can create our vision. Here are the kinds of questions to ask during the visioning process:

- What do you and the other human inhabitants want and need from the landscape? What can it offer? Possibilities include food, herbs, wildlife habitat, cut flowers, privacy, income, play space, or all of these. Research what's available, and go into a little detail, remembering that this is just the dreaming phase.
- What does the landscape and region need? Has previous abuse caused a problem that can be

corrected by good design? Does the soil need rejuvenating? Are trees dying, plants struggling? Would the land benefit from a pond, from wildlife habitat? Are rare native plants growing here that can be nurtured? Could the design regenerate and replenish a damaged landscape, and offer a chance of survival to endangered species?

- What are your skills, physical and financial resources, limitations, likes and dislikes? How much time and money are you willing and likely to spend on the design, implementation, and maintenance? Include children and any helpful neighbors in these considerations. A design cannot succeed without a realistic picture of the resources and limitations that constrain it.
- How should the new landscape feel? Like a forest, a Garden of Eden, a meadow, a sanctuary?
- What will you do there?
- What kind of food, herbs, medicinal plants, firewood, timber, or other products, can the land provide sustainably, for the long haul?
- Will the place have an overall theme or function such as education, sanctuary, demonstration site, simple living, or market gardening?

Let your imagination run free, and keep a list of the possibilities. When noting the items your want in the landscape, think in terms of what they do instead of giving them a static name. Rather than writing down "fence," call it a barrier, which invites far more possibilities: It could be a hedge, rock wall, trench, or even a moat. Instead of "compost pile" think "organic matter recycling." See the difference? Listing the pieces of the design by function rather than with an inert description will keep far more options open.

Planning

Now we sort through the observations and visions, clambering toward the future landscape. This portion of ecological garden design is the most demanding, but an abundance of useful tools exist to help us. I've broken this phase into three segments: priorities, analysis, and layout.

PRIORITIES. To make sense of what may be pages of notes, we need first to make priorities. What are the most urgent problems or desires that we need to address? Is it getting rid of the energy-gobbling lawn, redirecting runoff from the front walk, growing some food? Priorities can be personal, as in, "First I need a place to sit quietly; then I'll have the energy to build the rock walls I want." Examine the least important aspects of the vision too; perhaps these contradict the more important ones, or can just be dispensed with. If it helps, break priorities into several categories: personal, aesthetic, problems to be solved, environmental/ecological, and the like. See which categories and items leap out as the most important.

ANALYSIS. Now we can collect the design elements—plants, structures, tasks, functions—that will make our vision come alive. How do we choose and assemble them? The guiding principle here, once again, is that we're not creating a static collection of objects, but a dynamic, living landscape full of interactions between its inhabitants. This is the time to make a list of the things that will satisfy our vision. What kind of fruits go in the Garden of Eden? What species will attract the wildlife we want? Make detailed lists of species and structures. Later chapters and the appendix will offer many suggestions for this step.

These lists generate a lot of individual pieces. Next, and most important, is to see how the pieces of our design can be connected to create a living landscape. To do this, we need to think about how each element behaves. We can ask: What does this plant need to thrive? What harms it and thus should be kept away? What does it offer the other elements in the landscape? What can it take from them? What does it create? What does it destroy? Then we can search for other items in our visioning and planning lists that satisfy these needs, or add new elements if they're needed. If plant A needs lots of nitrogen, find a nitrogen-producing species to go alongside. Each clever linkage between design elements means one less job for the gardener, one less wheelbarrow load to schlep into or out of the garden. Each need not satisfied by another component of the design becomes work for the gardener; each product not used becomes pollution. The idea is to minimize both by designing wise connections.

Table 3-2 shows an example of this linking process using a pear tree. I've listed the pear tree's products, activities (such as casting shade), its intrinsic qualities (height, color, and so forth), and its needs, including some that aren't obvious. Using this list, we can try to connect the pear tree to the other plants and structures in our design in a way that will provide or use as many items on the list as possible.

With enough time, we could make a list like this for each element in our design. Given the constraints of the real world, where we never have enough time, we could just make lists for significant and representative elements (such as important plant species; "hardscape" features, including greenhouses, paths, and fences; and other items such as ponds and hedgerows). For the items for which we don't make lists, we can just try to think about them from this "linking" viewpoint, seeing the pieces of the design as dynamic, interacting entities that connect to each other.

With our lists in hand, we can now link the products, needs, and activities to other potential elements of a design. The box on page 36 looks at a few items on the pear-tree list that might pose problems or might inspire creative uses.

Using this linking technique, people have contrived ingenious interconnections in their garden designs. In Colorado, Jerome Osentowski attached a chicken coop to his greenhouse. This setup uses the birds' body heat to warm the plants, the carbon dioxide from their breath to stimulate plant growth, and the manure for fertilizer. He also employs the birds' natural scratching behavior to weed and till garden beds. The chickens eat bugs, too.

A trick used by other gardeners is to dig a pond on the south side of a greenhouse or group of fruit trees, where the reflected light aids in ripening and heating. Clever connections abound; we just have to imagine and design them.

To sum up this analysis segment: Each plant or structure in a garden design should have its needs

TABLE 3-2.

A PEAR TREE'S PRODUCTS, NEEDS, ACTIVITIES, AND QUALITIES

Products	Activities	Needs	Intrinsic Qualities
leaves	soil stabilization	water	color
wood	dust collection	nutrients	shape
seeds	soil loosening via roots	carbon dioxide	soil requirements
oxygen	nutrient transport	oxygen	climate requirements
water	wildlife habitat	sunlight	flavor
fruit	wind reduction	soil	scent
pollen	water purification	pollen	height
bark	mulch and soil building	pollinators	canopy spread
sap	water transport	protection from browsing, pests, and disease	root depth and spread
carbon dioxide	casting shade	pruning	

SOME PEAR TREE CONNECTIONS

PRODUCTS

Fruit: We should eat or preserve it all. If not, we should consider an animal to clean up fallen fruit, or neighbors or a charity to take the surplus.

Pollen: Our tree can pollinate other pears, or, combined with other pollen sources, provide food for bees. Do we want to raise honeybees?

Shade: We can grow shade-tolerant plants beneath the pear, or place the tree where the shade will be useful. Remember that it casts *seasonal* shade, so the tree could cool a building in summer but let needed light through in winter. We'll need to consider the final height of the tree (an intrinsic quality) when placing other sun-loving plants nearby.

Mulch and soil building: Leaves and roots will help build and loosen soil, but rotting leaves could cause fungal diseases (such as scab) if there isn't healthy soil life to break them down quickly. If we want to rake the leaves, we should plan where to locate paths and the compost pile.

NEEDS

Now let's consider the tree's needs, which may be trickier to deal with than the products.

Pollen: Is the tree self-fertile or does it need another pear tree for pollination? Do we want two fruit-bearing pear trees, or should the second be an ornamental variety?

Water: Is there adequate rainfall? Can we use water-conservation techniques, such as mulches and dense plantings under the tree to shade and hold water in the soil? Can these plantings provide for other needs too, such as . . .

Nutrients: Many plants pull nutrients from deep in the subsoil into their leaves, adding them to the topsoil at leaf-fall. We can underplant the pear tree with some of these accumulator plants (described in chapter 6 and the appendix). These plants can be mulched in place to build soil and offer nutrients. Meanwhile, can a nearby source of fertilizer suffice until the garden is producing its own?

Pollinators: Pollinator-attracting plants and beneficial-insect habitat should be near the pear tree. Can some of these plants also provide food, mulch, or plant nutrients?

Protection from browsers, pests, and disease: Do we need a deer fence? Can we use hedges or thorny plants to do this? How do we attract insects that will fight off pests?

Pruning: Should we choose a dwarf tree so we don't need an orchard ladder for pruning and harvesting? Can we use the cuttings to make a woody compost pile (see *hugelkultur,* chapter 4). Or shall we just let the tree take on a natural shape?

---

met by other design elements, and offer help to other elements. Dreaming up these connections often involves a cascading thought process—we choose a design element that we want, see what it needs and can offer, then find a desired element that meets some of those requirements, then see what connects to the second element, and so on. This process is intended to build a dense web of connections, but if done haphazardly can create a tangled mass of confused feedback loops and dead ends.

Fortunately, permaculture offers a system to help organize the process of designing connections, one that breaks it down into small chunks that can be easily grasped and managed. For that

technique, we need to look at the next segment in the planning step.

LAYOUT. One system that helps manage garden layout is called the Zone-and-Sector method. This method, used in permaculture, helps us decide where to place all the pieces of the garden so that they work with each other—and for us—most effectively.

The Zone-and-Sector method begins at the doorstep. Consider the house to be Zone o. Then place the plants and other landscape elements that you use most often, or that require the most care, closest to the house. Perhaps you like fresh herbs in nearly every meal. Where should you plant your herbs? The cofounder of permaculture, Bill Mollison, offers some guidance. "When you get up in the morning and the dew is on the ground," he says, "put on your woolly bathrobe and your fuzzy slippers. Then walk outside to cut some chives and other herbs for your omelet. When you get back inside, if your slippers are wet, your herbs are too far away."

In this system, the herbs should be placed in what is called Zone 1. Encompassing the area enclosed by a line about 20 to 40 feet from the house, Zone 1 contains what is used most often. A typical Zone 1 might hold intensively weeded and mulched garden beds, a patio or tiny lawn, a shady arbor, a cherry tomato plant or two, a dwarf fruit tree, and the loveliest and most delicate plants. Any elements of the design that need continual observation, frequent visits, or rigorous techniques—such as an espaliered tree or a trellised wisteria—belong in Zone 1.

This only makes sense. How often have you seen a weed-choked vegetable garden languishing 50 or 100 feet from a house? It's not on the way to anywhere, it's not under the kitchen window where sprouting weeds and past-due vegetables would alarm someone washing dishes. The little energetic hump created by the distance to the garden can be just enough to inspire neglect.

Zones are not neat concentric circles originating at the house. Their boundaries are permeable and bleed into one another. Zones are shaped and squeezed by topography, soil, available sunlight, native vegetation, and the homeowner's needs.

Zones help us organize the elements and the energy flows of our property in the right relationships, allowing us to weave order according to how often we use or need to care for something. Zones are based on dynamic relationships. Rather than thinking in terms of static categories— flower, vegetable, tree—we think of how we interact with the parts of our design. Items used every day, whether salad greens, cut flowers,

cherry tomatoes, or a patio, go right outside the door. If we like cucumbers in our daily lunch, we plant accordingly. In this new order, a vining cucumber that was previously relegated to a far-off vegetable garden becomes a wonderful choice for the arbor over an attached deck, where harvest is simple. A scented rose could crouch under a frequently opened window, wafting its fragrance indoors.

Look what's happening here. The edges of the house are beginning to blur a bit. Where does the building end and the garden begin? Ordering our landscape by use and not by shape or size fuzzes some of the old categories. Those espaliered dwarf pears against the fence—is that the orchard, the hedge, or, after the wood posts rot, perhaps the fence itself?

Good design suggests that we tailor our zones to our own lives. The gourmand will want a mesclun bed and herbs by the door, and baby carrots not much farther away. The "Come over to my place after work" type will give the patio and a cozy arbor pride of place.

Bring your garden close to home, particularly the plants you nibble every day. Vegetable gardens are ugly, you say? Then abandon straight-row gardening. Curve the garden beds, follow the contours of your yard—or create some. Think of the yard as a multifunctional landscape that provides food, beauty, habitat for beneficial insects, even its own fertilizer. In Zone 1, we can create attractive blends of perennials, annuals, salad herbs, shrubs, insect- and bird-attracting flowers, and nutrient-accumulating plants that build fertility.

I can attest to how well the zone method works. For years, our main garden was 100 feet from the house, its location and 8-foot deer fence a legacy from the previous owner. With marauding deer making outside-the-fence gardening a constant source of disappointment, we placed whatever deer-proof plants we could find near the house. Two small flower beds lay at the edge of the lawn, each surrounded by "temporary" deer fencing that was looking very permanent. Maintaining these gardens became a constant battle, in part because each was surrounded on all sides by grass that was forever encroaching upon the fertile, well-watered soil.

We refused to surround our home with a tall fence—the "concentration camp" aura of that arrangement was contrary to our hearts and to the openness of our landscape. But we also became less eager to visit the garden. So in the late afternoons, I would put on my boots, bid good-bye to Carolyn as if I were headed to the office, and trudge out to the garden, incommunicado until my work was done. And it felt like work—the garden was where I sweated, weeded, pruned, and dug.

For five years we watched as grass and our waning energy shrank each garden. Finally we agreed to change strategies, and built an unobtrusive fence to enclose a semicircle around half the house. It's not eight feet tall; a determined deer could leap it, but we try to offer them enough browse elsewhere to keep them busy. Inside the new fence, we sheet mulched heavily and planted a dense blend of useful and ornamental plants.

What a difference it's made! When we're chatting in the yard over a cup of coffee, it's nothing to stoop and yank a couple of tiny weeds. They don't get much beyond tiny, because we're always there to spot them. Grass can no longer encroach from all sides. Sandwich greens come from a mesclun bed outside my study door, as do some strawberries for breakfast, without a weary trudge. I distract myself from writing—far too often—by watching bees and butterflies work the yarrow, salvia, and valerian out my window. It's nothing to toss on a handful of mulch to shield a patch of bare soil, or squirt the hose on a drooping seedling. And best of all, we live in this garden, instead of just working there. Having had it both ways, using zones is the only way I'll garden.

Beyond Zone 1 is Zone 2. This is home to fruit

trees, terraced beds, large shrubs, berry bushes, ponds, and diversely planted hedges. It's also where the big production vegetable beds can go: potatoes, rows of canning tomatoes, trellises of pole beans. In one yard I've seen, Zone 2 holds a well-interplanted mix of shrubs, less-frequently picked perennial and annual vegetables, flowers, plus some orchard trees and a plastic greenhouse full of tomatoes. These are elements we don't visit every day, so management in Zone 2 isn't quite so intensive: spot-mulching instead of deep continuous mulching, automatic or large-scale irrigation instead of loving visits to each plant with a watering can. In a small yard, Zone 2 may begin only 15 feet from the door and end near the neighbor's fence. On a larger property, this zone may extend 50 to 100 feet from the house.

Permaculture locates forces such as wind, sun, and water each in its own *sector*.

Small animals such as rabbits, bees, or chickens will find their best homesite at the Zone 1/Zone 2 boundary. Compost should molder out there too. Ecological design is about placing the elements in the right relationship to each other, and careful thought can yield some time-saving placements. If the coop for a few urban chickens is on the way to a vegetable bed, we can toss kitchen scraps to the birds as we head out to weed, and on the return trip give the weeds to the eager birds at the coop in exchange for eggs. Why make three trips?

Zone 3 contains large, unpruned orchard and nut trees, field crops such as grains, and commercial gardens. Some of the trees may yield firewood, wood products, or animal forage. I've seen one suburban Zone 3 that holds walnuts, chestnuts, and bamboo—plants that need little attention and are harvested only once or twice a year.

Zone 4 usually applies to larger properties. It's home for grazing animals, and firewood and timber trees. It is where we gather native foods, herbs, or woodcraft supplies. This is a semi-wild, little-managed region.

Every property needs a Zone 5. It's the wild

TABLE 3-3.

THE ZONE SYSTEM: CONTENTS AND USES

	Structures	Plants	Garden techniques	Water sources	Animals	Human uses
Zone 1: Most visited; intensive use and care	greenhouse, trellis, arbor, deck, patio, bird feeders and bath, household storage, workshop	herbs, greens, flowers, dwarf trees, low shrubs, lawn	Intensive weeding and mulching, dense planting, espaliering	rain barrels, small ponds, greywater, household tap	wild birds, rabbits, guinea pigs, soil organisms, and beneficial insects	modify house microclimate, daily food and flowers, social space
Zone 2: Semi-intensely cultivated	greenhouse, barns, tool shed, shop, wood storage	staple and canning crops, small orchards, fire retardant plants	spot mulch, cover crops, seasonal pruning	well, pond, greywater, irrigation, swales	rabbits, fish, bats, poultry, soil organisms, beneficial insects	home food production, some market crops, plant propagation, wildlife habitat
Zone 3: Farm zone	feed storage, field shelters	cash crops, large fruit and nut trees, animal forage, shelterbelts, seedlings for grafting	cover crops, little pruning, moveable fences	large ponds, swales, storage in soil	cows, horses, pigs, sheep, goats, other large animals, soil organisms, beneficial insects	cash crops, firewood and lumber, pasture
Zone 4: Minimal care	animal feeders	firewood, timber, native plants	pasturing, selective forestry	ponds, swales	large animals, soil organisms, beneficial insects	hunting, gathering, grazing
Zone 5: Wild; unmanaged	none	native plants	unmanaged	lakes, creeks	native animals, soil organisms, beneficial insects	inspiration, foraging, meditation

land. Whether it's a corner of an urban lot dedicated to a wildlife thicket and a few rustling birch trees, or a nature preserve on the back forty, it is where we are visitors, not managers. We design the other four zones, but we enter Zone 5 to learn from it. There we observe, we play, we meditate, and we let the land be. Zone 5 is the instruction manual for the ecological garden and for keeping our lives in tune with nature.

Choosing the zone in which to place a design element depends on two things: the number of times we need to visit the plant, animal, or structure, and the number of times it needs us to visit it. The overall strategy with garden zones is to begin at the doorstep, design and develop the places closest to the house first, and gradually work outward. That way, we can keep a continuous area under control that gets as much attention as it needs, rather than having a hodgepodge of scattered patches that are easy to forget.

Zones help us place the pieces of our design in a useful relationship with each other and with ourselves. They tell us how to work with what is on the site. But the design elements also need to be arranged in the right relationship with a second set of factors: forces coming from outside the site, such as wind, sun, and water. Again, permaculture gives us a handy tool for working with these forces by

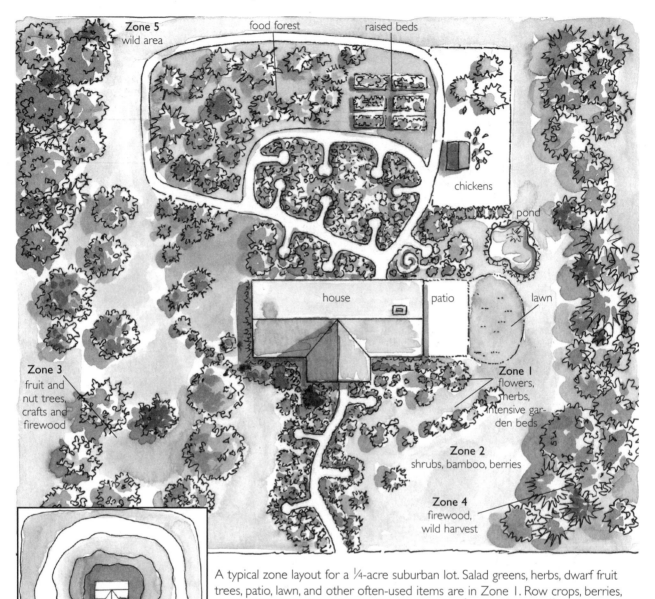

Zone 5
wild area

food forest

raised beds

chickens

pond

house

patio

lawn

Zone 1
flowers, herbs, intensive garden beds

Zone 2
shrubs, bamboo, berries

Zone 3
fruit and nut trees, crafts and firewood

Zone 4
firewood, wild harvest

Zone 1
Zone 2
Zone 3
Zone 4
Zone 5

A typical zone layout for a ¼-acre suburban lot. Salad greens, herbs, dwarf fruit trees, patio, lawn, and other often-used items are in Zone 1. Row crops, berries, useful shrubs, a pond, chickens, and a food forest are in Zone 2. Zone 3 holds larger fruit and nut trees, while Zone 4 is for foraging and firewood. A corner of the yard is left wild for Zone 5. The inset drawing shows an idealized pattern, from most-often used to least, of concentric zones around a house.

locating each one in its own specific *sector*. For example, the winds across a property usually come from a particular direction (the direction often depends on the time of year). Where I live in Oregon, rain-laden winter winds rage from the southwest. Thus the southwest is my winter wind

sector. In summer, cool breezes come down from Canada, so the summer wind sector is in the north. To use these observations, we can move various elements of the design around with respect to the wind sector until they work best. For example, we could try to buffer the effects of the winter wind with windbreaks or buildings, or take advantage of it with a windmill. But we might welcome the summer breeze by letting it flow unobstructed toward the house. By locating and mapping out the various sectors, the pieces of a design can be placed in proper relationship to the energies entering the site and use them effectively.

Here are several other sectors:

Sun: The sun sector varies with the seasons. In North America, the summer sun rises far to the northeast and sets in the northwest, so the summer sun sector is very large. Drawn on a property map, it spans nearly 270 degrees. The winter sun sector is far smaller, since in winter the sun rises and sets in the southern sky (see below).

View: The unpleasant sight of a neighbor's dilapidated garage would fall in what we might call the "ugly view sector," a vista to be masked by a screen of plants or a structure. But a gorgeous prospect of the ocean would be a view worth preserving or emphasizing.

Fire: My fire sector points at me from the south. Not only do I live at the top of a dry, south-facing hill that fire could race up quickly, but my neighbors, with their power mowers, chainsaws, pyromaniac children, and other incendiary devices, live to the south. Fire sectors should always be considered in a design, even in the city, and be left open, planted with fire-resistant species, or armed with sprinklers.

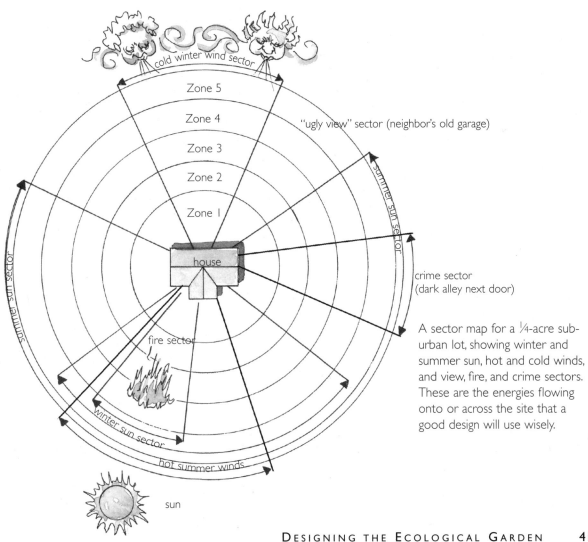

A sector map for a ¼-acre suburban lot, showing winter and summer sun, hot and cold winds, and view, fire, and crime sectors. These are the energies flowing onto or across the site that a good design will use wisely.

Wildlife: Every yard is penetrated by a wildlife sector, whether it brings marauding deer, a skulking raccoon, or a flock of cedar waxwings that flutter from a neighbor's cherry tree to yours. Wildlife can be deflected or welcomed by plantings and structures.

Other sectors include flooding and surface water, fog, pollution (noise, smells, power lines), and crime (a dark alley adjoining the yard).

The pieces of a design can interact with sectors in three ways. They can (1) block or screen out the forces entering through the sector, as with a windbreak or shade tree; (2) channel or collect energy for use, as does a windmill or greenhouse; or (3) open up the sector to use as much of the energy or view as possible, by removing whatever blocks the sector: vegetation, fencing, or other deterrent. Sector energies such as sun and wind are free energy. Think of this energy as another nutrient source, like free fertilizer or water. Just by placing a plant, building, path, or trellis *here* instead of *there* means that element is, in effect, being fed or otherwise improved by the sector's energy. Just sitting there, that greenhouse or windbreak or pond is benefiting the whole design.

To sum up, *zones* organize the pieces of a design by how often they are used or need attention, and *sectors* help locate the pieces so they manage the forces that come from outside the site. Using zones and sectors together, we can make the best use of the connections within a design. If we're building a greenhouse, for example, we'd want it close enough to the house to visit regularly (in Zone 1 or 2), near a faucet and tools, perhaps north of a pond to catch reflected light, in the sun sector, out of the winter wind sector to reduce chilling, probably away from the fire sector (though a metal and glass greenhouse with a sprinkler system might add to a firebreak), and maybe in the "ugly view sector" to screen that neighbor's nasty garage. Clever placements abound: A fragrant, evergreen oleander could go near a path in Zone 1 or 2 to enchant passersby with its scent, in the sun sector, in the

winter wind sector, and even in the fire sector, since it has fire-retardant properties.

Once we know what plants and structures we want in our design, we can use the Zone-and-Sector method to organize them. Using a base map, and sketching our ideas on overlays of tracing paper or clear plastic sheets, we can arrange the pieces of our design to connect sensibly with each other in their zones and sectors.

Sometimes when I'm stuck in the design process I use another technique, called random assembly, to break creative blocks. This consists of listing the design elements in a column:

fruit tree	hedgerow	trellis
greenhouse	pond	compost pile

I continue until all the major elements are listed. Then I make three copies of the list (cutting and pasting on a computer makes short work of this), and then prepare a second columnar list containing connecting words. Here are all the connecting words that I could think of:

around	in	facing
between	beside	into
before	is evolving	away from
after	and	over
hanging from	attached to	on
crossing	under	
instead of	near	

Make two copies of this list. Then cut out all five columns (three lists of elements, two of connecting words), and lay them beside each other, alternating elements with connecting words. Then slide the lists around, and read horizontally to see if a useful or inspirational placement results:

vine *over* greenhouse *above* pond
compost pile *near* toolshed *behind* hedgerow

This strategy gets us thinking in terms of connections between the design elements. Sometimes, of course, the placements are complete nonsense:

pond *hanging from* chickens *between* sauna

But often, a combination occurs that will jog creativity, pushing us to think in new directions. Sometimes by contemplating even a ridiculous combination, thinking about what would happen if it actually existed, we can arrive at new solutions for design problems. This system helps suspend our judgmental selves and frees us to innovate.

Development

In the previous steps, we determined what elements will be in the design and approximately where they will go. Now it's time to polish these rough ideas, working with the locations arrived at by the Zone-and-Sector method. Sketch in the various planting beds, trees, walls and fences, patios and decks, and other design elements. At first, don't go into any detail, just draw rough circles and outlines of the major components, showing their relative placement (this is often called a bubble diagram). Refine the connections between the components. Then sketch access routes (paths or roads) to the elements that need them. Try to minimize the number of paths. This may mean rearranging the components—trying to preserve their relationships—until the paths are most effective and occupy minimal space. This step is a bit tricky, but attention here will pay off in the long run in saved labor and a more harmonious layout. It's useful to refer back to the ideas in the "vision" step to keep the big picture in mind.

Once the layout has been refined on rough sketches, people with the skills or time may want to make more formal drawings and plans. Whether the documentation is of professional quality or not is up to the designer/gardener. Often just simple sketches will do, as long as they include distances, scale, and enough other detail to implement the design. Detailed documentation of the design is very important. Don't expect to rely on memory. It's frustrating to be about to install an expensive plant and not remember where it was supposed to go. Without maps and notes, that's exactly what will happen.

This is a good time to work on color schemes and other aesthetic points. Though the design process described here gives priority to ecological considerations, once the plants, structures, and other design elements are placed in the right relationships, we can select plant varieties whose foliage and colors go well together. Any good library will offer plenty of gardening books that cover design aesthetics. A few of my favorite authors in this category are Gertrude Jekyll, Penelope Hobhouse, Rosemary Verey, Ken Druse, and John Brookes.

Now it's time to schedule the installation. What needs to be done first? A combination of factors interact to shape this decision. These include:

- **Personal:** Is our most urgent desire food production, a patio, shade, a flower garden, or some other consideration?
- **Environmental:** Does the land most need soil building, erosion control, habitat, or something else?
- **Technical:** Will the design require earthmoving, concrete or stone work, or other hardscaping? These often must be done first to avoid disturbing the rest of the design, and to reduce the expense and potential for damage done by multiple bulldozer visits. Trees and shrubs should also be planted early in the work, conforming to the old advice, "the best time to plant a tree was ten years ago."
- **Seasonal:** What can be done during the season appropriate to the work? Earth moving in the wet season will ruin soil structure; planting in summer heat may bake the transplants.
- **Financial:** Is enough money available for the whole design? If not, what aspects make sense to phase in first?

To provide an "at a glance" guide to the design process, I'll sum up the steps once again, this time from the new viewpoints of ecological design and permaculture offered in this chapter.

1. OBSERVATION

Walk the site and make maps. Note what is there and how it interacts with its surroundings. Just observe, don't analyze. Make lists. Follow up with research into what was observed, the habits of species, soil types, and the like.

2. VISIONING

Keep ecological guidelines in mind. What can the place offer us? What does the site need from us? What are our limitations and resources? What should the design do?

3. PLANNING

a. ***Priorities.*** Rank the importance of the desires and problems that the design addresses. Consider personal, aesthetic, environmental/ecological, and other issues, as well as trouble spots and defects to correct.

b. ***Analysis.*** List the design elements that will satisfy the vision (plants, structures, functions, etc.). For each element (or for as many as is practical), list its products, activities, needs, and intrinsic qualities. Connect as many items as possible so that the needs of one design element are met by other elements, and so that it meets the needs of other elements.

c. ***Layout.*** Use zones to organize the pieces of a design by how often they are used or need attention, and sectors to locate the pieces so they manage wind, sun, and other forces that come from outside the site. The Zone-and-Sector method optimizes the connections between the design elements. Use the random-assembly method for brainstorming and to break creative blocks.

4. DEVELOPMENT

Sketch the locations of the design elements. Research species and varieties. Optimize paths and relationships in the design. Work with color and form. Then make working drawings and enough documentation to implement the design. Determine the steps of implementation.

5. IMPLEMENTATION

Install the design, and be flexible enough to deal with the surprises that appear when a paper design meets the real world.

Remember also to apply the wisdom of zones, even to the implementation phase: When possible, begin the installation at your doorstep and work outward.

Implementation

This phase of ecological landscape design is similar to installing any new landscape. Details can be found in any good home-landscaping book, such as Rita Buchanan's *Taylor's Master Guide to Landscaping* or Roger Holmes's *Home Landscaping* series. Follow this order of implementation:

- First, do any major earth moving. Grade the site to a rough contour, if needed. Dig any swales, ponds, and drainage ditches. Install utility lines and underground irrigation pipes and wires. Then backfill the trenches.

- Add any broadscale soil amendments and compost. Mulching and shaping of intensive Zone 1 beds can wait until later.

- Complete any *hardscaping,* the term designers use for wood, stone, concrete, and other constructed elements: walls, sheds, paths, fences, and the like.

- Make any final adjustments to the grade contours with rake and shovel.

- Lay down sheet mulches (see chapter for instructions).

- Install large plants, such as trees and major shrubs.

- Plant ground covers, nonwoody plants, lawn, and cover crops.
- Adjust mulches, and fine-tune the irrigation system, if any.
- Keep plants watered and help them get established by observing and caring for those that need a little extra attention.

In chapter 11, the section "Where to Begin" covers some aspects of implementation in detail. But remember that the people, plants, animals, and landscape involved are constantly changing and full of surprises. The design and its implementation may take unexpected turns when the shovel actually strikes the soil. Don't be too rigid, and be ready to revisit the early steps of the process to rework some aspects of the design so they will the fit changing circumstances.

NATURAL PATTERNS IN THE GARDEN

While describing the Zone-and-Sector method, I mentioned that vegetable gardens don't have to be ruler straight, but can have the same curves and meanders that give flower beds their visual appeal. Let me expand on that. Breaking away from straight lines can do far more than just add visual interest. Choosing and applying the right shapes and patterns in a landscape can also save space, reduce labor, enhance wildlife habitat, and help bring the plants, insects and other animals, and gardener into better balance.

What do I mean by the right shape and pattern? I'll begin with a simple example, and then move to a few richer and more elaborate ideas that play with pattern and shape.

The shape of a garden determines how much of its area can actually contain plants, as opposed to paths to make those plants accessible. Paths are a

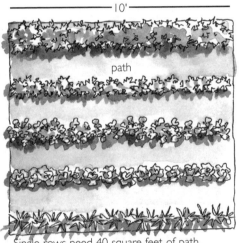

Single rows need 40 square feet of path.

A keyhole bed needs only 6 square feet of path.

Raised beds need 10 square feet of path.

Changing the shape of a garden bed—working with patterns—can reduce the area lost to paths as seen in these beds, each containing 50 square feet of planting.

BUILDING AND PLANTING
A KEYHOLE BED

To create a keyhole bed, begin with a circle of soil about 8 to 12 feet in diameter pierced on one side by a path to the center. Keyhole beds can be created by shoveling fertile topsoil into a horseshoe shape, but I prefer to build them by layering up, lasagna-style, leaves or other compostable organic matter, newspapers, and soil, using a technique called sheet mulching (see chapter 4 for details of the sheetmulch method). In a keyhole bed, the plantable zone is about as wide as in a standard raised bed: 3 to 5 feet across. The access path into the bed can be narrow, a foot or so wide, but the central circle of path needs to be big enough to turn around in, about 18 to 24 inches in diameter.

You can plant a keyhole bed using the Zone system. Put the most frequently picked plants closest to the center. That means herbs, greens, and other daily eaten veggies should border the central path. Behind these, place plants that get picked regularly over the growing season: tomatoes, peppers, bush peas and beans, eggplants, and others. These are still easy to reach without a stretch. At the back of the bed, install long-term crops and those that are harvested only once. These include potatoes, carrots, and other root crops, plus what I call the Red Queen veggies—cauliflower, iceberg lettuce, and cabbage—because it's "off with their heads" at harvest. These back-row plants might be a bit out of reach if the bed is more than 3 feet deep, thus what I am about to suggest will shock those gardeners who are zealous adherents of the double-dig method. To harvest these plants, step onto the bed (gasp!) and pluck. One footprint per season isn't going to annihilate soil porosity and structure. If the idea of stepping on light, fluffy soil is simply too appalling, lay down a board to stand on, which will limit compaction.

Keyhole beds abound with creative possibilities. A whole circle could be dedicated to tomatoes, with a few companion culinary herbs such as basil or chives at the inner margin. Or use the circular geometry to balance sun and shadow: Place crops that wilt in midsummer's full blaze to the east of taller sun-lovers, shading the tender ones in scorching afternoons. To trellis vining plants, curve a length of fencing around the bed. If salty coastal gales or the desiccating winds of the plains buffet the garden, plant tall sturdy crops such as Jerusalem artichokes or a stocky breed of sunflowers on the outside of the beds as a windbreak. Of course, keyhole beds work for flowers too, letting us stand, shears in hand, in a circle of brilliant color as we contemplate filling a vase or three.

Keyhole beds are round, and most yards are square. So what about the margins, those little triangles of unused ground at the corners of these beds—isn't that wasted space? Not at all. Every garden needs insect-attracting flowers, or perennial nitrogen-fixers such as Dutch clover, or a good wind-and-weed barrier at the edges to stop weed seeds blowing in from your neighbor's less-than-immaculate land. We could fill the margin with robust mulch-providers such as crotolaria or comfrey. It could be a perfect spot for a small fruit tree. Or we can just expand the bed to fill the corners. There's no rule that says a keyhole bed can't be square rather than round; it's the central path that defines it.

Planting more than one keyhole bed expands the possibilities. Keyholes can extend to the left and right of a central walkway.

An undulating path flanked by keyhole beds can wrap around a house to make an attractive Zone 1 garden.

A further modification of the keyhole scheme is the mandala garden, a set of four to eight keyhole beds arranged in a circle with one more bed in the center, and a path entering the mandala from one side. A mandala garden combines beauty and efficiency to create a magical effect. Few designs can fit more growing space into less area, and the more mystically inclined would say a mandala garden brings a spiritual aspect to a piece of ground.

part of the garden I've always regarded as a necessary evil. After working hard to build up the soil, it irritates me to pound a high percentage of fluffy loam into hardpan under my feet. Every bit of path is unusable real estate that could be devoted to a luscious crop of greens or a bed of sweet-scented blossoms. Fortunately, changing the shape of garden beds can minimize the land sacrificed to paths.

The most basic garden bed contains single rows of plants with paths between each row. In this layout, paths consume about half of the soil area. A raised bed garden, in which paths fall between every three or four rows of plants, is an improvement, sacrificing only about 30 percent of its ground to walkways while leaving the beds narrow enough for the gardener to reach the center. Here a simple change in geometry has eliminated almost half the path space. But we can do better, and create an eye-pleasing design while we're at it.

Keyhole Garden Beds

If we bend that rectangular raised bed into a circle—or more accurately, a horseshoe shape—even

Several keyhole beds can extend from a central path to create a garden with pleasing curves and plenty of accessible bed space.

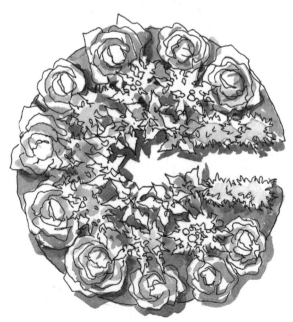

A keyhole bed planted with cabbages, tomatoes, and pathside greens and herbs in a space 8 to 10 feet in diameter.

more path will disappear. By a simple trick of topology, the path shrinks to a tiny keyhole shape, which gives this space-saving garden layout its name: keyhole bed.

Here's what happens. If we wrap a typical 4-by-15-foot raised bed into a circle with a small opening for a path, we cut the path down from about 22 square feet (figuring an 18-inch-wide path down one side of the raised bed) to 6 square feet. Less than a quarter of the ground is surrendered to paths. I won't torture you with the math that would prove this to the skeptical—as any publisher knows, each successive equation in a text puts half the remaining readers to flight.

Keyhole beds have aesthetics as well as mathematics going for them. Bringing curves into a garden eliminates that "soybean field" quality that

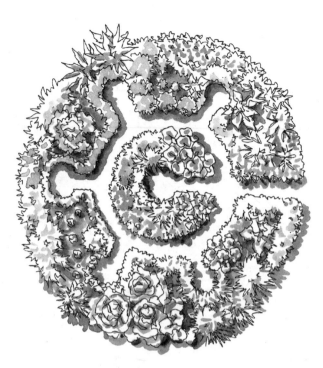

A mandala garden. A circular pattern of nested keyhole beds is both beautiful and space-conserving.

The Herb Spiral

We can go a little further into the use of shape and pattern in the garden. Let's say that we've become enamored of the marvelous benefits that can be had by using the Zone concept, so we're putting an herb garden along the path that starts at our back door. Okay, in goes the oregano, next to it a couple of types of thyme, then chives—we like chives, so let's plant five of them—and past those, a few parsley plants and a little mint. We add a dozen more favorite herbs and spices, and finish off with three varieties of sage. Soon, about twenty-five plants are dotted along the path, stretching well into the backyard. Those sage plants are pretty far away. Something tells me this arrangement will fail Bill Mollison's "wet slipper test." Plus, that little herb garden needs about 30 feet of path to give easy access, and every inch of path is one less inch of growing space.

What if we design the herb garden using a different pattern? Instead of a straight—or even meandering—line, let's fold up the path somehow so that the whole affair takes less space. We could just plunk the herbs into a standard raised bed, leaving a rather dull rectangular patch outside our door. That would save space, though some of the herbs might need quite a stretch to reach. But let's be more creative. Here's where a little knowledge of shapes and patterns comes into play.

This is a perfect spot for an herb spiral. An herb spiral coils up 20 or 30 linear feet of pathside plants into a roundish pattern about 5 feet across. It's not just a flat spiral, either. Here's how it works.

An herb spiral begins as a mound of good soil about 3 feet high and 5 feet across. To turn this mound into a spiral, place fist- to head-sized rocks in a spiral pattern that winds from the bottom inward to the top. Leave about a foot of soil between the tiers of the rock spiral

Now it's time to install the herbs, winding them up the spiral. This coils about 30 linear feet of row into a much smaller space. All the herbs can grow

emanates from ruler-straight beds and rows. With the exception of falling apples and other gravity-driven phenomena, nature never takes the shortest distance between two points. Instead, nature meanders, drifting in lazy undulations from here to there. It's humans who have become enamored of the unswerving, direct route. But in our gardens, we meet nature more or less on her terms. Just as a straight stretch of interstate highway invites narcolepsy, linear gardens are monotonous too. Curves and circles give surprise and whimsy to a garden. What a bonus that they happen to be more efficient.

One more benefit of keyhole beds: If we point the central path toward the south and locate tall plants such as tomatoes or sunflowers at the back, or northern edge, the bed creates a ∪-shaped sun bowl that traps warmth. The toasty microclimate inside is a good place for tender or heat-loving varieties.

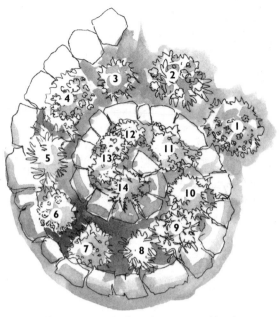

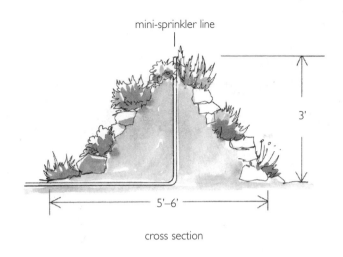

mini-sprinkler line

3'

5'–6'

cross section

1	feverfew	6	fennel	11	thyme
2	calendula	7	yarrow	12	oregano
3	coriander	8	sage	13	dill
4	parsley	9	echinacea	14	rosemary
5	chives	10	chamomile		

An herb spiral combines a two-dimensional pattern (a spiral) with a three-dimensional one (a mound) to form a beautiful and space-saving living sculpture that has several microclimates.

right outside the door, using only the path space necessary to walk around the spiral. Plus, mounding up the soil means we can reach the central herbs without bending over very far.

But this new pattern does much more than save space and effort. The herb spiral has slopes that face in all the directions of the compass. The south-facing slope will be hotter than the north. The east-facing side, which gets morning sun, will dry out earlier in the day than the west one. The soil at the bottom will stay wetter than that at the top. We've created an herb garden with different microclimates. So we plant accordingly, locating each herb in a suitable environment. Varieties that thrive in hot, dry climates, such as oregano, rosemary, and thyme, go on the sunny south side near the top. Parsley and chives, which prefer cooler, moister climes, find a home on the north side. Coriander, which seems to bolt in too much hot sun, can be stationed on the east side, protected from afternoon scorchings. Other herbs can snuggle into their best sites as well.

A few tips on building an herb spiral:

- To save on topsoil, place a few rocks or a heap of subsoil at the base of the mound, then build over that.
- To water the spiral easily, run plastic irrigation tubing ($\frac{1}{4}$ or $\frac{1}{2}$ inch) inside the mound, emerging from the top, and attach a mini-sprinkler.
- Consider sinking a small basin or tiny pond (1 to 3 feet across) at the bottom of the spiral. Water cress, waterchestnuts, and other edible pond plants can grow here.
- Built with attractive stone, an herb spiral can be an eye-catching central feature of any garden.

Other Natural Patterns in the Garden

Let's examine why the herb spiral offers so many rewards. This design winds a straight line into a spiral, and then drapes this two-dimensional pattern over a three-dimensional one—the mound of soil. The combination spawns a wealth of what are called

A few of the many spiral patterns found in nature.

he said. The central vein was thickest, the main branches from it were half the size, and from those extended tiny veinlets for ferrying nutrients to each cluster of cells. The veins themselves don't gather much light, so it behooves a plant to minimize them. "What if you designed a set of garden paths like that?" Kirk asked. "A big central path for a cart or wheelbarrow, smaller ones branching off of it for frequent foot traffic, and tiny tracks from those into each bed. You'd save a lot of space and have a natural flow pattern." I was struck by how original and useful Kirk's observation was.

Branching patterns are an efficient way to reach all the points in a large area, while moving the shortest distance possible. A single branch is also

synergistic effects—the unexpected benefits of a new collaboration that neither partner alone can offer. Clever use of natural patterns in garden design can often generate delightful bonuses.

Nature itself is full of these patterns. The spiral and its relative, the helix (a spiral stretched into three dimensions, like a corkscrew), are particularly abundant. Snail shells, the pattern of seeds in a sunflower head, ram's horns, hurricanes, galaxies, all form spirals. The pattern of leaves or branches extending from a stem often unwinds in a helix, which minimizes the amount of shade cast by each leaf on the one below. Spirals are often the result of growth or expansion.

Here are a few more of nature's patterns that are useful for gardeners.

BRANCHES. Branching patterns are used in nature to collect or disperse nutrients, energy, and water. Tree branches spread leaves over a wide area to better absorb sunlight. Forking roots gather nutrients and moisture.

We can apply these observations in the garden. During a slide show on garden design, Kirk Hansen, manager of Wild Thyme Farm in southwest Washington State, flashed an image of a leaf on the screen. "Look how the veins on this leaf use the least possible space to get nutrients to the rest of the leaf,"

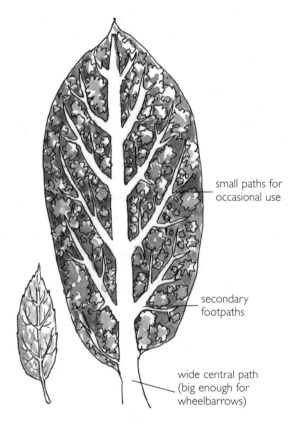

small paths for occasional use

secondary footpaths

wide central path (big enough for wheelbarrows)

Branching garden paths, modeled after a leaf. The pattern of a leaf's veins is a space-conserving way to deliver nutrients to the leaf cells without sacrificing precious light-gathering surface. We can use the same pattern for a garden's paths, which minimizes the growing area lost to our pounding feet.

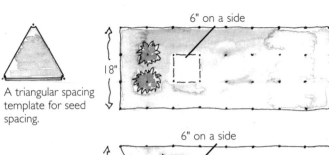

A triangular spacing template for seed spacing.

6" on a side

18"

Four rows of seeds planted 6 inches apart using rectangular spacing, need 18 inches of bed space.

6" on a side

15"

Using triangular spacing, the bed only needs to be about 15 inches.

A triangular net pattern allows more seeds to be planted in the same space than the more commonly used rectangular pattern.

easy to repair if damaged, and its loss has only a small effect on the whole system or organism. Anywhere collection or dispersal needs to be done in nature, you can find branching patterns: the tributaries of a river system, the seedheads of Queen Anne's lace and other umbel flowers, blood vessels, the forking zigzag of lightning bolts, or the ever-finer divisions of tubing in a drip-irrigation system. Branches are a common pattern in nature and in our gardens.

NETS. The net or mesh pattern is found in nature in spiderwebs, birds' nests, honeycombs, and the cracking of dried mud. Nets are patterns of expansion, contraction, and even distribution. Gardeners often create a net pattern when placing seeds in a raised bed, setting the seeds in a pattern of triangles to create equal distances between each seed. This pattern fits the most seeds into the space available.

In drylands, orchardists plant their trees in a net pattern to collect rain and runoff. Fruit trees are planted in small depressions, and the basins are connected by a network of shallow trenches. By this clever system, rain and runoff water falling over a large area is collected by the trench network and delivered to the base of the trees.

Trees in drylands can be planted in small depressions, called net-and-pan. The basins are then connected by a network of shallow trenches. The trench network collects rain and runoff water falling over a large area and delivers it to the base of the trees. Mulch also collects in the basins, building soil.

Nature uses net patterns to build soil and ameliorate harsh conditions, and we can take a leaf from her book for our gardens. I've seen shifting sand dunes stabilized via a net pattern of plants. The blustery winds on the dunes scatter grass or other seeds randomly over a large area, and as each plant grows, it creates a small shaded, windless patch around it. Bolstered by this self-created, benign microclimate, the plant sends out runners and colonizes new ground. Soon a netlike pattern of plants has captured and subdued a large patch of landscape, even though bare earth lies between the individual plants. Over time, the dispersed plants enlarge and finally connect, and the whole region has then been gentled and moderated, turned into mild and welcoming habitat.

We can use the same strategy in our yards. If our soil is poor and plants are few, instead of undertaking a labor- and money-intensive blitz to add topsoil and fill the place with plants all at once—a strategy that usually results in overwhelming work followed by a lot of dead plants—we can begin with a grid of small trees and shrubs spaced over the yard, much as nature does on the sand dunes. In the shelter of each sapling, we can add mulch and plant perennials, creating a network of mulched circles around the yard. Each tree and shrub is surrounded by a small zone of healthy soil and mild microclimate, ideal for growing. Over the next few years, we then expand each circle with mulch and plantings, until they touch each other and

One way to use the edge effect. A wavy edge can hold more plants, and expose more of their area to sun and beneficial insects, than a straight edge.

the entire property is rife with rich soil and lush vegetation. In this way, a net pattern can be used in the garden to gradually build fertility and a diverse array of plants, needing only a very manageable amount of labor and expense to do the job.

Along with spirals, branches, and nets, many other patterns occur in nature that can be applied to the garden. There are circles, waves, lobes, and fractals, as well as the complex swirling patterns of liquids and gases with exotic names such as Karman vortex streets, Ekman spirals, and Overbeck jets. If you would like to learn more about patterns and how they occur in nature and design, see the bibliography for further reading.

The Edge Effect

We've seen how coiling a row of herbs into a spiral and scrunching a rectangular garden plot into a keyhole bed shrinks the amount of path needed. These patterns do this by reducing the amount of the bed's edge in relation to its surface area. "Edge" is a key concept in ecology, so much so that ecologists speak of "the edge effect." Edges are fascinating and dynamic places, and I'd like to delve briefly into the ways that the edge effect can be used in the garden.

Edges are where things happen. Where a forest meets the prairie, where a river flows into the sea, or at nearly any other boundary between two ecosystems is a cauldron of biodiversity. All the species that thrive in each of the two environments are present, plus new species that live in the transition zone between the two. The edge is richer than what is on either side. Any fisherman knows this. He doesn't cast his lure into the center of the lake, but toward the shoreline where fish gather to feed on the flourishing life in the shallows.

We can see this edge effect in our own yards. Where do the most birds gather? Not in the middle of the lawn, but along the edge of a clump of trees or shrubs. Not deep in a thick mass of bushes, but on the twigs at the margin. So if we want to boost the biodiversity in our yards, we should

The benefits of increasing the edge in a pond. Though both ponds have roughly the same volume and surface area, the wavy pond has far more edge. Thus it can be surrounded by far more plants, and the extensive shallows offer more habitat for fish and aquatic plants.

increase the amount of edge. For a start, this means encouraging plantings of varying heights. A transition between, say, lawn and trees should be gradual, softened with increasingly large perennials and shrubs to increase habitat and variety. But there are many other ways to tinker with "edge" to gain the effects we want.

Sometimes it pays to minimize edge, as with the herb spiral and keyhole bed. Here, edge translates into waste space and more work. The decision to increase or decrease edge depends on what lies on either side of the edge, and what we want from it. Edges allow us to define spaces, break them up into manageable areas, and work with them. They are places of transition and translation, where matter and energy flow or stop, or often change into something else. Let's examine some of the edges found in a typical yard and how we can use them.

- **House/yard edge.** The outside walls of a house create varied microclimates. The south wall will be hottest and sunniest, so heat-loving and cold-tender plants can go here, often making it possible to grow plants found one or two USDA hardiness zones to the south. The west wall will be slightly cooler, and the north wall the coldest and darkest. We can fit our plants and work or play spaces into them accordingly.

- **Pavement/soil edge.** Paved surfaces collect water, so thirstier plants can be placed alongside sidewalks and driveways to catch runoff. Pavement also stores up heat on sunny days, so the adjacent soil will be warmer.

- **Fence/yard edge.** Fences and walls act as filters, stopping some flows and allowing others. Debris and snow will pile up against fences, collecting mulch and moisture. Fences can also be used as trellises, so running fencing in a zigzag will increase the area available for trellis and fence-side plantings, as well as making the fence more resistant to wind and creating a sheltered pocket in each concave "zig."

- **Plant/soil edge.** To increase the number of plants that can fit into a given space, place them in a wavy pattern rather than a straight line Plants at the edge of beds often yield more than the ones in the center, so patterns that increase edge in beds will boost production. Rows of tall plants can be alternated with short ones to achieve the same effect.

- **Plant/air edge.** I mentioned how a keyhole bed can be pointed south to create a sun-trap. Edges of garden beds and, on a larger scale, rows of shrubs and trees, can be sculpted into undulating shapes that contain cooler, windier lobes and protected, warm bays.

- **Water/soil edge.** The shape of a garden pond affects how many plants will fit at the edge. A perfectly round pond has the least edge, whereas a pond with lobes and bays, or in a starburst pattern, can hold an enormous number of bog plants and other moisture lovers. Also, the fingers of land extending into the pond will be drier in their raised centers. Land plants can thrive in the centers while boggy species can grow at the squishy margins. Varying the depth of the pond (another way to increase edge) will make room for more types of fish and water plants. Frogs and tadpoles can bask in the warm shallows while golden koi flash in the depths.

In general, straight lines and smooth shapes reduce the amount of edge, while shapes with lobes, notches, mounds, pits, crinkles, and crenellations will increase edge. Don't forget about extending the edge effect into the third dimension by varying the height and depth of plantings, soil, structures, and ponds. The importance of edges is simply one more manifestation of the role of connections in the ecological garden. Edges are not a static place, they are the result of a relationship between two or more dynamic pieces of the living landscape.

In the garden, we're working with live beings, not just shapes and colors. These creatures grow, set seed and multiply, and in time they die. Plants, insects, birds, and all the rest connect in a tight weave and enter each others' lives, creating and sharing among them food, shade, pollen, seeds, humus, perches, burrows, nests—a host of varied and valuable gifts. With a gentle, careful gaze we can peer into this wonderfully interlaced world and tease out some of the connections, transferring them to our own landscapes. Nature carries the instruction book for a sustainable world—it is up to us to read it and to preserve it.

In this chapter, I've tried to give an ecological view of garden design. Entire books—whole shelves of them—have been written about design, so a single chapter can only scratch the surface of this broad subject (though the rest of this book digs a little deeper). Design allows us to blend what we observe with what we desire. It is the way our dreams, sculpted by the limits of our skills, budgets, and materials, take form. Ecological design offers a way to harmonize people with the living landscape, a harmony that is often absent from many of the places we dwell. By connecting our gardens to the rest of nature, we can bring great beauty and abundance to ourselves, share this richness with other species, and regenerate the wholeness and diversity of life that is on the verge of being lost.

Now that we have an overview of garden ecology and ecological design, it's time to look at the individual parts of the garden.

PART TWO

The
PIECES
of the
ECOLOGICAL
GARDEN

Chapter 4

Bringing the Soil to Life

A LATIN AMERICAN FARMER once told a friend of mine, "Of course you have terrible soil problems in your country. What do you expect when you call it dirt?" In our culture, soil gets little respect. Most of the words for this fundamental substance are derogatory: When we want to know the worst about someone, we say, "Give me the dirt on this guy." Pornography is called "dirty." We hold at arm's length anything soiled, dirty, or muddy.

Yet soil is miraculous. It is where the dead are brought back to life. Here, in the thin earthy boundary between inanimate rock and the planet's green carpet, lifeless minerals are weathered from stones or decomposed from organic debris. Plants and microscopic animals eat these dead particles and turn them into living matter. In soil, matter crosses and recrosses the boundary between living and dead, and as we have seen, boundaries—edges—are where the most interesting and important events occur.

Most discussions about soil focus on what soil is: what it's made of, where it comes from, what its physical qualities are. Of course it's important

to know these things if we want to understand soil, but the physics and chemistry of soil are only part of the story. We also need to know what soil *does*. Soil is not merely some inert substrate to poke plants into. Soil is alive. One key to having a garden that's bursting with healthy plants, well-balanced insects, and thriving wildlife is to fill the soil with as much life as possible.

We can think of soil life as the base of a pyramid. Stacked upon this base are plants, then insects, and finally animals, each dependent on the creatures below it. The broader the pyramid's base—that is, the greater the number and diversity of soil organisms—the more plants will be supported by the soil. In turn, an extensive array of plants will attract a copious assortment of insects, and those plants and insects will provide food and shelter for a more diverse collection of animals at the top of the pyramid. Diversity builds diversity. The goal of this chapter is to give gardeners the knowledge and techniques for maximizing biodiversity in garden soil—for broadening the base of that pyramid upon which the rest of the ecological garden is built.

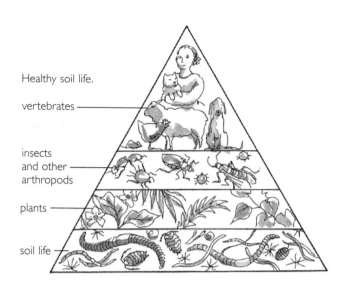

Healthy soil life.

vertebrates

insects and other arthropods

plants

soil life

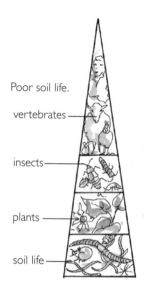

Poor soil life.

vertebrates

insects

plants

soil life

Healthy and diverse soil life supports a wide array of plants, insects, and vertebrates. Poor soil life can't support the same diversity or numbers.

How much life is in the soil? At least as much as above ground. When we look at a landscape, the plants and animals on the surface are obvious, but it's not easy to visualize how much life lies underground. With a few numbers, we can begin to glimpse the abundance. A teaspoon of good pasture soil may contain a billion bacteria, a million fungi, and ten thousand amoebae. It's hard to believe that anything else can fit into that teaspoon, but soil critters are small. There is still plenty of room for the clay, silt, sand, water, air, humus, and assorted small molecules that make up the rest of soil.

An acre of good pasture may support a horse or two, say about a half-ton of aboveground animals. But living in the soil of that acre may be 2 tons of worms and another 2 tons of bacteria, fungi, and soil animals such as millipedes and mites. That one-horse-per-acre soil may contain eight or ten horses worth of animals below ground. Vegetarians may be appalled, but much of gardening is actually raising animals: the tiny ones under the earth's surface. Elaine Ingham, cofounder of Soil Foodweb Incorporated, a firm that specializes in analyzing soil life, calls these swarms of subsurface livestock "microherds."

What are all those soil organisms doing, and how does that relate to gardening? Like most living creatures—except for a nearly hairless two-legged variety that spends much of its time *thinking* about things—soil organisms pass the hours searching for food, eating, and excreting. In all of these activities, they are moving nutrients around—food for themselves, food for other soil life (their wastes and their bodies, living or dead), and, most relevant to gardeners, food for plants. From a plant's perspective, the main role of soil organisms is to chew up matter that plants can't eat and transform it into palatable food. And soil is rich in food. In all but the most abused or leached-out soils, the earth contains plenty of material for soil life to turn into plant food: rock particles, and living and dead organic matter.

The soil organisms in a properly tended garden will furnish almost all the fertilizer that plants need. Soil inhabitants do this as they eat, excrete, reproduce, and die. In each of these activities, the life of the soil performs an alchemy upon organic matter and minerals in the ground. Through soil organisms, nutrients are broken down, consumed, transformed, rebuilt into body parts and energy-containing molecules, and broken down once more. And during these many-vectored flows of matter, a small surplus of nutrients constantly trickles to the plants. Just as bankers and merger specialists make their fortunes by skimming money from the colossal flows of commerce, so too do plants derive their sustenance by absorbing the surplus nutrients that whirl out of soil organisms' life cycles. Fertility comes from flow. A more vigorous soil life heaves more nutrients into the flux for plants to divert, releasing excess fertility during the cycle from raw material to living body to waste and back again. Here, as in so much of the ecological garden, the process, the activity, the relationship, is paramount. Healthy soil and plants are created not by the simple presence of nutrients and soil life, but by the briskness and depth of their flows and interconnections. Savvy gardeners know this, and will do all they can to feed the life of the soil.

SOIL LIFE: THE FIRST RECYCLERS

In nature, most fertility comes originally from the rocks. Rocks contain potassium, calcium, magnesium, and most of the other elements that plants need to build tissue and fuel their metabolic machinery. To convert rocks into food, plant roots and soil organisms secrete mild acids and enzymes that etch atoms loose from rock particles. In a sense, plants and soil microbes are miners, sluicing down rocks with caustic substances that carve away precious life-supporting ores. If we create healthy

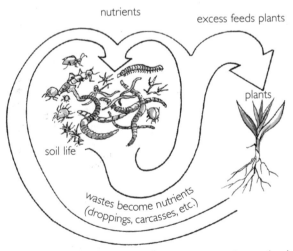

Soil life recycles organic matter, generating plenty of excess that becomes food for plants. The more soil life, the greater the flow of excess nutrients to plants.

soil in our gardens, the rampant soil life will coax an ample supply of nutrients from the rocks to supply most of our plants' needs.

Once these nutrients have been chiseled out of the stone, in a natural ecosystem they are husbanded with great care. Life is the great recycler, scrupulous in not letting go of any useful substance. An example from a typical northern forest illustrates this. Researchers found that the plants and soil of 1 hectare (2.5 acres) of forest contained about 365 kilograms of calcium. Of this, only about 8 kilograms (2 percent) was lost each year in runoff. Most of the forest's calcium—98 percent—was being recycled over and over, raining down in falling leaves or dying plants, then being decomposed and held by soil life, and transferred back to plant roots for another round. The washed-away 8 kilograms of calcium could easily be acquired by the forest each year: more than half that much splashed down as dissolved calcium in rainfall. The remainder of the lost calcium could be weathered from the rocks by roots and soil life. This 98 percent efficiency is a good bit better than the 30 percent or so that our cities strive for in recycling programs. And on heavily fertilized agricultural land, calcium losses range from 25 percent to 60 percent annually. To have a truly sustainable society, we will need to recycle as well as nature does.

How does life do such an incredible job of recycling, and how can we duplicate this economy in our gardens? To work toward an answer, let's look at the fate of a falling leaf as it composts into nutrients and is readied for a return to life.

It's early autumn, and the oak tree in an untended corner of your neighbor's yard is shedding its leaves. One dry leaf flutters down between tall blades of unmown grass, and settles on a patch of bare soil. At first, not much happens, because the leaf is too dry to be appetizing to any of the soil's many denizens (we'll assume your neighbor doesn't spray pesticides or herbicides on this corner of his yard, as these chemicals greatly diminish soil life). Also, this leaf, like most, contains nasty-tasting compounds to protect it from munching insects. The next morning, though, dew has wetted the leaf, and the protective chemicals have begun to leach out. A light drizzle accelerates the washing process. The leaf droops moistly against the soil. When the leaf is rinsed free of polyphenols and the other bitter-tasting compounds, and tenderized by moisture, the feast begins. Among the first at the table are bacteria that have lain dormant on the leaf surface. They revel in the moisture and begin to bloom, secreting enzymes that tear apart the long chains of sugar molecules composing the leaf cell walls. In just hours, the leaf is speckled with the dark blotches of bacterial colonies. Wind-borne spores of fungi also burst into life, and soon the white threads of fungal cells, called hyphae, knit a lacework across the leaf. Fungi hold a broad spectrum of enzymes able to digest lignin (the tough molecules that make wood so strong) and other hard-to-eat components of plants. This gives them a critical niche in the web of decomposers; without them, the earth might be neck-deep in fallen, undecomposable tree trunks.

Moistened by rain and softened by microbial feeding, the leaf quickly succumbs to attack by larger creatures. Millipedes, pill bugs (isopods), fly larvae, springtails, oribatid mites, enchytraeid worms, and earthworms begin to feed on the tasty tissue, shredding the leaf into small scraps. All of these invertebrates, together with bacteria, algae, fungi, and threadlike fungal relatives called actinomycetes, are among the first to dine on rotting organic matter. They are called the *primary decomposers.* Earthworms are the most visible and among the most important of the primary decomposers, so let's watch one as it feeds on our leaf.

The earthworm grabs a leaf chunk and slithers into its burrow. With its rasping mouthparts the worm pulverizes the leaf fragment, sucking in soil at the same time. The mixture churns its way to the worm's gizzard, where surging muscles grind the leaf and soil mixture into a fine paste. The paste moves deeper into the earthworm's gut. Here, bacteria help with digestion, much as our own gut flora help us process otherwise unavailable food. When the worm has wrested all the nutrients from the paste, it excretes the remains of the leaf and soil, plus dead gut bacteria. These worm-casts coat the burrow with fertile, organically enriched earth. Before long, bacteria, fungi, and microscopic soil animals will find this cache of organic matter and flourish in the walls of the burrow, adding their own excretions and dead bodies to the supply.

Fueled by the leaf's nutrients, the earthworm tunnels deeper into the ground, loosening, aerating, and fertilizing the soil. Autumn rain will trickle down the burrow, bringing moisture farther into the earth than previously. The soil will stay damp a little longer between rains. In spring, a root from the oak tree will find this burrow, and, coaxed by the easy passage and the tunnel's lining of organic food, will extend deep enough to tap that late-season moisture. The worm, with its fertile casts and a burrow that lets air, water, and roots penetrate the earth, will have aided the oak tree and much of the other life in the soil. Worms are among the most beneficial of soil animals: They turn over as much as 25 tons of soil per acre per year, or the equivalent of one inch of topsoil over Earth's land surface every ten years.

Meanwhile, on the surface, the feasting invertebrates continue to shred the leaf into tiny bits—or *comminute* it, in soil-specialist parlance. Comminution exposes more leaf surface—tender inner surfaces at that—to attack by bacteria and fungi, further hastening decomposition. Also, the small army of mites, larvae, and other invertebrates feeding on the leaf deposit a fair load of droppings, or frass, which also becomes food for other

> **The *primary decomposers*—invertebrates, bacteria, algae, fungi, and threadlike fungal relatives called actinomycetes—are the first to dine on rotting organic matter.**
>
>

decomposers (electron micrographs show that some decomposing leaves are nearly completely covered with frass, which adds up to an enormous amount of fertile manure). Any leaf bits that aren't fully digested on their first passage through a decomposer's gut are eaten again and again by one tiny animal after another until the organic matter is mashed into microscopic particles. Soil invertebrates such as worms and mites don't really alter the chemical composition of the leaf—their job is principally to pulverize litter. Their scurrying and tunneling also mixes the leaf particles with soil, where the fragments stay moist and palatable for others. In some cases, the animals' gut microbes can break down tenacious large molecules such as chitin, keratin, and cellulose into their simpler sugarlike components. The real alchemy—the chemical transformation of the leaf into humus and plant food—is done by microorganisms.

As the soil animals reduce the leaf to droppings and microscopic particles, a second wave of bacteria, fungi, and other microbes descends upon the remains. Using enzymes and the rest of their metabolic chemistry sets, these microbes snap large molecules into small, edible fragments. Cellulose and lignin, the tough components of

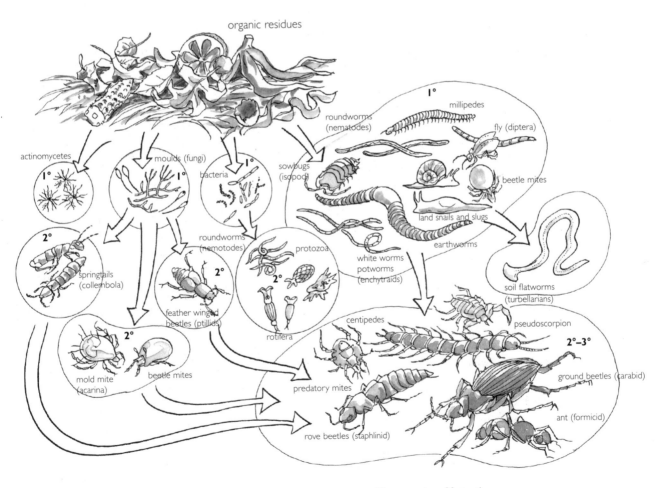

The soil food web. 1°=primary decomposers; 2°=secondary; 3°=tertiary.

plant cell walls, are cleaved into tasty sugars and aromatic carbon rings. Other microbes hack long chains of leaf protein into short amino acid pieces. Some of these microbes are highly specialized, able to break down only a few types of molecules, but working together this orchestra of thousands of species of bacteria, fungi, algae, and others fully decompose our leaf.

Besides breaking down organic matter, these underground microbes also build up soil structure. As they feed, certain soil bacteria secrete gums, waxes, and gels that hold tiny particles of earth together. Dividing fungal cells lengthen into long fingers of hyphae that surround crumbs of soil and bind them to each other. These mini-clumps give microbially rich soil its good *tilth,* the loose, crumbly structure that garden-ers and farmers strive for. Also, these gooey microbial byprod-ucts protect soil from drying and allow it to hold huge vol-umes of water. Without soil life, earth just dries up and blows away, or clumps together after a rain and forms clay-bound, root-thwarting clods.

The soil's microbes don't live very long—just hours or days. As they die, larger microbes and soil animals con-sume their bodies. Also, predators abound in the soil ecosystem. Voracious amoebae lurk in films of soil moisture, ready to engulf a hapless bacterium. Mold mites, springtails, certain beetles, and a host of other critters feed on the primary decomposers, and are called, in turn, *secondary decomposers.* Larger predators feed on the secondary (and some pri-mary) decomposers who have come to our leaf: These centipedes, ground beetles, pseudoscorpi-ons, predatory mites, ants, and spiders are the *ter-tiary decomposers.*

Although this order—primary, secondary, and tertiary decomposers—seems to suggest a linear hierarchy, the boundaries are not hard and fast. The frass and dead body of even the largest spider becomes food for bacteria and other primary decomposers, so it's hard to say who's on top. Soil ecology is a set of nested cycles, and a drawing of it would be laced with arrows, almost blackened with the interconnections that tie the life and death of each species to many of the others.

How Humus Is Made

Now our leaf is almost fully decomposed. How, then, does it become plant food—how does it return to life and reconnect to plants and to our garden? The leaf's contents (those that don't enter the atmosphere as gases) end up as one of two sub-stances: humus or minerals. Both are critical to healthy plants. We'll look at humus first.

As our leaf is shredded, chewed, and chemically dis-solved by soil organisms, some parts of the leaf decompose more quickly than others. The first tissues to go are those made of sugars and starches, which soil life quickly converts to energy, carbon dioxide, or more organisms. A little harder to digest are celluloses and some types of proteins, which are chains and sheets of tightly linked small molecules. Not all soil organisms have the special enzymes needed to break the crisscrossed bonds that hold these polymers together, thus these com-pounds decompose more slowly. Even tougher to break down are polymers known as lignins, which give wood its strength; chitins, which make up the armored coats of insects; and certain types of waxes. Only specialized soil organisms, particularly fungi, can break down these tenacious molecules.

Organisms that can't break down these hardy molecules nevertheless give it their best shot. Microbes work over these resistant compounds,

> **As they feed, certain soil bacteria secrete gums, waxes, and gels that hold tiny particles of earth together. These mini-clumps give microbially rich soil its good *tilth,* the loose, crumbly structure that gardeners and farmers strive for.**

nibbling and modifying the portions they can digest. In a process that is poorly understood, microbes and other forces of decomposition convert lignins and the other hard-core leaf compounds into *humus,* a fairly stable, incredibly complex group of molecules that only slowly undergoes further decomposition. Humus is made of carbon, oxygen, nitrogen, and hydrogen, bonded together in ways that make it difficult for soil organisms to attack.

In a sense, humus is the end of the road for organic matter—by the time our leaf's remains have reached the humus stage, decomposition has slowed to a snail's pace. Since organisms can't easily break down humus, it accumulates in the soil. It will eventually decompose, but in healthy soil, freshly composting debris arrives at least as fast as the old humus is broken down, resulting in a slow turnover and constant buildup of humus.

When pushed, soil organisms can decompose humus, but only grudgingly, and usually if there is nothing else to eat. If humus levels are dropping, it's a sign that the soil is in very bad shape. It means that easily digested organic matter is gone, and the inhabitants are, in effect, burning down the house to keep warm. Humus is critical to soil health, thus wise gardeners keep their soil rich in humus. For now we'll see why; later we'll learn how.

Of all the ingredients of soil, humus is by far the best at holding moisture, and will absorb four to six times its weight in water. Have you ever tried to pick up a wet bale of peat moss? It's monstrously heavy, and it will take months to dry out. Peat moss isn't exactly humus—it's organic matter that's been arrested on its way to becoming humus because peat bogs lack the oxygen for decomposers to finish the job—but hoisting a wet bale of peat moss can give some idea of how well humus holds moisture.

Humus also swells when it's wet, so humus-rich soil will gently heave upward after a rain. As this soil dries, the humus shrinks, leaving air spaces between soil crumbs. This expanding and shrinking process lightens the soil, acting a little like tilling, but with less upset to the soil life. In humusy, fluffed-up earth, roots and soil organisms can easily tunnel in search of nutrients, and these travelers further aerate the soil. Water penetrates the loosened soil more deeply, and is stored longer by the humus. Here is another life-enhancing positive feedback loop: Humus allows moisture and soil organisms to move deeper into the soil, where they create more humus, allowing yet deeper penetration, building humus again, and so on.

Where humus really excels is in holding nutrients. The humus molecule illustrated below shows that, from an atom's-eye viewpoint, the face that humus presents to the world is a bristling array of oxygen atoms. Oxygen has a strong negative charge, and in chemistry as in much of life, opposites attract. Thus, humus's many negative oxygen atoms serve as bait for luring lots of positively charged elements. These include some of the most important nutrients for both plants and soil animals: potassium, calcium, magnesium, ammonium (a nitrogen compound), copper, zinc, manganese, and many others. Under the right conditions (in soil of pH near 7, neither too acid nor too alkaline), humus can

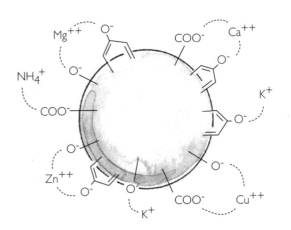

A chemical view of humus, studded with negatively charged oxygen atoms. Positively charged nutrients such as ammonium, potassium, copper, magnesium, calcium, and zinc are adsorbed to the humus. These nutrients can be pulled off the humus and used by plants and microbes.

pick up and store enormous quantities of positively charged nutrients.

How do these nutrients move from the humus to plants? Plant roots, as noted, secrete very mild acids, which break the bonds that hold the nutrients onto the humus. The nutrients are washed into the soil moisture, creating a rich soup. Bathed in this nutritious broth, the plants can absorb as much calcium, ammonium, or other nutrient as they need. There's evidence that when plants have supped long enough, they stop the flow of acid to avoid depleting the humus.

That's the direct method plants use to pull nutrients form humus. Just as common in healthy soil is an indirect route, in which microbes are the middlemen. In this type of plant feeding, roots release sugars and vitamins that are ideal food for beneficial bacteria and fungi. These microbes thrive in huge numbers close to roots, lapping up the plant-produced food and bathing in the film of moisture that surrounds the roots. In return, the microbes produce acids and enzymes that release the humus-bound nutrients, and share this food with the plants.

Microbes also excrete food for plants in their waste. Another big plus for plants is that many of the fungi and other microbes secrete antibiotics that protect the plants from disease. All of these mutual exchanges create a truly symbiotic relationship. Many plants have become dependent on particular species of microbial partners, and grow poorly without them. Even when the plant-microbe partnership isn't this specific, plants often grow much faster when microbes are present than in a sterile or microbe-depleted environment.

The Soil's Mineral Wealth

I said earlier that decomposing organic matter ends up either as humus or as minerals. We've covered humus, so let's look at the parts of our leaf that meet a mineral fate.

Like most living things, leaves are composed primarily of carbon-containing compounds: sugars, proteins, starches, and many other organic molecules. When soil creatures eat these compounds, some of the carbon becomes part of the consumer, as cell membrane, wing case, eyeball, or the like. And some of the carbon is released as a gas: carbon dioxide, or CO_2 (our breath contains carbon dioxide for the same reason). Soil organisms consume the other elements that make up the leaf, too, such as nitrogen, calcium, phosphorus, and all the rest, but most of those are reincorporated into solid matter—organism or bug manure—and remain earthbound. A substantial portion of the carbon, however, puffs into the atmosphere as carbon dioxide. This means that, in decomposing matter, the ratio of carbon to the other elements is decreasing; carbon drifts into the air, but most nitrogen, for example, stays behind. The carbon-to-nitrogen ratio decreases. (Compost enthusiasts will recognize this C:N ratio as a critical element of a good compost pile). In decomposition, carbon levels drop quickly, while the amounts of the other elements in our decomposing leaf stay roughly the same.

By the time the final rank of soil organisms, the microbes, are finished swarming over the leaf and digesting it, most of the consumable carbon—that which is not tied up as humus—is gone. Little remains but inorganic (non–carbon containing) compounds, such as phosphate, nitrate, sulfate, and other chemicals that most gardeners will recognize from the printing on bags of fertilizer. That's right: Microbes make plant fertilizer right in the soil. This process of converting organic, carbon-containing compounds into inorganic plant food is called *mineralization*. Minerals—the nitrates and phosphates and others—are tiny, usually highly mobile molecules that dissolve easily in water. That means that once organic debris is converted to minerals, or fertilizer is poured onto the soil, these nutrients don't hang around long, but are easily leached out of soil by rain.

Conventional wisdom has it that plant roots are the main imbibers of soil minerals, and that plants can only absorb these minerals (fertilizers) if they are in water-soluble form, but neither premise is true. Roots occupy only a very small fraction of the soil, so most soil minerals—and most chemical fertilizers—never make direct contact with roots. Unless these isolated, lonely minerals are snapped up by humus or soil organisms, they leach away. It's the humus and the life in the soil that keep the earth fertile by holding on to nutrients that would otherwise wash out of the soil into streams, lakes, and eventually the ocean.

Agricultural chemists have missed the boat with their soluble fertilizers; they're doing things the hard way by using an engineering approach rather than an ecological one. Yes, plants are quite capable of absorbing the water-soluble minerals in chemical fertilizer. But plants often use only 10 percent of the fertilizer that's applied, and rarely more than 50 percent. The rest washes into the groundwater, which is why so many wells in our farmlands are polluted with toxic levels of nitrates.

Applying fertilizer the way nature does—tied to organic matter—uses far less fertilizer and also saves the energy consumed in producing, shipping, and applying it. It also supports a broad assortment of soil life, which widens the base of our living pyramid and enhances rather than reduces biodiversity. In addition, plants get a balanced diet instead of being force-fed, and are more healthy. It's well documented that plants grown on soil rich in organic matter are more disease-resistant than plants in carbon-poor soil.

In short, in a properly tuned ecological garden we rarely need to use soluble fertilizers because plants and soil animals are perfectly capable of knocking nutrients loose from humus and organic debris (or clay, another nutrient storage source) with secretions of mild acid and enzymes. Most of the nutrients in healthy soil are "insoluble yet available." These nutrients, bound to organic matter or cycling among fast-living microbes, won't wash out of the soil, yet can be gently coaxed loose—or traded for sugar secretions—by plant roots. And the plants take only what they need. This turns out to be very little, since plants are 85 percent water, and much of the rest is carbon from the air. A fat ½-pound tomato, for example, only draws about 50 milligrams of phosphorus and 500 milligrams of potassium from the soil. That's easy to replace in a humus-rich garden that uses mulches, composts, and nutrient-accumulating plants.

A Question of Balance

Sometimes gardening books single out soil organisms as bad guys—they supposedly "lock up" nutrients, making them unavailable for plants. In an imbalanced soil, this is true. Soil life is much more mobile than plants and has a speedier metabolism. When hungry, microbes can grab nutrients faster than roots. As soil scientist William Albrecht says, "microbes dine at the first table." If the soil life is starved by poor soil, microbes certainly won't pass on any food to plants.

For example, a common soil problem is too little nitrogen. Nitrogen is used in proteins and cell membranes, and plants lacking this nutrient are pale and anemic. Gardeners are often admonished not to use wood shavings or straw as a soil amendment because it leads to nitrogen deficiency. This is because shavings and straw, though good sources of carbon, are very low in nitrogen (see table 4-1). These nitrogen-poor amendments are fine for use as mulch, on *top* of the soil, but when they are mixed into the soil with spade or tiller, decomposer organisms, who need a balanced diet of about twenty to thirty parts carbon for each part nitrogen, go on a carbon-fueled rampage. It's analogous to the whopping metabolic rush that a big

> **The process of converting organic carbon-containing compounds into inorganic plant food is called *mineralization*.**

TABLE 4-1.

CARBON TO NITROGEN (C:N) RATIOS IN COMMON MULCH AND COMPOST MATERIALS

Apple pomace	21:1
Bonemeal	3.5:1
Clover, flowering phase	23:1
Clover, vegetative phase	16:1
Compost, finished	16:1
Corn stover	60:1
Cottonseed meal	5:1
Fish scraps	4:1
Grain hulls and chaff	80:1
Grass clippings, dry	19:1
Grass clippings, fresh	15:1
Hay, legume/grass mix	25:1
Hay, mature alfalfa	25:1
Hay, young alfalfa	13:1
Leaves, dry	50:1
Leaves, fresh	30:1
Manure, chicken	7:1
Manure, cow	18:1
Manure, horse	25:1
Manure, human	8:1
Manure, rotted	20:1
Newspaper	800:1
Ryegrass, flowering phase	37:1
Ryegrass, vegetative phase	26:1
Sawdust, hardwood	400:1
Sawdust, rotted	200:1
Sawdust, softwood	600:1
Seaweed	19:1
Straw, oat	74:1
Straw, wheat	80:1
Urine, human	0.8:1
Vegetable wastes	12:1
Vetch, fresh hairy	11:1

Sources: Data taken from Robert Kourik, *Designing and Maintaining Your Edible Landscape—Naturally* (Metamorphic, 1986); The Farallones Institute, *The Integral Urban House* (Sierra Club, 1979); and Nyle C. Brady, *The Nature and Properties of Soils* (Prentice Hall, 1996).

dose of sugar can give you: a great short-term blast, but one that depletes other nutrients and leaves you drained.

To balance this straw-powered carbon feast, soil life grabs every bit of available nitrogen, eating, breeding, and growing as fast as the low lev-els of this nutrient will allow. The ample but imbalanced food triggers a population explosion among the microbes. Soon the secondary and tertiary decomposers (beetles, spiders, ants), spurred by a surge in their prey, are also breeding like fury. Whenever any valuable nitrogen is released in the form of dead bodies or waste, some tiny, hungry critter instantly consumes it before plants can. The plant roots lose out, because the microbes dine at the first table. This madly racing but lopsided feeding frenzy won't diminish until the overabundant carbon is either consumed or balanced by imports of nitrogen—from the air via bacteria that pull nitrogen from the air, from animal manure, or from an observant gardener with a bag of blood meal.

The same lock-ups occur when other nutrients are lacking in the soil. Until the soil life is properly fed, the plants can't eat. Conventional farming gets around this problem by flooding the soil with inorganic fertilizer, ten times what the plants can consume. But this, the engineer's approach rather than the biologist's, creates water pollution and problem-prone plants. The soil life, and the soil itself, suffer from the imbalance.

Here's what happens to soil life after overzealous application of chemical fertilizer. Pouring a big bag of inorganic fertilizer on the ground creates an excess of mineral nutrients. Now the food in short supply is carbon. Once again, the soil life roars into a feeding frenzy, spurred by the more-than-ample nitrogen, phosphorus, and potassium in typical NPK fertilizers. Since organisms need about twenty parts carbon for every one of nitrogen, it isn't long before any available carbon is pulled from the soil's organic matter and tied up in living bodies. These organisms exhale carbon dioxide, so a proportion of carbon is lost with each generation. First the easily digestible organic matter is eaten, then, more slowly, the humus. Eventually nearly all the soil's carbon is gone, and the soil life, starved of this essential food, begins to die. Species of soil organisms that can't survive the shortages go extinct locally. Some of these creatures may play critical roles, perhaps secreting antibiotics to protect plants, or transferring an essential nutrient, or breaking down an otherwise inedible compound. With important links missing, the soil life falls far out of balance. Natural predators begin to die off, so some of their prey organisms, no longer kept in check in this torn food web, surge in numbers and become pests.

Sadly, many of the creatures that remain after this mineral overdose are those that have learned to survive on the one remaining source of carbon: your plants. Burning carbon out of the soil with chemical fertilizers can actually select for disease organisms. All manner of chomping, sucking, mildewing, blackening, spotting horrors descend on the vegetation. With the natural controls gone, and disease ravishing every green thing, humans must step in with sprays. But the now-destructive organisms have what they need to thrive—the food and shelter of garden plants—and they will breed whenever the now-essential human intervention diminishes. The gardener is locked on a chemical treadmill. It's a losing battle, reflected in the fact that we use twenty times the pesticides we did fifty years ago, yet crop losses to insects and disease have actually increased, according to USDA statistics.

The other harm done by injudicious use of chemical fertilizers is to the soil itself. As organic matter is burned up by wildly feeding soil life, the soil loses its ability to hold water and air. Its tilth is destroyed. The desperate soil life has turned to feed on the humus itself, the food of last resort. With humus and all other organic matter gone, the soil loses its fluffy, friable structure and collapses. Clay-based soil compacts to concrete; silty soil desiccates to dust and blows away.

In contrast, ample soil life boosts both the soil structure and the health of your plants. When the soil food web is chock-full of diversity, diseases are held in check. If a bacterial blight begins to bloom, a balanced supply of predators grazes this food sur-

plus back into line. When a fungal disease threatens, microbial and insect denizens of your soil are ready to capitalize on this new supply of their favorite food. Living soil is the foundation of a healthy garden.

To Till or Not to Till

We've seen that organic matter keeps soil light and fluffy, and easy for roots to penetrate. What about mechanical methods for breaking up soil?

The invention of the plow ranks as one of the great steps forward for humanity. Farmers know that plowing releases locked-up soil fertility. Plowing also keeps down weeds, and thoroughly mingles surface litter with the soil. We do the same when we drag our power-tiller out of the garage and push the snorting beast through the garden beds in a cloud of blue smoke.

What's really happening during tilling? By churning the soil, we're flushing it with fresh air. All that oxygen invigorates the soil life, which zooms into action, breaking down organic matter and plucking minerals from humus and rock particles. Tilling also breaks up the soil, greatly increasing its surface area by creating many small clumps out of big ones. Soil microbes then colonize these fresh surfaces, extracting more nutrients and undergoing a population explosion.

All this is great for the first season. The huge blast of nutrients fuels tremendous plant growth, and the harvest is bountiful. But the life of the tilled soil releases far more nutrients than the plants can use. Much of the new fertility leaches away in rains. The next year, when the tiller returns, more organic matter burns up, again releasing a surfeit of fertility. The unused portion is again leached. After a few seasons, the soil is depleted. The humus is gone, the mineral ores are played out, and the prematurely exuberant soil life is depauperate. Now the gardener must renew the soil with bales of organic matter, fertilizer, and plenty of work.

Thus, tilling releases far more nutrients than

plants can use. Also, the constant mechanical battering destroys the soil structure, especially when perpetrated upon too-wet soil (and we're all impatient to get those seeds in, so this happens often). Frequent tilling smashes loamy soil crumbs to powder, and compacts clayey clods into hardpan. And a tilling session consumes far more calories of energy than are in a year's worth of garden-grown food. That's not a sustainable arrangement.

Better to let humus fluff your soil naturally, and to use mulches to smother weeds and renew nutrients. Instead of unleashing fertility at a breakneck, mechanical pace, we can allow plant roots to do the job. Questing roots will split nuggets of earth in their own time, opening the soil to microbial colonization, loosening nutrients at just the right rate. Once again, nature makes a better partner than slave.

BUILDING SOIL LIFE

Okay, enough theory. Let's get our hands dirty. What are some techniques for creating soil that gardeners dream of? To answer, I could end this chapter now with three little words: Add organic matter.

But I won't stop there. Techniques abound for building soil organic matter; different situations will call for different methods. These techniques break down into three broad categories: composts, mulches, and cover crops.

Compost: The Quick and Dirty Method

Most gardeners know the value of compost, and many excellent books and articles have been written about this "black gold," so I won't spend too much time recapitulating what's already out there. In brief, *compost,* the rich, humusy end product of decomposition, is made by piling surplus organic matter into a mound or bin, and letting it rot.

All homeowners generate excess organic matter: kitchen scraps, grass clippings, leaf piles, and debris from pruning and cleaning up a yardful of plants. Most of this can be recycled right on site,

and turned into a valuable source of soil life and nutrients for your plants. If you're not fussy, simply piling this stuff in a corner in your yard and waiting a few months is enough to generate compost. But the job can be done much more efficiently. The critical elements of a good compost pile are the right ratio of carbon to nitrogen, optimum moisture, and proper size.

Let's take size first. Chomping, multiplying microbes give off heat, which accelerates their growth and thus the breakdown of the pile's contents. But just as important, a hot compost pile will sterilize all the seeds found in yard waste. Piles smaller than about three feet on a side won't insulate the burgeoning microbe population enough to raise the temperature to the critical 130 to 150 degrees Fahrenheit necessary to kill seeds. Spreading cold-processed compost on the garden imports a host of weeds and other unwanted plants. I've seen tomato seedlings pop up by the hundreds in a flower bed after the addition of poorly prepared compost. Composters should thus save up their materials until they have enough for a 3-foot heap.

What to put in the pile? Different ingredients contain varying ratios of carbon to nitrogen, and although eventually almost anything organic will decompose, an overall ratio of 30:1 C:N is ideal. Table 4-1 gives the C:N ratios of many compostable materials. If you are the meticulous type, you can calculate a proper balance of high carbon and high nitrogen ingredients to yield 30:1. But for the less assiduous, here's a good rule of thumb: Green materials, such as grass clippings and fresh plant trimmings (and we'll also include kitchen waste here), are high in nitrogen. Brown items, such as dried leaves, hay, straw, and wood shavings, are high in carbon. The exception here is manure, which is high in nitrogen—consider it green. If you mix roughly half green with half brown, you'll approximate the ideal 30:1 C:N ratio. If high-nitrogen materials are in short supply, sprinkle in some blood meal or cottonseed meal for balance.

When building the pile, add the materials in layers no more than 6 inches thick. For a small pile, just jumble everything together by turning. Some gardeners suggest adding soil to the pile. My soil is so clayey that if I use native earth, I get reddish compost. I like my compost black, so I leave out the soil. But I do add some finished compost as I build the heap, which inoculates the pile with soil life and gives it a boost. When I'm feeling fanatical, I do two things. One is to inoculate the new pile with compost from another young pile if I have one, figuring that the species of soil organisms I'm transferring will be suited to the fresh pile's undigested debris. I'll also trek into the woods, a field, to a pond margin—a variety of ecosystems—where I'll grab a quart or two of soil from each, and add the blend. That way I'm maximizing the biodiversity of my soil life. Who knows what helpful predators and decomposers I might be importing?

The life of the compost heap needs water to survive. A good compost pile should be about as moist as a wrung-out sponge. If the ingredients are dry when the pile is assembled, it can take an astonishing amount of water to achieve the right moisture level. When I'm building a pile in August, I usually have a hose spraying on the pile the entire time I'm forking the dry debris in place (this is an excellent use for greywater, whose nutrient load gives the soil life an extra boost, and assuages my guilt about using so much water). I usually cover the finished pile with a tarp to retain moisture on sunny days and keep rain from leaching out the hard-won nutrients.

One age-old compost question is, to turn or not to turn? Turning a pile supplies oxygen, and speeds up decomposition. If you're in a hurry for compost, turn the pile as soon as the pile's initial blast of heat—which begins within days of a new pile's creation—begins to subside. This will restoke the metabolic fires of the pile's occupants with oxygen, and the compost will heat up again quickly. Each time the pile cools, turn it again. A properly made pile can be reduced to black gold in three weeks by well-timed turning.

However, I suggest that you plan ahead so that you'll have an ample supply of compost when you need it without turning a pile more than once or twice. That's enough to incorporate and rot down the outer layers of the pile.

Here's why. A less-turned pile won't rot down as quickly as a more ambitiously forked one, but each turning amps up microbial metabolism enormously. This drives the pile's contents further down the two-forked road of fully digested humus and totally mineralized nutrients. Mineralized nutrients can leach out of soil very quickly. Completely processed humus, while great for soil texture and drought resistance, won't feed as much soil life as less-digested organic matter. A slowly rotted compost, from my experience, still gets hot enough during that first heating-up to kill weed seeds, but seems to supply my plants with nutrients longer than the product of rapid turnings. My rule is: Turn for texture—when you need to quickly build soil structure—but rest the pile for long-term nutrition.

The best role for compost, as I see it, is to give a quick fertility boost to a limited area of soil—no more than a few hundred square feet. If you've just moved to a new garden and want productivity quickly, then compost will get soil fertility on the upswing rapidly. An inch or two of compost lightly spaded into poor soil, or, if you've got enough, several inches on top of depleted or compacted earth, will support very dense plantings. With plant production jump-started this way, a gardener can begin more long-term soil building.

I'm going to venture once more into the heretical here: Composting isn't my favorite way to build soil, and I try to do as little of it as possible. For one thing, it's a lot of work. All that sequestering of supplies, layering, watering, turning, and then carting the whole damn pile, load by load, onto the garden bed, shoveling it out, spading it in, and finally, raking the bed smooth. That's a bunch of materials handling, something that every efficient designer seeks to minimize.

But I also believe compost piles aren't the optimal way to raise your microherds, nor to take advantage of their work. Whenever I turn or move my compost pile, I know I'm murdering millions of

WOODY WAYS TO BUILD SOIL

Most of the techniques offered in this chapter involve the decomposition of readily broken-down organic matter such as grass and kitchen scraps. But most of us generate woody debris, too: tree prunings, logs, even rotten firewood or lumber scraps. We can't add these to the compost pile, but rather than burn or landfill them, we can use them to build soil too. Here's how:

HUGELKULTUR

In the carefully tended forests of central Europe, no scrap of wood is ever wasted. Branches and brushy prunings are used in a gardening technique called *hugelkultur*, or mound culture. To create a *hugelkultur*, pile up branches or brush a foot or two deep in a mound 4 to 8 feet long. Stomp on the pile to compact it a bit. Then toss compostable materials—grass clippings, sod, straw—into the pile. Sprinkle some compost on the mound, and top with an inch or so of soil. Then plant the *hugelkultur* with seeds or starts. Potatoes really love *hugelkultur*—I can start potatoes in these mounds a month earlier than in garden beds. Squashes, melons, and other vines do well here too.

The decomposing organic matter in *hugelkultur* beds raises the temperature just enough to boost plant growth. Another advantage: As the woody brush rots, it releases nutrients slowly, and also holds quite a bit of water. You don't need to fertilize or irrigate *hugelkultur* very often.

THE DEAD WOOD SWALE

Perhaps you've observed that rotting wood can hold a large amount of moisture. Late in a rainless Northwest summer, I've plunged my arm up to the elbow into a rotten log and brought out a fistful of damp pulp. By acting like sponges, downed logs may serve as critical moisture reservoirs for water-dependent species such as fungi and soil animals. Some naturalists theorize that roots and fungal mycelia may translocate water from these woody moisture caches to plants and fungi many feet away.

Rotting wood's talent for holding water is another of nature's tricks that can be applied in the garden. We can invert the *hugelkultur* idea and bury wood beneath our plants. Permaculturist Tom Ward digs trenches about 18 inches deep, tosses in woody trunks or rotten firewood, and then backfills the trenches with soil. On top of this, he plants blueberries. Tom told me, "I'm imitating how, in ponds and bogs, blueberries often root on floating logs. In my garden, all that wood is like a huge sponge sunk into the ground." The wood soaks up and holds soil moisture, and roots infiltrate this font of wetness and drink from it during drought.

Nearly any plant—not just blueberries—will grow well on a buried wood swale. Some people worry that the wood will lock up nitrogen, and thus they toss a nitrogen source into the swale (green compost materials or slow-release fertilizer) but I suspect that the wood decomposes so slowly that very little nitrogen is bound up by the microbes gnawing at the logs.

these wonderful helpers: smashing their homes, bludgeoning them and their children with my spading fork, desiccating all those who end up on the outer layer of the pile. I'm willing to break eggs to make an omelet, but only if I can't think of another way. I'd like my gardening to be a gentle art.

And morality aside, each disruption of the pile is a setback to the soil life. They're going through a complex ecological succession, a sweep through time from simple sugar-digesting species to protein-munchers to highly specialized lignin- and chitin-eating fungi. Each swipe of my fork disrupts this process. By the time I wheel my compost over to the garden and shovel it on, does the product still retain the maximum, optimum biodiversity? I don't think so.

Also, I think composting wastes nutrients. Each time I dig up my compost heap, underneath is a beautiful, foot-thick layer of black soil that's been created during the pile's dance from death to life. I usually trundle this rich earth to the garden too, but it's telling me that complex and life-giving metabolic liquors are oozing out of the pile, washing onto the margins and being wasted. I am loathe to see the results of my microherds' labors spilling useless onto the ground. Capture those nutritious juices, I say. I watch all those worms thriving under my compost pile, all the mites and millipedes, and I want them in my garden, shuttling nutrients to plants, not freeloading a foot below a plantless pile. I achieve these benefits by sheet mulching.

The Power of Sheet Mulch

Though the process took a number of years, I've been completely converted to composting in place, commonly known as sheet composting or *sheet mulching*. Sheet mulching is one of the basics in the ecological gardener's tool kit. It's a method of eradicating weeds and building soil that eliminates herbicides and avoids tilling, both of which rupture soil ecology. Sheet mulching is a variation on nature's way of building soil by accumulating and breaking down organic debris from the top down.

In its simplest form, sheet mulching is a two-step process: First, apply a layer of weed-suppressing newspaper or cardboard (or even cloth or wool carpet), and then top it with about a foot of organic mulch. Ideally this is done in fall, so that the mulch rots to become humusy earth over the winter. Also, the weed-stopping layer breaks down enough to let spring-planted seeds and transplants thrust their roots deep into the earth. For a more detailed description of sheet mulching, see the sidebar on pages 72–73.

Gathering the materials for sheet mulch is the most laborious and time-consuming part of the job; the rest is pretty painless. It's remarkable how much material it takes to really do it right. Fortunately, most of these items are free and easily available with a little research. If you choose materials appropriate to your bioregion, they will be easy to find. Timber country offers ample bark and sawdust, the coasts yield seaweed and salt hay, and the midcontinent and agricultural valleys always have a surfeit of straw, grain hulls, and other food-industry byproducts. In big cities, canneries, food processors, and produce distribution warehouses often generate plenty of organic waste. Utility companies or landscapers will often deliver chipped tree trimmings, and every neighborhood offers leaves in the fall. Put the word out that your looking for organic

matter, and someone else's problem will become your windfall.

Most gardeners know the benefits of mulch. A sprinkling of an inch or two of straw or shavings around plants helps conserve water, keeps soil cool on scorching summer days, suppresses weeds, and, mission accomplished, agreeably rots down into rich compost over the winter. Some gardeners have taken this idea and run with it, as in *The Ruth Stout No-Work Garden Book*. In her classic book, Ruth describes how 8 inches of spoiled hay applied to her garden beds built phenomenal, weed-free soil. I can vouch for the benefits.

At first I was a timid mulcher. Even after reading Stout's book, I didn't have the courage to wholeheartedly follow her instructions. Call it fear of mulching, but I would merely sprinkle down a stingy inch or two of straw to keep the soil moist when summer warmed up. I was afraid, I think, of somehow choking out the plants, or attracting slugs, or maybe growing some malignant fungus in the straw.

These drawbacks never materialized, and eventually I noticed the real benefits of mulching, beyond water retention: fewer weeds and bigger plants.

One observation mystified me for a time. Within a day or two of laying down mulch, I would find it strewn into the garden paths as if by some evil randomizing force. I would meticulously stuff it back in place, but soon, even with no evident wind, the mulch would be back in the paths. Then I saw the culprits: Robins and towhees, hunting for worms that now were migrating into the straw, since the soil was moist right up to the surface. It was observing this new interaction and understanding its implications that eliminated my mulching timidity. The mulch was clearly building a large worm population that in turn was boosting soil fertility. And the birds were helping too, pooping nitrates and phosphates into the straw.

Thus emboldened, I mulched half the garden under a foot of stable bedding, spoiled alfalfa hay, and straw. (Years ago, I had learned the hard way

THE ULTIMATE, BOMB-PROOF SHEET MULCH

Sheet mulch can be as simple as a layer of newspapers topped by 8 to 12 inches of nearly any mulch material. But if you want to build the perfect sheet mulch, here's how:

If this is your first sheet mulch, start small. Sheet mulch gobbles up a tremendous amount of organic matter—the roughly 2 cubic yards held by a full-sized pickup truck will cover about 50 square feet. But don't scrimp. It's much better to blanket a small area thoroughly than to spread the mulch too thin to smother weeds or feed the soil properly. Choose a site that's not more than 200 square feet, in the proper location for the intended plants, and preferably near the house. Remember your zones: Deeply mulched beds will soon be covered with a riot of plant life, and you want these awesomely productive areas right outside your door, to harvest the bounty or admire the many avian and insect visitors.

Here's a materials list for the perfect sheet mulch:

1. A 2- to 3-foot stack of newspaper, minus any glossy sections, whose inks contain metal pigments (the black and colored inks on standard newsprint are soy-based and nontoxic), or about 300 square feet of corrugated box cardboard without staples or plastic tape. You can also use cloth, old clothing, or wool carpet, provided they contain no synthetic fabric, but these take far longer to decay than paper.
2. Soil amendments, depending on your soil's needs: lime, rock phosphate, bonemeal, rock dust, kelp meal, or blood meal.
3. Bulk organic matter: straw, spoiled hay, yard waste, leaves, seaweed, finely ground bark, stable sweepings, wood shavings, or any mixture of these, ideally resulting in an overall C:N ratio of 100/1 to 30/1. Grass clippings are also good, but only when mixed with other, "brown" mulches, otherwise their high nitrogen content causes anaerobic—and smelly, slimy—decomposition. You will need about 4 to 8 cubic yards of loosely piled mulch, or 6 to 10 two-string bales of hay or straw.
4. Compost, about ¼ to ½ cubic yard (6 to 12 cubic feet).
5. Manure: ¼ to 1 cubic yard, depending on the concentration and amount of bedding mixed in. About 6 cubic feet of composted cattle manure or some other bagged product will be plenty.
6. A top layer of seed-free material, such as straw, leaves, wood shavings, bark, sawdust, pine needles, grain hulls (nut husks), or seagrass. You will need roughly 1 cubic yard or 2 to 4 two-string bales.

If you can't find every item, don't worry. Sheet mulching is very forgiving. As long as you have enough newspaper or cardboard, plus organic matter of almost any kind, you'll end up with great soil. Store your supplies near the chosen site so you won't have to move them too far on sheet-mulch day. Keep them dry, too.

The day before you mulch, water the site well unless the ground is moist from rain. The organisms that will be turning your mulch into rich earth can't work without water, and once the mulch is in place, it takes a lot of water to moisten the bottom layers. Conversely, it takes a long time for the layers to dry out—you've got lots of water storage.

After the water has soaked in overnight, slash down any vegetation. Don't pull up weeds—leave all the native organic matter right there, including the roots. Just clip, mow, scythe, or weed-whack everything down in place. It's great worm food, and the nitrogen-rich greens and roots will be a tasty starter for the decomposers. Remove any stumps or big woody pieces.

Next, add any soil amendments. If your soil is acid, sprinkle on some lime. For alkaline soil, a little gypsum or sulfur will help. A dusting of rock phosphate or bonemeal will supply phosphorus. Greensand, kelp meal, or rock dust will add trace minerals. Use a soil test or your own understanding of your soil's fertility to guide the type and quantity of soil amendments.

If your native earth is clayey or compacted, now is a good time to open it up a bit. Just push a spading fork into the ground, rock it a little, and pull it out. Do this across the entire mulch site. Don't turn the earth, just poke some holes into it and crack it open to allow better moisture and root penetration and soil-critter movement.

Then add a thin layer of high-nitrogen material. This can be manure, blood or cottonseed meal, fresh grass clippings or other lush greens, or cast-off produce from restaurants or markets. For concentrated matter such as rabbit manure or blood meal, sprinkle down enough material to just cover the soil. Grass clippings or bedding-rich manure should go down about an inch thick. While this layer isn't essential, it attracts worms and burrowing beetles, which will aerate and loosen the soil.

Now the fun begins: putting the sheet in sheet mulch. Lay down newspapers and/or cardboard to create a continuous light-blocking layer that will smother existing plants. Cardboard is very satisfying to use, since those big sheets, especially the ones from refrigerators and other appliances, cover the ground fast. Overlap the sheets by 6 inches or so to keep weeds from sneaking between them. Newspaper should be laid down ¼ to ½ inch thick.

As you spread out the sheets, wet them thoroughly from a hose. You'll want to do this frequently if a breeze comes up—watching your sheet mulch flap away is pretty demoralizing. Soak the sheets several times to make sure the water seeps through. If you're sheet mulching with a group, this is when hose-fights usually erupt, tugging any well-orchestrated work-party toward mayhem. Try not to walk on the paper, especially after it's wet, as this pulls the sheets apart and creates gaps. Pretend you're painting a floor: Start at one end and work toward the opposite side so you won't walk on your work.

Next, toss down another thin layer of nitrogen-rich manure, meal, or fresh green clippings. This will entice the worms up through the soon-to-be rotting sheets, and coax plant roots downward.

On top of this, pour on the bulk mulch, about 8 to 12 inches of loose straw, hay, leaves, or any of the other substances listed above. Weed seeds in this layer aren't a big concern, as a thick, seed-free stratum lies atop this one. Weed seeds seem to rot rather than germinate in the slowly composting mass.

Bales of hay or straw don't have to be fluffed up to their original grassy bulk. Just break the bales into thin "books" about 1 to 2 inches thick, and lay down about three thicknesses of these. Broken into several layers and moistened, the dense books will compost perfectly well.

To create an easily compostable sheet mulch, pay a little attention to the carbon:nitrogen ratio in the bulk mulch layer. If you're using high-carbon materials such as straw or, especially, wood shavings, sprinkle on nitrogen in the form of manure or blood meal, or "dilute" the carbonaceous mulch with perhaps one part clover hay, seaweed, grass clippings, or other high-nitrogen mulch for every four of high-carbon matter (see table 4-1 for a list of mulch materials and their C:N ratios). A mulch that is extremely low in nitrogen, such as wood shavings, will be very slow to rot down, and may cause anemic plant growth. You don't need a perfect C:N balance, just make such there's *some* nitrogen in the mix to feed the compost critters.

As you build this layer, spray on some water every few inches. This layer should be damp but not wet; you're looking for that wrung-out sponge state. This can take a surprisingly large volume of water; it may take a couple of minutes of soaking every few inches to achieve the damp-but-not-wet state.

Atop the bulk mulch, add an inch or two of compost. If this is in short supply, add compost plus whatever soil is on hand to reach the final thickness. Or, if the pile will have a few months to compost before planting, you can substitute manure or several inches of easily compostable material for this layer. But if you plan to plant the sheet mulch within a few weeks, a layer of compost will be necessary to act as a seedbed.

The final layer is 2 inches of weed- and seed-free organic matter, such as straw, fine bark, wood shavings, or any of the others listed above. Besides smothering weeds, this layer gives the project, in landscaper jargon, "that finished look," which will endear you to your more fastidious neighbors. For planting seeds and starts, push this layer aside to reach the compost/soil layer right below, just as you would with any mulch.

not to use fresh hay for top-mulching. A light mulch of fresh hay, laden with seeds, imported throngs of exotic weeds and grasses that took years to get under control. Straw, if harvested with a well-tuned combine, contains no seed; it's just the stems of grain plants. Hay is the whole stalk, seed-head and all.)

Since I was extending the garden into new territory, full of grass, I decided to employ sheet mulch for the new beds. By spring, my nasty red clay soil had darkened to chocolate brown, was seething with worms, and had begun to fluff to a marvelous crumbly tilth. I was sold. Oh, I still have a compost pile for seedling trays and soil emergencies, but sheet mulch and composting-in-place are my staple soil-building tools. Sometimes, instead of emptying the kitchen compost bucket into the compost pile, I tuck its contents under some mulch, where it rots very quickly.

By composting in place, I don't disturb the soil

organisms, so essential for ferrying nutrients to plant roots. An intact subterranean ecology develops, woven by silken fibers of mycelium, riddled with the channels of traveling microfauna, bound into perfect tilth by the gummy exudates and carbon-rich liquors of metabolism. Oxygen-gulping microbes colonize the upper layers of soil, and the shy anaerobes work their complex alchemy further below. Exploding populations of wriggling worms loosen the earth deep down, churning their nutrient-rich castings into the mulch. A thousand-specied hive of interlinked subterranean activity erects its many pathways of decomposition and resurrection as sowbugs, worms, mites, amoebae, and fungi swarm in fertility-building concert. Plants tap into this seething stew and thrive. And all this is cocreated by simply piling on a fat mattress of mulch.

Sometimes I've been less than meticulous in my sheet mulching, applying a layer of newspapers, moistening them, and then simply dumping a foot of used stable bedding upon them. Here I'm thinking long-term. I know that the wood shavings in the bedding will take a couple of years to break down, so plant growth won't be maximal until then. I'll use this technique in the more distant Zones 2 or 3, perhaps in circles around trees that

I want to underplant, or for garden beds I won't rely upon heavily for a while. For heavy food production or near-the-house insectary and ornamental plant beds, I strive more precisely to achieve the proper C:N ratio in the mulch.

Some of you may be wondering: Since sheet mulching doesn't have the volume necessary to hold in heat the way a compost pile does, how can weed seeds be sterilized? The answer is: They aren't. But most weed seeds need light or disturbance to germinate. This is why it's best to cover any seed-containing mulches with a couple of inches of straw, soil, bark, or other weed-free material. One of the beauties of deep mulch is that it never needs to be— never should be—tilled. What few weeds appear are easily pulled from the loose soil. To stop future weeds, just pile on more mulch. Thus weed seeds never really get a chance to sprout. They just rot.

Sheet mulch does have its weedy headaches. Bindweed, brought in via hay or other mulch, is the bane of sheet-mulchers, and can travel for yards beneath the paper layer. The same applies to Bermuda grass, whose rhizomes can tunnel forever through the tubes in corrugated cardboard, and gleefully emerge in a break for daylight at the edge of the mulch.

Another drawback to sheet mulch is slugs. In the

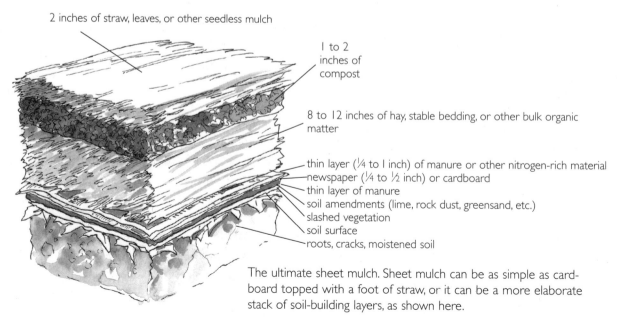

2 inches of straw, leaves, or other seedless mulch

1 to 2 inches of compost

8 to 12 inches of hay, stable bedding, or other bulk organic matter

thin layer (¼ to 1 inch) of manure or other nitrogen-rich material
newspaper (¼ to ½ inch) or cardboard
thin layer of manure
soil amendments (lime, rock dust, greensand, etc.)
slashed vegetation
soil surface
roots, cracks, moistened soil

The ultimate sheet mulch. Sheet mulch can be as simple as cardboard topped with a foot of straw, or it can be a more elaborate stack of soil-building layers, as shown here.

early phase of decomposition, slug populations can explode. I compensate by extra-heavy plantings of succulent greens such as lettuce (the slugs do the thinning). For less-easily seeded plants, make slug collars from tin (not aluminum) cans: Remove the top and bottom, cut down one side with tin snips, unroll the can, and cut 2-inch-high rings from it. Encircle tender plant stems with these. Slugs stay out, since they are irritated by the galvanic shock they receive from the metal coating.

STARTING PLANTS IN SHEET MULCH

A fresh sheet mulch won't be as productive as one that's six months old, hence it's best to prepare it in the fall. These beds seem to reach their prime the second season after construction, a productivity that doesn't fall off for several years and can be renewed by more mulch. But even a freshly built sheet-mulch bed is probably going to give plants a boost, as soil life blossoms within days, and there's plenty of fertility to be released in a foot of properly blended mulch. Starting plants in a new sheet mulch is a bit tricky, though. You can't simply sprinkle tiny seeds into the coarse, undigested mulch; they'll get lost.

If your sheet mulch hasn't broken down to soil by the time you want to plant, start seeds by making tiny pockets or trenches about 3 inches deep, filling them with soil or compost, and seeding these (this is why I keep that emergency compost pile). Seedlings and vegetable starts should also go into small soil pockets about three times the size of the plant's root mass. If the plant is deep-rooted, pull the mulch aside, slit the paper or cardboard in an X-pattern, and replace the mulch. Then plant above the slit, and roots will find the opening with no trouble. For shrubs or trees, either install them before sheet mulching and carefully work around them, or, after mulching, remove the mulch, slit the paper layer, peel the paper back, and dig a hole. Then place the plant in the hole with the root crown about an inch above the old soil level, and carefully replace the paper to minimize the chance of weed emergence. Either push soil up to cover the root crown and tamp it in place, or cover the crown with two or three inches of mulch, which in time will rot down to crown level. Don't bury the whole trunk in mulch or rodents will tunnel in and feast on the bark.

Sheet mulch, and deep mulching in general, is a fast and easy way to boost organic matter and soil life to prodigious levels. With the bottom of the biological pyramid—soil life—built on a broad, thick foundation of mulch, your garden will support a stunning diversity of plants, beneficial insects, and wildlife.

Cover Cropping for Fertility

To quickly but laboriously add fertility to soil, use compost. For intensively worked beds, I prefer sheet mulch. But for large areas, for long-term fertility, and for shifting the labor to nature's ample muscles, use cover crops.

Cover crops are planted specifically to build and hold soil and to smother weeds. They range from long-growing perennials such as red fescue and Dutch white clover for undisturbed cover, to short-term green manures meant to be slashed in place or lightly tilled in after a season, such as annual ryegrass and common vetch. The aim is the same: a solid cover of plants. Their leaves shield the soil from hammering rains and carpet the earth in fall with nutritious, humus-building litter. The dense planting crowds and shades out weeds. And their roots drive deep into the soil, loosening the earth, drawing up nutrients, and placing organic matter farther down than even the deepest plowing. This last is an oft-neglected benefit of cover crops.

Roots are nature's subterranean humus builders. Above ground, leaf litter does the job, but in the underworld, roots add organic matter in vast quantities during their constant cycles of growth and decay.

The most actively growing parts of roots are the root hairs, almost-microscopic threads growing from the very tips of roots. Root hairs lead an ephemeral existence, often living for only a few hours as they stretch toward zones of fertile soil. While alive, root hairs actively absorb nutrients and channel them to the main roots.

Plants and their roots don't grow smoothly and continuously, but in spurts. These growth periods are controlled by many overlapping cycles: day/night,

TABLE 4-2.

COVER CROPS

Annual Cool Weather Cover Crops

These crops are planted in the late summer or fall, and are mowed or tilled-in in the spring, while they are flowering and before they set seed (the time of maximum root growth, nitrogen content, and biomass). Most are hardy to 0 to 20 degrees Fahrenheit.

Common name	Botanical name	N-fixer	Soil preference	Tolerates poor soil	Height	Insectary	Comments
Austrian winter pea	Pisum arvense	•	heavy		2 ft.	•	hardy to 0°F
Barley	Hordeum vulgare		loam		2–4 ft.		mild winters only
Bell bean	Vicia faba	•	loam	•	3–6 ft.	•	opens heavy soil
Blando brome grass	Bromus mollis		many	•	2–4 ft.		drought tolerant
Clover, alsike	Trifolium hybridum	•	heavy		2 ft.	•	can take acid soils
Clover, berseem	Trifolium alexandrinum	•	many		2 ft.	•	hardy to 18°F
Clover, crimson	Trifolium incarnatum	•	loam	•	18 in.	•	hardy to 10°F
Clover, nitro Persian	Trifolium resupinatum	•	many	•	2 ft.	•	hardy to 15°F
Clover, red Kenland	Trifolium pratense	•	loam		2 ft.	•	short-lived perennial
Clover, sweet white	Melilotus alba	•	heavy		3–6 ft.	•	
Clover, sweet yellow	Melilotus officinalis	•	loam		3–6 ft.	•	drought tolerant
Fava bean	Vicia fava	•	many		4–8 ft.	•	hardy to 15°F
Fenugreek	Trigonella foenumgraecum	•	many		2 ft.	•	opens heavy soil
Fescue, zorro	Vulpia myuros		many		2 ft.		mix with legumes
Garbanzo bean	Cicer arientinum	•	many		3–5 ft.	•	slow in cold soils
Mustard	Brassica spp.		heavy	•	2–4 ft.	•	opens heavy soil
Oats	Avena sativa		many		2–4 ft.		mild winters only
Oilseed radish	Raphanus sativus		many		2–4 ft.	•	hardy to 20°F
Phacelia	Phacelia tanacetiflolia		many	•	2–3 ft.	•	hardy to 20°F
Rapeseed	Brassica napus		loam	•	2–3 ft.		opens heavy soil
Rye	Secale cereale		many		2–4 ft.		
Ryegrass, annual	Lolium multiforum		many		2–4 ft.		mix with legumes
Vetch, common	Vicia sativa	•	many		3–6 ft.	•	hardy to 0°F
Vetch, hairy	Vicia villosa	•	many	•	3–6 ft.	•	hardy to -10°F
Vetch, purple	Vicia atropurpurea	•	many		3–6 ft.	•	hardy to 10°F

Annual Warm Weather Cover Crops

These crops are planted in spring or summer, and are tilled or mowed before they set seed. With ample water and warmth, they can create enormous quantities of biomass.

Common name	Botanical name	N-fixer	Soil preference	Tolerates poor soil	Height	Insectary	Comments
Black-eyed peas	Vigna unguiculata	•	many		3–4 ft.	•	chokes weeds
Buckwheat	Fagopyrum esculentum		loam		1–3 ft.	•	chokes weeds
Cowpeas, red	Vigna sinensis	•	loam	•	1–2 ft.	•	drought resistant
Lablab	Lablab purpureus	•	many		5–10 ft.	•	drought resistant
Pinto beans	Phaseolus vulgaris	•	loam		2–4 ft.	•	drought resistant
Sesbania	Sesbania macrocarpa	•	many	•	6–8 ft.	•	drought resistant
Soybeans	Glycine max	•	many		2–4 ft.	•	mix with nonlegumes
Sudan grass	Sorghum bicolor		many	•	6–8 ft.		mix with legumes
Sunn hemp	Crotolaria juncea	•	loam	•	3–6 ft.	•	tolerates acid soil

Perennial Cover Crops

These are excellent for no-till gardens, and can be mowed to generate mulch and compost. Some of the shorter varieties, such as white Dutch clover, can be used as a living mulch, interplanted with other crops.

Common name	Botanical name	N-fixer	Soil preference	Tolerates poor soil	Height	Insectary	Comments
Alfalfa	Medicago sativa	•	loam		2–3 ft.	•	well-limed soil
Bird's-foot trefoil	Lotus corniculatus	•	many	•	3–5 ft.	•	drought resistant
Chicory	Cichorium intybus		heavy	•	2–3 ft.	•	opens heavy soil
Clover, stawberry	Trifolium fragiferum	•	many		1 ft.	•	needs moisture
Clover, white Dutch	Trifolium repens	•	many		6–10 in.	•	needs moisture
Clover, white Ladino	Trifolium repens	•	many		1 ft.	•	needs moisture
Clover, white New Zealand	Trifolium repens	•	many		1 ft.	•	needs moisture
Fescue, creeping red	Festuca rubra		many		2–3 ft.		
Orchard grass	Dactylis glomerata		many		1–2 ft.		
Ryegrass, perennial	Lolium perenne		heavy		2–3 ft.		
Timothy grass	Phleum pratense		heavy		2–3 ft.		needs moisture

wet/dry, cold/warm, and even by the comings and goings of soil organisms. Roots in particular are strongly influenced by wet/dry cycles. After a heavy rain or deep irrigation, the ground becomes saturated with water, and legions of root hairs die from lack of oxygen. This explains why some plants, such as cucumbers and squash, sometimes wilt after a rain, just when we expect them to brighten up again.

As the ground begins to dry after a rain, air flows into the now-empty soil pores. Fueled by fresh oxygen and moisture, root hairs and tips surge into growth, eagerly extending toward pockets of nutrients. Growth accelerates as oxygen levels rise and the soil, no longer water-saturated, approaches the perfect moisture range. But the cycle flows and ebbs: Water percolates downward, evaporates upward, and is sucked up and transpired by the plants themselves. Within hours, the soil becomes too dry for the tender root hairs. Without ample moisture, they start to wither and die. The plant becomes semi-dormant. If the soil dries further, as it so often does, whole root sections begin to die en masse, sloughing off and decomposing. With the next rain or irrigation, new roots begin the same odyssey, surging again into caches of fertility, but some of these soon die in the cycle between too wet and too dry.

Interlocked loops such as these reveal nature's complexity and intelligence: The wet/dry cycle drives the root-dieback cycle, which in turn tempers the rhythm of plant and soil organism growth. The thirsty plants themselves, as they consume soil water, then alter the wet/dry cycle. Wheels within wheels spin as humus, soil life, and plants all grow.

During this cycle, plants shed huge masses of roots, hourly, daily, constantly—not just in fall when the plants die. This decaying organic matter builds humus deep in the soil, and is one benefit of cover crops that can't be achieved any other way. Many cover crops send roots 10 or 15 feet deep. No plow will ever incorporate organic matter to a fraction of that depth.

Dozens of cover crops exist. How do you choose the best ones? As in so much of ecological gardening, diversity provides the key. While soil and climate conditions may suggest certain cover crops to try, your local microclimate or variations in soil can toss in a wild card. It's best to seed a number of varieties and record which ones thrive. Another benefit of diversity: Each plant type secretes its own array of sugars and other compounds from its roots. Each plant's particular chemical smorgasbord attracts a different community of soil organisms to it. This means that the more species of cover crop we plant, the more varied will be the soil life's diversity. As we've noted, this will subdue disease and boost plant growth.

The first decision to make in choosing cover crops is between annual and perennial plants (see table 4–2 for a list). If the goal is to build fertility in a temporarily dormant garden bed—say, over winter—annuals are the answer. But perennials are in order if you're preparing a future orchard's soil, or have a "back forty" section of yard you're not ready to wrestle with for a few years. Perennial clovers can also be used to cover garden paths or other areas. Masanobu Fukuoka, the brilliant author of *The One Straw Revolution,* uses perennial white clover as a permanent, living mulch in his garden beds. To plant crops, he simply opens up small areas in the clover and places seeds or transplants in the resulting gaps. This is a great example of stacking functions: The greenery suppresses weeds, the shade holds moisture in the soil, the blossoms attract beneficial insects, and nitrogen fixed by the clover boosts the growth of the other crops.

This leads us to a second set of choices: between nitrogen-fixing cover crops and non–nitrogen fixers. As many gardeners know, most members of the legume (pea and bean) family, plus certain other species (such as alder, Russian and autumn olive, and ceanothus) host symbiotic microorganisms that live in nodules among their roots. These bacteria and fungi "fix" nitrogen gas from the air by combining it with carbon to make amino acids and related molecules.

The microbes pass on any surplus to their host's roots, which absorb the nitrogenous compounds. The plant converts this gift into stems, leaves, and especially, protein-rich seeds. In return, the host plants reward their microbial partners with sugary root secretions.

Ancient farmers knew the value of legumes and other nitrogen-fixing plants. The Roman farm texts of Virgil and Cato both recommend that legumes be plowed into fallow fields. Experts both ancient and modern recommend that legumes be plowed in or mulched before the seeds set, because the plant drains nitrogen from stems and leaves at maturity and concentrates it in the seeds.

Some argue that nitrogen fixers do little good until they die, when they release the nitrogen locked in the plant and microbial nodules. I disagree, and both my own observations and those of researchers support me. I've seen corn planted with and without beans in the same garden, and the corn entwined by beans is decidedly larger. On Washington's Orcas Island, the Bullock brothers routinely plant a nitrogen-fixing shrub such as autumn olive or Siberian pea shrub in the same hole as a fruit tree. Douglas Bullock categorically states, "I've seen it, and I know that trees planted with a nitrogen fixer grow faster."

Don't believe the anecdotes? Let's go to the research. William King reports in the *Journal of Agronomy* that when he interplanted ryegrass and clover, he found, using radioactive tracer compounds, that 80 percent of the nitrogen in the ryegrass had come from the clover. The clover was pulling nitrogen from the air and feeding it to the ryegrass.

How does this work? A few paragraphs ago I described the constant growth and dieback of roots. That's the explanation. During the wet/dry soil cycle, the clover's roots slough off, as do the nitrogen-fixing nodules. Surrounding plants and microbes then absorb these nutrients as the roots and nodules decay.

Legumes offer many benefits. The Salina, Kansas-based Land Institute found during their prairie-building work that adding more legumes to a prairie seed mix increases the total number of species—legumes, grasses, and flowers—that survive. Nitrogen-fixing species abound in early successional ecosystems such as young fields, pioneer dune communities, and freshly burned forests. Ecological gardeners can take a lesson from this observation: When building soil or feeding hungry plants, go heavy on the nitrogen fixers.

But remember that balance is important. All that nitrogen must be balanced with carbon. Soil organisms consume ten to fifty times more carbon than nitrogen, so farmers always blend a grass or other nonlegume into their cover crops. A cover crop rich in nitrogen will rekindle the soil life's metabolic fires, burning prodigious amounts of carbon to balance the nitrogenous bounty. A too-rich nitrogen fuel can actually deplete more organic matter than the cover crop adds. For this reason, commercial cover crop mixes contain 10 to 40 percent oats, annual ryegrass, or other nonlegume.

Blending grasses with legumes provides one kind of balance in cover crops. Now that we've opened the door to biodiversity in cover crops, let's explore further. Grasses add carbon and build structure. Legumes increase soil nitrogen. What other roles can different cover crops perform?

Some cover crops are great at opening up heavy or compacted soils. Rapeseed and mustard have extensive root systems that punch through hard subsoil, aerating the earth and adding humus as the roots die. Alfalfa does the same, though it requires fertile soil to grow well. I've grown daikon radishes in heavy soil, let them flower, and then snapped them off at ground level. Each daikon will break up the clay and then rot, leaving a forearm-sized load of organic matter in the soil.

Other cover crops can mine the soil for nutrients, ferrying minerals from the depths into their leaves and thus, at leaf fall, to the soil surface. Chicory, a warm-season perennial, is renowned for its lengthy taproot, which seeks out pockets of potassium, sulfur, calcium, magnesium, and other minerals. Buckwheat converts insoluble phosphorus to a more plant-available form.

Many cover crops attract beneficial insects. The blossoms of buckwheat, phacelia, fava beans, many of the clovers, bell beans, mustard, and vetch are all abuzz with nectar-hunters soon after opening.

Thus, a cover crop mix can serve multiple functions. A blend of five to ten varieties sown into the soil can build humus, add nitrogen, mine minerals, bust up heavy soil, and beckon a wide array of helpful insects. Peaceful Valley Farm Supply carries a "Soil Builder Mix" that contains bell beans, winter peas, two vetch varieties, and oats (see the resources section). And that's just the beginning. I've seen old farm texts that list fifteen varieties in their cover crop mixtures, including four grass species, five clovers, plus yarrow, fennel, plantain, dandelion, and more. That kind of biodiversity will bring many forms of nature's energy—soil life, humus, minerals, beneficial insects, and more—to work in your garden.

SHARING THE WEALTH OF THE SOIL

An exuberantly healthy soil is the cornerstone of a sustainable garden. The virtues bestowed by a living, fertile soil are legion. When we pack the growing earth with organic matter, via thick mulch, self-renewing roots, and buried debris, we're beckoning the industrious workers of the soil. Worms, tiny beetles and mites, bacteria, fungi, and a host of other helpers arrive to feast on the offerings and upon each other. They churn and tunnel and munch and spawn, chiseling minerals from rock and humus, all the while loosing a veritable storm of fertility to be shared with plants. The plants themselves shelter, feed, and are nourished by whole communities of soil life in a mutually beneficent partnership. A vast commerce of shuttling minerals, sugars, acids, antibiotics, hormones, and all the molecules of life connect this thousand-specied hive together. For the price of a little mulch and a little care, rich and extravagant empires can be built beneath the earth, empires that will funnel their wealth upward to plants, and in turn to insects, to birds, to all wildlife, and to people as well. In the ecological garden, we do all we can to broaden this river of flowing fertility, and we start with the soil.

Feeding the soil engages us in a partnership that benefits all. By applying the techniques and the point of view offered in this chapter, the base of life's pyramid—the abundance of the soil—becomes broad and sturdy. Life builds on life. Whatever we plant in this rich earth will have a far greater chance of thriving; whatever we hope to feed, whether wildlife, ourselves, or perhaps just our senses, will be deeply nourished. And serendipities we never hoped for—a surprising new wildflower, a rare butterfly, or sturdier plants that bloom longer, fruit heavier, and grow in tough conditions—will grace our lives almost daily.

Chapter 5

Catching, Conserving, and Using Water

A GARDEN CAN BE a thirsty place. But in conventional garden design, water appears only by fortunate rainfall, or by the gardener's intervention, squirted through hoses and sprinklers that are fed by wells and pumps. Without a well-timed rain cycle, a gardener to lug hoses about, or a resource-intensive irrigation system, most gardens will droop and die. Ample moisture isn't the natural state of a typical garden. But in an ecologically based design, water is not an externally caused event—it is designed in, naturally present, naturally abundant. In the ecological garden, ample water, not drought, is the "default condition." A well-designed garden doesn't have to be nudged and babied and wheedled into health. It spontaneously cycles toward lush and vibrant growth, even when the gardener is absent and the skies are cloudless. Ecological design, as this chapter will show, lets us create gardens that survive the vagaries of weather without our constant care.

A water-wise design saves more than just labor and frustration. It conserves resources. Since most irrigation water is carried via pumps, turning on a sprinkler consumes energy that could be spared by good design. Also, the water's source is often a

dammed reservoir that blocks fish migration and floods once-wild land. Or the water may be pumped from a well whose source is unknown and thus unreliable. The well may tap an ancient aquifer—fossil water that someday soon will be depleted. An ecologically responsible gardener is sensitive to the limits of our water supply and the energy required to tap it.

This chapter will describe ways to be less reliant on distant, erratic, and expensive water sources. The methods for doing this, not so coincidentally, enhance the web of connections that link the pieces of the garden together. The result is not just less watering, but also a resilient, healthy backyard ecosystem.

This information isn't just for dryland dwellers. Even though much of the country receives ample rainfall, it rarely arrives in perfectly timed doses. The strategies that follow will help the garden survive not only drought, but the too-wet periods as well, through better drainage, storing rain for future use, and putting water where it is needed most.

To learn how to design a garden that is naturally water-wise, we look, as always, to nature. How does nature store water? Besides the obvious sources—lakes and ponds—nature holds water in plants, in the air, and in the soil. Water is cleansed and recycled in wetlands, breathed into the air by trees, collected and channeled by landforms. We can use all of these relationships as the basis for a garden that has a naturally healthy water cycle.

THE FIVEFOLD PATH TO WATER WISDOM

Recall the ecological design principle we introduced in chapter 2: "Each function is supported by many elements." A garden that captures, holds, and recycles its water will embody that principle. If a landscape relies on only one element or device for watering—perhaps an automatic sprinkler—then one small failure spells disaster. Given Murphy's Law, sooner or later that sprinkler will clog, break, or once too often miss the tender monkey-flower in the corner. But if we support the garden's water needs by multiple tricks, say by providing a layer of moisture-retaining mulch, plenty of rich soil that holds water, and a reliable irrigation system, the chance of all three systems failing at once dwindles to near-zero.

One of the finest examples I know of this principle at work is in the garden of Charles and Mary Zemach in Los Alamos, New Mexico. This oasis in the high desert, designed by Santa Fe permaculturist Ben Haggard, can last months between waterings. Yet this is no gravelly xeriscape. In the glare of desert summer, fruit trees bow under the weight of juicy plums and peaches, while delicately speckled pulmonaria and wispy maidenhair ferns shelter in cool shadows. Pale blossoms of mock orange and spirea peer from beneath an old apricot tree. Herbs such as burnet and French sorrel are posted near the front door, ready to enliven a salad. Here is tranquil beauty, more food than the Zemachs can eat, and abundant wildlife habitat. But in a city where water bills in summer can reach $300 per month, the Zemachs rely almost not at all on municipal water.

TABLE 5-1.

FIVE WATER-CONSERVING METHODS AND THEIR BENEFITS

Together these five techniques conserve moisture far more effectively and more certainly than any single technique, and the benefits extend far beyond water conservation.

Method	Benefits
High organic matter content	holds moisture
	adds fertility
	stores nutrients
	boosts soil life
	fluffs soil
Deep mulching	slows evaporation
	cools soil
	adds fertility
	boosts soil life
	smothers weeds
Water-conserving plants	need less water
	survive drought
Dense plantings	shade soil
	smother weeds
Soil contouring	catches water
	directs water where needed
	helps plants and soil life survive both wet and dry periods
	builds humus
	adds visual interest

The Zemachs' garden combines five complementary techniques to support the goal of ample water. The five are: building organically rich soil; contouring the landscape to catch water and direct it to where it is needed; including drought-tolerant plants when possible; planting densely to shade the soil; and mulching deeply. As proof of the deeply layered strategy's effectiveness, the plantings, only three years old at my visit, had survived a five-month drought the previous year.

A little contemplation of the Zemachs' strategy reveals a synergistic bonus. Because of their skillful combination, several of these techniques do more than just save water. They protect the plants from drought by keeping water in the soil, where plants can use it. Also, mulch and rich soil ensure a high level of organic matter, which boosts plant growth. And mulch, dense planting, and contoured land all protect the soil from erosion in the infrequent but fierce downpours of the Southwest. In a good design, well-chosen techniques interlock and complement each other to create synergies and yield serendipitous benefits.

Let's look at each element of this fivefold strategy separately to understand why the parts combine to offer more than just a simple sum.

Holding Water in the Soil

In the early phases of her garden's design, Mary Zemach had envisioned an ornate drip irrigation system, a plastic webwork of emitters and spitters and sprayers administered by an impressive control panel. Designer Ben Haggard waved this off, saying it would be an unnecessary expense. He then repeated one of permaculture's mantras: The cheapest place to store water is in the soil.

As I mentioned in the previous chapter, humus and other organic matter act as a sponge, swelling to greedily hold several times their weight in water. I've seen just how thirsty a good soil can be when I've sterilized humus-rich potting soil in the oven. The baked soil comes out of the oven bone-dry, so I add water to it before sowing seeds. A lot of water: 3 quarts of dry soil will easily hold 1 quart of water. This means that 1 foot of rich, moist soil blanketing a backyard holds as much water as a 3-inch-deep lake the same size. To build a pond or tank that holds that much water, or to buy the same number of gallons from the city would be frightfully expensive. Yet the soil will store the water for free. And soil is stingy with water. A rainstorm must first saturate the soil with water before a single drop trickles away as runoff. Plus, unlike pond water, moisture held in soil doesn't evaporate easily.

The key to the soil's capacity to hold water is organic matter. Research shows that soil with as little as 2 percent organic matter can reduce the

irrigation needed by 75 percent when compared to poor soils with less than 1 percent organic matter. Most urban and suburban soils are low in organic matter because developers often strip the topsoil from new subdivisions and sell it, and then replace the many inches of rich earth with a thin sprinkling of trucked-in topsoil. Before homeowners can achieve the lake-in-the-ground effect, they must build up that organic matter again to at least its pre-developer state.

The Zemachs built rich soil in their yard before the new plants went in. A landscaping crew stripped off the old grass, composted it, and added it back to the yard. The crew also tilled in several truckloads of compost from Los Alamos's yard-waste program, and many bales of peat moss. This created a foundation of plentiful organic matter and living soil.

Rich soil holds the water that keeps our rivers flowing and our lakes full, as a friend in northern California showed me vividly. I had stopped to see seed-grower George Stevens's farm on the banks of the Klamath River, and I asked him how often he irrigates. "Not much, not until late in the summer when the rains are long gone," George answered. He directed my eyes to the Klamath Mountain foothills that ringed the valley. "Those hills are why," he said. "Water drains out of that hillside soil very slowly. The hills take most of the summer to drain. The water travels underground and goes through my farm on its way to the river. It's right under our feet. These plants bring the water up." I understood. The soil, square miles of it lying on the rocky substrata of the hillsides and lapping down into the valley, was a giant sponge. It could hold massive quantities of water, and hold it for months. Over the dry summer, this sponge would dribble its water downhill, slowly draining into the Klamath. This explains why our rivers stay full instead of just draining dry after each rain. Sure, the rivers are fed by creeks, but what feeds

A *swale* is a shallow trench laid out dead level along the land's contours.

the creeks? There's no endlessly gushing faucet at the top. Water slowly seeps out of humic earth, drop by drop, the drops coalescing into a trickle, the trickles broadening into creeks. Each creekbank is a natural drainage ditch, collecting water that oozes from the moist earth over weeks and months. Rivers come from the soil, guardian of our water. By building our garden's soil, we can store whole rivers and lakes in our yards.

Contouring to Catch Water

The second water-holding technique that Mary used in her garden was sculpting the land to hold water. For example, in her yard is a circular patch of drought-tolerant Buffalo grass that has been contoured like a dish: The center of the circle is a few inches lower than the edges. It's a gentle concavity that you can hardly see, but the rain knows it's there. Rainwater collects in the depression and soaks in, reducing the need for irrigation. This is one of many self-watering spots in the design. Others have been created by making swales.

A *swale,* in this use of the term, is a shallow trench laid out dead level along the land's contours. A swale can be anywhere from one to several feet across, a foot or so deep, and whatever length necessary. You can think of a swale as a long skinny pond. The earth dug from the swale is piled on the downhill side to make a berm; a cross section of a swale looks like the letter S laid on its side. Surface and rain water run into a swale, spread out along its length, and slowly percolate into the soil. This underground water then seeps downhill, forming a lens of moisture that is held together by hydrostatic tension. The stored water creates an underground reservoir that aids plant growth for tens of feet downslope. Before rainwater can run into drains and gullies, swales intercept and hold it, and store it in the soil.

In the Zemachs' yard, aesthetics dictated that the swales be small and delicate, almost ripples in the ground. After all, this was a public space where the feet and gaze of friends and passers-by would fall; farm-scale ditches wouldn't do. So the swales have been laid out to curve in eye-pleasing lines, softened yet further by the leafy silhouettes

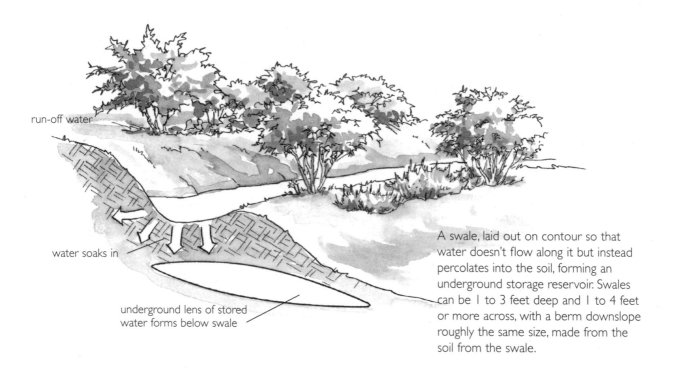

run-off water

water soaks in

underground lens of stored water forms below swale

A swale, laid out on contour so that water doesn't flow along it but instead percolates into the soil, forming an underground storage reservoir. Swales can be 1 to 3 feet deep and 1 to 4 feet or more across, with a berm downslope roughly the same size, made from the soil from the swale.

HOW TO MAKE A SWALE

First, if you're digging several swales, you need to determine how far apart to make them. A general rule of thumb is that the more rainfall, the closer swales should be to catch the heavier runoff. Where rainfall is 40 to 50 inches per year, swales should be about 18 feet apart, increasing to 50 feet apart for areas receiving only 15 inches of rain. For those in other rainfall regimes, use these numbers as guidelines to judge the appropriate distance between swales. This isn't rocket science, so exactitude isn't necessary. On steep slopes, and for compacted or nonabsorbent or clayey soils, runoff will be heavier, so bring the swales closer together.

Then lay out the swale lines on the level. For this you will need a leveling device. If you don't want to rent a surveyor's transit or buy an inexpensive peep-sight level, you can use a water level, a line level, or build your own A-frame level (see illustration). The critical point here is for the swale to be truly level so that water will infiltrate evenly and steadily.

Drive in pegs to mark the course of your swale. On hilly ground you may need to space your pegs about 6 feet apart to avoid height errors, but on flat ground (though no ground is truly flat!), every 10 or 15 feet will do. You'll be surprised to see that even on "flat" ground, a swale will undulate dramatically with changes in level.

Once the course is marked, begin digging. Where aesthetics aren't a concern, you can dig a rough trench 1 foot deep and about 18 inches wide, and mound the excavated soil along the downhill edge of the trench. For a gentler, less-visible swale, go only about 6 inches deep but wider (to 2 or 3 feet), and make the downhill berm wider too. Periodically check the bottom of the swale to make sure that it's level along its length. If you want, you can dig pits or other deep spots in the swale above water-loving plants to coax additional water to their roots.

The general principle is: the more water, the bigger and more numerous the swales. If gullywasher storms that dump 2 inches of rain regularly inundate your region, you'll want swales that can handle a lot of runoff.

After the swale is dug, you can partially fill it with mulch if you want, which will help hold and absorb water and make the swale less noticeable. A swale will be more stable and useful if it's planted along the berm. Most any plant will help, but trees and shrubs are ideal, because their deep roots will hold the berm in place, and the leaves will add humus to the soil. The shade will also slow evaporation.

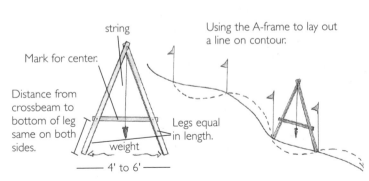

An A-frame level for laying out contour lines, made from 1x2 or 2x2 wood or metal. To calibrate, stand it upright and mark on the crossbeam where the string passes it. Then reverse the A-frame, setting each leg where the opposite one was. Mark the crossbeam again. The center is halfway between the two marks; mark it (traditionally, the object used for the weight is a beer bottle, but a rock or plumb bob will do). Or attach a bubble level to the crosspiece. To use the A-frame, place one leg at the beginning of the line to be laid out. Swing the other leg along the ground until the string aligns with the center mark. Mark this on-contour spot, and continue pivoting and marking until the line is laid out.

string

Mark for center.

Using the A-frame to lay out a line on contour.

Distance from crossbeam to bottom of leg same on both sides.

weight

Legs equal in length.

⎯ 4' to 6' ⎯

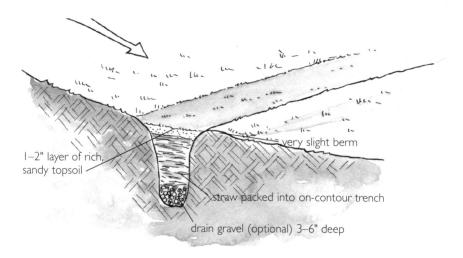

1–2" layer of rich, sandy topsoil

very slight berm

straw packed into on-contour trench

drain gravel (optional) 3–6" deep

Straw-filled swale. These can be used in more formal or well-traveled parts of the yard, where a standard swale would be too deep. An on-contour trench 1 to 3 feet deep is packed with staw or hay and topped with a thin layer of sandy topsoil. Most of the excess soil is removed, leaving only a slight berm downslope to stop runoff water. The swale can be planted, and will function about as well as a standard swale.

of plantings. Gentle swales lead from downspouts and along paths to the roots of shrubs, toward fruit trees, into perennial beds, all in soft arcs and windings. When the rain comes, each swale stops runoff and directs the water into the ground.

Mary says that in heavy rains some of the swales fill with water, but they rarely overflow. If they should spill over, another swale always lies just downhill to catch the excess water and coax it into the soil. And all these soft contours are almost invisible.

Swales aren't just for deserts. I was once skeptical that swales could be useful in my Northwest climate. Why would I want to catch water in winter when it's constantly raining? And when summer comes, we often go ninety days with no rain, so how could swales help during the dry season? But at some friends' urging, I dug a swale anyway, an 80-foot-long, 3-foot-wide affair on the slope below our house. It's made a tremendous difference, holding moisture long after the rains have gone. Come summer, above the swale the grass shrivels and browns within days after the rains stop. Below it, not only does the greenery remain verdant for weeks longer, but many new wildflower species have spontaneously appeared in the

slope

short swale

berm

contour lines

Fishscale swales. If existing trees or other obstacles make long swales impossible, shorter, overlapping swales can be dug to harvest runoff water.

welcoming microclimate. Humus is building, diversity is growing. I've found that letting water concentrate and soak in via swales will store it in the soil deeper and longer than if the water simply spreads across level ground. I'm sold on swales.

Swales can take many forms. In places where even the gentle undulation of a standard swale would be inappropriate, a level trench can be dug and stuffed full of straw or other absorbent organic matter. When the ground is planted and mulched, you'll never know this swale is there, but it will be thirstily intercepting water and storing it in the earth. If a long, yard-spanning swale is impossible because of trees and other obstacles, a series of short, overlapping swales above and below the obstacles will work. These are called fishscale swales.

Plants That Are Parsimonious with Water

Water-conservation technique number three is to use plants that are suited to the available water. Note that I'm not recommending only drought-tolerant plants. There are several ways to match plants to the water on hand, including using a mix of natives that are adapted to local climate, drought-tolerant varieties, and plants whose water use changes seasonally. Thirsty plants can be located where they can get water with minimal human effort. Plants should be in the right relationship with the overall climate, microclimate, landforms, soil, and surroundings. Here's how to do this.

Begin by using native plants where you can. Whatever the water regime in your locale, native plants are adapted to it. And your region's wildlife will appreciate the familiar food and habitat. Books abound on native plants for every region. A little research will uncover a wide array of natives for show, culinary and medicinal herbs, food, wildlife habitat, and a host of other uses.

Unless you're committed to a natives-only garden, you'll probably want to broaden the horticultural palette to include other plants. Now we can

move on to drought-tolerant plants. First some ecological background. Plants adapted to drought have evolved principally in two climate types: desert, where there just ain't no water, and Mediterranean climates, where summers are bone dry but winters are amply watered. "Mediterranean climate" in this sense means any region with a climate similar to that of the Mediterranean: much of North America's west coast, portions of western Chile, parts of South Africa, and of course, the Mediterranean coast itself.

Mediterranean-climate and desert plants differ in their approaches to water. Some desert plants can't survive for long with wet roots. If planted in, say, the American Midwest, desert plants may weather the corn-killing droughts, but be felled by a lengthy rainy spell. A Mediterranean-climate plant, however, is adapted to shifts between dry and wet, and may work better in nondesert climates. If rains in your region are irregular enough to droop common vegetables and flowers, Mediterranean plants will reduce both your water bill and drought headaches. As long as they are cold-hardy enough to survive the winter, Mediterranean plants are a good choice for outlasting the unpredictably dry spells in nearly every part of the country in this era of wild weather. Including them expands our selection of water-conserving species beyond native and desert plants. Table 5-2 lists some useful Mediterranean-climate plants. You can expand this list on your own by finding other varieties that hail from the world's Mediterranean zones.

What about all those luscious plants we love but that need regular water? Here, proper location is the answer. For starters, remember your zones. Stationing water-hungry plants where you'll see them, in Zone 1, will not only remind you to water them, but will make it easier to drag out the hose or watering can to quench their thirst.

Also, find and use the wet spots in your yard. Where does runoff accumulate? Often, driveways and sidewalks are sloped or crowned, and act as water catchments that direct rain to the adjacent soil. That's a good location for water-dependent

TABLE 5-2.

PLANTS FROM MEDITERRANEAN CLIMATES

These plants are from parts of the world with moist winters and dry summers. Though drought tolerant, they can survive wet periods far better than many so-called drought-tolerant plants that originate in deserts.

Common name	Botanical name
Almond	*Prunus dulcis*
Aloe vera	*Aloe vera*
Alstroemeria	*Alstroemeria ligtu*
Barberry	*Berberis vulgaris*
Bead tree	*Melia azedarach*
Blackberry	*Rubus fruticosus*
Bladder senna	*Colutea arborescens*
Borage	*Borago officinalis*
Cardoon	*Cynara cardunculus*
Fennel	*Foeniculum vulgare*
Fig	*Ficus carica*
Golden bamboo	*Phyllostachys aurea*
Golden garlic	*Allium moly*
Grape	*Vitis vinifera*
Hackberry	*Celtis* spp.
Hawthorn	*Crataegus* spp.
Hind's black walnut	*Juglans hindsii*
Honey locust	*Gleditsia triacanthos*
Italian stone pine	*Pinus pinea*
Lavender	*Lavandula angustifolia*
Lemonadeberry	*Rhus integrifolia*
Licorice	*Glycrrhiza glabra*
Lupine	*Lupinus* spp.
Madrone	*Arbutus menziesii*
Olive	*Olea europaea*
Oregano	*Origanum vulgare*
Oregon grape	*Mahonia aquifolium*
Quince	*Cydonia oblonga*
Quinoa	*Chenopodium quinoa*
Rock rose	*Cistus albidus*
Rocket	*Eruca vesicaria sativa*
Rosemary	*Rosmarinus officinalis*
Rue	*Ruta graveolens*
Sage	*Salvia* spp.
Salal	*Gaultheria shallon*
Scorzonera	*Scorzonerica hispanica*
Sea buckthorn	*Hippophae rhamnoides*
Sea holly	*Eryngium maritimum*
Snowberry	*Symphoricarus albus*
Summer savory	*Satureia hortensis*
Thyme	*Thymus vulgris*
Tree mallow	*Lavatera* spp.
Wormwood	*Artemisia absinthum*
Yarrow	*Achillea millefolium*

plants. Check near downspouts, under unguttered eaves, at low spots in the yard, beneath faucets, and near foundation drain outlets. Every property has its own microclimates, with specific sites that are a bit more moist than others. Do you have a spot in your lawn that stays green when the rest is beginning to brown? That's a likely candidate. Observe, assess, and then station your thirstiest plants in the naturally wet places. Contour the soil to catch water as suggested above. Let nature and gravity do your watering for you.

Dense Plantings to Banish Drought

The next step in this multilayered water strategy is to densely pack plants together to create shade. That way, the blanket of fronds and leaflets will block desiccating beams of summer sunlight before they reach the soil. This creates shaded, cool ground. Shading soil has been shown to reduce evaporation loss by over 60 percent. Shade, like mulch, also keeps root temperatures down, slowing the moist exhalations of transpiring leaves that would otherwise pump water into the sky.

Plants can also shade each other to reduce water loss. It's a rare plant that absolutely requires all the sunlight of a fourteen-hour summer day. In particular, cool-season vegetables such as brassicas and leafy greens do best when shaded for part of a hot afternoon. Many perennial flowers, including lady's mantle, astilbe, monarda, geranium, and others originated in forests or on shady riverbanks, and will flower with a half-day of sun. We can stack our plants in layers to hold moisture beneath the canopy, yet still harvest all the sunlight that each variety needs.

Watch how nature works in a forest. In spring, the first plants to leaf out are the tiny herbs and ground covers. Once these have gathered sunlight for a few weeks, building sugary sap and healthy roots, the shrubs above them begin to burst their buds. The low trees follow, and last come the spreading forest giants. By the time the heat of summer arrives, the canopy is nearly closed, and only a few dancing sunflecks shimmer on the forest floor. But by now everything is in full leaf, with branches arrayed in alternating whorls to catch the shifting rays and efficiently convert solar energy into sugars, starches, and the other molecules of plant life.

Once the forest canopy has closed, the air and soil beneath it stays far more moist than in the open. Desiccating sunlight can't reach into this grotto to dry the air and earth, and the temperature stays cool, further slowing moisture loss.

The time-delay approach used by nature can work in a garden, too. We'll cover the multilayered approach to gardening in detail in chapter 10, on forest gardens. For now, be aware that covering the soil in a blanket of plants will curtail water loss.

Mulching for Moisture

The final element in the fivefold water strategy is mulch. A 2- to 4-inch mulch layer (or more) will squelch moisture loss by slowing evaporation from the soil and by keeping plant roots cool, which will reduce transpiration (the movement of water into roots and out through the leaves). Organic mulches also soak up rain rather than letting it run off. And as organic mulches break down, they add humus to the soil, which compounds the soil's water-holding power. Mulches also prevent erosion, protect the soil structure, and soften temperature swings.

Mulch materials are nearly limitless: straw, alfalfa and other seedless hay, wood shavings, bark, leaves, corncobs, shredded cornstalks, seaweed, husks and hulls, even sand. For acid-loving plants, sawdust or pine needles work well. One warning: Mulched soil usually won't warm up in the spring as fast as naked earth, so for heat-loving plants, strip the mulch off in spring and replace it when the soil is warm.

Rocks can also be used for mulches. A mulch of stone may sound bizarre, but in dry country a rock mulch (1- to 4-inch-diameter pebbles a few inches deep) picks up morning dew and condenses it into the soil. During the day, hot air wafts through the cool, dark spaces between the stones. Moisture then condenses out of the warm air onto the chillier rock surfaces and trickles into the ground. In this way, a rock mulch can significantly boost the amount of water that plants receive. Rock mulches also hold heat, helping the soil warm up in spring and keeping plants toasty on chilly nights. A rock mulch can extend the growing season or help you grow hot-weather plants in cool regions.

By combining these five water-holding techniques—rich soil, contouring and swales, the right plants, dense plantings, and mulch—Mary Zemach makes her land far more drought-proof than if she had used only one method. Not only does this redundancy protect against the failure of any one method, but the combination of complementary techniques fuses to create a garden far less susceptible to drought than any one method alone. This synergy is one of the great benefits of gardening with ecological principles.

What if your garden's problem is too much water, not too little? Oddly enough, these same techniques can help, with little modification. They're not just for drought-proofing. More broadly, they moderate any extreme water conditions, dry or wet. Humus-rich soil and mulch can absorb vast volumes of water without losing the ability to hold air, and it's the lack of air that drowns water-logged plants. Plus, soil rich in organic matter drains better than nearly any but very sandy soil. And mulches, dense plantings, and contoured ground will help prevent pounding rains from causing soil erosion. In boggy yards where water really pools, dig swales just slightly off contour, at about a 2 percent grade, to carry water to an appropriate catchment (ideally a pond, creek, or a dry slope, but in the city, a storm drain may have to do).

CONSERVING WATER WITH CATCHMENT

You'll notice that Mary's multipronged approach to water wisdom doesn't include an irrigation system. She's never needed that imposing array of valves and sprinklers mentioned earlier. Because water is held so thriftily in the soil, the little irrigation that's needed can come from occasional brief sessions with a hose and watering can. However, even here, the Zemachs' yard takes its cue from nature. In an effort to use as little city water as possible, Mary has plugged into natural cycles and those of her own household. Much of her irrigation water comes from stored rainwater and from recycled domestic washwater, or greywater. As pumping water from the ground or over long distances becomes less economical, more people are turning to free, environmentally friendly ways of irrigating their gardens. Irrigation water doesn't need to be as clean as household tapwater, hence rainwater and greywater are practical alternatives. Let's look at rainwater first.

Harvesting and Storing Rainwater

Every home has a handy rainwater collection system built right into it: the roof. Rainwater splashes on rooftops, drips into the gutters, sluices through downspouts, and then goes . . . away, usually into a storm-drain system. Even in the desert, rainwater usually is treated as a problem to be disposed of, not as the valuable resource it is. I've watched countless acre-feet of rainwater collect on summer-baked parking lots, swirl uselessly down drains, and gurgle toward the ocean, while sprinklers hiss and stutter the last remaining bits of some fossil aquifer onto nearby lawns. Instead, those lawns could easily be watered by that parking-lot catchment system, or by rooftop-collected water.

How much water can a roof catch? The box on page 90 labeled "How Much Water Will Your Roof Collect?" gives a simple method for calculating just how much, and it's a lot. The average 2,000-square-foot, two-story house has over 1,000 square feet of roof (most houses plus the garage have far more). If that house is in a region receiving 40 inches of rain a year (the average for much of the United States), the roof will collect 25,000 gallons of water each year. That's enough to keep a 1,000-square-foot garden watered for 250 days of drought.

A 25,000-gallon tank is a little large for the typical backyard, but it's also rarely necessary. In the eastern half of North America, summer rain usually (though not always) falls every two or three weeks. To avoid using municipal or well water in that part of the country, we rarely need to store more than a couple of weeks' worth of irrigation water. How much water is that? A typical garden that covers 1,000 square feet (20 × 50 feet) needs roughly 100 gallons per day to thrive (and that's very generous water use). Two weeks' worth of water would thus be 1,400 gallons, which would fit into a circular pond 2 feet deep and 10 feet across, or a tank 5 feet high and 6 feet on each side. A pond or tank that size will easily fit into a typical yard.

We can further reduce the amount of water storage needed, of course, by using water-conserving techniques such as mulches, lots of organic matter, and drip irrigation. I know people who get most of their irrigation water from just four 55-gallon drums, one at each downspout. These drums are easy to camouflage with plantings and paint.

I recognize that rainless periods can last longer than two or three weeks east of the Mississippi, so for those who truly want to be water-independent and drought-proof, water storage needs to be larger. If you have the space and resources to build a large water tank or pond, then go for it. My point here is simply to show that it's easy to harvest rain, which greatly reduces our dependence on uncertain and energy-consuming water sources.

Those of us in the American West are in tougher shape, since rainfall is rarely sufficient for gardening. Outside help is essential. As I've said, a summertime stretch of ninety rainless days is common here in western Oregon. Water storage in the West simply needs to be larger. The 5,000-gallon rain-

PLANNING A WATER-HARVESTING SYSTEM

Since many books and articles have been written on ponds and other water storage systems, I'll not duplicate those efforts here by describing construction techniques. The bibliography lists several good sources. But here are some tips to help with planning. When designing a rainfall catchment system for your yard, consider these five factors:

1. **How much rain falls in a year.** The weather service will help here, although local features such as which side of a hill you're on or elevation changes can cause big variations in rainfall. A rain gauge, or a neighbor who has kept track of rain for years, is a more accurate source of information

2. **How much water is consumed.** By implementing the "fivefold water-saving strategy" described in this chapter, using drip irrigation, and watering only when needed rather than when an automatic timer decides, you can greatly reduce water consumption.

3. **The area of roof or other catchment available.** The amount of roof area available often depends on the pattern of gutters and downspouts; some sections of roof may not be usable without elaborate plumbing schemes. Pavement and other hard surfaces can also be called into service. I know someone who tosses a sandbag into the street gutter when it rains, thus diverting a huge volume of water up his driveway and into a swale to fill a pond and irrigate some trees.

4. **What size storage can be built.** Here, budget, space, and aesthetics are all factors. Tanks are more expensive than ponds, but take up less space. Ponds are generally much nicer to look at than tanks, but tanks can be hidden underground, or even, as in many houses built in the 1800s, built under the house.

5. **Where to place the storage relative to the catchment.** Use gravity when possible. If the storage can be higher than the garden, gravity, rather than a pump, can power the irrigation system. Again, aesthetics and ease of construction will also play a role in placement decisions.

Note that all of these factors except the amount of rainfall are controllable. This gives the gardener a lot of leverage. You can tinker with the four other factors to design the best system for your region.

A warning: The system I am describing is for irrigation water only, not for household use or drinking. Household systems require measures for keeping debris, dirt, bird guano, and other pollutants out of the water. Those methods are beyond the scope of this book, but are described in the permaculture and rainwater-harvesting books listed in the bibliography.

Awareness of the rainfall patterns in your area—not just how much it rains, but when—will help you design an effective water storage strategy. Rain that reliably replenishes a pond every few weeks will dictate a different approach than one forced by regular two-month droughts. But, as we will see in the next section, there are more ways to obtain water than turning on a faucet or praying for rain.

How Much Water Will Your Roof Collect?
First determine these numbers:

A = area of roof (area of ground covered by the roof, not total area of sloping roof)

R = rainfall in inches per year
Then calculate:

$$\frac{A \times R}{12} = W \text{ cubic feet}$$

This is the number of cubic feet of rain your roof collects each year. Since a cubic foot contains about 7.5 gallons, to convert to gallons, calculate:

$$W \times 7.5 = \text{rainfall in gallons per year}$$

Here's an example: a 30-by-36-foot roof covers 1,080 square feet. If the average rainfall at that site is 35 inches, Area x Rainfall = 1,080 times 35, which equals 37,800. Dividing this by 12 inches gives 3,150 cubic feet of water. To convert to gallons, multiply 3,150 by 7.5; this yields 23,625 gallons of rainwater per year collected by the roof.

---

water tank in my own yard, sunk in the ground and camouflaged with a deck and grape arbor, only lasts through six weeks of drought. By the time you read this, we should have a large pond to provide water through the summer.

Ponds are a pleasing way to store water. Beyond the practical benefits, on a hot day the sight of sparkling water edged by lush greenery seems to drop the temperature by ten degrees.

The secret of storing water in a pond is depth. By digging a 12-by-12-foot garden pond 4 feet deep instead of the usual 2, you can store over 4,000 gallons of water. Obviously, if you're pulling water from the pond for irrigation, you will have to develop some strategies for protecting plants and fish when the water level drops toward the bottom. One possibility is to have one pond strictly for irrigation, and a second, smaller one for finny and leafy inhabitants.

To see how a pond can be both a landscape focal point and a practical water source for the garden, let's look at what forestry consultant and permaculturist Tom Ward did in his Ashland, Oregon, yard. Tom has built a 3,000-gallon pond on the uphill side of his vegetable garden. "After we dug the hole for the pond," Tom told me, "we lined it with three coats of a product called plastic cement, troweled onto bird netting for reinforcement." He could have used a rubber or plastic liner, but chose a less-expensive but more labor-intensive method. The pond is fed by downspouts from the house next door and from a shed in the lot behind Tom's. Both neighbors responded readily to his request for their runoff water.

The pond was new when I visited, but Tom intended to stock it with edible fish and a variety of useful and attractive plants. However, the pond's benefits extend beyond its boundaries. A swale runs alongside the pond. Overflow dribbles out of the pond, down a rock waterfall, and into the swale. The water is captured by the level swale and sinks into the soil. Tom's vegetable garden is just downhill from the swale, and the expanding lens of subterranean wetness from the swale moves down the slope toward the crops like a slow underground tide. The pond and swale thus form a subsurface irrigation system for the nearby garden. Once again, placing the pieces in the right relationship lets nature do the work, and substantially cuts Tom's reliance on municipal water.

At the outlet end of the swale, about twenty feet from the waterfall inlet, Tom has planted blueberry bushes. Any water that flows the entire length of the swale and spills out the far end is captured by these shrubs.

This is a fine example of ecological design. The pond harvests rainfall from his neighbors' roofs, the swale collects any surplus from the pond, and the garden and blueberries benefit from moisture taken in by the swale. Tom has integrated a pond into his garden that is attractive, practical, and connects once-separate elements—even from beyond his own property—into a healthy, smoothly functioning whole.

Closing the Cycle with Greywater

The typical American family uses 100 to 200 gallons of water a day in their home (not including irrigation water). Though some of that household water goes down the toilet as "blackwater," most of it leaves via sink, shower, and laundry drain, contaminated only by a few drops of soap, the odd flake of dead skin, and a smattering of the bacteria that coexist peacefully with us. This is greywater, nearly pure but just dirty enough to be unfit for direct human reuse. However, plants and soil organisms will gratefully accept the watery part of greywater, and eagerly consume the solid and dissolved contents as food.

Reusing greywater reduces pollution and the strain on sewage and septic systems. Just as we now separate our compostable garbage and recyclables from landfill-bound trash, it makes sense not to combine easily reusable, almost-clean greywater with toilet wastes.

Does the idea of using wastewater in the yard

seem, well, a bit unsavory? Don't worry. By following a few simple guidelines, you can easily reuse greywater with no health risk, odor, or any other unpleasantness. Far from it. Greywater can be an important resource, helping to build yet another resilient, life-enhancing cycle into the ecological garden. Let me describe greywater's benefits; then we'll see how to add this new resource to the garden's living structure.

In earlier chapters, I described the crucial role of the decomposers that make up the detritus cycle. In a healthy ecosystem, the decomposers play as large a part, both physically and energetically, as the producers (such as plants) and the consumers (animals). The decomposers transform the wastes and corpses cast off by the living into the raw feedstocks of life, ready to be cycled once more as the breath and bodies of animate beings. Yet in most human ecosystems, including our yards, the detritus cycle is sadly lacking. Without decomposers and their products, organic matter becomes as rare as precious gems. (I've known gardeners who, when they move, take their compost pile with them.) Ecological gardening attempts to restore the detritus cycle to its rightful, central role by using deep mulches and composting, and by avoiding pesticides. Incorporating greywater is one more method to do this.

Greywater closes a loop. The usual linear flow of water through a household goes like this: We import and use clean water and items such as soap and food in the home ecosystem, mix them together to create dirty water, and send this very dilute waste out of our house (and our awareness) through the sewer. This greywater is often piped through a massive sewage system, processed in an expensive treatment plant, and eventually dumped into a river, lake, or ocean. In this way, valuable resources are speedily converted to garbage, yielding along the way only a fraction of the energy and value they contain, and costing lots of money to clean up.

In contrast, reusing greywater creates a tight cycle and uses far less energy. In such a system, water, food, and biodegradable soaps are imported into the household ecology, mixed with a little dirt and skin effluvia in shower and laundry, and sent into the soil or a backyard wetland. There, the whole melange is processed by the microbes and plants in the yard. The result is not "waste," but clean water and fertilizer, ready for recycling. The soaps and food bits are transformed into soil, trees, and flowers in the garden. These nutrients have now been absorbed into the home ecosystem to be whirled into the eternal dance from leaf to litter and back again. With a greywater system, instead of burdening a sewage treatment plant, most of the water used in the household grows our plants and is lofted into the air by transpiration, cooling us on a hot day, and wafting high into the sky to return soon as rain. Each time greywater flows into the garden, new fertility is added, captured, used, and reused by the plants and animals that live there. With every shower or load of laundry, this circle's connections grow thicker and stronger, and the garden grows greener.

Although the amount of soaps, food, and other material in greywater may seem trivial, it adds up over time, building biomass, becoming plants and wildlife and food. And obviously, the water involved, at about 100 gallons a day, is by no means trivial. I've seen greywater systems that have quickly and dramatically boosted the fertility and lushness of a yard. There's something magical in creating these simple cycles, as if nature recognizes the service and showers us with her gifts in return.

If we think of a garden as a living being, then a greywater system acts as one of its organs, a sort of liver and kidneys that process waste and liquid. These "organs" are missing from most gardens. No one can function without kidneys; the only substitute is the elaborate machinery of life support. Our gardens are the same. Given a full complement of "organs," a garden comes to life. Then we can withdraw resource-gobbling life-support systems such as automated sprinklers and doses of

TIPS FOR USING GREYWATER

- Greywater is a legal gray area. The southwestern states are the most greywater-friendly, but even their building codes mandate systems that are more complex than necessary. Many greywater systems have been built without code approval, yet function safely. I'd advise becoming aware of the codes in your area before building a greywater system.

- Avoid watering food plants directly with untreated graywater. Greywater should be applied to the base of nonfood plants or fruit trees and shrubs. It can also be delivered by subsurface irrigation using perforated leach lines, like a septic system. The risk of disease or toxicity from greywater is slight, but putting greywater directly on food is asking for trouble. Once greywater has been processed by passing through microbes and plants in an artificial wetland or other system, its contaminants will have been removed or detoxified. It can then be collected if desired, and used for food-plant irrigation.

- Be careful of what you put in a greywater system. Chlorine bleach, detergents containing boron (borax), and some household chemicals and solvents are toxic to plants and should never go in a greywater system. Hydrogen peroxide–based bleaches are safe to use. If you must use chlorine or boron, install a diverter valve so that your laundry outlet can be temporarily sent to the septic tank or sewer (that is, treated as blackwater).

- Most common detergents will make greywater quite alkaline, which is hard on most plants. Many stores now sell detergents that are greywater compatible and are labeled as such.

- In climates where the ground freezes more than a few inches deep, greywater systems may not work in the winter. Here it's a good idea to be able to divert greywater back into the sewer or septic system until spring thaws.

- Don't store greywater for more than a day or two. The normally low numbers of bacteria can multiply quickly in the nutrient-rich water, and create unpleasant smells at best, and health hazards at worst. Get greywater on the ground quickly.

- Greywater is too "lumpy" for drip irrigation systems unless filtered by sand or some other fine filtration system. Lint, hair, and other debris will quickly clog pumps and pipes or openings less than ½-inch across. Use large-diameter hose and pipes to deliver greywater, or invest in an appropriate filter system.

fertilizer. A greywater system helps a garden be more self-sustaining.

A thorough guide to greywater systems is beyond the scope of this chapter. Good books and articles have been written on the subject. My favorite resource is *Create an Oasis with Greywater* by Art Ludwig (see bibliography). This easy-to-read booklet describes how to choose and install a range of greywater systems. For now, the present chapter will look at a few simple greywater setups, to show how easy and sensible it is to incorporate greywater into the ecological garden.

The simplest possible greywater system—maybe too simple for most people—is a basin in the sink. When it's full, just empty the basin into a well-mulched garden bed. The mulch will absorb the greywater instead of letting it run off, and mulch contains ample soil life to quickly and hungrily process the greywater's contents. Avoid pouring greywater directly on vegetation, as soaps or oils could clog leaf pores or otherwise harm the plant.

For those who would like to recycle their greywater but don't want to be sloshing outdoors with a full soapy basin every few hours, the next level is what greywater guru Art Ludwig calls a "drain to mulch basin" system. This involves a little do-it-yourselfing or hiring a plumber to tap into the outlet of a washing machine, tub, or shower, and to isolate it from the drain lines that carry toilet wastes. Rigid plastic drain pipe (ABS) is then connected to the drain to carry the greywater out of the house. Outside the house, more ABS pipe or flexible, *nonkinkable* 1-inch hose (such as spa-flex PVC) directs the greywater downhill into a mulched swale or to mulched basins around trees. The outlet hose *must* be unkinkable—not just a garden hose or irrigation polypipe. A kinked hose can cause a drain to back up or burn out a washing-machine pump. See the illustration on page 94 for details of this setup. This system can be varied to include a 30- to 55-gallon drum outside the house to temporarily hold the greywater. The

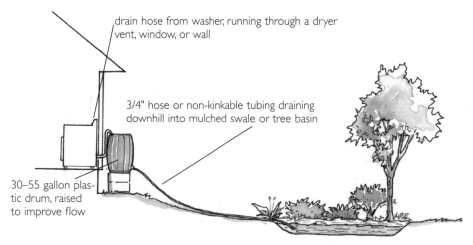

drain hose from washer, running through a dryer vent, window, or wall

3/4" hose or non-kinkable tubing draining downhill into mulched swale or tree basin

30–55 gallon plastic drum, raised to improve flow

A washing machine set up to pump greywater into a drum that will then drain to a planted, mulched swale or tree.

Redrawn with permission from Create an Oasis with Greywater, *by Art Ludwig (Oasis Design 2000).*

ideal example is one created by Penny Livingston, at her home north of San Francisco.

Penny's greywater system is a set of four shimmering ponds, complete with water plants, fish, and ducks. Greywater from bath and laundry first flows through a small marsh that brims with bog plants and ornamental grasses. This artificial wetland, just a few feet across, removes most of the greywater's contaminants and converts them into vegetation. The mostly clean water then trickles over rocks through three small ponds, where it is joined by rainwater from the roof of Penny's backyard office, home of the Permaculture Institute of Northern California. The

drum will cool water that's too hot for plants, and briefly store large volumes of water, such as a tub's contents, that flow too fast for a narrow-diameter outlet hose.

This arrangement, which provides regular doses of 10 to 30 gallons from a shower or laundry load, is ideal for trees, shrubs, and large mulched beds. The flexible hose outflow can be moved from bed to bed every day or two, so that no single area will get too soggy. Ludwig's booklet also describes systems that drain to multiple beds, so you won't have to move a hose around.

Some very complex greywater systems exist, full of automatic backflush pumps, multistage filters, and leach-field distribution lines. However, for me, the next step in greywater technology beyond the "drain to mulch basin" system is no more mechanically complicated, but far more biologically rich. An

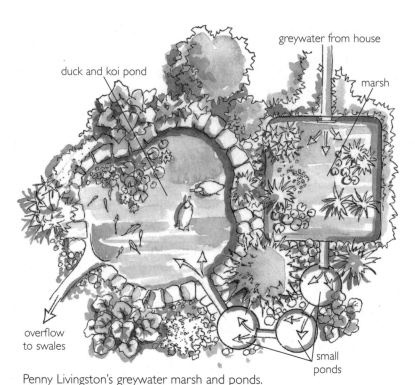

greywater from house

marsh

duck and koi pond

overflow to swales

small ponds

Penny Livingston's greywater marsh and ponds.

Ducks bob happily in clean, treated greywater that has been purified by a backyard wetland.

final destination is the duck pond, a deep 10-by-10-foot affair that glimmers with golden koi and ripples with the splashes of mallards. The ducks serve as water-quality monitors. In the system's early days, before the marsh was installed, the ducks wouldn't swim in the not-clean-enough water. That was because the residual soap in the ponds washed the oil from their feathers, resulting in sinking ducks. Now, the marsh-cleaned water suits them perfectly.

The pond network is strategically located just south of the office so that winter sun is reflected through the windows, brightening the building's interior. A patio and arbor lie beside the pond, where Penny and the rest of the staff sit on pleasant days or on any other excuse to enjoy this soothing spot.

Penny's backyard was my introduction to the dynamic nature of greywater. During a visit, I quickly learned that when I showered, the pond network came alive, so some mornings I would dash, half-dressed and dripping, from the shower to the ponds to watch the show my bathing had triggered. As my shower's water surged into the tiny wetland, plant-filtered water flowed out, over the rocks, past the meditating Buddha and under the dwarf peach tree, filling the first pond to overflowing. The second pond topped up, then the third, and water soon cascaded into the final pond. The gentle surge of water set the ducks bobbing, and their soft quacks sounded like laughter.

Here was living, dancing water that needed no pump to force its liquid motion. With greywater, every yard, no matter how landlocked or desert-bound, can gurgle and splash with the lively rhythms of moving water, without pumps or huge utility bills. And these simple systems give a tremendous boost to the diversity of plants and wildlife that a yard will support while decreasing water consumption. Adding water to a yard creates a whole series of new edges, and new flows of both energy and living beings, as any pond owner knows. Treated and cleaned in a backyard wetland, greywater not only provides this bounty guilt-free, it eases the burden on overtaxed sewer systems.

WATER BRINGS THE GARDEN TO LIFE

If I were designing a landscape from scratch, I'd try to incorporate nearly every idea in this chapter. That way, the garden would be nearly self-watering, sparing the gardener from most of the work and expense of irrigation. But the reasons go much deeper. Catching water from rooftops spares our overtaxed municipal supplies and groundwater aquifers. Thinking of the soil as the best place to store water encourages deep mulching and other practices that also create fertility and abundant soil life. This, in turn, keeps plants healthier. Using greywater allows us to

CREATING A BACKYARD WETLAND

Wetlands are nature's way of purifying and recycling water. As dirty water wends sluggishly through a marsh or bog, the resident plants, microbes, and animals dine leisurely on the water's contents, converting pollutants to biomass and purifying the water. Cities from Shelburne Falls, Massachusetts, to Arcata, California, have copied nature, building "artificial" wetlands to process municipal wastewater. Many of these projects are beautiful, threaded with paths for nature-lovers who gather to watch the waterfowl, otters, and other creatures that thrive in the restored habitat. The know-how for building these wetlands has trickled down to homeowners, coincidentally at a time when growing bog and water plants is very popular. By creating a backyard wetland for greywater, we can meld the beauty of water gardens with ecological responsibility.

Building a backyard wetland is relatively straightforward. It's really just a shallow pond, filled with gravel, covered with mulch or soil, and planted with bog and water plants. The water level is kept below the top of the gravel to thwart mosquitoes. Greywater enters the wetland, passes through the gravel, is purified by the plants and attendant microbes, and exits to a pond, swale, or irrigation system (running greywater through irrigation pumps and sprinklers may require additional filtering). Table 5-3 suggests some plants for this wetland. The plants in the first section of the table—cattail, bulrush, reed canary grass, and canna lily—are essential for treating greywater, and all greywater wetlands should contain a majority of one or more of these species. They are special water-cleaning plants, able to supply oxygen to their roots and to the soil nearby. This creates an aerobic zone around each root, resulting in countless aerobic and anaerobic microsites in the wetland and plenty of edge between them. These diverse micro-niches support many different kinds of pollution-eating microbes. A wetland lacking these special plants might not clean water effectively.

Once a preponderance of the essential plants are in place, other plants, such as those in the second section of table 5-3, can be added to increase diversity.

Greywater wetlands only function effectively when the plants are growing. Gardeners in very cold climates should install a diverter valve to direct water to the sewer or septic system when the plants die back in winter. This also will keep the outdoor greywater plumbing from freezing.

To build a backyard greywater wetland, select a site that is downhill from your home's greywater outlet so the wetland can be gravity-fed (otherwise you'll need a sump pump or other power-using system). As a rule of thumb for sizing the wetland, it takes about 1.25 square feet of wetland to process 1 gallon of greywater per day, thus a family that produces 100 gallons of greywater daily would need a wetland roughly 10 by 12 feet. This can be any shape: a long trench, a circle, a wavy-edged pattern that maximizes the edge effect, or even more than one wetland in series or parallel.

The wetland should be 12 to 18 inches deep, and lined with a plastic pond liner. If your soils are relatively impervious clay, you may not need a liner. Local building codes may offer guidelines for size and materials, although home greywater wetlands are a little avant-garde for most codes to even consider. Many of the systems I know of are of the guerrilla variety, or have required special code variances.

Once the wetland is dug and lined, install plumbing as per the diagram. Then fill the liner with ½- to 1-inch round gravel. The wetland can be covered with mulch or an inch or two of topsoil to help get plants established. Then add the plants. Now greywater can begin to fill the wetland.

The water depth is controlled by a water-level box such as that shown in the diagram on page 98. By changing the height of the pipe, the water level can be adjusted to the optimal height, about 2 inches below the top of the gravel (this will prevent mosquito growth). If you want to be extra nice to the plants, once a month or so pull the level control pipe all the way off to drain the wetland. Once it's drained, reinsert the pipe. Periodic draining aerates the bottom of the wetland, helping roots get deeply established.

TABLE 5-3.

Essential Plants for a Graywater Wetland

One or more of these varieties should make up the majority of any graywater wetland, as they are particularly effective at purifying water.

WETLAND PLANTS

Common name	Botanical name	Comments
Bulrush	*Scirpus validus*	
Canna lily	*Canna* spp.	ornamental
Cattail	*Typha* spp.	wildlife value
Reed canary grass	*Phragmites communis*	can be invasive, accumulator

Additional Wetland Plants

Arrowhead	*Sagittaria* spp.	ornamental
Chokeberry	*Aronia* spp.	wildlife value
Comfrey	*Symphytum officinale*	mulch, insectary
Cranberry	*Vaccinium macrocarpon*	wildlife value, foliage
Elderberry	*Sambucus* spp.	ornamental, wildlife
Hedge hyssop	*Gratiola virginiana*	aromatic, ornamental
High-bush blueberry	*Vaccinium corymbosum*	wildlife value, foliage
High-bush cranberry	*Viburnum trilobum*	wildlife value, foliage
Horsetail	*Equisetum* spp.	accumulates nutrients, can be invasive
Lotus	*Nelumbo lutea, N. nucifera*	ornamental
Ostrich fern	*Matteuccia pennsylvanica*	ornamental
Pickerel weed	*Pontederia cordata*	ornamental, invasive
Soft rush	*Juncus effusus*	fiber plant
Spike rush	*Eleocharis* spp.	
Sweet flag	*Acorus calamus*	ornamental, can be invasive
Water canna	*Thalia* spp.	ornamental
Yellow iris	*Iris pseudoacorus*	ornamental

harvest and use both water and fertility that would otherwise be wasted. And wetlands and ponds are beautiful and incredibly productive garden features that attract a marvelous range of wildlife.

The result is one step closer to a home ecosystem. Each rainfall is captured by rooftops and sent, not to a storm-drain's banishment, but to where it can be used, just as a tree harvests water with its leaves and directs it to its roots. In this garden, rain collects in cisterns and ponds, is slowed by gentle contours and swales, and then is stored in the soil to be slowly released and used, mimicking a natural watershed. Plants form a continuous cover, keeping the soil moist, cooling the air, offering a home to plentiful wildlife, and pleasing the eye and palate with their bounty. When the human inhabitants of this ecosystem use water in their home, bog plants thrive and grow, ponds and waterfalls gurgle, and the glint of flowing water reflects on the leaves overhead. Who would choose the mechanical hiss of automatic sprinklers drenching a sterile lawn over this verdant paradise?

All of the techniques in this chapter help us think of our gardens as living systems, humming with energy and busily shuttling nutrients to and fro. These living places are laced with a webwork of interdependent pathways and feedback loops, with plants, soil, insects, microbes, birds, and

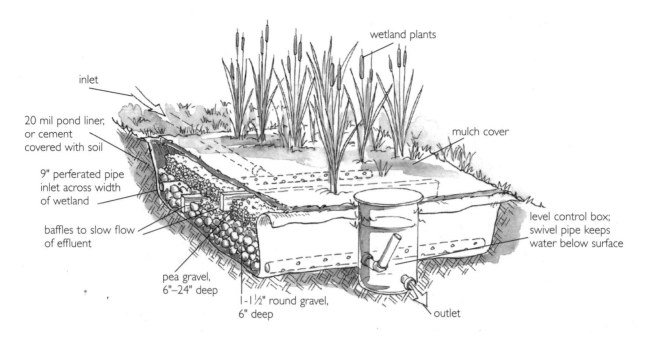

inlet

20 mil pond liner,
or cement
covered with soil

9" perforated pipe
inlet across width
of wetland

baffles to slow flow
of effluent

pea gravel,
6"–24" deep

1-1½" round gravel,
6" deep

wetland plants

mulch cover

level control box;
swivel pipe keeps
water below surface

outlet

A greywater wetland.

others all connected via water. Without water, there is no life.

With a conscious, ecological design, water becomes an integral part of a landscape: designed in, not added on. In a well-designed garden, perfectly watered plants—not parched, not drowned—is the natural state. Drought and flood are foreigners here. A healthy garden tunes its relationship with water toward harmony, using rich soil, ponds, a wetland, and the intelligence of the gardener to survive both drying and drenching.

Chapter 6

Plants for Many Uses

IN MOST GARDENS, each plant is chosen for a single purpose. A silver maple tree in the front lawn, for example, has probably been selected for its stunning fall foliage, while a spreading white oak in back is for shade. Those shasta daisies in the perennial bed? Their white blossoms accent the hues of nearby plantings, while the cylindrical juniper against the house may have been the only shrub narrow enough to fit between two windows. This is how most conventional landscape designs work: a selection of isolated pieces placed together because they look nice. Nature never works this way. Natural plant groupings form through dynamic relationships among species and the environment—yet nature always manages to create landscapes that rival and often surpass the beauty of human designs. And natural landscapes work: They harvest water, build soil, minimize disease, reproduce themselves, have copious yields, support an enormous diversity of species, and function in dozens of other ways that we hardly recognize. All this while looking pretty.

In this chapter, I'd like to lay the groundwork for understanding how plants actually work together. We'll explore the different functions that plants can have—the roles they play in the ecological theater—plus how they cooperate and aid each other, and how they change and are changed by their environment. Then we'll see how to select plants that fill the needs of both the gardener and the landscape.

Of course, we want to live in an attractive landscape. But if we can go beyond what plants look like, and examine what they are doing, we can begin to create gardens that have the health, resilience, and beauty of natural ecosystems while yielding abundant gifts for people and for other species.

THE MANY ROLES OF A TREE

As I've said, when we look at a plant, we often see it as doing one thing. Take the hypothetical white oak I referred to above. Some homeowner placed that tree in the backyard to create a shady spot. But even this single tree, isolated in a lawn, is giving a rich performance, not simply acting as a leafy umbrella. Let's watch this oak tree to see what it's doing.

It's dawn. The first rays of sunlight strike the canopy of the oak, but most of the energy in these beams is consumed in evaporating dew on the leaves. Only after the leaves are dry does the sunlight warm the air within the tree. Above the oak, however, the air has begun to heat, and a cloud of just-awakened insects swirls here. Below the canopy, it's still too chilly for insects to venture. The insects roil in a narrow band, sharply defining the layer of warm air above the tree. Together the sun and the oak have created insect habitat, and with it, a place for birds, who quickly swoop to feast on the swarm of bugs.

In the cool shade of this tree, snow remains late into the spring, long after unprotected snow has melted. Soil near the tree stays moist, watering both the oak and nearby plantings, and helping to keep a nearby creek flowing (early miners in the West frequently reported creeks disappearing once they'd cut nearby forests for mine timbers).

Soon the sun warms the humid, night-chilled air within the tree. The entrapped air dries, its moisture escaping to the sky to help form clouds. This lost moisture is quickly replaced by the transpiring leaves, which pump water up from roots and exhale it through puffy-lipped pores in the leaves called stomata. Groundwater, whether polluted or clean, is filtered by the tree and exits through the leaves as pure water. So trees are excellent water purifiers, and active ones. A full-grown tree can transpire 2,000 gallons of water on a hot, dry day. But this moisture doesn't just go away—it soon returns as rain: Up to half of the rainfall over forested land comes from the trees themselves (the rest arrives as evaporation from bodies of water). Cut the trees, and the rain disappears.

Sun striking the leaves ignites the engines of photosynthesis, and from these green factories, oxygen streams into the air. But more benefits exist. To build sugars and the other carbon-based molecules that provide fuel and structure for the tree, the leaves remove carbon dioxide from the air. This is how trees help reduce the level of greenhouse gases.

As the leaves absorb sunlight and warm the air within the tree, this hot, moist air rises and mixes with the drier, cool air above. Convection currents begin to churn, and morning breezes begin. So trees help create cooling winds.

But closer to the ground, trees block the wind. The oak's upper branches toss in the morning breeze, while down below the air is still. The tree has captured the energetic movement of the air and converted it into its own motion. Where does this energy go? Some scientists think that captured wind energy is converted into the woody tissue of the tree, helping to build tough but flexible cells.

Trees make excellent windbreaks: A tree placed on the windward side of a house can substantially reduce heating bills.

The morning breeze carries dust from the plowed fields of nearby farmland, which collects on the oak leaves. A single tree may have 10 to 30 acres of leaf surface, all able to draw dust and pollutants from the air. Air passing through the tree is thus purified, and humidified as well. As air passes through the tree, it picks up moisture exhaled from the leaves, a light burden of pollen grains, a fine mist of small molecules produced by the tree, some bacteria, and fungal spores.

Some of those spores have landed below the tree, spawning several species of fungus that grow symbiotically amid the roots, secreting nutrients and antibiotics that feed and protect the tree. A vole has tunneled into the soft earth beneath the tree in search of some of this fungus. Later this vole will leave manure pellets near other oaks, inoculating them with the beneficial fungus. That is, if the owl who regularly frequents this oak doesn't snatch up the vole first.

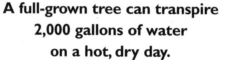

A full-grown tree can transpire 2,000 gallons of water on a hot, dry day.

This tree's ancestors provided Native Americans with flour made from acorns, though most suburbanites wouldn't consider this use. Now, bluejays and squirrels frolic in the oak, snatching acorns and hiding them around this and neighboring yards. Some of these acorns, forgotten, will sprout and grow into new trees. Meanwhile, the animals' diggings and droppings will aid the soil. Other birds probe the bark for insects, and yet others depend on the inconspicuous flowers for food.

Later in the day, clouds (half of them created by trees, remember) begin to build. Rain droplets readily form around the bacteria, pollen, and other microscopic debris lofted from the oak. These small particles provide the nucleation sites that raindrops need to form. Thus, trees act as "cloud-seeders" to bring rain.

As the rain falls, the droplets smack against the oak leaves and spread out into a fine film, coating the entire tree (all 10 to 30 acres of leaves, plus the branches and trunk) before a single drop strikes the ground. This thin film begins to evaporate even as the rain falls, further delaying any through-fall. Mosses and lichens on this old oak soak up even more of the rain. We've all seen dry patches beneath trees after a rain: A mature tree can absorb over ¼ inch of rain before any reaches the earth; even more if the air is dry and the rain is light.

The leaves and branches act as a funnel, channeling much of the rain to the trunk and toward the root zone of the tree. Soil close to the trunk can receive two to ten times as much rain as that in open ground. And the tree's shade slows evaporation, preserving this moisture.

As the rain continues, droplets leak off the leaves and splatter on the ground. Since this tree-drip has lost most of the energy it gathered during its fall from the clouds, little soil erodes beneath the tree. Leaf litter and roots also help hold the soil in place. Trees are supreme erosion-control systems.

The water falling from the leaves is very different from what fell from the sky. Its passage through the tree transmutes it into a rich soup, laden with the pollen, dust, bird and insect droppings, bacteria and fungi collected by the leaves, and many chemicals and nutrients secreted by the tree. This nutritious broth both nourishes the soil beneath the tree and inoculates the leaf litter and earth with soil-decomposing organisms. In this way, the tree collects and prepares its own fertilizer solution.

The rain eases toward sundown, and the sky clears. The upper leaves of the tree begin to chill as night falls, and cold air drains down from the canopy, cooling the trunk and soil. But this chill is countered by heat rising from the day-warmed earth, which warms the air under the tree. The leafy canopy holds this warmth, preventing it from escaping to the night sky. So nighttime temperatures are warmer beneath the tree than in the open.

The leaves, however, radiate their heat to the sky and become quite cold, often much colder than the air. All these cold surfaces condense moisture from the air, and the resulting dew drips from the leaves and wets the ground, watering the tree and surrounding plants. Leaves can also gather moisture from fog: On foggy days the mist collects in such volume that droplets trickle steadily from the leaves. On arid but foggy coasts, tree-harvested precipitation can be triple the average rainfall. By harvesting dew and fog, trees can boost available moisture to far beyond what a rain gauge indicates.

As we gaze at this huge oak, remember that we're barely seeing half of it. At least 50 percent of this tree's mass is below the ground. The roots may extend tens of feet down, and horizontally can range far beyond the span of the tree's branches. We've already learned how these roots loosen and aerate soil, build humus as they grow and die, etch minerals free from rocks with mild acid secretions, and with sugary exudates provide food for hundreds or even thousands of species of soil organisms that live with them.

Roots bring nutrients from deep in the ground, and the tree converts them into leaves. When these leaves drop in the fall, carbon and minerals gathered from the immense volume of air and earth surrounding the tree are concentrated into a thin layer of mulch. Thus, the tree has harvested a diffuse dusting of useful nutrients, once sprinkled over thousands of cubic yards of soil and air, and distilled them into a rich, dense agglutination of topsoil. In this way, trees mine the sparse ores that surround them and build fertility and wealth. This wealth is shared with many other species, which root and burrow, feed and build, all nourished by the tree's gatherings.

But there is more: This tree's roots have threaded toward those of nearby oak trees and then fused with them. A tree's roots, researchers have shown, can graft with those of its kind nearby, exchanging nutrients and even notifying each other of insect attack. Chemical signals released by an infested tree prompt its neighbors to secrete protective compounds that will repulse the soon-to-invade bugs. If an oak has grafted to its neighbors, does it remain an individual tree? Perhaps trees in a forest are more like branches from a single subterranean "tree" than a group of individuals.

The ways in which a single tree interacts with other species and its environment, then, are many. I've barely mentioned the swarms of insects that this oak supports: gall wasps and their hymenopteran relatives, beetles who tunnel into twigs and bark, and all manner of sucking and chewing bugs and their many insect predators. Then there are the birds who feed on these bugs. And we shouldn't forget the myriad nearby plants that benefit from the rain and nutrients collected by this tree.

Through this tree, we glimpse the benefits of ecological thinking. Instead of viewing a tree simply as something that looks nice or provides a single offering such as apples or shade, we can now begin to see how deeply connected a tree is to its surroundings, both living and inanimate. A tree transforms wind and sunlight into a variety of daily-changing microclimates, harvests nutrients, builds soil, pumps and purifies air and water, creates and concentrates rain, and shelters and feeds wildlife and microbes. Add to all this the better-known benefits for people: fruit or nuts, shade, climbing and other fun for kids, and the beauty of foliage, flowers, or form. We start to see how tightly enmeshed is a simple tree with all the other elements in a landscape. Now we can begin to imagine the richness of a landscape of many plant species, all interconnected by flows of energy and nutrients, nurturing and being nourished by the animals and microbes that flap and crawl and tunnel among them.

Each plant modifies its environment. These changes in turn support or inhibit what lies nearby, whether living or not. Recognizing that plants don't stand alone can radically affect the way we place the features of our gardens.

> **A tree transforms wind and sunlight into a variety of daily-changing microclimates, harvests nutrients, builds soil, pumps and purifies air and water, creates and concentrates rain, and shelters and feeds wildlife and microbes.**

MULTIPURPOSE PLANTS

We've seen how one oak tree has many qualities. This oak isn't exceptional; all species are just as multitalented, albeit in different ways. What good does this knowledge do us? Granted that a plant can harvest rain, build soil, attract insects, and do umpteen other things, how do we use this in our yards?

When we understand a few of the roles that a particular plant can play, we can place that species so that it complements what is nearby. Any given plant can have a positive or negative relationship with nearby plants, animals, structures, and limitations of soil, light, wind, and water. Acknowledging and using these relationships can benefit the plant, its neighbors, the environment, and, not incidentally, the gardener.

We can choose plants according to function—and not just one function. These multiple and often overlapping uses of plants allow us to have some real fun in garden design. For example, if a yard contains a dry spot in poor soil under a shade tree, that's a perfect place for a drought- and shade-tolerant, nitrogen-fixing shrub such as indigo *(Indigofera tinctoria),* which incidentally is a good green manure and attracts insects to its lovely purple blossoms. Other nitrogen-fixing shrubs can take extreme cold, such as Siberian pea shrub *(Caragana arborescens);* drought-tolerant, N-fixing shrubs that revel in full sun, including wild lilac *(Ceanothus* spp.*);* and just about every other permutation you could ask for. Want an insect-attracting, deer-proof, and edible flower with medicinal properties? Try bee balm *(Monarda didyma).* For a plant that yields salad greens and poultry forage, and has roots that break up clay soil and make a coffee substitute when roasted, use chicory *(Cichorium intybus).* How about a nitrogen-fixing shrub that is great for erosion control and hedges, with edible berries that are packed with vitamin C? That would be sea buckthorn *(Hippophae rhamnoides).* The combinations can even be whimsical. At a recent workshop, one student listed twenty medicinal plants that could also be used for toilet paper.

To see how multifunctional plants can be used in the landscape, let's look in some detail at a few species with many functions and some ways to take advantage of them. Then I'll describe some general roles that plants take on.

Maximilian sunflower
(Helianthus maximilianii).

MAXIMILIAN SUNFLOWER. Just south of our house, we've planted a mixed border filled with shrubs, herbs, and flowers. Below this, the ground angles downhill. On this slope, we've placed a hedge of Maximilian sunflower, *Helianthus maximilianii.* Maximilians are one of the few perennial—not annual—sunflowers, which is a benefit right there because I don't have to plant them every year. They grow 5 to 7 feet tall and sport 4-inch yellow blooms in the late fall, giving a fine flash of color when most everything else is spent. A big plus for me is that deer don't eat them—in fact, the stems are covered with a coarse fuzz that discourages deer from poking through them. The plants aren't invasive, but they grow thickly, forming a superb deer barrier that deters the hungry beasts from strolling up the hill to munch on our mixed border. In winter, I trim the stalks to about 4 feet high, and the deer really hate the stiff spikes that remain. The bare stems, a potential eyesore, are downhill and thus hidden from our view. But the trimmings, especially when I cut them to the ground in early spring, are copious and create plenty of biomass for mulch or compost.

The benefits continue. Maximilians, a relative of Jerusalem artichokes, have edible shoots that are delicious raw or cooked. The seeds are attractive to birds (they also yield a useful oil, but I confess I'm not following up on this aspect). They are very hardy, to -30 degrees Fahrenheit. The plant is very drought-tolerant, which is great because it's just far enough from a faucet that I don't care to water it often. It can tolerate many soil types, all the better since I'm growing it in some very nasty red clay.

Below the Maxies sprawls a grassy savanna that I'm slowly converting to a food forest (more about that in a later chapter). Here, the sunflowers' thick growth stanches the tide of grass that would love to spread uphill into the mixed border.

So here's a plant that I've placed in this particular spot primarily to create a deer barrier, but that is also quite pretty, has edible parts, attracts birds, generates mulch, stops grass invasion, and is very low-maintenance. It's an excellent multifunctional plant.

GOUMI. I'll offer a second many-purpose species. Goumi *(Elaeagnus multiflora)* is a relative of Russian olive, hardy to 10 degrees Fahrenheit, that was bred in Asia to yield tasty berries. The red, ¾-inch fruits thickly festoon this 6-foot-tall shrub in late summer, and are good eaten out-of-hand, but are more often made into jams, sauces, and pies. The berries are very high in vitamin C, contain compounds that help break down fats in the blood, and are reputed to reduce cholesterol levels. Birds love the berries too. Where I live, wild turkeys gather to feast on goumi berries and those of other Elaeagnus shrubs.

Once established, goumi is very drought tolerant, so it's a good wildlife shrub for the far, unwatered margins of the yard. Deer do a little nibbling of the leaves and young growth, but I've never seen them strip and annihilate an entire shrub as they do with so many other woody plants.

Spring finds goumi vibrant with hundreds of fragrant, cream-colored flowers that are adored by bees and other pollinators. The leaves of goumi are attractive too. Gray-green on top and silver below, in a breeze they shimmer and sparkle as the light catches the bright undersides.

One heavyweight benefit of goumi for the ecological garden is that it fixes nitrogen. Elaeagnus species bear root nodules that harbor a nitrogen-producing filamentous fungi called *Frankia,* making these shrubs one of the few N-fixers outside the pea family. Goumi's gift of nitrogen boosts the growth of neighboring plants, thus many gardeners interplant this or other N-fixers among plants

Goumi *(Elaeagnus multiflora).*

that don't fix nitrogen. Nitrogen-fixing shrubs also help restore soil and, interspersed in a young landscape, can speed the repair of battered land. The fast-growing greenery can be slashed back heavily to yield mulch.

Ecological landscapers often go heavy on N-fixers such as goumi in the early phases of a design to build fertility and create a supportive environment for other plantings. Later, as the landscape matures and these pioneer qualities are less needed, different shrubs can be gradually substituted for many of the N-fixers.

Thus, in goumi we have a nitrogen-fixing perennial that attracts insects and birds, offers healthful food, needs little care, nurtures young landscapes, generates plenty of mulch or compost, and bears lovely foliage, flowers, and fruit. That's a multifaceted plant.

MAYPOP. Moving from shrubs to a different growth form, let me offer a vining passionflower, Maypop *(Passiflora incarnata),* as our next many-talented species. This fast-growing climber is native to the southeast United States, and is hardy to 0 degrees Fahrenheit. Like all passionflowers, Maypop offers an exquisite and exotic-looking blossom; this one has a lemony fragrance. The flowers attract bees, butterflies, and admiring humans, and develop into an edible fruit about the size of a hen's egg that tastes

Maypop *(Passiflora incarnata)*.

a little like apricot. (You will notice that food forms a common theme through these selections; though not essential for my regard, edibility considerably raises my esteem for a plant.) The fruit can also be used for jam and juice. Even the young leafy shoots are edible, and can be chopped raw into a salad or cooked as a green.

Vining deciduous plants fill an important niche. Trellised on the sunny side of a house or patio, or over a greenhouse, they leaf out in early summer just as the heat comes on. This creates much-treasured shade, keeping a house cool or allowing an unbearably hot space to become usable in summer. Then when the warm weather ends, the leaves drop and sunlight can stream in again. Vines such as Maypop can also climb up bare tree trunks or into nonflowering shrubs to provide color with their blossoms.

Maypop won't shade out other shrubs, as it leafs out late in the spring, giving other plants a chance to get started. In climates with heavy winter freezes, Maypop dies back to its roots. But it's a vigorous grower, leaping from 18-inch sprouts in June to as much as 25 feet of growth by fall. Spreading can be a problem: The roots can send up

new plants 15 feet away, though usually only a few of them each year.

Maypop, then, attracts insects and birds, has edible parts, and is ideal for trellising, creating a seasonal shady spot that's bright with exotic blooms and offering tasty fruit and greens.

BAMBOO. Bamboo is the queen of the useful plants—whole books have been written in loving description of her many roles. More than 1,580 human uses for bamboo have been found, including paper, flooring, poles, food, baskets, bridges, fans, fences, hats, acupuncture needles, and xylophones. Thomas Edison used bamboo for the filament of his first successful lightbulb.

Yet bamboo, so important in Asia that it is often called "the brother," gets a bad rap in this culture. Many temperate varieties are "running" (monopodial) bamboos, which if placed wrongly will seemingly sprint across the ground via fast-growing

Black bamboo *(Phyllostyachys nigra)*, one of hundreds of useful bamboo species.

rhizomes. The most common question asked about bamboo seems to be, "But won't it take over?"

In my mind, and in that of many bamboo-loving *bambuseros,* the benefits vastly outweigh the relatively easily overcome drawbacks. Here are some of bamboo's uses in a typical yard: Birds use the leaves and twigs for nests, and bamboo stands attract bush tits, chickadees, song sparrows, and many others to warble from within the dense, rustling foliage. The canes have endless uses around the home, whether for trellis uprights and overhead lattice, an eternal supply of garden stakes, temporary (or permanent) fences, or a Huck Finn–style fishing pole for the kids. For those with a little tool savvy, bamboo poles can be transformed into furniture, flutes, wind chimes, mats, handmade paper, and—literally—a thousand other items.

Bamboo is deer-proof, so suburban and rural gardeners can add it to the "outside-the-fence" plant list. The roots, like those of other grasses, don't expand in girth, thus it can be planted over septic drain-fields without fear of clogging the pipes. On steep slopes, it's a natural for erosion control because its rhizomatous roots interlace into a tough webwork. Bamboo has been used for restoration work, healing clearcuts and other abused lands (in Vietnam bamboo has thrown a green bandage over landscapes defoliated by Agent Orange). Bamboos vary in hardiness, from tropics-only species to those that will survive below-zero temperatures.

It's a beautiful, restful plant. Few sights and sounds are as soothing after a wearying workday as a shady, sussurating grove of bamboo, enfolding and quieting a space within a forest of soaring green canes that arch overhead. A bamboo grove, however small, is a meditative place that quiets the outside world.

With dozens of species to choose from, a homeowner can select varieties ranging from knee high to 40 or 50 feet tall, and thicknesses from pencil size to 4-inch timber bamboo. The shapes and colors vary too, with straight, curved, or zig-zag stems; green, golden, striped, bluish, or black canes; and solid, variegated, or striped leaves.

Bamboo is also food. The young shoots of most varieties are edible and delicious when steamed or sautéed. In fact, the best way to control bamboo's potentially rampant growth is to eat any shoots that venture outside the chosen bamboo zone. Now that's stacking functions!

Here are a few other tips for control: Remember to think like bamboo. It needs water to thrive, and the rhizomes run most furiously in loose soil. Thus, in the arid West, bamboo can be thwarted by simply not watering outside the desired growth area. In wetter climates, plant bamboo next to a pond, compacted path, or gravel driveway (a sidewalk or paved driveway might stop the plant, but in some cases the rhizomes really enjoy the lack of competing roots and zip under the pavement, bursting joyously into daylight on the other side). For the truly bamboo-fearful, nonspreading clumping bamboos—called *sympodial,* as opposed to running, or *monopodial* bamboos—are available.

For physical containment, fiberglass roofing sheets (metal won't last more than a few years) can be sunk 20 inches deep in the ground, sloping slightly outward to deflect rhizomes upward. Or a similar barrier of concrete can be created. Some growers dig out a bed about a foot deep, line and edge it with a pond liner, and fill it with soil.

But the very best way to contain bamboo is to use it. It is a plant that seems to cherish an active relationship with people, often languishing without human companions. So eat any errant shoots, thin out and use the poles when they are three or four years old, and perhaps with some creativity you can add to the long list of known uses for bamboo.

These are just a few examples of multifunctional plants. In the appendix, I've listed many others along with their roles, but the list is far from exhaustive. Nearly every plant is multifunctional, and only the gardener's imagination sets limits on how many ways a plant can be used. The key here is to remember that plants don't merely supply *products*, such as fruit and flowers. More importantly, plants are busily performing *processes* such as soil building and water harvesting. Viewing plants as dynamic, not static, requires a subtle shift in thinking—after all, plants just seem to sit there most of the time. But with experience, we can learn to see plants as active participants in the garden ecology. In the next section we'll examine some of the roles plants play.

THE ROLES OF PLANTS IN THE ECOLOGICAL THEATER

We'll never know all the roles that plants play. We can see the obvious activities, such as shedding leaves and casting shade. And with some observation we can understand that plants build soil and nurture insects. But many of the jobs plants perform are hidden from our eyes: pulling nutrients from deep in the soil and sharing them with microbes or even with other plants via entwined and connected roots. Or pumping nitrogen into the soil to prepare barren ground for colonization. I'm sure there are other quiet relations among plants and the rest of the world that we don't even glimpse. Thus, any list of plant's roles must be incomplete, as we mere humans aren't equipped to detect all the subtle activities of the green world. Here I'll attempt to describe the roles plants play that are important for the ecological garden, knowing that they surely have other, more subtle vocations as well.

MULCH MAKERS. Plants build soil in many ways, and one is by the continual rain of leaves, flowers, twigs, and bark that patters upon the earth as the seasons turn. All this debris quickly composts into rich humus. Every plant drops litter, but some are truly prodigious mulch makers, and it is these that we especially welcome when the soil is young or has been abused. Mulching is simply composting in

place, but it brings other benefits such as moisture retention, soil cooling, and habitat creation.

Soft-leafed plants make mulch the fastest. These include artichoke and its relative cardoon, rhubarb, comfrey, Jerusalem artichoke, ferns, reeds, and nasturtium. Many varieties used for "green manure" cover crops can be used for mulch, such as the clovers (especially sweet clover, which grows 5 feet tall), vetches, many grasses and grains (such as oats, wheat, and barley), mustard, crotolaria, and buckwheat. These plants and many others can be slashed or mowed down, often several times a season, and used as mulch wherever needed. Obviously, mulch plants should be used before they go to seed or you'll have mulch growing in your beds (which in the right circumstances could be desirable). If the mulch looks too messy, it can be tucked under a layer of straw or wood shavings.

Woody plants can make great mulch too. Many shrubs, especially nitrogen fixers such as alder, *Elaeagnus,* scotch broom, and ceanothus, break down very quickly. Trimmings from shrubs and trees that have small branches (pencil-thick or thinner) are fine for mulch; there's no need to send them through a chipper as long as they're in contact with the soil, which greatly speeds rotting. A tall pile of brush won't break down nearly as fast as some stomped-down branches that get ground contact. Again, if aesthetics are a factor, brush can be mulched out of sight or under a more attractive top layer.

Then there are living mulches. A soft undercover of greenery offers many of the same benefits as dry mulch, plus those of living plants (flowers, habitat, and so on). Living mulches include dwarf yarrow, thrift, Ajuga, wild strawberry, stonecrop (*Sedum* spp.*),* periwinkle (*Vinca minor*) and white clover.

NUTRIENT ACCUMULATORS. Certain species draw specific nutrients from deep in the soil and concentrate them in their leaves. The long taproots of these plants dredge up important nutrients such as potassium, magnesium, calcium, sulfur, and others. As these plants lose their foliage in fall, the nutrients build up in the topsoil. Such plants are obvious candidates for the ecological garden, since they keep nutrients cycling within the yard and reduce the need for purchased fertilizers.

Nutrient accumulators include yarrow, chamomile, fennel, lamb's quarters, chicory, dandelion, plantain, and many more. The list is long, and different plants pull up different nutrients; you can find such a list in Robert Kourik's book *Designing and Maintaining Your Edible Landscape.*

You'll note that many of these plants are considered weeds. In nature's more tolerant scheme, most weeds make their living as pioneer species—tough, sun-dependent, fast-growing, and short-lived. These early colonists invade bare or depleted soils, where one of their roles is to accumulate nutrients in their roots and leaves. Each fall, these plants die and rot, pumping a fat load of minerals into the soil. The enriched earth is then ready for the next successionary phase of less ephemeral, more fastidious plants such as perennial herbs, shrubs, and trees.

> **Ecological gardeners turn the features of *pioneer plants* to advantage, letting them draw nutrients from deep in the earth to create fertile, balanced soil.**

Ecological gardeners turn the features of pioneer plants to advantage, letting them draw nutrients from deep in the earth to create fertile, balanced soil. As the soil improves, nutrients will begin to recycle from leaf to soil and back again. No longer will deep roots be required to tug scarce nutrients from the depths. The accumulator plants will then be redundant, and will begin a natural decline that the gardener can accelerate by pulling them up and replacing them with other varieties.

NITROGEN FIXERS. A third group of soil-building plants we have met before: the nitrogen fixers. These plants harbor bacteria or fungi among their roots that extract nitrogen from the air and convert it to plant-available form. Though arguments still rage about how and when these plants deliver their nitrogenous bounty to the soil, there is no doubt of their benefit. Some people believe that nitrogen fixers must die to release their nutrients, but both research and my own experience show that live N-fixers are at least as growth-boosting as dead ones.

Most plants in the pea family (legumes) fix nitrogen, as do ceanothus, mountain mahogany, buffaloberry, and *Elaeagnus* species such as goumi, and Autumn and Russian olive. Nitrogen fixers come in all sizes, from ground covers such as clover, to shrubs, to trees such as black locust, alder, and acacia. These fast-growing plants can be slashed down or trimmed to provide a rich stock for mulch or compost.

SOIL FUMIGANTS AND PEST REPELLENTS. Some plants secrete compounds that repel a few specific pests in the soil or above. Examples include nasturtium, false indigo, elderberry, and certain marigolds. Nasturtiums seem to deter whitefly, though the data are a bit ambiguous. The wild marigold, *Tagetes minuta*, repels soil nematodes, although cultivated varieties, such as *T. patula* and *T. erecta* are less effective. The rule seems to be: The more highly bred and less odoriferous the marigold, the less effective as a pest deterrent. Some hybrid marigolds, in fact, stunt the growth of nearby plants and attract pests. Pest-repellent plants are not well researched, and I'd advise planting them in limited quantities.

INSECTARY PLANTS. Plants that attract beneficial insects are legion: Almost any pollen- or nectar-producing flower will lure our six-legged friends. Beneficial insects fall into two main groups: *pollinators,* needed for fruit and seed set; and *predators,* which gobble up the bugs that munch our plants. These insects will be covered in more detail in chapter 7. A few choice insectary plants are yarrow, buckwheat, lavender, golden marguerite, bee balm, and many clovers. Nearly all of the celery or carrot family (the Apiaceae), which includes fennel, Queen Anne's lace, dill, and coriander, are excellent insectary plants. Other plant families that are loaded with insect-attracting species include the onion or lily family (the Lilaceae), the sunflower or composite family (the Asteraceae), and especially the mint family (the Lamaceae). Not only will insectary plants improve your garden's health, but the flash and shimmer of multicolored buzzers and flutterers will both delight the eye and attract many varieties of birds to eat them, further increasing your yard's biodiversity. Chapter 7 contains a special section on insectary plants.

FORTRESS PLANTS. I use the term "fortress plants" for species that prevent invasive plants from swarming into more delicate areas of the garden. They work by producing a wall of thick growth above and below ground that shades out and physically restrains invaders. They'll stop the rampages of grass, weed seeds, creeping vines such as bindweed, and other unwanted marauders. Some, like the above-mentioned Maximilian sunflower, secrete mildly toxic compounds that inhibit seed germination and root growth. Other fortress plants include comfrey, Jerusalem artichoke, lemongrass, red-hot poker, and any other thickly growing perennial with a dense root system.

SPIKE ROOTS. When soil is compacted or clayey, plants are excellent tools to restore tilth and fluffiness. Many species have deep, soil-busting taproots that are perfect for the job. These include daikon (Japanese radish), chicory, comfrey, artichoke, and dandelion. Others, such as mustard, rapeseed, and alfalfa, don't have a single taproot but instead thrust a massive, fibrous root system deep into the earth to accomplish the same soil loosening. You can use these plants in either of two strategies: Sow them into a future orchard or garden to work a year or two before the final planting; or intercrop them among the beds or under trees to continually break up the soil. An added bonus of spike roots is

that most of these species will add organic matter as their giant root systems decay. After they've done their work, these plants can be cut down, shaded out by taller plants, or sheet mulched. (Comfrey will be tough to get rid of, but persistent sheet mulch is effective).

WILDLIFE NURTURERS. In the late 1970s, gardeners began to discover the joys of attracting wildlife to their yards, not only via bird feeders and salt licks, but by choosing plants that sheltered and fed the animals they loved. If you choose appropriate plants, rare birds, mammals, and butterflies—not deer and raccoons—will appear. A few of my favorite wildlife plants include dogwood, elderberry, chokeberry, blueberry, native roses, hawthorn, ceanothus, and various wild cherries. Chapter 7 contains a table listing more. With so many plants to choose from, a wildlife zone need not be a brushy tangle, but can be attractive as well as functional.

SHELTERBELTERS. Plants can create effective windbreaks and shelterbelts to modify harsh winds, keep out unwanted browsers such as deer, screen an unwanted view, or create ∪-shaped sun-traps for warmth. Shelterbelt species are limited only by the designer's imagination, as these hedges can be delightfully multifunctional. For a large windbreak, why not mix together some junipers and hollies for year-round protection, fruiting trees and shrubs for food, nitrogen fixers such as black locust and laburnum—which incidentally are beloved by bees—and some wildlife species? As a rule of thumb, windbreaks should be constructed to allow 40 to 70 percent of the wind to pass through them (if they are denser, they create turbulence downwind). They will protect an area two to five times as long as the windbreak is high. A hedge of shorter plants can shelter garden beds, but remember that these, too, can be multifunctional. I've used Maximilian sunflowers and Jerusalem artichokes around my garden, and I know of other gardens protected by bamboo, basketry willows, wildlife shrubs, or berry bushes.

A U-shaped sun-trap. Open to the sunny south side, but closed to winds by a semicircle of plants, the microclimate of this suntrap is warm and protected, and suitable for tender plants. Evergreens can be planted on the north side as a year-round windbreak.

garden beds

Deciduous plants can also be used for their seasonal shade. Trellised on the south or west side of a building, over a deck, or even over a roof, their shade will drop the temperature substantially, yet let in sunlight in bare-branched winter.

A tangle of thorny shrubs can thwart plant-munching deer (or discourage trespassers). I've redirected deer with a hedge of osage orange, hawthorn, native roses, Manchurian plum, gooseberries, and a few nonthorny wildlife species mixed in for filler. Once these are established, the deer can nibble on the outside to their heart's content, but they can't get through.

In this necessarily incomplete listing of plant functions, I've omitted purely human-oriented uses such as edible species, flowers for cutting, timber trees, and craft material. My focus is on the ecological role that plants can play, and I'll leave it to the clever gardener to note the many uses for people that these plants also have. A well-designed ecological landscape will benefit all of nature, humans included. When a garden supports pollinators, builds soil, discourages pests, and moderates climatic extremes, its gifts for people will also be marvelously abundant, flowing from the landscape almost as a byproduct. Those spike-rooted artichokes (whose leaves make great mulch) just happen to be edible; that group of wildlife shrubs yields berries for a tangy jelly (and incidentally hides the neighbor's house); the bamboo windscreen, in addition to sheltering a chickadee family, also provides tomato stakes and edible shoots.

By recognizing that plants and the other elements of a garden can serve many purposes, we can create richly connected, productive landscapes that relieve the gardener of many tasks that nature will gladly do. Why make compost when you can have plants that build their own soil? Why weed when a living mulch will smother any unwanted invaders? It may take a little work to design and install a well-working ecological garden, and there may be some trial-and-error before all the pieces fit perfectly, but in the long run, understanding that in nature "nothing does only one thing" will result in lively, dynamic landscapes.

ANNUALS AND PERENNIALS

You may have noticed that nearly every plant I've mentioned in this chapter is a perennial. That's not

TABLE 6-1.

A SAMPLING OF COMMON EDIBLE WEEDS

Common name	Botanical name	Edible part
Burdock	*Arctium lappa*	root
Chickweed	*Stellaria media*	leaf
Chicory	*Cichorium intybus*	leaf, root, flower
Cleavers	*Galium trifidum*	leaf
Dandelions	*Taraxacum officinale*	leaf, root (roasted), flower
Dock, curly	*Rumex persicarioides*	leaf, root
Dock, yellow	*Rumex crispus*	leaf, root
Epazote	*Chenopodium ambrosioides*	leaf
Garlic mustard	*Allicaria officinalis*	leaf, root, seed
Goldenrod	*Solidago* spp.	flower (for tea or spice)
Knotweed	*Polygonum cuspidatum*	shoot
Lamb's quarters	*Chenopodium album*	leaf
Lettuce, wild	*Lactuca scariola*	leaf
Mint	*Mentha* spp.	leaf
Mustard, wild	*Brassica* spp.	leaf, flower, seed
Pigweed	*Amaranthus retroflexus*	leaf, seed
Pineapple weed	*Matricaria matricarioides*	leaf (for tea)
Plantain	*Plantago* spp.	leaf, seed
Purslane	*Portulaca oleracea*	leaf
Queen Anne's lace	*Daucus carota*	leaf, flower, root
Shepherd's purse	*Capsella bursa-pastoris*	leaf, seed, seedpod
Sorrel, sheep	*Rumex acetosella*	leaf
Sow thistle	*Sonchus oleraceus*	leaf
Stinging nettle	*Urtica dioica*	leaf (cooked)
Wintercress	*Barbarea vulgaris*	leaf

a coincidence. Sure, my garden has its share of tomatoes and peppers and beans. But I'd trade them in a minute for perennial varieties if they existed. I don't grow many annual flowers since there seems to be a fine perennial substitute in nearly every case. And many of my salad greens are either perennial such as French sorrel, perennial kale, and Good King Henry, or self-seeding such as arugula, chard, red mustard, and lettuce. In part, the cause is simple laziness: Why slave over seed trays, grow lights, cold frames, and transplanting when I don't have to? But I prefer perennials for ecological reasons, too.

Planting annuals every year means disturbing the soil, which is rough on the soil life and brings weed seeds to the surface where they germinate. Tilling to prepare a seedbed also flushes the soil life with oxygen, and the revved-up little critters burn a lot of organic matter in response. This uses up nutrients that could otherwise be feeding plants. Plus, the bare soil erodes in the rain and wind.

Perennials, on the other hand, eliminate the drawbacks of tilling, plus they hold the soil in place year-round with their roots and prevent erosion with nearly continuous cover. Their roots often go far deeper than those of annuals, so they can tap water and nutrient reserves. This means less irrigation and fertilizing.

That big root system is part of what ecologists mean when they say that perennials have more "standing biomass" than annuals. *Standing biomass* is simply the part of the plant that's permanent, such as branches and large roots, as opposed to seasonal, such as fruit or deciduous leaves. Let me give an example to show why standing biomass is important. I grow perennial kale (*Brassica oleracea* var. *ramosa,* sometimes called tree collards), which resembles annual kale but reaches 5 feet in height and has a thick trunk. When I pick leaves from my perennial kale for a dinner, I'm removing much less of the plant than if I were to snip a head of cabbage for the same meal. The remaining biomass on the perennial kale—the leaves, stem, and roots— helps it recover from harvest much faster than the cabbage (if indeed the cabbage survives my assault). The roots grab nutrients, the remaining foliage captures sunlight, and the plant quickly sprouts new leaves. The plant rebounds speedily from my harvest. I've removed only a tiny percentage of my garden, leaving plenty of biomass behind to keep all those important nutrients cycling and recycling. The biomass *is* the garden's essence; remove it, and everything stops.

Also, by removing only a bit of the biomass, the larger cycles of the garden ecosystem remain more intact than if I hacked down a head of cabbage (to me, harvesting annuals is like small-scale clearcut logging). The perennial kale continues to offer habitat and food for bugs and birds, the roots harbor soil life, the leaves shade the soil, and so forth. That's a lot more than a stub of cut-off cabbage will provide.

As we saw in chapter 2, ample standing biomass is a quality of mature ecosystems such as forests, and in ecological gardening we're trying to create mature ecosystems, rather than immature, pioneer systems such as vacant lots, conventional lawns, and farmland. Mature ecosystems need far fewer inputs since they cycle nutrients internally. Perennials, with their permanent roots and stems, are a feature of mature ecosystems, annuals of immature ones.

Perennials can replace many (though not all) annual plants. Fruit and ornamental trees; bushes for berries, blossoms, and wildlife; shrubs, vines, herbs, edible greens, and flowers all come in perennial varieties. Hundreds of books describe perennial plants. But one niche is tough to fill with perennials: vegetables. Most fruits are perennial, and perennial greens abound, but not many temperate-climate veggies return each year. The only ones commonly used in the United States are asparagus, rhubarb, and artichoke. Egyptian or walking onions, which set shallotlike bulbs above ground on stalks, can be added to the list. A perennial broccoli exists, called Nine-star, that must be picked before it sets seed or it may die. Another that I've already mentioned is bamboo, with edible shoots. Scarlet runner beans are perennial in mild climates (USDA Zone 8 and above). In the tropics, tomatoes and peppers are perennial too, but not in most of the continental United States.

Let's broaden the horizon with some less-familiar perennial vegetables. (I thank Eric Toensmeier of the Perennial Vegetable Seed Company and Ken Fern of Plants for a Future for introducing me to many of these varieties. See Resources for their addresses and other seed sources.)

Perennial Vegetables

Garlic chives (*Allium tuberosum*) have tangy leaves and flowers, and make an attractive ornamental as well.

Perennial groundcherry (*Physalis heterophylla*). A wild relative of the tomato, hardy to at least -20 degrees Fahrenheit, with small golden berries that are tangy and sweet.

Groundplum milkvetch (*Astragalus crassicarpus*) has pods that look like plums, with a pealike flavor and purple flowers. It also fixes nitrogen.

Sea kale (*Crambe maratima*) has broccoli-like heads, and shoots that can be blanched and eaten. The leaves are edible too.

Lovage (*Levisticum officinale*) is an old European vegetable whose stalks, seeds, and leaves are edible, and have a strong celery-like flavor. The huge flowers attract beneficial insects.

Mitsuba or Japanese parsley (*Crytotaenia japonica*). A perennial parsley that prefers moist, shady spots, and can tolerate -20 degrees Fahrenheit or below.

Ramps or wild leeks (*Allium tricoccum*) have tasty, flat, and broad greens and edible bulbs, and incidentally thrive in shade.

Udo (*Aralia cordata*) is a Japanese plant that grows to 9 feet or more. The blanched shoots are eaten, either sliced very thin and soaked in ice water, or boiled in several changes of water. Prefers partial shade.

Watercress (*Nasturtium officinale*) has edible stems and leaves, and grows in streams and flowing water. It can be invasive.

Chinese water lotus (*Nelumbo nucifera*) has edible roots, young leaves, and seeds that taste like chestnuts. An aquatic, it's hardy to Zone 6 if planted in deep soil and water.

WEEDS AND OTHER WILD FOOD

Another low-maintenance source of food lurks at the garden's margins. These are the weeds, a highly subjective category of maligned plants that even the United States Department of Agriculture admits are simply "plants that interfere with human activities." But one person's weed is another's treasured specimen. A surprising number of so-called weeds have edible greens, including dandelion, chicory, pigweed, lamb's quarters, chickweed, sheep sorrel, and cleavers. In Ashland, Oregon, permaculturist Tom Ward has cultivated an intimate relationship with his weeds. He has encouraged edible weeds in his lawn, and prepares diverse and highly nutritious salads from his front yard. "Domesticated greens like lettuce can't compare with wild greens," Tom says. "When we bred out those tangy or slightly bitter flavors, we bred out the nutrition. There's probably more nutrition along the edges of most gardens—in the weeds—than in the crops. So mothers should be telling their children not, 'Eat your greens,' but, 'Eat your weeds.'"

Weeds are supremely multifunctional plants. They are the pioneers, covering, protecting, and fertilizing bare soil, preparing it for others. Many weeds are superb nutrient accumulators—in fact, that is often their primary role, pulling widely scattered nutrients from deep in the earth and concentrating them in the surface soil. That also explains why they are so nutritious: They accumulate minerals in their tissues. Weeds can also tell the gardener about soil conditions. Some weeds, such as curly dock and horsetail, grow in ground too moist for most fruit trees. Eastern bracken and silvery cinquefoil point to soils that are acid, while white campion and salad burnet reveal alkaline soil.

In addition to these uses, weeds furnish critical food and habitat at various times of the year for songbirds, gamebirds, and other wildlife. Insects that feed on abundant spring weeds afford crucial nourishment for hungry nesting birds, while weed seeds help carry many animals through lean winters.

Weeds have been our partners at least since the dawn of farming. Many weeds are semidomesticated, once-major food plants used by early humans, tried but found wanting as full-scale agricultural crops. Perhaps they had too much genetic variability or didn't set seed regularly. Thus, they fell by the wayside—quite literally—yet were so well adapted to our landscapes that they have followed us ever since. Other weeds coevolved with humans because they thrive in the disturbed or cultivated soil at our settlements. Wanted or not, they have lurked at the edges of our culture since culture began.

Many of the weeds in North America are imports, brought with food, animals, ship's ballast, or via less obvious avenues. Plantain was named white-man's foot by Native Americans because its tiny seeds lodged in the wooden soles of early colonials' boots. As the colonists blundered about the unfamiliar woods, plantain seeds dropped and sprouted, revealing where the Europeans had walked. Plantain is often cursed as a noxious weed, yet like so many others, it offers both food and medicine to those who understand it.

Acknowledging the usefulness of weeds can eliminate some of the warlike sentiments that we often bring into the garden. I want my garden to be a place of relaxation and sustenance for me and others, but if I grow furious at every sprout of chickweed or sheep sorrel, the garden becomes merely one more trigger for high blood pressure. Now I see weeds as my allies, protecting soil that I've inadvertently left naked, quietly boosting fertility until I'm ready to plant. And most of them are a source of food, which further raises them in my esteem. Not incidentally, eating them becomes a way of controlling them too.

Native plants offer another source of low-maintenance food, though without special training not many of us will make a meal from natives. Unless you're a serious survivalist, you probably won't do more than snack on the occasional huckleberry, currant, or wild strawberry. Food is one of the least compelling reasons to include native plants in the garden; their value for wildlife habitat and biodiversity preservation is far greater. Natives play an important role in the ecological garden, but share the landscape with many useful non-native plants.

Perennial Herbs

To expand the list of edible perennials yet further, we can include several herbs, especially those that can be used in quantity. Some examples are **chives, fennel, lemongrass,** and **garden cress.** Many other herbs are perennial, such as oregano, sage, marjoram, and other culinary herbs, but as they are never eaten in substantial amounts, it might be stretching things to include them.

Perennial Greens

Then there are a number of perennial greens. These include **French sorrel** *(Rumex scutatus),* **Good King Henry** *(Chenopodium bonus-henricus),* **dandelion greens** *(Taraxacum officinale),* **perennial kale** *(Brassica oleracea ramosa),* and **Turkish rocket** *(Bunias orientalis).*

Roots and Tubers

We can sneak a few roots and tubers into this list. I consider them marginal perennial foods, because you must disturb the soil to harvest them, and if you harvest the entire root, it doesn't matter if it's a perennial—the plant is gone. But by leaving a section of the root, or allowing the plant to grow large enough to send out smaller roots, some species can be perennialized. They include **Jerusalem artichoke, salsify** or **oyster root, Chinese artichoke, horseradish, shallots, garlic, cinnamon vine** or **Chinese yam, American groundnut, burdock,** and **chicory.**

Even plain old **potatoes** left in the ground will grow and form new tubers, but they seem to become woody and small if left in for more than a year or two.

A group of ancient Peruvian tubers is now becoming popular, so let's add them to the list. These include:

Mashua *(Tropaeolum tuberosum)* is a vining nasturtium with a small, peppery tuber that becomes deliciously sweet upon baking.

Oca *(Oxalis tuberosa)* grows 3-inch tubers with a lemony flavor.

Yacon *(Polymnia edulis)* is a frost-tender plant with large, crisp, and juicy tubers.

Perennialized and Reseeding Annuals

Some annual plants can be "perennialized." For example, if **leeks** are allowed to set flowers, many small bulblets will form at the base. If you pull only the main stem and bulb, the bulblets can grow the following season.

We can stretch the list still further by including plants that reseed naturally. Good choices here are **arugula, chard, lettuce** (though eventually lettuce reverts to its more bitter ancestor), **red mustard, corn salad** *(Valerianella locusta),* and **lamb's quarters.** Many common vegetables, such as tomatoes, brassicas, and squash, will self-seed, but they too-easily hybridize or revert to wild types, giving flavorless or unpredictable varieties.

You can see that the perennial food garden can contain a wide variety of crops. Supplement these with the better-known perennial fruits, berries, and herbs, and you can have a very low maintenance, ecologically sound way of producing food.

MICROCLIMATES FOR THE GARDEN

Whether perennial or annual, a plant will thrive only under the right growth conditions. A drought-loving rosemary bush that will drown too close to a downspout will perk up in a hot, sunny corner. But a sweet woodruff that is withering in the sunny site will sigh in relief when shaded by some nurturing shrub. Each plant requires a certain range of soil type, acidity, temperature, light, moisture, and other factors. I've described how to improve soil and moisture conditions. Now let's see how to change the climate in your yards—the microclimate—to support the plants we want. The right microclimate is important to a plant's survival.

In turn, the plants we choose will change the

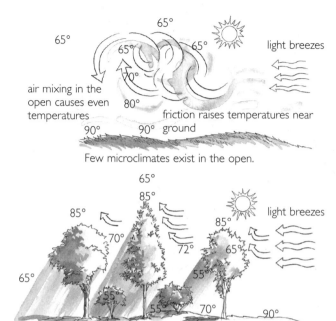

65°

65°   65°

65°   65°   light breezes

air mixing in the   70°
open causes even
temperatures   80°
                friction raises temperatures near
90°   90° ground

Few microclimates exist in the open.

65°

85°

85°

70°   85°

72°   65°

65°

55°

55°   70°   90°

Many microclimates form when trees block air mixing, reduce radiative heat loss, and cast shade.

environment around them. Some species—pioneers in particular—bring on their own destruction, changing soil pH and fertility until other species, better adapted to the new conditions, can easily crowd them out. Other plants wage environmental war to squelch competition by secreting mild toxins or casting such dense shade that nothing else can survive. Vegetation can also make a homesite more or less hospitable for the people who live there. My neighbors cut down all the trees south of their house to improve their view, only to find that summer temperatures soared 10 degrees hotter as the sun blistered the now-exposed earth. A scalding breeze now scorches them where cool shade once refreshed.

In contrast, Seattleite Kevin Burkhart trained a hardy kiwi vine onto wires over the southern half of his roof, and the seasonal shade has significantly lowered the summer temperature of his home. Yet after leaf fall, the bare vines don't block Seattle's scanty winter light. An added plus—stacking functions again—is the huge harvest of delicious fruit that Kevin enjoys in autumn.

We can think of the give-and-take between plants and their environment as *microclimate gardening*. With a little background, and of course, some observation, we can identify the right microclimates for our greenery, and understand how nearby plants will affect our environment in turn.

The big force that creates most microclimates is heat transfer. I won't get too technical here; heat transfer is simply the movement of energy from one place to another. Heat transfer occurs when the sun sends radiant energy to the earth, when warm ground radiates heat to the sky, or when wind mixes hot air with cold.

That warm spot on the south side of your house, where snow melts soonest, exists because of heat transfer, and is a good lesson in microclimate. If your house weren't there, the sun would still heat the ground, but most of the resulting warmth would simply radiate back to the open sky. The rest would be swept away by the wind.

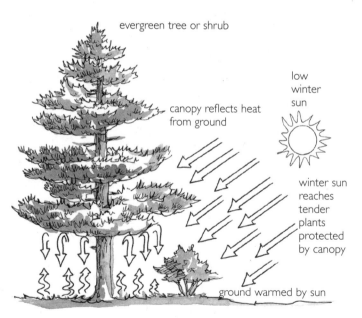

evergreen tree or shrub

low winter sun

canopy reflects heat from ground

winter sun reaches tender plants protected by canopy

ground warmed by sun

Using microclimates to protect tender plants. When sensitive plants are placed near the edge of an evergreen tree canopy, the rays of the low winter sun can warm them, and the tree canopy holds in the ground's heat. This can allow plants too tender for the climate (by one or two USDA hardiness zones) to be safely grown.

When the south wall of your house enters the scene, the picture changes dramatically. Sun heats the ground just as in the open, but now the sunlight also warms the south-facing wall. The wall's warmth then bounces onto the ground, warming the earth further. That's heat transfer. Also, the heat radiating from the ground—which in the open would disappear skyward—is partially blocked by the wall, and can't escape. A vertical wall blocks up to two-thirds of heat loss from a nearby "radiant body"—the ground in this case. (Let's not go into the math—microclimatology is called "the mathematician's paradise" because of the dense formulae that choke most books on the subject.)

The wall also alters heat transfer in a third way: It blocks air movement, preventing cool air from mixing with the warm air against the wall. A chilly wind over that hot spot would conduct heat from the ground. By stopping these gusts, the wall reduces the windchill factor (which is simply the rate that a breeze sucks heat away from a "radiant body," most commonly your shivering torso).

The mixing of air is a key element in creating microclimates. When wind sweeps across a bare plain, the air at head height or above mixes well. Temperatures from that height to a few hundred feet above are fairly even due to good air mixing. At the ground, however, friction slows the air and prevents good mixing. On a sunny day, the temperature an inch from the ground can be 20 degrees hotter than at eye level. A steep vertical temperature gradient forms: uneven air mixing. If we add some trees, walls, and houses to this bare plain, friction of the wind against these obstacles causes turbulence. Eddies of stillness form; pockets of hot air gather. Uneven air mixing now occurs horizontally as well as vertically. Microclimates are born.

We can use this very basic overview to find—and create—useful microclimates in the yard. Trees, shrubs, and other vegetation alter the way heat transfer and air mixing occur. A leafy canopy, even that of a good-sized herb, will block sunlight during the day, slowing the warming of the ground beneath it, At night, that canopy prevents the escape of heat from the earth to the sky, so temperatures below any plant won't fluctuate as much as in open ground. Also, the air below the greenery is more humid, and moist air uses more energy to heat than dry air. This further reduces temperature swings.

The benefits of a canopy become even more apparent in winter, when the sloping rays of the horizon-skimming sun reach under the leaves of, say, an evergreen shrub to warm the soil, but at night, the leaves block heat loss. Tender perennials can shelter there. Overhanging eaves of a house can have a similar effect, especially on the south and west side, creating another spot for less-hardy or warmth-loving plants. This all means that cold-sensitive plants can survive under canopies and eaves in climates where, in the open, they would be frozen out. Protection like this can often let the gardener use plants suited to one USDA zone farther south.

Just as capturing warm air is important, eliminating cold air is critical too. Cold air drains downhill, so it's important not to block its escape routes. I know of some gardeners who planted a fine stand of bamboo just downslope of their garden, only to find that it stopped cold air drainage, turning their garden into a chilly frost pocket. They moved the bamboo, and the garden warmed considerably. Thus, slope can affect microclimate, too. Since cold air sinks, orchardists know that fruit trees on high ground can survive frosts that blacken the blossoms of trees just a few feet lower. This knowledge can be used in reverse: In regions with late frosts, gardeners often set fruit trees in the coldest part of their yard (for example, in a low spot, or on the northeast side of the house) so the trees will stay chilly. That way they won't bud out until late in spring, after the final frosts.

> **We can think of the give-and-take between plants and their environment as *microclimate gardening*.**
>
>

We can use more than just theory to find microclimates; we can observe them. A perfect time to locate warm and cool spots is just after a light frost. Watch which places lose the hoary rime of ice the soonest. These may be ideal sites for starting early flowers or cool-weather vegetables. The plants themselves can tell you too. I have three Lattarula fig trees, but one, in a little south-facing bowl against a hedge, holds its leaves long after the other two are bare, and leafs out earlier. That tells me it's in a great spot for other cold-sensitive or late-fruiting plants.

If you have pets, they'll let you know where the hot spots are. North Carolinian Jeff Ashton has written that since his dog, Dakota, has gotten a bit elderly, he's become picky about where he naps. Using the same instinct that cats employ to identify favorable microclimates on top of the fridge or water heater, Dakota has helped Jeff locate several warm sites in his yard. Jeff then uses these hot spots for specialized plantings (we hope Dakota is agreeable to being relocated).

Insects are savvy microclimate users. Bees often sleep inside daffodil blossoms because on a sunny morning the flower's interior can be 15 degrees Fahrenheit warmer than outside (due mainly to reduced air mixing). The bees heat up to flying temperature bright and early, and are out pollinating much sooner than their outside-sleeping companions.

Color creates microclimates too. A dark wall absorbs heat; a light one reflects light. Researchers found that peaches grown against a dark wall grew faster, but didn't ripen fruit any earlier than in the open. However, when peaches and grapes were grown against a light-colored wall, the fruit set was heavier and earlier. The reflected light had more of an effect on fruiting than the heat.

The color of the soil also affects microclimate. Light-colored soils heat up slower than dark ones. Maori farmers darken their soil with a sprinkling of charcoal to help it heat up in spring. Tibetans toss dark rocks on snow-covered fields to speed the thaw.

Soil density matters as well. A dense clay warms far slower than a fluffy, sandy soil. And mulch, with its many insulating air pockets, can keep soil from freezing, but greatly retards the warming of soil in spring. Pull mulch aside when spring temperatures rise to help speed soil heating.

By understanding microclimates, we can find better homes for our plants, but we can also use our plantings to make our own homes more comfortable. Deciduous trees on the south side will cool a house and yard dramatically in summer, yet let in light in winter. On the windward side of a house (in this country, usually the west), evergreens can block winter winds. Here in Oregon, winter storms come from the southwest, so conifers should be located there. Summer breezes here come from the north, so I plant trees and high shrubs only sparsely in that direction.

I've mentioned the benefits of planting deciduous vines on arbors, trellises, even roofs and walls. Summer temperatures can be lowered substantially this way. Shading a yard works the same way, especially with a high canopy of trees. The sun doesn't penetrate, but breezes can still waft through the open space beneath the treetops. Now that the trees and shrubs around our house are beginning to mature and cast ample shade, not only do we stay cooler on those withering August afternoons, but I don't need to water these and the other plants they shelter nearly as often.

Anywhere that slope or shape or density or color alters the way heat enters or leaves, anywhere friction or other forces change the mixing of air, this is where microclimates form. Microclimate gardening can extend the growing season by weeks, reduce heating and cooling bills substantially, and make living in any site far more pleasant.

NURSES, SCAFFOLDS, AND CHAPERONES

Now that I've shown how plants can be used to alter microclimates, and introduced the concept of nutrient-accumulating species, I'd like to combine the two notions. Melding these two concepts yields

TABLE 6-2.

NURSE PLANTS

All of these plants are fast growing and can take harsh conditions, though they should be watered and fertilized while getting established. Other plants can be planted beneath and near them to benefit from their protection, leaf litter, and nutrient accumulation.

Common name	Botanical name	Comments
Acacia	*Acacia* spp.	Nonhardy N-fixing trees
Alder	*Alnus* spp.	N-fixing trees and shrubs
Autumn olive, Russian olive, goumi	*Elaeagnus* spp.	N-fixing shrub, edible berries
Black locust	*Robinia pseudoacacia*	N-fixing tree
Bladder senna	*Colutea arborescens*	N-fixing shrub
Bush clover	*Lespedeza thunbergii*	N-fixing shrub
Casuarina	*Casuarina* spp.	Nonhardy N-fixing tree
Crimson-spot rock rose	*Cistus ladanifer*	Fast-growing shrub
Elderberry	*Sambucus nigra*	Shrub with edible berries
Flowering quince	*Chaenomeles* spp.	Small deciduous ornamental tree
Golden-chain tree	*Laburnum anagyroides*	N-fixing small tree
Hackberry	*Celtis occidentalis*	Drought-tolerant shrub
Hebe	*Hebe salicifolia*	Fast-growing shrub
Hybrid broom	*Cytisus* x *spachianus*	N-fixer. Hybrids are not invasive, unlike nonhybrids
Mesquite	*Prosopis* spp.	N-fixing, droughttolerant tree
Mulberry	*Morus* spp.	Pioneer tree, but can tolerate shade
Sea buckthorn	*Hippophae rhamnoides*	N-fixing shrub, edible fruit
Siberian pea shrub	*Caragana arborescens*	N-fixing shrub
Silk tree, mimosa	*Albizia julibrissin*	N-fixing tree
Spanish broom	*Spartium junceum*	N-fixing shrub
Tree mallow	*Lavatera* spp.	Small shrub to medium tree
Tree of heaven	*Ailanthus altissima*	Tolerates pollution, invasive
Wild lilac, buckbrush	*Ceanothus* spp.	N-fixing shrub
Willow	*Salix* spp.	Small tree or shrub for moist areas

a powerful gardening technique: using plants to modify both soil and microclimate to spur the growth of other flora. Species that do this are called nurse, chaperone, and scaffold plants.

In many ways, creating an ecological garden is a restoration project. The soil in most yards is poor, important species are missing, and healthy cycles are broken. Thus, people who restore damaged landscapes for a living—restoration biologists—have some things to teach us.

One trick the restorationists have learned from nature is the use of *nurse plants*. These are species that create shelter and other favorable conditions in which more delicate plants that would otherwise never survive can get a start. In Roxanne Swentzell's

New Mexico garden, she and permaculture designer Joel Glanzberg, who helped create the site, planted Siberian pea shrubs and other nitrogen fixers along a swale to provide shade and nutrients for less-hardy plants. This nurse-plant strategy helped overcome some inhospitable conditions.

In Roxanne's yard, Joel showed me a black walnut tree about eight years old that towered over a tired-looking Russian olive. The Russian olive, though it had grown 10 feet tall, was now clearly struggling. They had planted it to shield the young walnut from the withering sun, as well as to pump nutritious nitrogen into the soil, boost organic matter and soil life, and mulch the eroded ground with leaf litter. Now in deep shade and possibly suffering from years of the walnut's toxic juglone secretions, the Russian olive's work was done. Its walnut protégé had thrived under the Russian olive's care, then overtopped it and, a little sadly, driven it into decline.

This is often the fate of nurse plants, to be spurned by the youngsters they coddled into maturity. Sometimes it's possible to save a desirable nurse plant by pruning back its competitors, but often the best nurse plants are short-lived pioneers that rarely survive more than a decade or two, so their decline, though lamentable, is natural.

Many nitrogen fixers make great nurse plants, since their symbiotic microbes forcefeed them nutrients, even in poor soils, so they grow quickly (think of the astounding growth of wisteria and alder, both nitrogen fixers). Other candidates are the fast-growing species found in young shrub communities. See table 6-2 for a list of potential nurse species.

Nurse plants can be used in several ways. In the example above, Joel and Roxanne employed nitrogen-fixing shrubs as what I call *chaperone plants*. These are species that protect seedlings from harm until the juveniles are ready for life on their own. Chaperone plants are common in nature. Piñon pines under the protection of oak tree canopies survive far better than pines in the open. And mesquite, a nitrogen fixer, chaperones seedling saguaro cacti by sheltering them until the saguaros are tough enough to take the full desert sun. As with many chaperone species, mesquite's benefits are manyfold. In addition to providing fertility and shade, mesquites also aid saguaro reproduction, Mesquites are the favorite nest-trees for white-winged doves, who feed saguaro fruit to their young. The nestlings regurgitate the seeds, which then sprout in the shaded, rich litter beneath the mesquites.

Understandably, chaperone plants for shade are more needed in hot-sun climates toward the south. But many plants, especially shrubs and small trees for the understory layers of the garden, will profit from sun protection during their early years.

Woodland plants evolved in the dappled sunlight beneath the forest canopy, and can be fried by even the mild sun of a Maine summer. Plus, chaperones bestow more than just shade. Their roots loosen the soil, build humus, and secrete sugary juices for beneficial microbes; the leaf litter creates mulch and keeps soil moist; and the leafy canopy slows evaporation and forms a microclimate that damps temperature swings and holds humidity.

This is why nurse plants are used by many gardeners to restore battered landscapes and build biodiversity. On Orcas Island, the Bullock brothers swear by them. As I mentioned in chapter 4, the brothers poke a nitrogen-fixing shrub or small tree alongside the fruit and nut trees they plant, sometimes even in the same hole. When the protected plant is mature, or if the chaperone begins to compete with it, they slash the chaperone back for mulch. They aver that this "two plants in every hole" system speeds growth immensely, and not just from sun protection.

A second use for nurse plants is as *scaffolds*. Here, the helpers' physical presence lets young or otherwise-vulnerable plants get established. Then, like the temporary staging that workers use for erecting buildings, the scaffold plants can be removed or used for a different job. For example, ornithologist David Wingate relied on scaffold plants when he attempted to create habitat on a denuded island for an endangered Bermudan bird, the cahow. In the 1960s, Wingate tried to restore the native cedar forest, destroyed by overgrazing and a subsequent blight, that was once the cahow's home. But fierce ocean winds scoured down the seedling trees. So he turned to non-native scaffold plants, tamarisk and the fast-growing nitrogen-fixer casuarina, to create a windbreak, and replanted cedars in their shelter. The cedar forest quickly grew, and was tough enough to withstand Hurricane Emily in 1987. Wingate has since guided the vegetation closer to its native composition by girdling many of the scaffold plants (removing a ring of bark from around the trunk). This kills them but leaves them standing, reducing the ecological stress on the cedars that wholesale removal of the scaffolds might cause.

Other uses of scaffold plants are to hold soil in place on eroding hills and gullies, to stabilize and catch windblown soil, and to create thorny or dense fencing that protects young plants from deer and other animals. Thus, scaffold plants can be placed thickly in these trouble spots. Once the scaffold plants' mission is accomplished and other, more permanent vegetation is established, the scaffolds can be removed.

Nurse plants can also create wildlife habitat and attract new species. For example, the wild chile, or chiltepine, increasingly endangered by development, requires nurse plants to protect it from strong sun. Scientists noticed that the wild chiles grew mainly under hackberry bushes, even though many other shrubs provided similar shelter. In part, this was because hackberries create denser shade than most other shrubs. But the big factor was the hackberry's superior wildlife habitat. Several species of birds that are insensitive to the fiery-hot taste of chiltepine fruit prefer hackberry bushes for perching and nesting. The denser shade and tasty fruit makes hackberries a favored bird hangout. The birds thus dispersed most of the seeds of the chiltepines they'd eaten under hackberries.

Hackberries and other wildlife plants can serve many functions. They can protect tender or rare plants, attract animals, and put out the welcome mat for animal-imported species such as the chiltepine. Here we get a sense for the interconnectedness of natural communities and how they are assembled. A Johnny Appleseed–like broadcasting of chiltepine seed probably won't save this rare species. It is connected to a set of chile-insensitive birds, and both are tied to the hackberry. So creating supportive plant communities via nurse plants and other network-building techniques will furnish places for many species to thrive. This increases the odds that new species will survive, whether they're chosen by the gardener or imported via squirrel fur and bird poop.

SUMMARY: MIXING THE MANY FUNCTIONS OF PLANTS

Ecological gardening moves away from the "one role for each plant" philosophy. Plants are intimately connected to the sun, soil, water, and air, to each other, to insects and other animals, and to people. Also, they transform all that they are tied to. When we understand the multiple roles that plants can play, we can link together their many functions in intelligent ways. Then we can design gardens full of resilient, interconnected networks of life.

Through creative choice of plants, a simple hedge, for example, becomes not merely a screen but a deer-blocking, wind-reducing, wildlife- and people-feeding, mulch-producing, insect-attracting source of medicinal plants and craft materials. Curve it around the north side of a garden, and it becomes a sun-trap. And that's just getting started; a clever designer could probably come up with ten more roles for that hedge.

In thinking of plants not simply as passive objects but as active, dynamic performers, we can begin to see some of their many roles. In this chapter, I've pointed out that plants can play a wide range of ecological parts, as mulch makers, nutrient accumulators, nitrogen fixers, insect attractors, pest repellents, fortress plants, spike roots, wildlife nurturers, and shelterbelters. Any functioning ecosystem—or ecological garden—almost certainly needs plants that play each of these roles. A few species that fill these functions have been described in this chapter, and more are listed in the appendix.

How do we combine all these performers? The final section of this book, "Assembling the Ecological Garden," will show how. But for now, we need to look at one more important piece of the ecological garden.

Chapter 7

Bringing in the Bees, Birds, and Other Helpful Animals

MY WIFE, CAROLYN, loves birds. To attract them, she hung a feeder from a tree in our front yard, and we both enjoyed the chickadees, goldfinches, grosbeaks, and others that flocked to this seed-stuffed larder. As the birds scrambled to eat, they flung seed to the ground in pattering cascades. The fallen seed first drew ground-feeding towhees, and then a covey of California quail. These larger birds would scratch and claw in their search for seed, and I noticed that the quail roto-tilled the ground thoroughly, leaving behind speckles of guano, a phosphorus-rich fertilizer.

Then, for various reasons, we moved the feeder. The quail-worked ground, now birdless, quickly grew lush and green with grass and wildflowers. Those quail and other ground-scratchers had acted as birdseed-powered tractors, scratching out all the vegetation, loosening the soil, and adding a little bonus of fertilizer. The same thing is happening in the feeder's new spot, but this time I have plans to plant some herbs and shrubs after the birds have worked their magic.

It's comforting to know that while I sit in my lounge chair and sip tea, the birds are tilling and fertilizing a new garden bed for us. We haven't enslaved the quail, just taken advantage of their byproducts. We've just put the feeder in the right place. In ecological gardening at its best, that's all the work that's necessary: putting things in the right relationship. Nature will do the rest.

Those busy birds illustrate how animals can be one of the gardener's most powerful allies. In the wrong place, an animal can wreak havoc, but when the garden's elements are in the right relationships, animals can eliminate a lot of labor for the gardener. Animals include not just the feathered and the four-legged varieties, but insects, spiders, and the zillion-legged soil critters too. They all can help us.

My simple "quail tractor" barely scratches the surface of what animals can do for the garden. Animals don't just till and fertilize: They pollinate, disperse, and process seed, prune vegetation, eat pests, dispose of waste, circulate nutrients, and provide food for us if we wish. By attracting birds, small animals, and insects to our yards, we not only increase biodiversity, but make our gardens more balanced, disease-free, and productive as well.

From an ecological viewpoint, animals are a critical part of the home ecosystem: the *consumers*. Remember that the cycle of energy and matter in an ecosystem whirls from producers to consumers to decomposers, over and over. Without all three roles, the cycle is broken and the ecosystem won't work. The principle producers are plants, who turn sunlight into leafy and woody tissue. The decomposers, as we have seen, live mostly in the soil, working their alchemy to transform organic matter for reuse. The consumers are primarily animal: humans and other mammals, insects, birds, and all the rest. Animals are opportunists, living off the bounty produced by plants. But animals aren't mere parasites; we have our place. Animals, though a tiny portion of the total biomass of nature, are the "regulators" of an ecosystem. Whether they are loggers removing whole forests, browsing deer or cattle eliminating a tasty species, or gypsy moths defoliating an oak grove, animals channel and control huge flows of matter and energy through ecosystems.

From an ecological viewpoint, animals are a critical part of the home ecosystem: the *consumers*.

Animals control the growth rates of many other species, by pollinating, dispersing seeds, grazing, hunting, and choosing where to drop manure. Add to this their trampling, burrowing, scratching, and browsing, not to mention the large-scale effects of human endeavors, and we see that animals have altered the face of the planet.

Without animals, a garden can't function. We need them, in the right place and numbers. In this chapter, we'll look at the ways that animals of many types can work in the garden. First we'll examine the role of insects, and see how to attract and nurture beneficial ones. Then we'll do the same with birds and other wildlife. Last, we'll see how small domestic animals, such as ducks, rabbits, and chickens, can play a valuable part in the garden, even in the city.

MORE GOOD BUGS THAN BAD

Not long ago, I visited Occidental Arts and Ecology Center, an environmental learning institute north of San Francisco renowned for its marvelously productive organic gardens. Ecologist Brock Dolman was leading a tour, and one of the participants asked Brock how he dealt with a noxious insect that ravaged local crops. "I'm not a good one to ask about insect pests," Brock answered. "These gardens are in such good ecological balance that no single pest ever does much harm. All the pests here have natural enemies that keep them in check. So we've never had to become experts on specific bug problems."

This perspective is a far cry from that of most conventional agriculturists. The main emphasis of most agricultural extension agents, Master Gardener clinics, and numerous textbooks—not to mention several multibillion dollar industries—is on pests. A gardener who confesses ignorance about problem insects must be living in another, more benign universe.

Insects aren't high on most gardener's lists of favorite things. It's too easy to notice the bug-ravaged leaves of broccoli and ignore the benefits of pollination and the role of pest-killing predator insects. Yet most insects are either helpful or neutral. Only a minority harm plants. Without insects, there would be very little for us to eat, no compost or topsoil, few birds, fewer mammals—they're an essential, major thread in the web of life. Biologist E. O. Wilson calls them "the little things that run the world." Yet most gardeners hate them: On a visit to a hardware store I overheard a man ask, "What can I get to kill all the bugs in my yard?" I nearly began shrieking.

There's no doubt that insects damage food plants and ornamentals. Fourteen percent of all crops are lost to insects and disease, according to the USDA. However, there's more to that number than meets the eye, as fifty years ago, crop loss was only 7 percent. Three factors have caused this alarming trend. The first is loss of soil fertility. Healthy plants need healthy soil, and we've lost or impoverished much of ours. The other two causes fit with this chapter's theme, because they are responsible for the death of the beneficial insects that once kept pests in check. These are fencerow-to-fencerow "clean" cultivation, and heavy and ill-timed pesticide use.

Up until a few decades ago, farmers divided their fields with many-specied hedgerows, and left wild vegetation along creeks and back pastures. The diversity of plants in these untamed places gave a home to a wide variety of insects, who sheltered among the leaves and supped from the nectar and pollen of the many blossoms. Spiders and birds also thrived in these thickets. Whenever pests swarmed into the adjacent fields, predators were waiting in the wings to gobble up this new food source. With all of nature standing ready in hedgerows and fallow fields to right any imbalance, pest problems rarely got out of hand.

Then, the advent of herbicides and high-powered tractors, and the incentive to squeeze every dollar from farmland destroyed the good bugs' habitat. The broad, wildlife-filled hedgerows were replaced with wire fence or removed to make larger, tractor-tilled fields. Herbicides eliminated the wild places, which were seen as unproductive and sources of weed seed, pests, and disease.

The second blow of the one-two punch that knocked out beneficial insects was widespread insecticide use. The ecology of pests and their predators tells us how this contributed. Insects that feed on plants reproduce at staggering rates, quickly surging to astronomical numbers. But the insects that prey on these pests reproduce more slowly and are far fewer in number. This is because a predators' food supply is less abundant (there are more leaves to eat than bugs), and it takes more energy to hunt than it does to mill around and graze. Less energy is available for predator breeding than for that of their prey. Just as a predator such as an owl is fairly uncommon and has only a few offspring per year, a predaceous lady beetle doesn't reproduce as quickly or prolifically as its prey. Predators always occur in much smaller numbers than their prey. This makes them vulnerable to extinction when conditions are bad.

Also, a time lag falls between the breeding of prey and of their predators. An outbreak of aphids can reach pestilential proportions in a week or two (frighteningly, aphids can give birth to already-pregnant young). Although lady beetles—you may know them as ladybugs or ladybird beetles—will reach the scene quickly and decimate the aphid population, if there isn't enough habitat for lady beetles to shelter and breed, there won't be enough of them to quell the outbreak. And now the hedgerows and wild places where they lived are gone.

A rich food-source such as aphids will trigger the lady beetles to breed, but lady beetles need time to lay and hatch eggs. The young larva, which look like alligators, are predators just like mom, but they take a few days to get going. Hence the time lag before their numbers can build. Meanwhile, the aphids are multiplying to astounding numbers.

Unfortunately, just about the time the lady beetles reach the numbers necessary to control the aphids, the farmer or gardener notices the outbreak and sprays insecticide. This kills most of the aphids and the lady beetles. The fast-breeding aphids recover within a few weeks, but the lady beetles, who have no food until the aphids are in good supply, remain at critically low numbers. Just when the lady beetles, feeding on the small population of aphids, begin to breed again, the gardener sees that a few aphids are still out there. Fearing another plague, he sprays again, really hammering the struggling lady beetles. A few rounds of this cycle and the lady beetles are all dead, while some aphids are bound to survive. Now the pests are predator-free and can multiply unchecked, and the farmer—or gardener—is on an expensive and toxic insecticide treadmill. He or she has eliminated nature's safeguards, and must spray and spray, or take the time—and the short-term crop loss—to restore the natural balance.

How can we create gardens that have this balance and that provide what beneficial insects need? First, we need to get to know these helpful insects a little. We can distinguish four types of beneficial

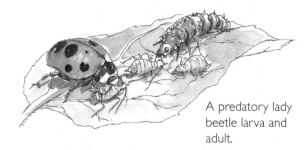

A predatory lady beetle larva and adult.

insects: predators, parasitic insects (or parasitoids), pollinators, and weed feeders. Let's look at each in turn.

Predatory Insects

Predators come from several different groups, or orders, of insects: beetles, true bugs, flies, wasps and their relatives, and a few smaller orders. They eat their prey either by chewing them with fierce mandibles, or piercing them with tubelike mouth parts and sucking out the body fluids (it doesn't sound pretty, but just wait till you hear how parasitoids use their prey). Some are specialists, preying on only one or a few species, but many eat anything that comes their way, whether helpful or harmful. In many cases, both the adult and immature insect are predators. Lady beetles are a prime example: The voracious young have huge, powerful jaws on a crocodile-like body. These larvae look nothing like the cute spotted adults heralded in nursery rhyme.

Spiders, though they are arachnids and not insects, are superb predators, so allow me to add them here. Spiders shelter in dried grass and mulch, which provide the high humidity and refuge from temperature changes that they prefer. A cleanly cultivated garden is poor habitat for them: Researchers found thirty times more spiders in mulched gardens than in unmulched ones, and far less insect damage to plants.

Parasitic Insects

Parasitic insects, called *parasitoids,* are small wasps and flies that lay their eggs inside other insects or insect eggs. This is one of nature's more gruesome stories, a sample of which I'll share here. One species of the group of parasitic wasps called braconids hunts down cabbageworm caterpillars. On finding its prey, the wasp thrusts its sharp ovipositor, or egg-laying tube, into the caterpillar and pumps twenty to sixty eggs into the hapless creature. The cabbageworm is perfectly alive when this happens. In two or three weeks, the wasp eggs hatch inside the cabbageworm and begin to feed. Death is slow for the cabbageworm, as the wasp larvae avoid eating vital organs until they are almost ready to emerge. Finally, the growing larvae chew their way out through the caterpillar's flesh, killing the miserable host and leaving an empty, wrinkled husk behind.

I don't doubt that the makers of the film *Alien* got their inspiration from parasitic wasps. Other parasitic wasps lay their eggs on leaves, where caterpillars will eat them. Once consumed, the eggs hatch inside the caterpillar and the whole ghoulish story begins again.

Parasitoids are often specialists, preying on only one or a few species of pest, so they rarely harm helpful insects. Most adult parasitoids are not carnivorous, and feed mainly on pollen and nectar (perhaps they got flesh-eating out of their system at a young age). Flowers and wild vegetation near or in the garden are critical for their survival.

Many parasitic wasps are barely visible to the eye, and most are stingless, so those averse to bees and wasps have nothing to fear from these helpful insects.

A parasitic braconid wasp injecting eggs into a cabbageworm larva.

Pollinators

The link between plants and animals is dusted with pollen. Without insects to begin fruit and seed growth by fertilizing flowers with pollen, humans would starve. Vegetable gardens and orchards would be bare except for corn, grapes, and a handful of other wind-pollinated plants. Flower beds wouldn't exist.

The story of coevolution between plants and insects is a long one, stretching back tens of millions of years to the end of the dinosaur age. Back then, insects learned that protein-rich pollen was excellent food, and flowering plants found that pollen-covered insects were more effective than the wind in delivering their male DNA to a female ovary. A partnership began. Plants developed easily reachable pollen organs, bright flowers as signals to bugs, and nectar sacs brimming with sweet sugars to further reward the industrious pollinators. In turn, insects grew pouches to hold freightloads of pollen, extendable mouth parts to delve deep into blossoms, and in some cases, the ability to buzz loudly at just the right frequency to send pollen boiling out of the blooms.

The best-known pollinator is the European honeybee. Imported with many of America's food plants, these honeybees are generalists, pollinating almost anything they can reach. But honeybees, bred like many other domestic animals for docility and high yield, aren't as tough as wild bees. Recently they've fallen prey to parasitic mites and diseases that have killed up to 80 percent of their colonies. This means that native and other pollinators are more important than ever.

Fortunately, native bees and wasps and their imported kin are abundant. The Maya and other Native Americans cultivated local bees both for pollination and for their honey, often keeping several species of them in their dooryard gardens. Remember too, that predator and parasitic insects, like the rest of nature, play multiple roles. They can be pollinators as well. Many insects imported to battle pests have naturalized and now pollinate both native and exotic plants.

I've mentioned that most of our food crops and many weeds are not native; neither are a large percentage of their pollinators. Imported beneficials play major roles in pollinating many exotic species that came from the same region. Scientists found that when European honeybees were kept away from the invasive weed star-thistle, also from Europe, thistle reproduction plummeted. This suggests that it will be very hard to eliminate many weeds unless we kill off their insect allies, a difficult or even undesirable goal. Given a welcoming environment, exotic insects, like exotic plants, eventually become part of their new ecosystem.

Weed Feeders

Not all pest insects chomp solely on vegetables and prize flowers, though I know it seems that way. Some insects specifically eat unwanted plants. For example, purple loosestrife, rampantly invasive in the United States, is a valued wildflower in its native Europe, where it is controlled by a large web of natural enemies and competitors. A beetle and a weevil that feed only on loosestrife have been brought from Europe to control the invasive plant and in experiments have left only dead stumps where loosestrife once thrived. Then there is the larva of the yellow agapeta moth, which eats the roots of several knapweed species. Certain flea beetles dine on leafy spurge, a rangeland weed that sickens cattle.

Of course, importing a new insect is risky, as it

A tawny mining bee pollinating an apple blossom.

TABLE 7-1.

HOST PLANTS FOR BENEFICIAL INSECTS

	PLANT				INSECT ATTRACTED				
Common name	Botanical name	Bloom time	Ladybug	Tachinid fly	Minute pirate bug	Hoverfly	Parasitic wasps	Big-eyed bugs	Lacewing
Alfalfa	Medicago sativa	sum–fall			•			•	
Alpine cinquefoil	Potentilla villosa	spr	•			•	•		
Angelica	Angelica gigas	mid–late sum							•
Basket of gold	Alyssum saxatilis	early spr	•			•			
Buckwheat	Fagopyrum esculentum	early fall	•	•	•	•			
Bugle	Ajuga reptans	late spr or early sum	•			•			
Butter and eggs	Linaria vulgaris	sum–fall			•	•	•		
Butterfly weed	Asclepias tuberosa	sum	•						
Caraway	Carum carvi	sum				•	•		•
Coriander	Coriandrum sativum	sum–fall	•			•	•		•
Cosmos "white sensation"	Cosmos bipinnatus	sum–fall				•	•		•
Crimson thyme	Thymus serpyllum coccineus	sum		•		•	•		
Dandelion	Taraxacum officinale	spr, fall	•						•
Dill	Anethum graveolens	sum	•			•	•		•
Dwarf alpine aster	Aster alpinus	sum				•			
English lavender	Lavandula angustifolia	sum				•			
Fennel	Foeniculum vulgare	sum	•			•	•		•
Fern-leaf yarrow	Achillea filipendulina	sum–fall	•			•	•		•
Feverfew	Chrysanthemum parthenium	sum–early fall				•			
Four-wing saltbush	Atriplex canescens	sum	•			•			•
Gloriosa daisy	Rudbeckia fulgida	late sum–fall				•			
Golden marguerite	Anthemis tinctoria	spr–fall	•	•		•	•		•
Goldenrod	Solidago virgaurea	late sum–fall			•	•			
Hairy vetch	Vicia villosa	sum–fall	•		•				
Lavender globe lily	Allium tanguticum	sum				•	•		
Lemon balm	Melissa officinalis	sum		•		•	•		
Lobelia	Lobelia erinus	sum				•			
Marigold "lemon gem"	Tagetes tenuifolia	sum–fall	•			•	•		
Masterwort	Astrantia major	sum				•	•		
Maximilian sunflower	Helianthus maximilianii	late sum	•						•
Orange stonecrop	Sedum kamtschaticum	sum				•	•		
Parsley	Petroselinum crispum	sum		•		•	•		
Pennyroyal	Mentha pulegium	sum		•		•	•		
Phacelia	Phacelia tanacetifolia	late spr–early sum		•					
Poached-egg plant	Limnanthes douglasii	sum				•			
Purple poppy mallow	Callirhoe involucrata	sum				•	•		•
Queen Anne's lace	Daucus carota	sum–fall	•			•	•		•
Rocky mountain penstemon	Penstemon strictus	late spr–sum	•			•			
Spearmint	Mentha spicata	sum				•			
Spike speedwell	Veronica spicata	sum	•			•			
Statice	Limonium latifolium	sum–fall				•	•		
Stonecrops	Sedum spurium & S. album	sum				•			
Sulfur cinquefoil	Potentilla recta 'warrenii'	sum, early fall	•			•	•		
Sweet alyssum	Lobularia maritima	sum				•	•		
Tansy	Tanacetum vulgare	late sum–fall	•	•			•		•
Wild bergamot	Monarda fistulosa	sum				•			
Wood betony	Stachys officinalis	spr–sum				•			
Yarrow	Achillea millefolium	sum–early fall	•			•	•		
Zinnia	Zinnia elegans	sum–frost				•	•		

A GALLERY OF BENEFICIAL INSECTS

Though thousands of species of bugs are beneficial to gardeners, most of them fit in a few major categories. Here are the principal insect allies of the gardener.

Predatory beetles include the familiar lady beetle, also called ladybugs or ladybird bugs. They feed mainly on aphids, but also eat mites, soft-bodied insects, and insect eggs. They overwinter in leaf litter, under rocks, and in other protected places. Ladybugs and their ferocious-looking alligator-like larvae consume fifty to five hundred aphids each day. When hungry, the adults can survive on nectar and pollen from shallow flower clusters such as yarrow and sunflower, but they greatly prefer insects.

Other important predaceous beetles are the iridescent green- or blue-winged beauties known as ground beetles, which feed on potato beetle eggs and others, and rove beetles, which consume cabbage maggots, onion maggots, and other root maggots.

Lacewings are found all over North America, green lacewings east of the Rockies, and the smaller brown lacewings in the West. The larvae are voracious predators of aphids, mealybugs, thrips, caterpillars and their eggs, mites, and scales. The young have hollow mandibles through which they suck the body fluids of their victims. Larvae spin yellow, pea-sized cocoons on leaves that hatch in about two weeks. Some adults eat aphids and mealybugs, but others rely on pollen and nectar for food. If adults are released where no other food exists, they will eat each other.

Predatory wasps include both social and solitary wasps. Social, colony-forming wasps such as yellowjackets and paper wasps attack caterpillars, eating them or feeding them to their larvae. Solitary wasps, such as digger wasps, do not form colonies but make one-critter nests, and feed on weevils, crickets, and caterpillars. Some predatory wasps paralyze their prey with a surgically accurate sting to a specific nerve bundle, leaving the victim alive but helpless in the nest for the larvae to consume at leisure. Most adults need pollen and nectar for food. Composite flowers (such as daisy, chamomile, golden marguerite) and mints (spearmint, peppermint, catnip) will attract and feed predatory wasps as well as hoverflies and robber flies, described below.

Parasitic wasps fall into three main groups. The braconids are tiny, often brightly colored wasps that lay their eggs on or in cabbageworms, tomato hornworms, and other caterpillars. Gardeners can sometimes spot caterpillars studded with dozens of eggs, usually the work of braconids. A second group, chalcids, are small (1/32-inch) wasps that parasitize mealybugs, aphids, and the larvae of moths, beetles, and butterflies. They may be golden colored or black. The third group, ichneumonid wasps, insert their characteristic long ovipositor into moth and butterfly larva and lay eggs within. All these wasps rely on pollen and nectar as adults. Plants with tiny flowers, including fennel, angelica, coriander, dill, and Queen Anne's lace, provide their favorite food.

Syrphid flies, which include hoverflies (also called flowerflies), and robber flies, are members of the Diptera, the fly order, though many of them look like bees. They are stingless. Hoverfly larva eat aphids, mealybugs, leafhoppers, and scale, hoisting their prey aloft like wineskins while draining their innards. Adults feed on pollen and nectar, and can be lured by keeping blossoms blooming all season. Robber flies are large and attack many insects, including useful or harmless ones, so it is the grub- and egg-eating larval stage that is most helpful.

Tachinid flies also are dipterans, and are dark and bristled like houseflies. They are parasitic, injecting their hosts with eggs or maggots, or leaving eggs on leaves to be consumed by hosts, inside whom they will hatch. One species, *Lydella stabulans,* is often written about because the young sometimes hatch inside their mother and consume her from within. When not eating mom, tachinids destroy stinkbugs, caterpillars, cutworms, armyworms, and the larvae of gypsy moths and Japanese beetles. Adults need flowers, since they feed on nectar and pollen as well as aphid honeydew.

Minute pirate bugs and their relatives, insidious pirate bugs, are true bugs (order Hemiptera), about 1/8-inch long, black with white wing patches. Both adults and young feed by sucking juices through a needle-like beak. They eat thrips, spider mites, insect eggs, aphids, and small caterpillars. Spring- and summer-flowering shrubs and weeds will entice them to stay, since they eat pollen and plant juices when they can't find prey. Pirate bugs particularly like elderberry, mountain ash, hairy vetch, and wild and domestic buckwheat.

Big-eyed bugs are about 3/16-inch long and silver-gray, resembling tiny cicadas with bulging eyes. They have a distinctive waggle when they walk. Both the adults and young feed by sucking juices from their prey through a needle-like beak. They munch eggs and larvae of bollworms, tobacco budworms, and all stages of whiteflies, mites, and aphids. Big-eyed bugs also eat seeds—planting sunflowers boosts their numbers. They also feed on nectar and like cool-season cover crops such as clover.

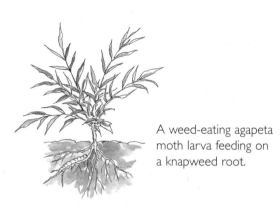

A weed-eating agapeta moth larva feeding on a knapweed root.

may misbehave in its new home by attacking valued species. This is a fairly esoteric field that most gardeners probably shouldn't pursue on their own, but if your property is being invaded by a well-known exotic such as loosestrife, you could contact your county extension agent to learn if a specific weed-feeding control insect is appropriate. But we're tinkering with a complex system here, so be cautious.

ATTRACTING BENEFICIAL INSECTS

Now that we've met our insect friends, we can put out the welcome mat for them. Like all animals, insects need food, shelter, water, and the right conditions to reproduce. Let's look at some ways to provide them.

Table 7-1 is a list of insect-attracting plants and the beneficials that frequent them. These plants may offer pollen and nectar, foliage for the larvae to feed on, or habitat for prey species; they all furnish food in some form. Many of these flora are very attractive and can (and should!) be included in even the most formal garden bed. Note that plenty of these plants are multifunctional, yielding food, herbs, medicine, or other bonuses.

Without a reliable supply of prey, predators and parasitoids won't stay around. This is another benefit of hedgerows or weedy spots, which always harbor a few aphids and other prey, encouraging beneficials to lurk about. Some gardeners fear that weeds or other "trap crops," as noncrop prey homes are called, are the breeding source for pests, but research shows that their value as snack bars for good bugs far outweighs any possible harm from pests. It seems counterintuitive, but having a few pests around is better than having none at all. If you temporarily eliminate all pests (and temporarily is all that's possible), good bugs will disappear too, leaving you defenseless when the faster-breeding pests return.

Helpful bugs also require shelter, which includes dense foliage, mulch, dead brush and leaves, and rock piles and walls. Shrubs, hedges, and thick perennial beds are ideal. Research shows that many beneficial insects overwinter or lay eggs in dead vegetation, so gardeners should delay their postseason cleanup until spring. That fastidiously neat garden is poor habitat for beneficials (isn't it wonderful to find sound ecological reasons for procrastinating?).

Drinking water isn't usually a concern, since many insects get moisture from nectar or foliage. Some species of bees and wasps drink from open water, however; other insects have an aquatic larval stage, so it's never a bad idea to have a pond or other water feature.

Offering food, shelter, and moisture goes a long way toward creating the right conditions for beneficials to reproduce. Food also needs to be available at the right time, and here diversity is once again the key. Grow many species of flowers so that several types are always in bloom to give beneficials a better chance at fattening up enough to breed. Many-specied hedgerows, wild and weedy spots, mixed and perennial borders, and flowers sprinkled in vegetable beds all provide habitat. You could take a scientific approach and select specific plants for individual beneficials, or you could be like me and use the shotgun method: Plant everything under the sun and enjoy the resulting orgy of buzzing, flittering, iridescence, nectar-slurping, pollinating, and garden health.

Remember too that no insect is an island. All organisms evolved in concert with others, and bugs are no different. They have plant and animal partners, and if we can re-create these partnerships in our gardens, better balance and fewer problems will result. A good example of this is the sunflower plant. Sunflowers are native to North America, and over 150 species of insects, including weevils, beetles, and caterpillars, feed on their foliage, roots, flowers, and seeds. When large-scale commercial planting of sunflowers began in the 1970s, some of these pests moved from wild to domestic sunflowers. Yet only a few became significant problems. That's because an equally enormous array of predator and parasitic insects—over 100 species—had also evolved with the sunflower-eating bugs, and were on hand to squelch outbreaks. Dozens of insects have evolved as sunflower pollinators, too.

This gives a glimpse of how complex plant-insect relations are. We can think of plants and their insect companions as occurring in orchestras—or as mini-ecologies—each playing a role, each being in balance with dozens or hundreds of species. This is one advantage to working with native plants: The partners needed for healthy growth and reproduction (including soil microorganisms, rodents, or birds) are likely to be on hand. But after several centuries of commerce and travel between continents, plenty of the partners of exotic plants have arrived here too. Many of the beneficials buzzing in an ecologically designed American landscape came from other countries, yet they can find their way to a healthy garden's welcoming habitat with little effort.

Many garden-supply companies sell beneficial insects, and this is one sure-fire way to obtain them. But it would be silly to buy expensive bugs if you don't offer them habitat. They'll just head to greener pastures, or at best, eat the nearby pests and then die without reproducing. Perhaps for farms or large gardens with rows and rows of vegetables, buying insects is a short-term solution, but I've never resorted to it, and my yard hums with helpful bugs. Besides, an ecological garden won't have rows and rows of monocultured veggies, but a diverse array of many varieties blended together, including flowers. To attract beneficials, just plant flowers and provide habitat, and the beneficial insects will come—and stay.

Each year, I add more useful flowers, and I'm astounded at the almost exponential increase in insect life. Insectary plants do more than just attract insects. A garden laden with bug-attracting plants can—and will—be multifunctional. My plants are healthier, and my garden is simply prettier. Plus, the scientist in me gets to scrutinize dozens of tiny stingless wasps and weirder critters as they flit from blossom to blossom. Also, many of these flowers are edible; I can pop calendula, bee balm, mustard, borage, or many other blooms into a salad, or use foliage from these and others as herbs. The medically inclined can make tinctures and salves from insectary plants. Because insects are a big part of the avian diet, I've seen a jump in bird visitors too. The relationship between plants, insects, and birds is fascinating, and one we'll explore next.

THE GARDENER'S FEATHERED FRIENDS

My story of the "quail tractor" at the beginning of this chapter hints at the roles birds can play in the ecological garden. But as with insects, many gardeners don't welcome birds into the garden or orchard with unambiguously open arms. Birds can decimate a berry crop, peck holes in fruit, and scratch up small seedlings. Often these problems arise because good bird habitat is lacking, and the birds are reduced to making do with what's available (in other words, your plants). I'd argue that in a well-designed, balanced landscape, birds do far more good than harm. They are supreme insect predators, attacking both leaf-munching caterpillars and flying bugs. Many birds eat seeds, reducing the number of weeds. In return for this food, they leave small gifts of rich manure. Individual bird droppings may not amount to much, but when a gardener concentrates manure by hanging a feeder or by some other tactic, plenty of fertilizer can accumulate. Birds also scratch the soil, simultaneously tilling the ground, removing insects and weed seeds, and uprooting weed seedlings. Some small birds are good pollinators. And then there is the simple joy that birds bring, with their bright plumage, burbling song, nest-building and family-raising, and their endlessly varied behavior as they hunt, court, stake out turf, and socialize. A yard without birds seems a sterile place.

To see how to attract birds to the landscape and to benefit from them, let's once again take the ecological view. What kind of habitat gives birds all that they need? Once we've answered that, we can see how to blend bird habitat, and all the gifts birds offer, into the garden.

Imagine a backyard of bare ground. A little bare earth is useful for birds, who will take dust baths in dry soil to subdue mites and other parasites. Birds also eat grit to aid digestion. But without shelter from predators and the elements, no bird can live here. Occasional visitors might come to pluck worms or ground-dwelling insects from this empty place, but they will not stay for long.

Allow a low ground cover to carpet the soil, and the friendly microclimate and greenery will attract several types of insects. Now ground-nesting birds such as meadowlarks and certain sparrows may appear to feed on bugs and seeds. These two types of food foster diversity in bird residents: Insect-eating birds have long, slender beaks to pluck insects from foliage, while the bills of seed-eaters are short and thick to crack tough seeds. As the environment grows more complex, bird anatomy and behavior diversify as well. The implication: More species of birds can coexist in complex habitats than in simple ones.

Bring in a little more plant diversity: tall grasses. Thick, high grass offers birds protection from predators, but also hampers bird flight. Birds that live in tall grass are different from ground-nesters. They have short wings and tails to nimbly maneuver through the grass, hopping rather than flying.

This is still a fairly impoverished home. Let's add some shrubs, which foster diversity in several ways. One is by moving firmly into the third dimension, height. This provides perches for birds, where they can sit and watch for prey rather than hopping about in continuous search. Sit-and-wait hunting conserves energy, leaving more for breeding and social behavior. Perches also encourage flying, so the wings and tails of shrub-dwelling birds are bigger than the sawed-off stubs of grass residents. Also, birds that hunt bugs on the wing have broader bills to raise the odds of nailing insects with each swoop. Nests, now off the ground, are safer, cooler, and drier, so more nestlings survive.

Perching birds are superb seed dispersers and can bolster plant diversity on their own. Researchers found that when they provided perches in a field, the number and variety of seeds brought by birds skyrocketed. If we offer the birds a few shrubs for perching, they'll introduce many new plant varieties on their own. This in turn will attract new insects, which will bring more new birds, who will ferry in more seeds, and up and up the cycle builds.

Another boost to diversity offered by shrubs is from woody tissue. Grass and herbs have soft stems and foliage, thus insects can munch them with ease. But the woody stems of shrubs will thwart a soft-mouthed bug. Woody stems offer a whole new niche, welcoming insects with tough jaws or piercing mouth parts. Thus, a shrub-filled landscape is home to yet more species of insects, and that means more types of birds to eat them.

Within the shrubby canopy, small birds are protected from predators. These birds can hop from twig to twig, snapping up insects. They have sharp, pointed beaks to poke into small places in search of food. Here come some more new species.

The move to the third dimension really boosts diversity, opening up many new opportunities for food sources and consumers of that food. As the habitat diversifies, more and more birds find niches, and create more variety in turn. Also, a combination of herbs and shrubs will nurture not only the birds dependent on each, but new species that colonize the edge between the two habitats. Once again, the whole is more than the sum of the parts.

Now we can add some trees to the mix. The

combination of tree trunk and canopy creates a new structure, where birds can glide in the open expanse below the crowns. More flying birds will arrive, and bigger ones too, since thick branches can support large birds. And once again, this creates new insect niches. The tree trunks, with thick bark and broad surfaces, allow new species of bugs to feed, hide, and lay their eggs. The birds who eat these bugs need specialized beaks to probe the bark, and an anatomy modified to hang sideways on trunks instead of perching upright. So trees hike bird diversity yet further. Life among the trees is safer, too. Birds and nests in the canopy are protected from predators lurking on the ground, who must now learn to climb for their food.

This shows how a diverse habitat, with many shapes, sizes, and varieties of plants, attracts birds (and insects) of many species and lifestyles. Birds play a critical role in any ecological garden, for the reasons given at the beginning of this section. Although some people landscape their yards specifically to attract birds, every yard can have some bird-friendly elements in it. Of course, we can design so that most of these elements will have more than one function, benefiting the human and other occupants and contributing to the health of the entire mini-ecosystem. Let's see specifically what needs to be included in the ecological garden to bring birds into it, and how those pieces fit in.

An ideal, diverse habitat for birds will have four key elements. They are:

1. **FOOD.** Bird foods fall in three main categories: fruits and berries, insects, and seeds and nuts. Some birds are specialists, eating mostly from one group, while others aren't so fussy. Hummingbirds and a few others also drink nectar, but even hummingbirds get over half their nutrition from insects. To feed a wide variety of birds, a garden needs insectary plants (many of which offer nectar, too), grasses and herbs that yield seeds, and shrubs and trees with nuts, fruit, and berries. A wide variety of species to continuously provide food over a long season is best. Many fruits and berries hang on into winter, and

these species will invite birds all year. Table 7-2 is a brief list of plants that are all around useful ones for birds and have other functions as well. A more comprehensive list of plants that feed birds would fill many pages, so I will refer the reader to the bibliography for some good books on the subject.

2. **WATER.** The most natural source of water for birds is a pond or small stream with shallow edges. An alternative is a bird bath or other container less than 2 inches deep. A shrub or other shelter very close by will give birds an escape route and allow them to check out the water from a safe perch. Birds will also frolic in a sprinkler or other moving water.

3. **SHELTER AND PROTECTION.** Birds know that death from predators or bad weather is always near. Thus, food and water offer little enticement for birds unless accompanied by shelter from the elements and protection from predators. Dense shrubs, tangles of vines, plants with thorns, and leafy tree canopies all provide safe havens from predators. Thick evergreen foliage will shelter them from wintry winds, heavy snows, and extreme cold. For nesting, birds need plants whose foliage will exclude rain, hot sun, and sharp-eyed predators. Birds often nest at specific heights, so a diverse array of shrubs and trees will offer potential homesites to many species. Wide, dense plants are useful, since lots of birds prefer to nest deep inside a broad hedge or bush.

4. **FOOD AND HABITAT DIVERSITY.** To attract and nurture numerous birds from many species, a yard should furnish many food sources that stretch yields over the whole year, diverse places for shelter and protection, and plenty of private spots at varying heights for nest sites. To provide all this, a landscape needs plants from each of seven overlapping categories:

Evergreens: Evergreen trees and shrubs with needles (pine, fir, cedar, spruce, yew, hemlock, juniper, and others), and to a lesser extent, broadleaf evergreens (holly, arbutus, large bamboo, eucalyptus, bayberry) offer winter shelter, summer nesting sites, and escape cover. Some of these provide buds, seeds, and sap for food.

Grasses and forbs: Tall grasses, annual and perennial flowers, and herbs provide cover for birds that feed or nest on the ground. Many offer seeds and nectar or are hosts for insects.

Nectar-producing plants: Nectar-producing plants with red tubular flowers (such as *Penstemon barbatus,* trumpet vine, columbine) are irresistible to hummingbirds. Larger nectar-producers (including sugar and big-leaf maple, *Elaeagnus,* honeysuckle, banksia, black locust) are used by orioles and other small birds to supplement their diet.

Summer-fruiting plants: Plants that produce fruits or berries from May through August are the mainstays of many bird-attracting gardens. Varieties include blackberry, blueberry, cherry, chokecherry, honeysuckle, raspberry, serviceberry, mulberry, elderberry, and wild plum, but there are dozens more.

Fall-fruiting plants: Migratory birds must build up fat reserves for their long voyage southward, and nonmigratory varieties need plenty of food to survive winter freezes. Fall-fruiting plants are essential for this; they include dogwood, mountain ash, snowberry, sea buckthorn, buffaloberry, and cotoneaster.

Winter-fruiting plants: Especially valuable are plants whose fruits cling to the branches into winter. Some of these fruits need repeated freezing and thawing to be palatable. Winter fruits include black chokecherry, snowberry, sumac, highbush cranberry, many varieties of crabapple, barberry, hawthorn, strawberry tree, bittersweet, eastern and European

wahoo, hardy kiwi, medlar, Virginia creeper, and chinaberry.

Nut and acorn plants: These include oaks, hickories, butternuts, walnuts, buckeyes, chestnuts, piñon and stone pine, and hazels. These trees also provide good nesting habitat.

Most of these plants will complement any home landscape, and many are multifunctional, offering food as well as beautiful foliage and flowers. A few, such as buffaloberry and sea buckthorn, are nitrogen fixers. In turn, the birds these plants attract will provide entertainment and insight into animal psychology as they forage, nest, and interact. They'll help keep insect problems in check, while their gifts of fertilizer and tilling can be significant too. The next section shows how to consciously harvest these animal benefits, using them to improve the garden.

OTHER BACKYARD HELPERS

The chances are good that your grandparents, whether they were farmers or not, kept small livestock. Before World War II, the sound of clucking chickens or the sight of rabbit cages was common in backyards even in the cities. On apartment rooftops, flocks of pigeons cooed and groomed in specially built lofts and dovecotes. Not a few ice boxes were stocked with meat and eggs from homegrown animals, and feathers or fur often found a use as well. Manure, of course, went to the garden (or sometimes to other uses: Citizens in Elizabethan England were exhorted to raise pigeons, since bird guano yielded phosphate for gunpowder).

But in the postwar era, small livestock disappeared from urban and suburban yards. It was easier to buy meat, eggs, and even composted manure at the store than to raise small livestock. Many towns passed laws against keeping these animals—especially roosters, whose unpredictable crowing disturbed the sleep of nine-to-five commuters.

The past few years have seen a resurgence of small animals in backyards. Anti-chicken ordi-

TABLE 7-2.

USEFUL PLANTS FOR BIRDS

NAME OF PLANT		PROVIDES					
Common name	Botanical name	Seeds	Insects	Fruits	Winter fruits	Shelter and cover	Nest sites
Alder	*Alnus* spp.	•					•
American cranberry	*Viburnum trilobum*			•	•		
Amur cork tree	*Phellodendron amurense*				•		
Amur honeysuckle	*Lonicera maackii*				•		
Apple and crabapple	*Malus* spp.			•	•		•
Ash	*Fraxinus* spp.	•					•
Autumn olive	*Elaeagnus umbellata*			•	•		
Barberry	*Berberis* spp.					•	•
Bayberry or wax myrtle	*Myrica* spp.			•	•		
Birch	*Betula* spp.	•	•				
Blackberry and raspberry	*Rubus* spp.			•			
Blueberry	*Vaccinium* spp.			•			
Buckthorn	*Rhamnus* spp.					•	•
Cherry	*Prunus* spp.			•			
Dogwood	*Cornus* spp.			•			•
Douglas fir	*Pseudotsuga menziesii*						•
Eastern red cedar	*Juniperus virginiana*				•	•	•
Elderberry	*Sambucus* spp.					•	•
Elm	*Ulmus* spp.		•				•
Euonymus	*Euonymus* spp.	•					
European cranberry	*Viburnum opulus*			•	•		
Fir	*Abies* spp.					•	
Firethorn	*Pyracantha* spp.			•			
Greenbrier	*Smilax* spp.					•	
Hackberry	*Celtis* spp.				•		
Hawthorn	*Crataegus* spp.			•	•		•
Holly	*Ilex* spp.			•	•		•
Honeysuckle	*Lonicera* spp.			•			
Maple	*Acer* spp.	•	•				•
Mountain ash	*Sorbus* spp.			•	•		
Mulberry	*Morus* spp.			•		•	•
Pine	*Pinus* spp.					•	•
Rugosa rose	*Rosa rugosa*				•		
Russian olive	*Elaeagnus angustifolia*			•	•		•
Serviceberry	*Amelanchier* spp.			•			•
Smooth sumac	*Rhus glabra*				•		
Spicebush	*Lindera benzoin*			•			
Spruce	*Picea* spp.					•	•
Staghorn sumac	*Rhus typhina*				•		
Sycamore	*Platanus*		•				
Toyon	*Heteromeles arbutifolia*			•			
Tulip tree	*Liriodendron tulipfera*				•		
Willow	*Salix* spp.		•				
Wolfberry	*Lycium* spp.			•		•	•

nances have begun to topple (sometimes allowing hens but not roosters), and chicken yards, duck ponds, rabbit hutches, and even pens for dwarf pot-bellied pigs are cropping up in suburb and city. Some of this renaissance is spurred by a desire for humanely raised, hormone- and antibiotic-free meat, but even vegetarians or those unwilling to butcher their own animals are finding advantages to small livestock.

Small animals suited for the backyard are legion, and include chickens, turkeys, pigeons, ducks, quail, peafowl, as well as rabbits, guinea pigs, and pot-bellied mini-pigs. Geese and guineafowl, though also small animals, are a little too noisy for the city or suburbs.

If animals are intelligently raised, their advantages are also multifold: they can fertilize, till, clip grass, weed, eat scraps and leftovers, hunt insects and slugs, process compost and yard waste, and warn of intruders (okay, rabbits and guinea pigs aren't great alarm-sounders). Feeding kitchen scraps to a hen is more efficient than composting the scraps directly, since the bird will convert the waste to meat, eggs, and useful activities such as weed-eating, and then produce nearly as much fertilizer as you'd get from composting. If we're eating these animals or their eggs, cycling wastes through animals captures more stored energy than direct composting. That's because in a compost pile the scraps would be converted to soil life, which we don't eat, instead of chicken, which we do (a proportion of the scraps will be converted to carbon dioxide and other gases, no matter what eats them).

We can think of other benefits of raising animals. When small animals are housed in or adjoining a greenhouse, their body heat warms it in winter, and they boost plant growth with carbon dioxide from their breath. Less tangibly, they can entertain us for hours, become our companions and friends, and teach adults and children about the cycles of birth and death. With all that, their ability to provide us with food seems almost trivial.

Does raising livestock in the city or suburb

seem shocking? It's a matter of perspective. We raise dogs and cats with nary a second thought, yet they require expensive feed and intense care, their excrement is extremely noxious, they destroy property, and barking dogs and love-smitten cats are every bit as noisy as roosters. Their benefits do include companionship, and dogs make great burglar alarms, but if you're looking at tangible benefits, other small animals provide far more with less trouble. We've just gotten used to dogs and cats, and I'd like to see us expand our small-animal horizons. I love dogs and cats, but they can raise hell in the garden, while many other animals are garden assets and can provide useful labor and fertilizer as a byproduct of their daily activities, as well as fur and meat.

Sometimes the biggest obstacles to keeping animals in the city are the neighbors, who may need to be educated gently about animals' benefits and trouble-free nature. I know several people who quieted their neighbors' worries by supplying them with occasional eggs or meat.

Chicken Tractors

The secret to using small animals effectively in the garden is a small mobile pen, called an animal tractor (see the illustration on page 135). By keeping livestock in a small moveable space, animal tractors let the gardener decide where the animal will work best, rather than allowing the critters to wander and wreak havoc in freshly seeded beds. The pens concentrate the animals' weeding, tilling, and manuring in a small space, which is the key to successfully melding animals and gardens. With an animal tractor, you can have weed-free, surface-tilled, perfectly manured raised beds with only a few minutes of (your) work per day.

Chickens are ideally suited to animal tractors, although ducks, rabbits, pigs, and guinea pigs have been used in these mobile pens. Andy Lee has written an entire book on the subject, *Chicken Tractor,* which I recommend to anyone planning to use an animal tractor.

A chicken tractor is a bottomless pen on wheels

that fits over a garden bed. A typical one might be 4 feet wide by 8 feet long, and about 2 feet high. It's an open wood-frame box, covered on the sides with 1-inch chicken wire (poultry netting), roofed with plastic panels, having wheels or skids at one end and a door to let the birds in and out. Inside, food and water containers hang from the roof, and in some models, perches project from the sides. There are other designs, but that's the gist. To move the pen, just lift one end and roll it on the wheels or skids. Animal tractors work best with garden beds as wide as the tractor, and ideally, in lengths that are an even multiple of the tractor length.

The number of birds per tractor varies with the breed, but as a rule of thumb, a laying hen needs 4 square feet of room, while a broiler need 2 square feet. Thus, a 32-square-foot tractor can hold up to eight layers or sixteen broilers.

You can use a chicken tractor to build soil in three basic ways: rotation, sheet mulching, and deep mulching.

In the *rotation* method, first thing in the morning you wheel the pen and chickens to an unused garden bed. The birds can stay inside while you move it—they'll scurry along inside the pen. Withhold their feed until they've been on the new bed for an hour or so. The hungry birds will eat the vegetation inside the tractor. Let the birds weed, till, and manure the soil all day. The next morning, wheel the tractor down the bed to the next fresh spot, and sprinkle some mulch on the first bed. Rotate through all the unused beds. This system requires that some of your garden beds go fallow part of the time so the chickens have soil to improve. Andy Lee's garden is twice as big as he needs, which lets him rotate chicken tractors through each bed every other year.

As the tractor leaves each raised bed, you can sow a cover crop of buckwheat, or winter rye and vetch, and bring the chickens back to eat and till it again when the cover crop is about 4 inches high. Not only does this boost fertility and soil life enormously, but it cuts down on chicken feed bills. The result is superb soil with little labor, plus eggs and meat if you wish.

To *sheet mulch* with chickens, leave the tractor in one spot for several days. Each day, add about an inch of mulch, and let the chickens work over the mulch and add manure to it. When the mulch is about 4 inches deep, move the chickens to a new spot and repeat the process. This way, you (and the

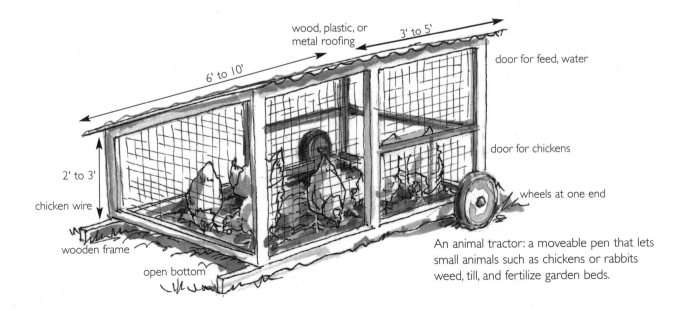

wood, plastic, or metal roofing

3' to 5'

6' to 10'

door for feed, water

2' to 3'

chicken wire

door for chickens

wheels at one end

wooden frame

open bottom

An animal tractor: a moveable pen that lets small animals such as chickens or rabbits weed, till, and fertilize garden beds.

chickens) are adding both nutrients and organic matter to the soil. The mulch binds the nitrogen and other nutrients in place while the whole mixture composts. Treat this bed as you would any new sheet-mulched bed, and plant it with seedlings in soil pockets or seeds in a top layer of potting soil.

You can also use a chicken tractor to make a *deep mulch* garden bed, useful in gardens too small to move the tractor every day or where the soil is very poor. Leave the chicken tractor in one place and add about an inch of mulch each day. After about five weeks—or the time it takes broilers to grow from chicks to mature—you'll have a thick raised bed to plant. Andy Lee warns that leaving the tractor in one place this long may give predators—dogs, skunks, foxes—time to dig under the pen and attack the birds. He recommends laying chicken wire on the ground around the pen and pinning it in place to frustrate digging predators.

Both mulch techniques work well on sloped as well as level ground. On a slope, the chickens—and gravity—will leave the mulch thicker on the downhill side of the pen, resulting in a level, terraced bed.

Chickens can also graze free-range in the garden, where they will glean insects, slugs, and weed seeds, but it's best to keep an eye on them in case they find a crop they really like, such as berries or tomatoes. Wait until garden plants are mature before letting the chickens into the garden, as poultry will happily eat tender seedlings. If you allow the birds into the garden in the late afternoon, they won't be there long enough to do any damage, and will naturally return to their coop or tractor at dusk, sparing you the trouble of a lengthy chicken chase.

Growing some of the chicken's food will cut down on costs and reduce imports to your site, but it's not realistic to expect to grow all their food. A hen needs about 80 pounds of grain a year, which could be grown on about 1,000 square feet. The numbers add up fast: Feeding a small flock of eight hens would require an 80-by-100-foot garden and countless hours of labor to grow and harvest the food. Instead, I'd suggest growing multifunctional plants around the yard to supplement the chickens' diets, which will cut costs and provide valuable vitamins and fresh foods. These plants could be nicely integrated into the garden design, supplying habitat, food, nutrients, and all the other needs of the ecological garden, rather than just the single function of chicken feed. And growing chicken forage creates yet another closed cycle for the garden. As the chickens build the soil, the resulting food plants will be healthier and more lush, and the chickens in turn grow stronger and more productive.

Table 7-3 lists some plants that can be included in a chicken yard or integrated into a landscape for chicken forage.

Ducks, Rabbits, Worms, and Other Small Animals

Animals not well suited for tractors but useful in the garden are ducks, and their relatives the muscovies. Penny Livingston's ducks, those inhabitants of her greywater pond system, patrol her garden rigorously for slugs and insects, leaving behind a little fertilizer. Many of the plants in table 7-3 are suitable for ducks as well as chickens.

Ducks are gentler on plants than chickens and don't scratch much, thus they don't need close supervision in the garden. Khaki Campbells and Indian Runners are good egg layers, while Pekins and Improved Mallards are bred for meat. Muscovies, a South American fowl intermediate between ducks and geese, are very quiet, making them good candidates for the urban or suburban yard.

A nonfeathered animal that works well in a tractor is the rabbit. You'll need to put a chicken-wire bottom on the tractor, since rabbits are burrowers and will quickly tunnel out of a bottomless pen. They don't scratch the way chickens do, so they're less effective tillers, but their manure is high in nutrients, and they're voracious vegetarians that will quickly eliminate weeds.

Rabbits can be grown as pets or for their prod-

Table 7-3.

PLANTS THAT PROVIDE POULTRY FORAGE

Common name	Botanical name	Comments
Trees		
Black locust	*Robinia pseudoacacia*	pods can be ground
Fruit trees	Various	fallen or fresh fruit
Mulberry	*Morus* spp.	fruits eaten
Nut trees	Various	cracked nuts for feed
Oak	*Quercus* spp.	acorns high in protein
Pistachio	*Pistacia* spp.	nuts eaten
Honey locust	*Gleditsia triacanthos*	pods can be ground

Shrubs

All fruits and many of the greens of these shrubs can be eaten by poultry.

Autumn olive	*Elaeagnus umbellata*	
Barberry	*Berberis* spp.	
Boxthorn	*Lycium* spp.	
Buffaloberry	*Shepherdia* spp.	
Coffeeberry	*Rhamnus* spp.	
Currant	*Ribes* spp.	
Elderberry	*Sambucus* spp.	
Hackberry	*Celtis* spp.	
Hawthorn	*Crataegus* spp.	
Manzanita	*Arctostaphylos* spp.	
Privet	*Forestiera* spp.	
Russian olive	*Elaeagnus angustifolia*	
Serviceberry	*Amelianchier* spp.	
Siberian pea shrub	*Caragana arborescens*	edible pods

Herbaceous plants

The seeds, flowers, and greens of these herbaceous plants can be eaten by poultry.

Alfalfa	*Medicago sativa*	
Buckwheat	*Fagopyrum esculentum*	
Chickweed	*Stellaria medea*	
Chicory	*Cichorium intybus*	
Cleavers	*Galium aparine*	
Clover	*Trifolium* spp.	
Comfrey	*Symphytum officinale*	
Fennel	*Foeniculum vulgare*	
Pigweed	*Amaranthus retroflexus*	
Rye	*Secale cereale*	
Shepherd's purse	*Capsella bursa-pastoris*	
Swiss chard	*Beta vulgaris*	

Seed crops

Amaranth	*Amaranthus*	
Barley	*Hordeum vulgare*	
Corn	*Zea mays*	
Millet	*Panicum miliaceum*	
Oats	*Avena sativa*	
Quinoa	*Chenopodium quinoa*	
Sunflower	*Helianthus annuum*	
Wheat	*Tritium aestivum*	

ucts. Angoras provide wool (French angoras are easier to raise than the English variety, which can develop eye problems, and must be brushed daily or their hair will mat). For those so inclined, a few rabbits can provide meat for a family. Five breeding rabbits, each birthing per year an average of three litters of five kits, will yield ample meat for a typical family. That's an intensive breeding rate, and someone who cares for their rabbits will let the mothers rest every other year or the exhausted animals will die young. Good breeds for meat include California and New Zealand rabbits. Their fur also has commercial value.

Since rabbits don't eat insects or scratch the soil, some gardeners think they aren't ideally suited to animal tractors. Instead they employ rabbits in the garden by combining rabbit hutches with worm bins to naturally process manure into a perfect compost (see the illustration on page 138). This technique links two animals together, and like all well-connected relationships, provides benefits—great compost and fat worms—and solves problems, by conscientiously utilizing rabbit manure and urine.

In this system, a wire-bottomed rabbit hutch should be elevated on posts. Below the hutch, set an open wooden or plastic bin 18 to 30 inches deep and big enough to catch the droppings. Place shredded newspaper plus peat moss or shredded dry leaves into the bin to a depth of 6 inches. The bin will collect rabbit manure, urine, and spilled food. Once this bin is full, add one to three hundred red worms to it, cover the box, and set it aside. Place a second box containing the newspaper/peat moss mixture under the rabbit hutch. By the time the second bin is full, you should have beautiful worm compost in the first box. These worm bins can also process kitchen scraps. Worm bins are a first-rate composting system that can be used indoors. The virtually odorless bins are ideal for creating compost in northern winters, when the outdoor compost pile is a frozen lump. I'd advise checking the bibliography under worm composting for more details on constructing and using worm bins.

With animals, we extend the reach of our garden into yet another kingdom of nature. In the rich soil teem the unseen wonders that bring the dead back to life, the decomposers who work their magic on wood and leaf, on bone and chitin. Above ground are the plants, green marvels who capture the sunlight and build sugar and sap, the flowers, fruits, and seeds that feed us all. And now we bring in the animals that flit and buzz, scamper and scratch, nibble and manure. Animals are the final link in nature's cycle. They are nature's mechanics, accelerating growth here with seed dispersal and fertilizer, retarding it there with a vigorous browse and trample. They haul nutrients and seeds great distances, from places of abundance to a dry bare patch used for a dust bath. They process seed heads through their bodies and hooves, mashing seed into the soil, trimming branches, thinning the hordes of bugs. Without animals, our labor is doubled and redoubled, and we must pollinate, spray, dig, cart and spread fertilizer, and fill the thousand other tasks easily and cheerfully done by our marvelous cousins. Without animals, nature just limps along; in a garden we must supply the crutch. By creating a garden that nurtures our two-, four-, and more-legged friends, we close the cycle and shift the burden more evenly, letting nature carry her share.

worm bin

A rabbit hutch combined with a worm bin. The rabbit manure is quickly converted into rich compost by the worms.

PART THREE

ASSEMBLING
the
ECOLOGICAL
GARDEN

Chapter 8

Creating Communities for the Garden

It's time to assemble the pieces of the ecological garden. We know that our garden needs water, which is stored best by the soil but also held within plants, and in ponds and cisterns. Our garden's soil is alive, charged with fertility and bursting with microbes to shuttle that fertility to plant roots. Rooted in this living soil are the plants themselves, in all the many roles they play. The plants we've chosen will collect and cycle the earth's minerals, shade the soil and renew it with leafy mulch, and yield fruits and greens for people and wildlife. In the ecological garden, animal companions abound. Birds scratch the soil, scatter seed, munch malevolent larvae, and leave an offering of phosphate-laden droppings. Here are insects to subdue pests and to pollinate the many flowers. Perhaps, too, this garden holds a few chickens, ducks, or rabbits for soil tilling, weed and bug control, and for a gift of manure. In the wilder edges, deer pass by to prune and harvest; mice and voles scuttle off with seed—some of which, far off and forgotten, will sprout to widen our garden's reach yet further.

But these are merely the pieces. Left unconnected, water, soil, plants, and animals create little more than a collection of fragments: pretty potsherds that hold nothing until glued back together. These fragments, as should be clear by now, do not come to life until they are assembled in the proper relationships. In this chapter, we'll examine those relationships.

We'll begin our work of connection simply, blending a few plants together to glimpse what synergies emerge from their juxtaposition. Then we'll create communities of plants using both wild and domesticated varieties. Each member of these communities supports, enhances, and is benefited by the others. Although our communities are based on plants, their participants extend beyond the floral realm to include insects, birds, mammals, soil organisms, and people.

INTERPLANTING AND BEYOND

Vegetable gardeners have some experience in creating plant communities. Food-growers have long attempted to avoid the drawbacks, both aesthetic and ecological, of large blocks of a single crop.

Garden monocultures deplete the soil, provide a sumptuous feast for pests, and look quite dull. To avoid these faults, many gardeners practice *interplanting,* mixing different varieties together to save space and avoid solid clumps of one vegetable. Interplanting strategies, while usually limited to vegetables, illustrate some of the principles of combining varieties that work together to deter pests and aid each other in other ways. Once we've learned the basics of interplanting, we can broaden our spectrum, and look beyond vegetables toward garden plant communities that benefit not just people but all of nature.

One simple interplant mixes onions, carrots, and lettuce in the same garden bed. These three plants have different leaf forms, light requirements, and rooting depths. The cylindrical leaves of onions grow virtually straight up, casting little shade. Feathery carrot leaves bush out a bit, but don't create deep shadows. Lettuce, although it forms a solid mass of greenery, is short, and casts its shade below the other plants. The three leaf forms fit well together, allowing ample sunlight to bathe each plant. Also, lettuce needs less sun than onions and carrots, so the slight shade cast by the latter two won't impede lettuce's growth. And last, the roots of these three plants don't compete for space: Onions are shallow rooted, lettuce reaches to intermediate depth, and carrots go straight down. Each searches for nutrients in a different place. These three vegetables, with their varying shapes, light requirements, and rooting patterns, can be interplanted very successfully.

Though interplanting saves space, it doesn't go far enough for me. Most interplanting, like the above example, simply combines plants to avoid negative interactions, such as competition for space or light. This form of interplanting doesn't blend plants into dynamic, interactive associations the way nature does. What's more, interplanting

> **Many gardeners practice *interplanting,* mixing different varieties together to save space and avoid solid clumps of one vegetable.**
>
>

rarely capitalizes on the mutual benefits plants can provide each other, such as deterring pests or transporting and storing nutrients.

A second technique, *companion planting,* takes advantage of some of these mutual benefits. For example, planting sage near carrots reputedly repels the carrot fly. Carrots themselves are thought to exude a substance that stimulates the growth of peas. Companion planting is a step in the right direction, but unfortunately, many traditional combinations turn out, in careful trials, to provide no benefit. Surprisingly, some old recipes produce detrimental effects. Robert Kourik, in his excellent book, *Designing and Maintaining Your Edible Landscape—Naturally,* summarizes a wealth of research that debunks many old-time companion-plant recipes. For example, gardeners have long edged their beds with marigolds to deter pests, and Kourik notes that certain marigolds, especially Mexican marigolds *(Tagetes minuta)* can repel harmful soil nematodes. However, other varieties of marigold actually attract pests, and most simply don't help at all. I've seen gardens randomly strewn with marigolds as a general panacea, but the research makes me wonder if the benefits extend beyond offering something nice to look at.

Hence I'm skeptical of planting basil with tomatoes in hopes of bigger beefsteaks—to choose an old-time companion recipe at random. Companion planting in its highest form can create beautiful mixed beds of flowers and vegetables. In its simplest and most common mode, however, companion planting merely combines plants in what is not far from monoculture: nice orderly beds of two or perhaps three species—static, perfectly weeded, and ecologically dead. Can't we do better?

Gardening Goes Polycultural

What if we could blend the best qualities of interplanting and companion planting? Interplanting combines crops that minimize competition for sun and nutrients. Companion planting blends varieties that enhance each other. Natural plant communities, tuned by billions of years of evolution, do both. Why not emulate these plant communities in our gardens?

Plant communities are dynamic, not static. As we saw in chapter 2, they are constantly changing their composition, swapping species in and out as ecological succession lurches on. In succession's early stages, aggressive pioneer plants—usually annuals—colonize bare earth. As they grow and die, their leaf litter scatters mulch upon the soil. Their roots crack open the hard ground, and after death, decay into fingers of humus that fan deep into the soil. The ground has now been prepared for later, more choosy species. Conditions are right for longer-lived perennials to move in to this now-fertilized ground, followed by shrubs. Eventually, if rainfall is ample, trees appear.

The living plants themselves create conditions attractive to other species. When pioneers move in, the once-bare ground, with its uniform temperature, humidity, and sunlight, is subdivided by plant life into myriad habitats and microclimates. Beneath the pioneers' leafy protection, the soil becomes moist and cool, a perfect milieu for seeds of new species to germinate. Soon the once-naked earth is swaddled in plants of contrasting height, width, leaf size and shape, succulence, scent, flower form, reflectance and absorbance, and a host of other qualities. Diversity cascades upon diversity. As microclimates multiply, favorable conditions evolve for yet more species. Niches abound, and new varieties will move into these niches, attracting more insects, more birds, more life.

The typical vegetable garden, however, has only one niche: loamy soil, at neutral pH, in full sun. (Okay, we all don't have gardens like that. Your garden may have acidic clay hardpan that's shaded by a neighbor's tree, but most gardeners aspire to have the so-called ideal conditions listed above. This ideal reduces a diverse ecology to an impoverished uniformity.) The many plants that grace our gardens were collected from hundreds of ecological niches that differ in soil type, available sunlight, and many other variables. Sentencing our garden plants to a single uniform habitat erodes the broad potential available to us. A garden that offers varying soil, light, and temperature enlarges the palette of species that will thrive there.

One of the biggest factors that shapes the garden environment is the plants themselves. Our plants co-evolved in dynamic environments, molded by neighboring plants. Species evolved under tree canopies, amid grasses and herbs, or shouldering their way between shrubs, but never alone, always competing and cooperating with the other members of their communities. Isolating these mostly gregarious plants and plunking them into beds and borders extracts them from their original niches.

To re-create or mimic the original niches of our now-domesticated plants, we can use a gardening technique called polyculture. Polycultures are dynamic, self-organizing plant communities composed of several to many species.

Interplanting and companion planting are very elementary forms of polyculture, which in its simplest definition means growing many plants together. But in more sophisticated polycultures, the plants themselves tune their environment to the best conditions for their growth. Given the chance, heat-shunning lettuces will snuggle for protection under a leafy canopy of cauliflower. Slow-germinating wildflowers will bide their time in the moist shade of an early-leafing currant bush. We can encourage these

> **Polycultures are dynamic, self-organizing plant communities composed of several to many species.**
>
>

IANTO EVANS'S POLYCULTURE

Prepare a garden bed, allowing about 20 square feet of bed for each person who will be fed from the polyculture.

Two weeks before the last frost: Indoors, start about ten cabbage plants per 20 square feet of bed. The cabbages should be ready for transplanting a month or so after the seed mixture below is sown. To extend the season, choose both early- and fall-maturing cabbages.

Week One (at the last frost date in your region): In early spring, sow seeds of radish, dill, parsnip, calendula, and lettuce. For a lengthy harvest season, select several varieties of lettuce. A mix of loose leaf, romaine, butter, iceberg, and heat-tolerant varieties such as Summertime or Optima will stretch the lettuce season into summer.

Broadcast all the seeds over the same area: You're creating a mixed planting. Cover the entire bed with a light scattering of seed (sow each seed type separately—don't mix the seeds and toss them all onto the bed, because the heavy seeds will be flung the farthest, and you'll wind up with all the radishes on one end, and all the parsnips at the other). Sow at a density of about one seed every couple of square inches. Then cover the seed with about ¼ inch of compost, and water gently.

Week Four: Some of the radishes should be ready to pluck. In a few of the gaps left by the radishes, plant cabbage seedlings about 18 inches apart.

Week Six: The young lettuce will be big enough to harvest. The dense sowing of lettuce will yield a flavorful mesclun blend when the plants are young. With continued thinning, the remaining lettuce will grow up full-sized. If you've chosen varieties carefully, you'll be crunching lettuce for up to four months.

Late Spring/Early Summer: When the soil has warmed to above 60 degrees Fahrenheit, plant bush beans in the spaces left by the lettuce. If more openings develop in early summer, sow buckwheat and begin thinning their edible greens shortly after they appear. The next crops to harvest after the lettuce will be the dill and calendula (calendula blossoms are edible and make a tasty addition to salads). The early cabbages will be coming on at about this time too, followed in midsummer by the beans. Parsnips are slow growing and will be ready to eat in fall and winter. As gaps in the polyculture appear in early autumn, mild-winter gardeners can plant fava beans; others can poke garlic cloves into the openings, to be harvested the following spring.

relationships to flourish in our gardens. By blending a carefully chosen but highly diverse assortment of varieties, we can create gardens in which plants nestle together in minimally competitive patterns, bolster each other with beneficial interactions, and shift their composition in ecological succession, all combining to provide a lengthy and varied harvest of food, blossoms, and habitat.

We'll look at a simple polyculture system that introduces this ecological gardening technique, followed by a more elaborate version. Afterward, I'll present guidelines for designing your own polycultures.

Traditional societies have long used polycultures, but most of these employ plants unfamiliar to most North American gardeners. Recognizing the need for polycultures based on European and American varieties, a team headed by Ianto Evans, a transplanted Welshman living on our West Coast, pioneered several temperate-climate polycultures in the 1980s. Ianto is an inventor, teacher, and architect who spoons out his accumulated wisdom in thoughtful and sometimes curmudgeonly dollops. He has traveled often in the less-developed world, and his creations, which include new bean varieties, fuel-efficient woodstoves, and sculpted earthen houses, temper industrial technologies with the wisdom of traditional cultures. Ianto's polycultures follow suit, infusing indigenous knowledge into Western gardens.

After observing polyculture gardens used in traditional cultures, Ianto extracted a set of basic principles that allowed him to blend common vegetable varieties into combinations that would ripen, one variety after another, over many months to give up to nine months of continuous food. His efforts, originally limited and tentative, gradually evolved into polycultures of up to thirty species, and his work has been continued by others.

Ianto devised a seven-variety polyculture that mimics natural succession and fills ecological niches—and a garden bed—densely. As the early-germinating plants in this polyculture grow, they create habitat for the other members of the assemblage, and they attract beneficial insects for pollinating as well as fighting pests. The thick planting forms a living mulch for the soil, curtailing evaporation and the need for water. This polyculture yields a steady harvest for several months from a very small space. All these benefits stem from placing the plants in the right relationship, one that takes advantage of the dynamic qualities of living beings.

Ianto's polyculture blends early-sprouting radishes, insect-attracting and edible dill and calendula, lettuce, parsnips, cabbage, and nitrogen-fixing bush beans. Detailed instructions for planting this polyculture are given in the box on page 144.

How do the elements of this polyculture interact? The fast-growing radishes cast shade, which keeps the soil moist and cool. This protects slow-germinating seeds—particularly the parsnips—from the desiccating sun. Strongly scented dill and calendula will confuse insects searching for tender young radishes. Dill also hosts tiny predatory wasps that attack cabbage loopers. Cabbages, which grow through the fall and into winter, protect the soil from erosion by heavy rains. Beans add nitrogen to the soil. The variety of leaf shapes and root depths minimizes competition for sun, space, and nutrients.

The polyculture as a whole provides enough diversity to bewilder most pests. The thick planting creates a living mulch that protects the soil from sun, rain erosion, and heat, thus conserving soil texture, humus, and moisture. I've pushed my hand into a polyculture on a blazing summer afternoon and found the lower leaves and soil deliciously cool and moist. Also, since most plant niches are filled, weeds are denied easy access. The

JAJARKOT'S ADVANCED POLYCULTURE

To create Jajarkot's polyculture, prepare a garden bed, allowing 20 to 30 square feet of space for each person to be fed.

One month before your last frost date: Start a few seedlings each of cabbage, cauliflower, or broccoli indoors. Select a blend of varieties that will ripen over a long season.

Week One (at the last frost date in your region): Create an edible ground cover by densely sowing a mix of mustard greens (Osaka purple mustard, tat tsoi, mizuna, garden cress, and the like) and other cool-season greens such as arugula, garden purslane, and shiso. In regions where spring is warm (May temperatures reaching 80 degrees Fahrenheit), also sow buckwheat. Young buckwheat greens are delicious in salads or stir-fried.

Then add some salad crops. Lightly sow the seeds of radishes, chard, lettuces, and carrots among the previously sown seeds.

Herb seeds go in next. Sow fennel, dill, and coriander, somewhat more densely than the salad crops, since they don't seem to germinate as well.

Now add legume seeds to the mix. Push fava beans, bush peas, or a blend of these, into the soil roughly 1 foot apart.

Add some of your favorite alliums, such as onions, garlic, garlic chives, or leeks. Plant either seeds or starts of these, about 6 to 12 inches apart.

Weeks Two to Four: Begin harvesting the edible ground cover. Don't just trim the leaves; pull the whole plant to create openings. Take care not to disturb the young beans or alliums. Pull a few of the young herbs to thin them out; they'll make a tangy addition to salads and stews. In some of the resulting gaps, plant cabbage, cauliflower, or broccoli seedlings about 18 inches apart.

Late Spring/Early Summer: When soil temperatures reach 60 degrees Fahrenheit, plant basil and bush beans in the openings.

As the spring warms up, many of the greens will bolt. Speed up your harvesting of these to eliminate them before they set seed. Alternatively, if you want to naturalize these greens in your garden, let a few go to seed, then pull the whole plant and lay it on the soil to compost and reseed. Continue harvesting all plants as they mature or crowd.

overall yield is greater than if the plants were grown in monocultural blocks covering the same area. And this polyculture offers a long and varied harvest from just one major sowing and a few minutes of later care.

Further Adventures with Polycultures

Others have expanded upon Ianto's work, adding new species to his seven-part polyculture. A village self-development organization in Nepal, the Jajarkot Permaculture Program, has created an enlarged polyculture that, with the modifications I have made, can be planted in spring in most North American gardens.

This polyculture begins by planting a dense ground cover of edible greens interspersed with slower-growing salad plants and herbs. As these are harvested, beans and other vegetables take their place. In all but the most bitterly cold regions, this polyculture can yield food for six to eight months of the year. In northern climes, installing spun row cover or greenhouse plastic over the bed can extend the productivity of this planting well into the fall and spring.

With Jajarkot's polyculture (see box on page 145), you'll be harvesting herbs for a month or two—longer if you trim some of the dill, fennel, coriander, and basil rather than pulling the whole plant. Salad greens will yield for three to four months. The early brassicas and peas will come on by late spring, and bush beans, favas, and alliums in summer. If you've chosen a few fall-heading brassicas, these will be ready for your table in autumn.

The interactions and benefits of Jajarkot's polyculture are much the same as in Ianto's, just on a larger scale. The several umbelliferous herbs attract beneficial insects. A variety of legumes fixes nitrogen, and the fava beans also attract parasitic wasps. Once again, the dense greenery shades and protects the soil and excludes weeds. And of course, the lengthy harvest is a big benefit for the gardener.

Designing Your Own Polycultures

Temperate-climate polyculture design is still in its infancy. Plenty of research still needs to be done to develop successful combinations and to broaden the number of plant varieties that work well. I encourage gardeners to experiment with their own polyculture versions. A polyculture that succeeds in one climate, such as my native Northwest with its long, cool spring and fall, might bolt or bake in the hotter "shoulder seasons" of the South or Midwest. To help gardeners design polycultures, Ianto Evans has developed a set of guidelines based on his long experience. His time-tested tips are:

1. *Seed several varieties of each species.* This lengthens the harvest season, provides information on the best types to plant, and more fully occupies ecological niches.
2. *Don't sow seed too thickly.* The recommended sowing rates on seed packets are based on heavy thinning. You'll be eating nearly every plant, so you'll be "thinning" after your plants are at least adolescent size, which is later than in conventional gardens. If you sow ten species, reduce your sowing density accordingly, to about 10 percent of the suggested rate. I've found that one seed per couple of square inches is plenty; any more than that and you'll be overwhelmed with hundreds of tiny salad plants about one month after sowing. This not only makes harvesting/thinning tedious, but the speedier-growing greens can overwhelm the less sturdy herbs.
3. *Begin your harvest early.* Harvest your plants, especially greens, when they begin to crowd, not when they are mature. Overcrowding will inhibit rapid growth. Young plants are especially tasty, as the continuing infatuation with baby vegetables demonstrates.
4. *Mix plant families, not just species.* Closely related plants compete for the same nutrients, so a polyculture that's heavy on the brassicas

(broccoli, cauliflower, cabbage, kale, Brussels sprouts) or any other single genus won't grow well. In addition to preventing fertility shortages, diversity will confuse pests in search of big blocks of their favorite food.

5. *Include many seeds of fast-growing, shallow-rooted species.* Radishes, mustard greens, fenugreek, and buckwheat will cover the soil quickly to thwart weeds, and will get your harvest off to a fast start. You'll eat a lot of these small plants, so plant them the thickest.

6. *Overlap the harvests.* To extend the harvest season, plant several varieties of each species, each with a different ripening time. For example, leaf lettuce is ready for the salad bowl much sooner than head lettuce. In addition, blend fast-growing vegetables with slow ones; early-season crops with late. Examples are radishes followed by cabbage, or peas followed by bush beans followed by fall fava beans, or spring herbs such as dill succeeded by summer basil.

7. *Avoid root and light competition.* Sprawling plants such as tomatoes and potatoes may not be appropriate for polycultures; they'll shade out many other plants. A preponderance of root crops will compete for soil space. Think about the mature size and shape of each variety before you plant, and avoid competition.

8. *Harvest whole plants.* With the exception of some long-lived herbs that can be prevented from bolting by regular trimming, polyculture plants should be pulled up whole. This allows room for the other many contenders for the same space. Be gentle; don't disturb the roots of adjoining plants. Harvest from the densest zones, and select plants whose harvest will release their slower companions from competition.

9. *Save a few plants for seed.* Let a few of the healthiest individuals of each species go to seed, for natural reseeding or for seed saving. Plants saved for seed should, if possible, be left on the north side of the bed, so they won't shade the other flora.

10. *Examine your polyculture every day.* Things happen fast in polycultures. After about three weeks, your polyculture will be at maximum density, and will need daily harvest to continue rapid growth. The payoff is a nice salad or stir-fry every day. Your polyculture will appreciate this daily attention: As the Chinese say, the best fertilizer is the gardener's shadow.

GUILDING THE GARDEN

By now, readers who are wildlife gardeners are growing impatient with all this talk of lettuce and broccoli. The above polycultures reside firmly in the realm of vegetable gardening. They are heavily cultivated, omit native plants, and allow few roles for wildlife beyond insects. These polycultures, while more "natural" than clean-cultivated row crops, are still a far cry from wild ecosystems. We need to remedy this. I began with these vegetable-based polycultures because they illustrate some of the basics of assembling plants into interactive communities, without being overwhelmingly complex. It's time to consider a wider variety of species that can more closely mimic a natural plant community. In these systems, the needs of humans are balanced with those of the rest of nature.

The more complex polycultures mentioned above have some of the qualities of natural communities. Polycultures undergo succession, offer many niches, and play a large role in creating their own structure, as do plant communities and ecosystems. We can think of ecosystems as very intricate polycultures, with far more complex interactions. Because ecosystems are so multifaceted, they can behave in more interesting and adaptive ways than simple systems. In ecosystems, we see qualities such as succession, predator-prey relations, adaptation to fire, climate control, and so on, that you won't see in conventional farms and gardens. The ability to develop patterns and qualities such as these make ecosystems far more robust, more adaptive, and less prone to disaster than most human-designed systems—such as our gardens. What qualities of ecosystems can we use in our gardens to nudge our yards into more ecological patterns?

Here's one useful quality: Ecosystems are fundamentally cooperative places. Yes, there is plenty of competition, but the underlying dynamic is one of mutual aid. In an ecosystem, microbes build soil, soil nourishes plants, plants feed animals, and animals disperse seed and leave their waste and corpses to be transformed by microbes into soil. Here spins a cycle of mutual interdependence, rich with many specific partnerships.

We can re-create some of these partnerships in our gardens. I'm not talking about simple companion planting, with its nebulous and difficult-to-identify fellowships. Let's begin with qualities we can easily spot. Plants display outward, measurable characteristics, such as nitrogen fixation, insect attraction, and mulch production. By identifying and combining these qualities, we can create the floristic equivalent of a mutual-aid society in our garden.

Nature, as we saw in chapter 2, binds plants into interdependent communities and associations. Indigenous people, too, have crafted plant combinations that weave synergies among species. In the past two decades, ecological designers also have blended plants into communities that contain partnerships. Permaculture calls these imitations of natural associations *guilds*.* Formally defined, a guild is a harmoniously interwoven group of plants and animals, often centered around one major species, that benefits humans while creating habitat. The remainder of this chapter explores the role of guilds in bringing nature's dynamics into our own gardens.

Guilds are an attempt to bridge the broad gap between conventional vegetable gardens and wildlife gardening by creating plant communities that act and feel like natural landscapes, but that include humans in their webwork. Vegetable gardens benefit only humans, while wildlife or natural gardens specifically exclude people from their ecological patterns.

Gardens for wildlife are immensely valuable, but they are only a partial answer to habitat loss. As I've said before, if we ignore the material needs of humans in our urban and suburban landscapes, we're doomed to continue our voracious consumption of wild land for factory farms and tree plantations. Ecological gardens, using guilds and the other tools described in this book, help our developed land to blossom into nourishing places for both humans and wildlife.

The Three Sisters (or is it four?)

Let's begin our exploration of guilds with a very simple example that illustrates some essential principles. Then we can proceed to more complex guilds—ones that go beyond vegetables.

Familiar to many gardeners is the Native American triad of corn, beans, and squash, a combination often called the Three Sisters. The trio qualifies as a guild because each of these plants supports and benefits the others. The cornstalks form a trellis for the bean vines to climb. The beans, in turn, draw nitrogen from the air, and via symbiotic bacteria convert the nitrogen to plant-available form. These nitrogen-fixing bacteria, scientists have recently learned, are fed by special sugars that ooze from the corn roots. The rambling squash, with its broad leaves, forms a living parasol that densely covers the ground, inhibiting weeds and keeping the soil cool and moist. Together, the Three Sisters produce more food, with less water and fertilizer, than a similar area planted to any one of these three crops in isolation. Jane Mt. Pleasant, an agronomist at Cornell University who has blended her Iroquois heritage with her research, has shown that yields of this guild, measured in calories, are about 20 percent higher than corn grown alone in an equal-sized plot.

---

* The term *guild* is used by ecologists to mean something slightly different (a set of different species that use a common resource in a similar way, as in "the guild of seed-eating birds"). This overlap is unfortunate and potentially confusing, but permaculture's use of the term *guild* is well established, and I will stick with this common usage rather than introduce another term.

Look at how many interconnections this guild bears. Beans furnish nitrogenous fertility for themselves, the corn, and the squash; squash shades soil for the benefit of all three; corn feeds the bean-hugging bacterial nodules and creates a trellis for the beans. Three plants, weaving at least eight connections. The Three Sisters guild is a perfect place to begin creating a richly connected garden.

In the Southwest, a fourth "sister" is found in this guild: Rocky Mountain bee plant (Cleome serrulata). Often found growing near former Anasazi settlements—it's virtually an indicator plant for ancient ruins—this 2- to 5-foot-tall, pink-flowered cleome is a powerful attractant for beneficial insects that pollinate beans and squash. The young leaves, flowers, and seedpods of bee plant are edible, and native people boiled and ate them, or made a paste from the plant for later use. Bee plant also accumulates iron, and is the source of a deep-hued paint used to create the characteristic black designs on Anasazi pottery. Songs and blessings of New Mexico's Tewa people mention corn, beans, squash, and bee plant, indicating that this multifunctional flower is an integral member of a sacred plant pantheon.

I was pleased to learn of this fourth sister, as it connects the web of this guild's beneficial interactions with the insect realm. Part of the strength of the corn/beans/squash triad comes from its tie-in with a nonvegetable domain: that of the symbiotic nitrogen-fixing bacteria carried by the beans. And now, by adding a fourth plant to the guild, the web's pattern strengthens further, drawing insects into the network. Lured by bee plant, these nectar-slurpers will pollinate the squash and beans (corn is wind pollinated), ensuring good fruit set. By extending the Three Sisters, we've moved into three kingdoms: animal, plant, and bacterial. Creating this connectedness allows us to draw upon three billion years of life's wisdom for aid.

The lesson here is that by hooking into the cyclical rhythms of many-kingdomed nature, a guild can capitalize on enormous sources of energy and experience. Focusing only on food plants sucks

GROWING THE THREE SISTERS GUILD

Mark out a series of planting holes about 3 feet apart (to calculate how many holes you need, figure that you'll get about four or five ears of corn per hole). Then poke three or four kernels of corn into each hole, and cover with an inch of soil. Your favorite sweet corn variety will do, although Native Americans developed shorter, multistalked cultivars specifically for this guild, such as Black Aztec, Hopi white, or Tarahumara sweet corn, so you might consider a similar many-stalked variety. When the corn sprouts, start mounding the soil up around the young stalks. Don't cover the sprouts, just build up earth around the base. These mounds, by exposing soil to the air and sun, will warm the sprouts, speeding their growth. The mounds also improve drainage. Don't thin the corn—you want two or three stalks per mound, hence the greater-than-usual distance between mounds.

About two weeks after planting the corn, select some pole beans—not a bush variety—and coat the seeds with a legume inoculant specific for beans (available from many seed suppliers). This ensures that the all-important nitrogen-fixing bacteria find a happy home among the bean roots. Plant two or three bean seeds into each corn mound.

At the same time you start the beans, plant squash or pumpkins between each mound. Don't use zucchini; grow a vining squash variety that will sprawl over the soil.

Aside from these planting instructions, grow the Three Sisters by following the guidelines on each vegetable's seed packet. After harvest, leave the stalks, vines, and other organic debris on the ground to compost in place. This returns some of the extracted fertility to the soil and protects the ground from erosion. Although much of the bacterially fixed nitrogen will be concentrated into the protein-rich bean pods, plenty will remain in the vines and roots, ready to go back to the earth.

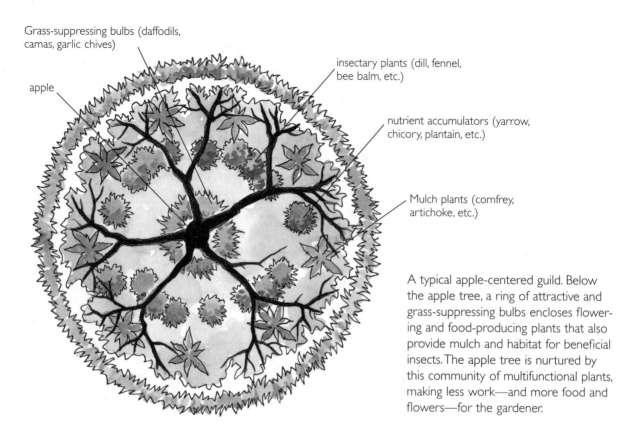

Grass-suppressing bulbs (daffodils, camas, garlic chives)

apple

insectary plants (dill, fennel, bee balm, etc.)

nutrient accumulators (yarrow, chicory, plantain, etc.)

Mulch plants (comfrey, artichoke, etc.)

A typical apple-centered guild. Below the apple tree, a ring of attractive and grass-suppressing bulbs encloses flowering and food-producing plants that also provide mulch and habitat for beneficial insects. The apple tree is nurtured by this community of multifunctional plants, making less work—and more food and flowers—for the gardener.

fertility from the soil while giving little in return. In contrast, offering a little something extra—a habitat for bees, a home for soil organisms—ties the small cycles of our garden into the generous and large cycles of nature. Growing a few early-blooming flowers encourages bees and other beneficial insects to stick around when the fruit trees need pollination and the aphids begin to swarm. Leaving last fall's leaves to compost on a flower bed nurtures a healthy crop of worms to till and aerate soil and to deposit nutrient-rich worm castings down among the roots. Our small offerings bring large rewards. In effect, if we buy the first round of drinks, nature picks up the tab for dinner and a show. We can leverage our assets into a not-so-small fortune by piggy-backing onto the pooled resources of the natural economy. By making nature our partner, our yields multiply, and risk of failure declines.

The addition of bee plant boosts the Three Sisters into a more powerful foursome. This illustrates a useful rule for guild design: Start with something known and basic, and gradually add connections. We now have a hint about creating our own guilds. Let's see how a more complex guild is constructed, and then we can develop more guidelines for building our own.

Building an Apple-Centered Guild

Courses in permaculture often proffer, as an introduction for students, a basic guild whose dominant member is an apple tree. Just as the Three (or four) Sisters bolster each other, the members of this new guild support the apple tree in numerous ways: by luring beneficial insects for pollination and pest control, boosting soil tilth and fertility, reducing root competition, conserving water, balancing fungal populations to counter diseases such as scab, diversifying the yield of food, creating habitat, and several other functions. The result is a healthier apple tree and a varied ecology. Also, this biological support replaces human intervention, shifting the gardener's workload onto the broad back of nature.

The apple guild is a useful learning tool. It illustrates some general principles of guild building. I'll describe an apple guild briefly, and then we can examine it in more detail to see how each piece functions.

In the center of a typical apple guild, not too surprisingly, is an apple tree. Under the tree's outermost leaves, at the *drip line,* is a ring of thickly planted daffodil bulbs. Inside the bulbs is a broken circle of lush comfrey plants, each topped with purple blossoms that buzz with bees. Within these circles are two or three robust artichoke plants. Dotted between these grow flowers and herbs: yellow bursts of yarrow, trailing orange nasturtiums, and the airy umbels of dill and fennel. A closer look shows a number of plants that are normally considered weeds, such as dandelion, chicory, and plantain. Crowding between all this flora is a thick ground cover of clover, and we can spot some fava beans and other legumes growing in the dappled sun beneath the branches.

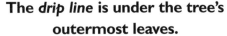

The *drip line* is under the tree's outermost leaves.

Each species in this guild performs a valuable function. Just as an automobile needs parts that perform certain functions—steering, power, braking—organized in the proper relationship, every guild has elements to do the tasks—disease control, fertilizer production, pollination—necessary for the guild to be healthy and low maintenance. Good guild design lets nature perform all these jobs by fitting different plants and animals into each role. If we leave out one of the guild's pieces, we're stuck with performing that part's task. And if we're short-sighted enough to simply plant an apple tree in isolation, we have to do it all: spraying for disease, watering, fertilizing, and importing bee hives for pollination. No wonder fruit trees are considered high maintenance. Conventional orchards have broken the gears that mesh our fruit trees into the rest of nature.

Now that we have an overview of this guild, let's dive in and examine its pieces to see how they fit together to create a harmonious community. In keeping with ecological gardening's emphasis on processes rather than pieces, I've organized the guild members by function instead of plant type. You've seen most of these plant functions before, in chapter 6, but here I relate them more specifically to guilds. These are the elements that are common to almost every well-designed guild.

THE CENTRAL ELEMENT. In this guild, we've chosen an apple tree as the centerpiece, though almost any fruit tree could be substituted. Usually the central element is a food-producing plant, though other types of guilds may feature wildlife-attracting or nitrogen-fixing trees, or perhaps a timber-producer. Apple trees come in many sizes, from 30-foot-tall standard trees to 6-foot mini-dwarfs, with semi-standards, semi-dwarfs, and dwarf trees in between. All are fine for guilds, but obviously, a small tree won't support as many associated plants as a big one. The size you choose will be based on your property size, how high you like to reach or climb to harvest, and other similar variables. The tree should be pruned to an open shape to allow light to reach the plants below.

GRASS-SUPPRESSING BULBS. The shallow roots of bulbs keep grasses from moving into our guild. Grasses, though planted deliberately by many orchardists, are surface feeders and thus vie for nutrients with trees, whose principal feeding roots also lie near the surface (where most nutrients reside). Eliminating grasses near fruit trees will lessen the need for fertilizer.

Bulbs should be planted in a circle at the drip line of the tree based on its full-grown size. Since bulbs curtail their growth in early summer, they won't rob water from the tree as the heat comes on. Useful bulbs include daffodils, camas, and alliums (preferably perennial alliums such as garlic,

garlic chives, ramps or wild leek, or Egyptian onions rather than annual onions).

Daffodils are particularly useful bulbs, as they contain toxins that animals abhor. Deer eschew the aboveground parts, and gophers are repelled by the bulbs. Planting one circle of daffodils around the trunk and a second thick circle of them at the drip line will temper the depredations of browsers, burrowers, and bark-chewers.

Bulbs such as camas and alliums, besides occupying ground that would otherwise be choked with grass, are edible. Camas bulbs were a principal food of western Native Americans, and are having a resurgence among wild-food enthusiasts.

This selection of multifunctional bulbs can yield food, protect from pests, and reduce grasses. You've probably noticed that they look nice, too. In general, bulbs for this guild should be spring flowering and summer dormant, and ideally have at least one function beyond shouldering aside the grass, such as edibility, pest repellence, or beneficial-bug luring.

INSECT- AND BIRD-ATTRACTING PLANTS. The tempting blossoms of flowering plants will lure pollinators for boosting fruit set, and attract predatory wasps that feast on pestiferous larvae such as borers and codling moths. Choices include edible herbs such as dill, fennel, and coriander, as well as many of the insectary plants described in chapter 6 and listed in the appendix. If you want to be a fanatic, the commercial orchardists tell us, select flowers that will bloom just before and after—but not during—apple blossom time, so pollinators will be abundant but not distracted by competing blooms. For home orchards, I suspect this is less than critical.

A few flowering shrubs such as butterfly bush and fuchsia, or perennials such as red-hot poker and salvia varieties, placed not necessarily under the tree but nearby, will encourage insectivorous birds, who will probe the apple tree's bark crevices for larvae and eggs.

MULCH PLANTS. Growing mulch under the tree eliminates trudging around with a compost-filled wheelbarrow, since the guild will build its own soil. Mulch makers include soft-leafed plants such as comfrey, artichokes, cardoon, rhubarb, clovers, and nasturtiums, all of which can be slashed and left to compost in place. A ring of comfrey around the tree can be hacked down four or five times a summer. As the nutrient-rich greenery rots, it delivers a huge dose of minerals and organic matter to the soil. The resulting thick layer of compost is home to a thriving and diverse population of worms, fungi, bacteria, and other helpful denizens of the soil. This rich and living soil will suppress diseases, because the churning soil life competes fiercely for food and habitat below the ground. With all the resources divvied up pretty evenly between the soil's many inhabitants, no one microbial species can get out of balance and become a pest. This means that buildups of harmful fungi such as apple scab are less likely—there's too much competition and too many predators for a single-species population explosion. In contrast, a clean-swept and chemically fertilized orchard floor, devoid of organic matter, ensures that the only fungi able to thrive will be pests, since they are adapted to feeding on the one remaining source of food: your trees.

NUTRIENT ACCUMULATORS. Examples of plants that accumulate nutrients are chicory, dandelion, yarrow, plantain, and others found in the appendix. The deep taproots of these plants plunge far into the mineral soil and dredge up important nutrients: potassium, magnesium, calcium, sulfur, and others. As the guild matures, nutrients will begin to recycle within the guild rather than requiring extraction from mineral soil by deep roots. The accumulator plants will then become redundant, and begin a natural decline that the gardener can accelerate by pulling them up and replacing them with others.

NITROGEN FIXERS. I've mentioned the benefits of nitrogen-fixing plants throughout this book, so it should be no surprise that they are a critical component of guilds. Adding nitrogen fixers to guilds is one more way of keeping nutrients cycling within the plant community and reducing the need for fertilizer and other inputs. Since all-important nitrogen is so freely available from the air, it seems silly to be constantly lugging bags of it into our gardens.

The list of potential N-fixers for guilds is long, and includes clovers, alfalfa, lupines, cowpeas, beans, peas, vetch, and others listed in the appendix. Which is best? I opt for the perennials, such as Dutch or New Zealand white clover, alfalfa, or lupine. However, many of the others, including vetch and some beans, reseed freely, giving them nearly perennial status. Cowpeas and fava beans are edible, which stacks yet another product into the guild. In late summer, I usually poke one or two dozen fava seeds into the soil beneath each of my fruit trees, and the following spring, harvest the pods and mulch the stalks in place. Gardeners not similarly blessed with mild winters can start favas in early spring for summer harvest and for mulch material.

SOIL FUMIGANTS AND PEST REPELLENTS. Certain plants exude substances that repel pests. Examples are nasturtiums and certain marigolds. Their merits and drawbacks were presented in chapter 6. Pest-repellent plants are the least understood of the guild members, and although nasturtiums seem to be beneficial in guilds, few other pest repellents have been well tested, and should be used with caution, as they may repel beneficials as well.

HABITAT NOOKS. Piling up stones, logs, or brush near the apple guild, and creating small ponds and puddles, will attract lizards, frogs, snakes, and birds. I've tucked individual and piled-up rocks unobtrusively around our yard, and vast numbers of helpful garter snakes and lizards nest under them. Now I can't move a rock without uncovering a reptilian home. That's okay—I want a ready crew of these beneficial animals for gobbling up slugs, leaf-eating insects, and harmful larvae.

Predators such as these are important for preserving balance. If any prey species—caterpillars, aphids, slugs, or the like—finds a home in the lush garden and begins to reproduce exuberantly, a waiting population of predators will cull their numbers with chilling efficiency.

These are the roles that should be filled in any guild. Guild design is still a young science, and as we learn more about the connections necessary to build a thriving plant community, we may need to insert other roles into our guilds. So far, ecological gardeners around the country have had good results from a blend of grass suppressers, insect and bird attractants, nutrient accumulators, mulch plants, nitrogen fixers, soil fumigants, and pest repellents, all surrounding a central food-producer tree.

Several Pieces, Many Functions, One Guild

You'll note that many of the apple-guild members have more than one function. Clover and alfalfa are nitrogen fixers, but they also attract bees. Plantain and yarrow sequester nutrients and are medicinal as well, artichokes produce both mulch and food, and mineral-collecting dandelions and chicory are also edible. The winner in the multifunctional sweepstakes is comfrey, which yields mulch and medicine, attracts insects to its flowers, pulls potassium and other minerals from the soil into its leaves, and can be made into a tea for drinking or for fertilizing the garden. Clever guild designers will choose as many multifunctional guild members as they can. This begets a guild that swells with connections, which, as we saw in chapter 2, makes a plant community—and our garden—flexible, responsive, and robust. Plants acting in community can survive weather extremes, soil problems, pest invasions, and other onslaughts far better than can isolated species.

All that remains to create the apple guild is to fit the plants together. The illustration on page 150 shows one arrangement that will work in most gardens. To decide how many plants to use, let the mature size of the central tree be the guide. A dwarf or semi-dwarf apple tree will support fewer guild members than a large standard tree, and will require smaller plant varieties. With dwarf trees, I'd avoid climbers such as vetch, which might trellis up the apple and shroud it with vines. Also, artichokes are probably too large to fit under a dwarf tree. Think about each plant's habits and mature size when you construct your array. As a rule of thumb, the larger the plant, the fewer of its kind in the guild: one apple, one or two artichokes, several comfreys, a dozen insectary plants, dozens of bulbs, hundreds of clovers.

One potential drawback to our apple guild: Come harvest time, the apple tree may be surrounded by a thicket of vegetation that will ensnare the legs of an orchard ladder. Fortunately, by the time mid- to late-fruiting apple varieties are ripe, much of the undergrowth will have died down and harvest will be easy. But harvesting summer apples will necessitate a bit of care during ladder placement. However, there's no hurry—this isn't a commercial orchard, and the extra bounty and reduced maintenance bequeathed by the guild should balance any slight inconvenience felt while parking the ladder.

This guild restores nature's role as the gardener's partner, transforming a solitary apple tree into a plant community that immensely lightens the human workload. By creating a guild such as this one, gardeners weave a strong web that builds fertile soil and mulch, attracts pollinators and pest-fighting insects, reduces fungal disease, provides a diverse array of food, flowers, and herbs, creates wildlife habitat, and reduces water and fertilizer use. These benefits stem not just from choosing the right parts—the right plants—but also from placing the guild's parts in the right relationship.

Chapter 9

Designing Garden Guilds

To DESIGN OUR OWN GUILDS, we need to go back to nature. A natural community of plants has a life of its own, one that we'd like to imitate in our guilds. A healthy plant community recycles its own waste back into nutrients, resists disease, controls pests, harvests and conserves water, attracts insects and other animals to do its bidding, and hums along happily as it performs these and a hundred other tasks. To lay the groundwork for building our own guilds, we ought to look at natural communities—what they're made of, how they're organized, and how the pieces are connected. Although simply copying the guilds found in this book may satisfy some gardeners, more experimentally inclined readers may want to create their own guilds. The next few sections show how. Also, not all guilds are appropriate for every soil, climate, and terrain, thus knowing how to customize guilds without severing their interconnections is useful.

This chapter offers two techniques for creating your own guilds by analyzing natural plant communities. The first method is based on intimate, firsthand knowledge—hanging out with a plant community long enough to see interrelationships between the various members. The second technique is more of a "paint-by-numbers" approach for those lacking the time for lingering meditations in the woods. This method uses plant identification books and library research to assemble a guild. (A note on nomenclature: when I refer to a *community,* I mean a natural grouping of species in the wild. A *guild,* on the other hand, is a human-made assemblage that mimics a natural community.)

After learning about guild design, we'll see how to combine several guilds to create landscapes that offer an incredibly diverse assortment of fruits, vegetables, and wildlife habitat while minimizing the gardener's work by letting nature do her share.

AN INTIMATE WAY OF GUILD-BUILDING

Every region has its own set of plant communities, whether we're in the oak-hickory woodlands of the Northeast, the chaparral of California, the saguaro-mesquite lands of the low desert, or the Southeast's pine forests. Local field guidebooks, especially the more recently published ones, often list the dominant plant communities of the region.

A brief walk with a field guide through the native plant communities where we live (or those remaining near our city or suburb in nature parks and preserves) will teach us which species regularly occur together. Each community has an almost palpable feel, and as we become more experienced, we can sense the shift from, say, a dry and open oak-hickory woods to the cool dampness of a maple and beech grove. Soon we can see relationships. We might note that currant bushes seem to thrive beneath the maples, but they are thin and rare below the oaks; or that squirrels extend the spread of oak woods by stashing and forgetting acorns.

Eventually, our observations will allow us to understand natural plant communities well enough to build analogous guilds of plants appropriate for our yards. By blending a native community's original species with similar domesticated plants we can try to re-create the community's original interconnections while tilting the community's offerings a bit into the human realm. We'll take a look at how one experienced naturewatcher designed a successful guild, and then we'll use this example to generate some general rules for guild-building.

Solanaceae are *narcissistic*—that is, they thrive on the leaf litter of members of their own family.

Arizona permaculture designer Tim Murphy has created a guild centered on a walnut tree, based on his intimate knowledge of a walnut-containing plant community. Let's follow Tim's observations, reasoning, and hunches to see how an experienced guild-builder uses nature to design a useful plant assembly. Since walnuts grow in much of the United States, this example of guild creation can be applied by gardeners all over the country.

The walnut tree is one of the patriarchs of the plant kingdom. My old home in Illinois had a huge black walnut over the back deck, and on many mornings I lounged in its soothing shadows with a good book and a mug of coffee. Along with shaded

pleasures, walnut trees offer many other benefits. They yield delicious nuts, and delight us with the scampering of squirrels among the branches in search of the tree's bounty. Even the nutshells have uses, for dye and abrasives. Walnuts also provide premium-quality timber that brings in a hefty sum and is a cabinetmaker's delight. The trees are drought tolerant, too, and can thrive in the arid western states as well as in less harsh locales.

Choosing companion plants for walnuts is tricky because this genus is *allelopathic*—that is, the plants secrete a toxic substance (in this case, one called juglone) that suppresses competing plants. Very few species can thrive under the canopy of a walnut, and vegetation near the trees is often stunted. But once again, observing nature nudges us toward a solution. By observing what juglone-tolerant species naturally associate with these stately trees, Tim Murphy has evolved a guild of walnut-friendly plants.

Murphy noticed that in Arizona a vigorous pioneer shrub called hackberry (*Celtis* spp.) often sprawls in the dry shade of walnut trees. Hackberry's leaves and berries yield good wildlife forage, making this shrub a candidate for the ecological garden. Since hackberries seem to thrive beneath walnut trees, the shrub's growth is evidently not squelched by juglone. Like walnuts, hackberries secrete a competition-suppressing substance; an intriguing harmony vibrates between these two allelopathic birds-of-a-feather. The toxins from the two species almost seem to complement each other. Juglone, though stunting the growth of many plants, doesn't have much effect on grass, whereas hackberry's toxins inhibit grasses and other shallow-rooted plants.

Here is a subtle interweaving that leaves a highly specialized niche. What rare combination of qualities results in plants that can grow amidst walnuts and hackberries, unscathed by this broad spectrum of toxicity? We can look to nature to tell us what grows with walnuts and hackberries, but how their companions survive in toxin-laced soil is little understood. We know only superficialities about plant relations and are reduced to simple, empirical observations at this point. Some plants can tolerate walnut and hackberry toxins, and many cannot.

To create a useful guild, we need to find more species that can survive this allelopathic bath. Tim has noted currants growing under a walnut canopy. An odd thing about these currants: Tim generally finds them under walnut trees only when hackberries are present. Why is that? Does the mingling of walnut and hackberry create some currant-enhancing condition? Tim offers up a few hypotheses for the walnut/hackberry/currant confederation. He notes that decomposing walnut leaves and husks release insect-repelling citronella fumes. Since aphids and other soft-bodied bugs are a prime currant pest, the odor of citronella wafting through currant leaves may protect this low shrub. Also, cur-

rants probably benefit from the absence of competing grasses under hackberries, and the dappled shade cast by these larger chaperones provides the half-gloom that currants favor. Perhaps, too, the berry bushes profit from some subterranean molecular commerce between the microbial associates of walnut and hackberry roots. A combination of these and other, less obvious qualities may explain the allure that walnuts and hackberries hold for currants.

These three plants—walnuts, hackberries, and currants—furnish the foundations of a guild. The three species provide nuts and timber, habitat for wildlife, and berries for munching or jam. That's still a meager harvest, though. Can we build on this framework?

Tim has recorded two other species found under hackberries: chiltepine (*Capsicum aviculare*) and wolfberry (*Lycium* spp.). Chiltepine, a perennial, is the feral parent of the chile pepper and bears habañero-hot half-inch fruits. Wolfberry is a

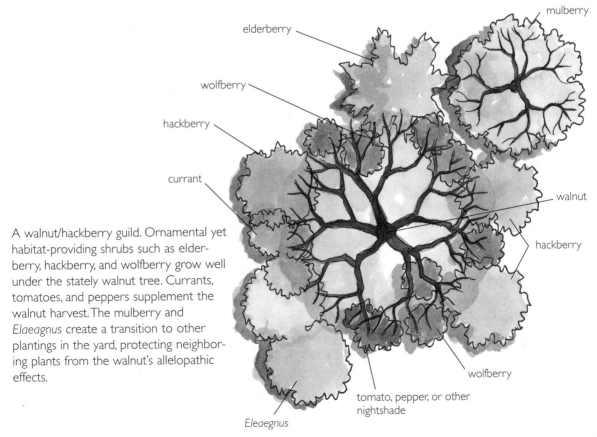

A walnut/hackberry guild. Ornamental yet habitat-providing shrubs such as elderberry, hackberry, and wolfberry grow well under the stately walnut tree. Currants, tomatoes, and peppers supplement the walnut harvest. The mulberry and *Elaeagnus* create a transition to other plantings in the yard, protecting neighboring plants from the walnut's allelopathic effects.

thorned shrub that drops its leaves in severe drought and holds berries relished by birds. Both are members of the Solanaceae, the nightshade family, which also includes tomatoes, peppers, potatoes, and eggplants. Tim notes that the Solanaceae are *narcissistic*—that is, they thrive in the leaf litter of members of their own family. This raises the possibility that certain of the domesticated Solanaceae could fit into the walnut/hackberry guild (it's well known that potatoes are stunted by juglone, but the pepper and tomato branch of the family seems less sensitive, and could provide good candidates).

Now we have a framework for a nature-based guild: Walnuts, hackberries, currants, and perhaps peppers or tomatoes. Let's flesh out this skeleton yet further. Nitrogen-fixing plants are obvious candidates to plug into our guild. Their ability, via symbiotic bacteria, to convert atmospheric nitrogen into fertility-giving nitrate means they simultaneously enhance soil ecology and accumulate nutrients. These multiple functions brand them near-mandatory components of guilds. Most nitrogen fixers are legumes, the plant family that includes beans and peas. A few other plant families also bear nitrogen-fixing members. For the walnut/hackberry guild, Tim proposes a nonleguminous nitrogen fixer called Russian olive. Other members of Russian olive's genus, *Elaeagnus*, will also work, as the drought-tolerant *Elaeagnus* species seem insensitive to juglone. The berries of wild Elaeagnus are prime wildlife food, and domesticated varieties, such as goumi and *Elaeagnus × ebbingei* sport fruit good enough for humans. Native plant enthusiasts may want to include indigenous nitrogen fixers such as ceanothus, or, in the southwest, Apache plume *(Fallugia paradoxa)*.

Finally, Tim suggests placing other walnut-tolerant species near the margins of the guild to buffer juglone's effect on other plants. Candidates include mulberries, elderberries, black locusts, and acacias. The last two also fix nitrogen and are beloved by bees. Beyond this buffer zone, useful plants not tolerant of juglone, such as fruiting trees and shrubs, can be woven into the assemblage.

How to assemble this guild? The illustration on page 157 gives one possible arrangement. Just as in the apple guild, the rule for determining numbers is: the bigger the plant, the fewer in the guild. Begin with a single walnut tree. Around it, within the roughly 20-foot circle that will be the future drip line of the walnut, plant one to three each of hackberry, currant, wolfberry, and *Elaeagnus* or other N-fixer. Then scatter the solanaceous plants (peppers, tomatoes, eggplants) in the interstices. In northern climates with their reduced sunlight, sprinkle these last toward the brighter margins of the circle. In the south, these vegetables will appreciate the walnut's dappled shade. Radiating outside of this circle, place the mulberries and other buffer plants.

The resulting varied array will create a lively web of connections to beckon many ancillary components: birds to spread seeds and guano, insects for pollination, soil microorganisms to release and transport nutrients, and small mammals to till, prune, and fertilize.

Several gardeners have installed variations of this guild. Los Alamos resident Mary Zemach has put many of Tim's observations to work in her own walnut/hackberry guild, which also holds currants, wolfberries, elderberries, silverberries, and *Elaeagnus*. Mary acknowledges that her guild is still an experiment, but when I visited, the plants were thriving.

GUILDS FOR BOOKWORMS

The most successful guilds are those designed after prolonged observation of a natural community. These guilds have the best chance of clicking into the dynamic relationships that wild plant communities embody. But gaining enough knowledge to design on the basis of prolonged observation takes special dedication. For ecological gardeners who haven't the time or inclination to spend hours—or years—with a natural community, I present a more academic, armchair method of guild design. Remember, though, that nothing substitutes for

USING NATURAL PLANT COMMUNITIES TO GUIDE GUILD DESIGN

Based on the work of Tim Murphy and other guild designers, we can develop some guidelines for creating guilds from local plant communities. Here are some questions to ask that will help select plants for useful guilds.

1. What is the dominant tree species of the community? Is it useful for humans, via nuts, fruit, particular beauty, animal feed, or other benefit? Is a related tree even more useful?
2. Which plants are offering food to wildlife? What wildlife uses them? Are these animals desirable in the yard?
3. Are any plants capable of providing food for humans? Do any plants in the community have domesticated relatives that can provide fruit, berries, tubers, greens, herbs, or other products for people?
4. Which species are common to more than one community, as opposed to those unique to only one? These may be possible buffer or transition plants to connect a guild to the rest of the yard.
5. Does any species show exceptional insect damage, or have large numbers of harmful insects living on it? This might not be a desirable variety.
6. What species generates most of the leaf litter? Would it make a good mulch plant?
7. How well, and by what mechanisms, does the community withstand drought or flood? Some desert plants shed their leaves in extreme dryness, a useful quality but not an attractive habit for a major planting.
8. Do any plants have bare ground or stunted vegetation near them? This may simply be due to deep shade, but if sunlight reaches the soil near this plant, the species might be an allelopath and worthy of caution.
9. Are any plant families heavily represented in the community? If so, domesticated relatives might be successfully substituted.
10. Does the community contain any known nitrogen fixers or other nutrient accumulators? These may be critical members and necessary for a related guild.

The answers to these questions will generate a list of species that can form the backbone of a potential guild.

observation, and even a brief field trip to a plant community can yield critical insights that books can't give.

The armchair method begins with a search for lists of the major plant communities native to your area. This information resides in ecology books and journal articles in university libraries or online databases. This literature is abundant and dense, and may require some digging to extract the relevant nuggets. In my own neck of the woods, I would begin by searching under "Plant Communities, Oregon" in a university library catalog or database index. In your search, plug in your own state's name. When the lengthy list of references comes up, watch for titles such as "Plant Associations of (your state)," or "Vegetation of (your county)." If you know the dominant native tree in your region, you can narrow down the search by seeking research on that species. I have a handy paper called "The *Quercus garryana* Forests of the Willamette Valley," which describes the Oregon white oak forests that rule the dry hillsides of my region.

If this research process seems daunting, some legwork can be circumvented by calling the nearest college botany department and asking where to find descriptions of the plant communities of your area. Someone in the department will know the name of the best books or journal articles for you, and may even be willing to give an impromptu telephone lecture on local plant communities.

Here's how I would build an armchair guild for my bioregion. On my bookshelf sits the bible of plant communities for my locale, *Vegetation of Oregon and Washington,* by Jerry Franklin and C. T. Dyrness. Though it's more than twenty years old, the species lists are still valid. Thumbing through this book, I see that plant communities are listed not only by region, but also, bless the authors' hearts, by climate and soil preference. My house hugs the brow of a south-facing hillside that bakes to withering dryness in summer, thus I need to find a plant community that's native to my area and tolerates hot, dry, clayey slopes. Franklin and Dyrness suggest that Oregon white oak, *Quercus garryana,* will thrive in my conditions. This is no surprise, as both my woods rambles and the paper cited above have taught me that Oregon white oak loves it here. It's reassuring, though, that the professors and I agree.

White oak communities, Franklin and Dyrness reveal, come in several varieties, each named for the most prevalent understory shrub. These communities are called white oak/hazelnut, white oak/serviceberry, and—gulp—white oak/poison oak, which unfortunately is all too common around here. Each community contains a dozen or more associated plants that are listed in the text or in a table.

Next, I scan these lists for species that are useful in themselves, or have relatives that yield food, habitat, or other gifts. My goal is to use the original community members or related substitutes to create a guild with a structure similar to the native community, but one that provides products for humans in addition to its many natural functions. The white oak/hazelnut community has excellent

TABLE 9-1.

**MEMBERS OF THE
WHITE OAK/HAZELNUT COMMUNITY**

Common name	Botanical name
Oregon white oak	*Quercus garryana*
California hazelnut	*Corylus cornuta*
Pacific madrone	*Arbutus menziesii*
Mazzard cherry	*Prunus avium*
Black hawthorn	*Craetagus douglasii*
Saskatoon serviceberry	*Amelanchier alnifolia*
Creambush oceanspray	*Holodiscus discolor*
Round-leaved snowberry	*Symphoricarpos albus*
Thimbleberry	*Rubus parviflorus*
Trailing blackberry	*Rubus ursinus*
Sweetbriar rose	*Rosa eglanteria*
Broad-petaled strawberry	*Fragaria virginiana*
Poison oak	*Rhus diversiloba*
Yerba buena	*Satureja douglasii*
Sweet cicely	*Osmorhiza chilensis*
American vetch	*Vicia americana*

potential, since it includes several nuts, fruits, berries, and herbs. The members of the community are shown in table 9-1.

With a little exploration and fine-tuning, the white oak/hazelnut community can be transformed into a very useful guild. Let's walk through the species list.

Oregon white oak has subtle virtues. It's a lovely shade tree, and mature specimens bear abundant acorns cherished by wildlife. Oaks often swarm with birds probing the bark for insects. The acorns were a major protein source for Native Americans, roasted whole or ground into flour. White oak acorns contain less bitter tannic acid than others, and thus don't require the complex leaching process that renders many acorns palatable. They also make excellent animal feed. Will suburban gardeners eat acorns? I confess I've only experimented with them, and I'd wager their acceptability as food is limited. The tree also takes a decade or more to bear acorns, so they're not an ideal human food plant. Oak wood is valuable timber, but unless you've got some acreage, cutting down a major yard tree is potentially disastrous, and it certainly disrupts the guild.

Thus, white oak's food value for humans is limited, and its timber value in a suburban yard is doubtful. Is Oregon white oak useful enough to hold down a guild? Here is my reasoning: If I demanded that every guild's central tree provide me with copious food, I might substitute an oak relative, the chestnut, and hope that it wove well into this guild. I might even rove far afield and experiment with a fruit tree or other species, especially if I could take advantage of a mature specimen already present. But with all of oak's gentle benefits, especially for wildlife, plus its status as one of our most charismatic trees, I'm inclined to overlook its slight food value for humans. For me, the oak is a fine focal tree for a guild. I grow other trees for fruit and nuts.

The second major component of this oak community is the California hazel. No major substitution is needed here, just a little domestication. Hazelnut is a very useful plant. The hazelnut genus has been bred into a suite of heavy nut-producers such as European and Turkish filberts, filazels, hazelberts, and the tree hazel or trazel. Not only are the shrubs attractive, but birds love hazelnuts too, and you'll probably share your harvest with them, like it or not. With white oak and a domesticated hazelnut, we're on our way to a useful guild.

Often the Oregon white oak community harbors another tree species, Pacific madrone. Here we have several choices. The madrone is an outstanding tree, luring immense flocks of birds to munch the prolific flowers and berries. Its smooth red bark is gorgeous, flaking off each summer to bring in birds in search of insects under the cracking fragments. Should the tree come down, the firewood is denser than walnut and burns hot and long. The genus *Arbutus* also contains several ornamental species that could be substituted, but my suggestion for using this genus is to plant madrone's close relative, the strawberry tree, *Arbutus unedo,* which bears edible, somewhat seedy fruit. However, I'm hesitant to place both oak and madrone—large trees with limited food value—into a guild, especially in a small yard. Unless you live on a half-acre or more, you might declare that this guild just ain't big enough for the both of them, and drop the arbutus altogether.

The understory of the white oak community holds two small trees, mazzard cherry and black hawthorn. Co-opting these species into our guild is easy, since each is useful in wild or domesticated form. Mazzard cherries are relished by birds, though humans will find the fruit good only for an occasional sour mouthful or for pies. Mazzard is also a commonly used cherry rootstock, available at nurseries grafted onto sweet or pie cherry scion wood. These grafted cherries could be introduced into our guild. The second small tree, black hawthorn, is not only beautiful but a superb wildlife plant as well, with berries that carry many

birds through the winter. It's a close relative of the pear, and can be easily grafted to become a pear-bearing variety. Pruning will keep these two already-small trees at manageable height. With cherry and hawthorn, we now have an understory that generates food for wildlife and humans.

The white oak community, as the list shows, is loaded with berries. Serviceberry (also called juneberry or saskatoonberry) has been domesticated into varieties that yield excellent fruit, so let's plug in some of these. Thimbleberries are a treat known to all Northwest hikers; they rival raspberries for flavor. Two species of blackberry twine among this community, but for the sake of your skin's integrity, I'd substitute the thornless variety. Snowberry doesn't taste very good to humans, since the fruits contain soapy saponins, but birds savor the plant. Snowberry is related to honeysuckle, which suggests a possible ornamental and wildlife-attracting substitute. And finally, the strawberries are an obvious choice for a tasty ground cover.

Why on earth, you ask, did I include poison oak? This rash-producing shrub and its relative, poison ivy, remind me of the "Police Line—Do Not Cross" ribbons that cordon off crime scenes. The plants move into abused, chewed-up land and cloak it with a protective, human-deterring barrier. Poison oak seems to say, "You humans messed this up; now stay away while it heals." Gardeners obviously won't want to plant poison oak, but a harmless near-relative, lemonade berry *(Rhus inte-grifolia)* bears flowers that can be steeped in boiling water to make a tangy drink. The flowers secrete nectar for insects, and birds enjoy the berries. A Southwest native, lemonade berry is hardy enough (USDA Zone 7) to survive in my Oregon yard. One drawback: Lemonade berry even *looks* like poison oak, so a gardener might accidentally grub it out during a robotic weeding frenzy.

Sweetbriar rose illustrates the line we're trying to tread between wild and domestic. You could use the native species, or select a different variety, such as *Rosa rugosa,* that bears large, edible hips for both you and animals. But I recommend that you shun the heavily domesticated hybrid roses; their pollenless blossoms lack wildlife value, and they demand incessant care. For guild plants in general, choose the less-domesticated varieties. Humans, adaptable generalists that we are, can learn to savor new, wilder tastes. Animals are often less flexible, and have nutritional or taste requirements that are missing from highly bred cultivars.

The remaining shrub, oceanspray, is also called ironwood because its stems are steel-hard and slow to burn. Native people fashioned arrow shafts, digging sticks, and eating utensils from the wood, which suggests potential carving projects to me. Also, the shrubs swarm with birds, who eat the seeds and hide among the dense twigs.

Three small plants finish our list. Sweet cicely (*Osmorhiza chilensis,* not to be confused with an eastern plant called sweet cicely, *Myrrhis odrata,* which also has edible leaves, seeds, and young roots) has an anise-flavored root used for seasoning, and the flowers attract butterflies and other insects. Yerba buena is a trailing, aromatic herb whose leaves produce a mild sedative effect when steeped as a tea. American vetch fixes nitrogen, but I might swap it for the more readily available common vetch.

Our white oak guild now contains plants for food, birds and mammals, insects, herbal medicine, and nitrogen fixation, which covers most of the necessary roles of any guild. The only obvious omission from the list is a heavy-duty mulch plant such as comfrey or artichoke. I'd recommend a few mulch plants initially to jump-start biomass production, and then eliminate them later when the guild fills in. The guild will accumulate plenty of leaf litter once it's mature. Also, my intuition tells me a few more insectary plants (herbs such as dill or fennel, or suitable natives) and more nitrogen fixers (perhaps beans and clover, or the native, insect-attracting ceanothus) are also in order. The

insectary plants will ensure good pollination and fruit set, which is important since we'll be harvesting this guild's products intensively. Also, we're pulling products out of the ecosystem's loops, thus we need to replace what we've withdrawn by importing nutrients via nitrogen fixers as well as mulch and nutrient accumulators.

In summary, the armchair method of guild construction begins with a library or Internet search to identify a plant community that suits your region, soil, and climate. Then, list the component species and gather either these native varieties or domestic cultivars. Try to balance both your own desire for food and other products with the needs of the wild creatures who will also depend on your guild. If you're not familiar with the plants you've listed, consult native plant books and nursery catalogs to become acquainted. If the new guild lacks any of the elements listed in the above section on the apple-centered guild, fill in the gaps with species listed in this chapter and in the appendix. Also, I strongly urge that you trek out into nature and find a living example of the native community, if only to get a cursory feel for its patterns and structure. Then plant the guild, stand back, and wait to see what connections emerge.

CREATING A SUPER-GUILD

A single apple or walnut tree—let alone an oak—isn't going to provide a terribly varied diet, even as part of a guild. There's a limit to how many apples or nuts a gardener will eat. However, several different tree-centered guilds can be combined to boost both the food choice and the overall biodiversity that a garden provides. One obvious solution is to substitute other types of fruit and nut trees—peaches, almonds, plums, persimmons—for apple and walnut trees in guilds. This creates an orchard made of guilds. But any orchard, even one with a remarkably diverse understory such as ours, acts as a beacon to summon fruit-chomping pests. Also, if the only trees in our yard are fruit-bearers, neatly pruned into open form, uniformly blossoming, all looking like—well, fruit trees—then the landscape will be visually boring and will lack the biodiversity that's possible and necessary for a thriving ecosystem.

If the garden is large enough, we can be more subtle than simply growing a bunch of fruit trees. Just as we combine nitrogen fixers, insectary plants, and other multifunctional flora to create dynamic guilds, we can weave together trees of diverse uses to create a "super-guild." Guilds, each based on a different type of tree, can act as subunits of a larger, multi-tree super-guild, and be integrated to create a more deeply connected community. Our backyard ecosystem will then shift to a higher level of complexity. Think of the various guilds as organs in a body, combining to form a healthy and long-lived organism that is capable of much more elaborate behaviors than the components alone. Our guilds can do the same, altering microclimates, attracting new species, changing the look and feel of our landscape, and restoring it to health.

How can we assemble a set of guilds that will create a complete landscape? The walnut/hackberry guild developed by Tim Murphy hinted at a method. Tim's suggestion of using "buffer plants" to protect fruit trees from the effects of a walnut tree's toxic secretions pointed at one route for extending and connecting guilds. Bill Mollison, in *Permaculture: A Designers' Manual,* elaborates on the value of buffer plants. If we planted a walnut guild next to an apple guild, the apple tree would suffer from juglone poisoning. Instead, Mollison says, we can select useful buffer trees to fit between and link incompatible species.

What makes a good buffer tree? First, buffer trees should (obviously) be compatible with the trees we're trying to link. A tree harmed by juglone isn't a good choice for a walnut buffer (a few trees unfazed by walnuts are listed below). Second, in keeping with our desire to find beneficial interactions among and within guilds, we should keep an eye out for buffer trees that have a positive effect on one or both of the guilds to be linked. Nitrogen fixers, mulch-producers, and bird- or insect-attracting plants come to mind. Third, species that offer food, animal forage, lumber, or some other useful product should be among our candidates. We want to stack as many functions as possible into our buffer plants. Some species to

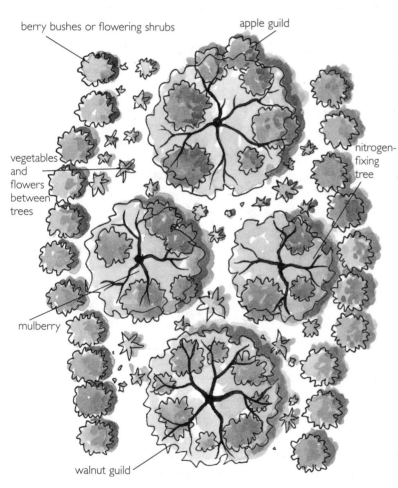

berry bushes or flowering shrubs

apple guild

nitrogen-fixing tree

vegetables and flowers between trees

mulberry

walnut guild

An orchard super-guild. The nitrogen-fixing tree (black locust, acacia, tagasaste, alder, or the like) and mulberry are underplanted with useful shrubs and flowers (such as mulch plants and insectary plants). Rows of berry bushes and flowering shrubs fill the alleys between the trees, and any open space holds vegetables and flowers.

connect walnut and apple guilds (and potentially, many other guilds) that satisfy one or more of these criteria include:

- **Mulberry trees.** Unharmed by walnut exudations, mulberries come in many attractive cultivars (white, Russian, Illinois, Olivett). Some homeowners complain that mulberry fruit creates a gooey, staining mess, but intelligent placement (avoiding the driveway and play areas) will minimize this drawback. Also, if the backyard ecosystem is in good health, the abundant wildlife will greedily consume the berries. Mulberries are quickly gobbled up by domestic fowl as well, thus a few chickens or ducks in the yard will quickly clean up any dropped fruit.
- **Nitrogen-fixing trees and large shrubs.** Most nitrogen fixers tolerate walnut toxins. Black locusts work well here, having attractive foliage, generous blossoms that bees love, and rot-resistant timber for fence posts. Other attractive trees that add fertility to soil include acacia, red or black alder, golden-chain tree, silk tree, and mountain mahogany. Large nitrogen-fixing shrubs, such as Russian olive and wax myrtle, also make good buffer plants.

A combination of fruit, nut, and buffer trees—for example, apple, walnut, mulberry, and a nitrogen fixer—creates an array that maximizes beneficial interactions and minimizes the negative. Here are some of the benefits: A nitrogen fixer boosts the growth of all three other trees by adding fertility to the soil. Mulberries not only buffer apples from walnut toxins, but research indicates that apples actually profit from mulberry companionship. The guilds-*cum*-buffers offer a liberal assortment of food that won't bore human palates, and the blossoms, fruit, and shelter will attract many species of wildlife.

The illustration on page 165 provides a layout that places each tree-based guild to best advantage. How will this pattern play in suburbia? Ten to twenty medium-sized trees can be tucked into a typical suburban quarter-acre without shrouding the inhabitants in a gloomy Black Forest. Two iterations of our four-tree "super-guild" gives us eight trees, which leaves ample space in the yard for other species that will raise biodiversity yet farther. The illustration opposite shows one way of creating a larger super-guild orchard.

There is a tangible contrast between a sterile yard that is studded with isolated, out-of-place specimen trees in ecological disconnection, and this thriving semi-tamed woodland that is vibrant with wildlife, dripping with fruit and nuts, and echoing with the voices of children playing hide-and-seek among flower-spangled shrubs.

GUILDS AREN'T PERFECT

I don't want to claim that guilds are the answer to all gardening problems. The advantages of guilds—reduced human intervention, less fertilizer and other inputs, a harmony between people and wildlife, and the magical synergy of plant communities—are obvious. The drawbacks are more subtle. First, guilds consume a lot of space. One or two guilds will fill most of a small city lot. In addition, guilds are slow to establish. A fruit tree takes several years to bear. Even shrubs need a few seasons to mature. To nudge a guild into early productivity, annual vegetables and flowers can be planted between the young, more permanent guild elements. As the perennial plants begin to bear, both the space and the need for annuals will diminish.

Another weakness: Since a guild's many plants act in close concert, tracing the source of a difficulty—say, stunted fruit on an apple tree—can be challenging. Is the problem due to root competition? An allelopathic interaction? A pest harbored by another guild member? In a guild, plant A may aid plant B which benefits C which inhibits A, so where do you start tracing a negative interaction?

Oregon permaculture teacher Tom Ward has experimented with guilds and knows their complexities. "Guilds were first developed in the tropics, where there is little soil," Tom notes. "Allelopath toxins are harbored in the soil, but because tropical soils are shallow, allelopaths can't build up to toxic levels and are rarely a problem there. Negative interactions seldom occur. Without allelopaths to worry about, guilds are simpler to design in the tropics than they are here in the temperate zone."

In contrast to the tropics, temperate forests and prairies have deep soil. In the thick temperate soil layer, toxins secreted by microorganisms and allelopathic plants can accumulate. Thus, a diverse array of plant species may be shuttling among their roots an equally complex chemical freight. This varied assortment of sugars, lignins, alkaloids, and what-have-you can have unpredictable effects on nearby plants. Soil-born toxins make temperate guild design more difficult.

Also, guilds are often site-specific. What works in New York may be completely inappropriate for California. Tom Ward points out that there is no handy list of guilds for every garden. "You're given an example or two," Tom says. "Nobody has ever put together a book of generic guilds because they are so specific to site. You have to use observation to figure out what plants grow well together in your region."

Several of the guilds cited in this chapter—the Three Sisters, the apple guild, and the walnut guild—are attempts at "universal" guilds that should thrive in most North American conditions. The Oregon white oak guild is a more site-specific guild, presented as an exercise in design based on local native plants. No, there isn't a "Book of Guilds" for every site. For the most part, temperate-climate guilds are a recent invention, only about twenty years old, and much remains to be learned and attempted. Perhaps readers of this book will help advance this young and very promising field.

Gardening with guilds forces a different attitude toward harvesting as well. You don't gaily traipse down a row of clean-cultivated vegetables, filling a bushel basket with one crop. Guild harvests are reminiscent of the hunter-gatherers: You pluck a few greens, some peppers and tomatoes, a few herbs, and a small basket of fruit and berries for dessert.

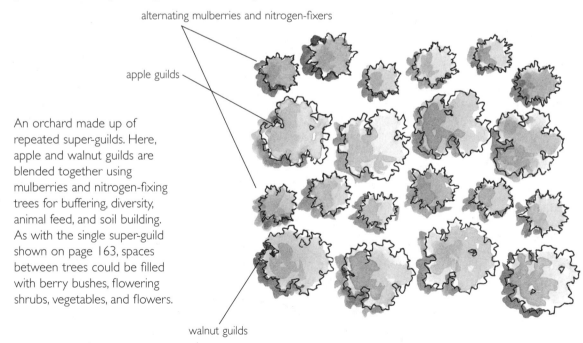

alternating mulberries and nitrogen-fixers

apple guilds

An orchard made up of repeated super-guilds. Here, apple and walnut guilds are blended together using mulberries and nitrogen-fixing trees for buffering, diversity, animal feed, and soil building. As with the single super-guild shown on page 163, spaces between trees could be filled with berry bushes, flowering shrubs, vegetables, and flowers.

walnut guilds

Some plants aren't appropriate for guilds, particularly vegetables that are insistent on full sun. Most guild-gardeners have small beds of annual vegetables for bulk harvesting tucked here and there. However, gardeners who grow a significant portion of their own food have found that guilds, supplemented with annual beds, can approach the ecological ideal of minimal inputs and maximum diversity.

Nature-based growing systems such as guilds do entail a change in thinking. Tom Ward cites a story told about Masanobu Fukuoka, the sage-like founder of the Natural Farming movement. Fukuoka's method involves permanent cover crops interplanted with vegetables and perennials, all with minimal tending. "One day," Tom relates, "Fukuoka was asked, 'If we grow our fruit trees the way you recommend, with no pruning, how do we harvest the apples and what do we do with them?' Fukuoka's answer was, 'You shake the apples out of the tree and make cider, or feed them to pigs.' His point was, you go in a whole other direction."

Though not to that extreme, guilds ask for a subtle adjustment of our relations with our environment. The order of a conventional row-crop garden is the order of the machine. This regimentation invites us to view plants as mechanical food factories. We fuel them with fertilizer, service them with rakes and hoes, and measure their production in bushels, bins, and tons. We view the plants as part of our dominion. In a guild, we are but one living being among many others, and like all the other animals enfolded by this community, we nurture and are nurtured by an almost-wild place. We prune and cull, as do the deer and mice. The fruit we leave does not rot on the ground to breed disease; it is gladly devoured by our many companions. We turn over a bit of soil, and the worms turn over yet more. We participate rather than rule. With guilds, we can begin to shed the mantle of command, and return to nature the many responsibilities we have unnecessarily assumed.

Chapter 10

Growing a Food Forest

GARDENING WITH GUILDS brings us one step closer to landscapes that look and act like natural ones, but that have been tweaked just a bit to benefit people as well as the rest of nature. However, even guilds are just pieces of a larger whole. Now it's time to tie guilds and the other ideas presented in this book into a unified, ecologically sound landscape.

In chapter 2, I described the process of succession, the evolution of a landscape over decades from bare ground through fast-growing pioneer species to a mature ecosystem. When not interrupted by fire or other disaster, the end result of succession nearly everywhere is forest. Even in the arid Southwest, dryland forests of ironwood, mesquite, and saguaro cactus blanketed what is now desert, until the sheep-grazers' depredations and the lumbermen's axes destroyed them. Given a few inches of annual rain and the respite of a handful of years between wildfires, tree and shrub seedlings will sprout on almost any ground, patiently outwait the other vegetation, and create a woodland. This is why, as noted earlier, suburbanites must constantly weed and chop out woody seedlings from their well-watered lawns and garden beds. The typical yard, with its perfect regimen of irrigation

and fertilizer, is trying very hard to become a forest. Only the lawn mower and pruning shears prevent the woods from taking over.

So why fight this trend toward woodland? Instead, we can work with nature to fashion a multistoried *forest garden,* a food- and habitat-producing landscape that acts like a natural woodland. In a forest garden, the yard is a parklike grove of spreading fruit trees, walnuts, chestnuts, and other useful trees. In the bright openings are smaller persimmon trees, plums, cherries, pawpaws, and a few ornamentals such as golden-chain trees and pink-flowered silk trees (which just happen to fix nitrogen). Catching the sunlight farther down, dancing with birds, are flowering shrubs and berry bushes. Occasional honeysuckle and hardy kiwi vines wind up tree trunks, leaving a trail of blossoms and fruit. Beneath all this and in the bright edges are beds of perennial flowers, vegetables, and soil-building mulch plants. Plant guilds weave this many-layered garden into a cohesive whole, and the many-functioned flora extends a welcome to helpful insects, birds, and other wildlife, as well as to people.

A food forest such as this isn't as unconventional as it may sound. I'm not talking about a gloomy mass of light-defeating trees, but an open, many-layered edible woodland garden with plenty of sunny edges. Many yards already contain most of the elements of a forest garden: a few tall trees in front or at the back edge, some shrubs for a hedge or berries, a vegetable patch, a few herbs, and a flower bed. But in the typical yard these elements lie separate and disconnected. A forest garden simply integrates all these pieces into a smoothly working whole.

At its essence, a forest garden has several layers, as does a natural forest. A simple forest garden contains a top layer of trees, a middle level of shrubs, and a ground layer of herbs, vegetables, and flowers. Each plant is chosen for the role or roles that it will play, whether for food, wildlife habitat, herbal medicine, insect attraction, soil building, or any of the other functions that we've covered throughout this book. The major trees and shrubs are spaced to let the sun fall between, and plants in the lower layers are placed in sun or shade according to their appetite for light.

A forest garden has a different feel from other garden styles, in large part because trees are a major element, integrated into and defining the other layers. Certainly, conventional gardens mingle shrubs and nonwoody perennials of varying heights in the traditional mixed border. And nearly every yard contains a few trees. But in a forest garden, trees—their leaves arching overhead, trunks thrusting skyward, branches enfolding the space—control the landscape's character. We're not strolling in an exposed group of bushes and flowers, our heads above most of the foliage, we're nestled within a sheltering yet open canopy of trees of all heights. The trees predominate, yet without smothering.

With a tree-filled forest garden, we have enlisted as our allies the most powerful and productive vegetation on the planet, the aristocrats of the plant world. I briefly described the many and

important roles that trees play in chapter 6. I believe that trees—as full, integrated partners, not merely as scattered specimens—are a prerequisite for a healthy, sustainable landscape.

Trees' ability to produce soil-enriching leaf litter, fill the earth with humusy roots, quell temperature swings, hold moisture, arrest erosion, and offer tiers of habitat for animals is unparalleled, and in the forest garden they're on our side. And for productivity you can't beat trees. An acre of wheat provides a mere 1 to 2 tons of grain, while an acre of apple trees yields 7 tons of fruit, and an acre of honey-locust trees explodes with 15 tons of protein-rich pods—without annual replanting.

Trees reach deep into the earth for nutrients and water, and far and wide into the sky for solar power. They are life's largest, most effective natural collectors of energy and matter. So by incorporating trees as integral elements of the garden, we're putting heavy hitters on our team. Trees, though they share the space with many other species, define the forest garden and distinguish it from other landscape styles.

The wealth of trees, shrubs, and other flora we have to choose from means that the forest garden can be as varied as a forest itself, and as individual as its owner. Some gardeners will want a veritable food forest, where the constant rain of ripe fruit and luscious berries almost warrants wearing a hard hat. Others will pitch their mini-forest toward blossom and beauty, selecting plants to create a tall, thick cascade of color and many-textured foliage. Utilitarian souls may sculpt a garden that yields income from medicinal tinctures, craft wood, bamboo poles, rare seeds, nursery plants, or grafting stock. Or the gardener can mix and match the styles to tailor a garden that combines food, beauty, habitat, species preservation, and income.

A garden that uses trees and shrubs to reach far

> **We can work with nature to fashion a multistoried *forest garden,* a food- and habitat-producing landscape that acts like a natural woodland.**

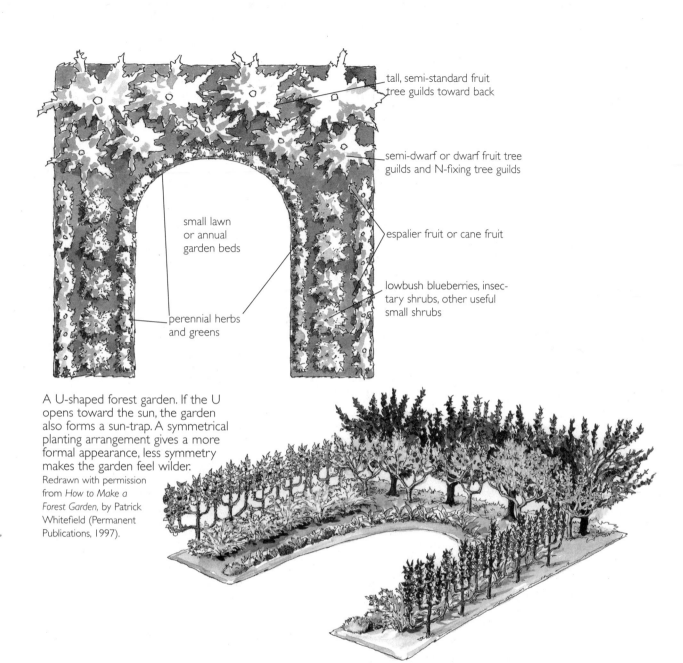

tall, semi-standard fruit tree guilds toward back

semi-dwarf or dwarf fruit tree guilds and N-fixing tree guilds

espalier fruit or cane fruit

lowbush blueberries, insectary shrubs, other useful small shrubs

small lawn or annual garden beds

perennial herbs and greens

A U-shaped forest garden. If the U opens toward the sun, the garden also forms a sun-trap. A symmetrical planting arrangement gives a more formal appearance, less symmetry makes the garden feel wilder. Redrawn with permission from *How to Make a Forest Garden*, by Patrick Whitefield (Permanent Publications, 1997).

into three dimensions offers maximum wildlife habitat, the largest possible crop yields for the space, and the greatest possibilities for edge and diversity. It won't hurt property values either, as the most desirable neighborhoods are always those with well-developed trees. On hilly land, forest gardens are also the most ecologically sound way to develop steep slopes, since the trees and other perennial plants hold soil in place and eliminate erosion-producing tilling.

The illustrations on this page and the next show some of the possible forms that a forest gar-den can take. Shapes, heights, spacing, and overall size can be altered to suit the site conditions and gardener's preferences. A large yard provides enough room for full-sized trees, while in a smaller property, dwarf and naturally small species can fit together to provide biodiversity. Northern gardeners will want a more open array of trees to allow the not-so-strong sunlight to reach the ground layers, but southerners may desire dense spacing to provide needed shade.

Forest gardens raise the obvious question: Don't the upper layers cast too much shade for the lower

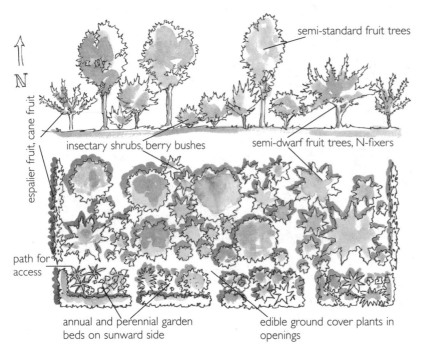

semi-standard fruit trees

espalier fruit, cane fruit

insectary shrubs, berry bushes

semi-dwarf fruit trees, N-fixers

path for access

annual and perennial garden beds on sunward side

edible ground cover plants in openings

A forest garden for a rectangular yard. Large trees are placed far apart so that light can reach shrubs and smaller trees. Vegetable or flower beds are located on the sunward side.

plants? Part of the answer is that proper tree spacing and shade-tolerant plants will keep lack of light from being a problem. But to be perfectly honest—especially for northern gardens where the sun is weaker—fruit yields and flower density won't be as large in the shady parts of the understory as in full sun. I'm growing currants and gooseberries, two shade-tolerant bush fruits, in both full sun and under some pear trees, and the sunnier plants bear more fruit. But the guild-grown shrubs require less water, have lusher, darker foliage, and are still packed with plenty of berries. Plus, the shrub-filled, sun-dappled margin under the pear tree offers far more, ecologically, aesthetically, and for my palate than if I were just growing grass.

Forest gardens offer the same advantages as guilds, and then some. Nearly every cubic inch is filled with greenery, flowers, or fruit. This riot of vegetation into three dimensions furnishes vast amounts of habitat for birds, small animals, and beneficial insects. Pest problems dwindle. And once established, forest gardens are low maintenance, since the thick vegetation cover reduces water needs, smothers weeds, and renews soil through self-mulching and natural soil building. Because the forest garden holds mostly perennial and self-seeding plants, it also needs no tilling and little seasonal replanting.

At the Bullock brothers' several-acre food forest on Orcas Island, Doug Bullock listed some other benefits of forest gardening. "Sheer biodiversity is part of it," he told me. "We get birds and other animals here that no one else has seen for years. But the best part is the food—it's unreal!" We stood beneath a plum tree bent nearly double with fruit, and I nodded as Doug continued, "Every summer we have about twenty students here for three weeks. And there's enough fruit right here to feed them. Think about it: twenty people grazing for weeks on plums, peaches, and berries, and when they're gone there's still tons of fruit on the trees for us."

Because Doug and his brothers have populated their food forest with a wide variety of plants, every month of the year brings fresh fruit or vegetables: cool-season salad greens in midwinter, berries in late spring, and branch-breaking loads of fruit in summer and fall. Even in December, their exotic medlar trees bear a fruit that tastes like cinnamon-spiced pear butter.

EXPERIMENTING WITH FOREST GARDENS

Because temperate-climate forest gardening is so new, only a few mature forest gardens exist on this continent, though many more are being developed. I visited several while researching this book.

A BRIEF HISTORY OF FOREST GARDENS

Forest gardening is a young field for North American gardeners, but it has a long history. Food forests have existed for millennia in the tropics, though early anthropologists didn't recognize them as gardens at all. Accustomed to row crops and annual vegetables, the first white visitors to tropical home gardens assumed that the small fields of manioc, beans, or grain that lay near African, Asian, and South American villages provided most of the inhabitants' food, while the areas surrounding the houses looked like untamed jungle. Only after prolonged and unprejudiced observation did anthropologists comprehend that virtually every plant surrounding the dwelling was useful in some way. The tall trees were timber and firewood producers or nitrogen fixers, while the shorter ones bore mangoes, papayas, avocados, and other marvelous fruits. Beneath these were shrubs for food, fiber, and wood products. The herb layer was filled with medicinal, edible, and ornamental plants. Rampant growth was slashed back several times each year and used for mulch or animal fodder.

But because these plants were arranged in guilds and by function, rather than in neat lines and beds, scientists had no idea that they were looking at an ecologically sound, carefully worked-out scheme for producing nearly everything the occupants needed. Sadly, many of these wonderful food forests have been replaced by Western-style cash-crop agriculture, making the once self-reliant inhabitants dependent on fertilizers, pesticides, and imported, processed food and other goods.

Fortunately, a number of visionaries saw the immense value of these tropical forest gardens. One was Robert Hart, an Englishman who not only studied tropical food forests but transplanted many of their concepts to temperate gardens. His book, *Forest Gardening*, was the first to describe forest gardening for the Northern Hemisphere. A second useful book is *How to Make a Forest Garden*, by Patrick Whitefield. Both these books are written primarily for a British audience. See the bibliography for more information on these books.

One site that illustrates the transition from raised-bed to forest garden was that of Jerome Osentowski, near Aspen, Colorado. Jerome faces some tough gardening challenges, as he lives 7,400 feet above sea level. Frosts can occur during any month. When I visited him, in September, his garden was still lush and green, but he expected the first killing frosts of autumn soon.

For years, much of Jerome's income came from growing organic salad greens for the upscale markets and restaurants of Aspen. But supplying this finicky market year-round took arduous labor, and after a decade or so, a somewhat exhausted Jerome was open to alternatives. Many of the former salad beds now held small trees and shrubs. In one, celery and a few heads of lettuce dotted a sunny edge below some young trees.

"The food forest was a natural evolution of this place," Jerome told me as we walked toward the heat-holding rock terraces of his young forest garden. "After years of growing annual vegetables, a lot of fertility had leached down to where the short roots of the salad greens couldn't get it. So I went to fruit trees, with their deep roots, to get at all those nutrients."

I asked Jerome what species he had planted. Swinging his arm to encompass the slope, he said, "Let's start with the trees. We've got apples—there's one with five different varieties grafted onto it. Apricots, plums, some native Douglas firs, and New Mexico locusts for nitrogen. The trees are young, not really in production yet. But the shrubs are really giving us a lot of food now." He pointed out the understory of black and white currants, gooseberries, bush cherries, cranberries, and Siberian pea shrubs. Bamboo and willow were sprouting vigorously, and several varieties of grapes, along with scarlet runner beans and squash, entwined the other vegetation. Strawberries and miner's lettuce swarmed over the rock terraces.

"We've got a lot of medicinal herbs, too," Jerome continued. "A nice market crop if we want it. Echinacea, St. John's-wort, astragalus, artemisia, lots more." We admired the lush cascade of greenery. "What makes this place work, though, are what I call the *compañeros*, all the guild companion-plants." He showed me the rich array of soil-building and insect-attracting species: nitrogen fixers such as pea shrubs, fava beans, clovers, fenugreek, and alfalfa; bee plants such as borage and comfrey; other insectary species including fennel, celery, dill, and coriander; and strongly scented pest-confusers such as horseradish, Mexican marigold, garlic mustard, and walking onions. These many-functioned plants reduce Jerome's share of the pest control and fertilization duties, and augment the web of ecological connections among the forest garden's inhabitants.

The rock terraces are essential to mitigating the harsh mountain climate. The mass of the stones absorbs heat, which softens temperature swings, warms the plants at night, and fights frost. "The rock terraces were important in helping the young plants survive." Jerome told me. "They get shaded now in the summer, but they still store heat in winter and especially in spring when the plants need it most." During winter, the rocks, snow cover, and mulch combine to prevent the ground from freezing even when temperatures swing below zero. This allows slug-eating snakes and other beneficial wildlife to survive the cold season.

The garden is surrounded by a tall deer fence, and a complete guild was designed to grow upon it. Hops and sweet peas trellis up the woven wire, and Russian olive and gooseberry form a green shrub layer. Sunflowers stretch skyward. Clover and strawberries cascade along the ground, interspersed by garlic in the root zone. In a forest garden, every site offers new opportunities for creative design.

Though food is one obvious benefit here, Jerome told me of the forest garden's real value. "As I phase out the salad-green operation, I can get income from the medicinals and tinctures, and

from nursery stock and scion wood for grafting. But I've found that's not the most valuable part. I learn from all this. And so do my students who come up here for the classes at Central Rocky Mountain Permaculture Institute." The real value-added product of the forest garden, Jerome points out, is the inspiration, knowledge, and renewal that comes when humans and the rest of nature mesh in a healthy, vigorous, and diverse setting.

THE SEVEN-STORY GARDEN

The basic forest garden contains three layers: trees, shrubs, and ground plants. But for those who like to take full advantage of every planting opportunity, a truly deluxe forest garden can contain as many as seven tiers of vegetation. As the illustration below shows, the seven layers of the forest garden are tall trees, low trees, shrubs, herbs, ground covers, vines, and root crops.

Here are these layers in more detail. Table 10-1 suggests plant species for each layer.

1. THE TALL-TREE LAYER. This is an overstory of full-sized fruit, nut, or other useful trees, with spaces between to let plenty of light to the lower layers. Dense, spreading species—the classic shade trees

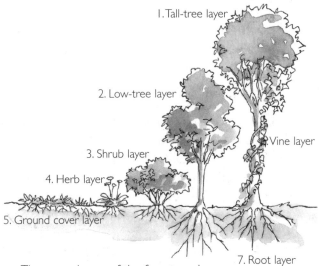

The seven layers of the forest garden.

such as maple, sycamore, and beech—don't work well in the forest garden because they cast deep shadows over a large area. Better choices are multifunctioned fruit and nut trees. These include standard and semi-standard apple and pear trees, European plums on standard rootstocks such as Myrobalan, and full-sized cherries. Chestnut trees, though quite large, work well, especially if pruned to an open, light-allowing shape. Chinese chestnuts, generally not as large as American types, are good candidates (see table 10-1 for botanical names of all species mentioned here). Walnut trees, especially the naturally open, spreading varieties such as heartnut and buartnut, are excellent. Don't overlook the nut-bearing stone piñon pines. Nitrogen-fixing trees will help build soil, and most bear blossoms that attract insects. These include black locust, mesquite, alder, and in low-frost climates, acacia, algoroba, tagasaste, and carob.

Since much of the forest garden lies in landscape Zones 1 and 2, timber trees aren't appropriate—tree-felling in close quarters would be too destructive. But pruning and storm damage will generate firewood and small wood for crafts.

The canopy trees will define the major patterns of the forest garden, so they must be chosen carefully. Plant them with careful regard to their mature size so enough light will fall between them to support other plants.

2. THE LOW-TREE LAYER. Here are many of the same fruits and nuts as in the canopy, but on dwarf and semi-dwarf rootstocks to keep them low. Plus, we can plant naturally small trees such as apricot, peach, nectarine, almond, and mulberry. Here also are shade-tolerant fruit trees such as persimmon and pawpaw. In a smaller forest garden, these small trees may serve as the canopy. They can easily be pruned into an open form, which will allow light to reach the other species beneath them.

Other low-growing trees include flowering species such as dogwood and mountain ash, and some nitrogen fixers, including golden-chain tree,

silk tree, and mountain mahogany. Both large and small nitrogen-fixing trees grow quickly and can be pruned heavily to generate plenty of mulch and compost.

3. THE SHRUB LAYER. This tier includes flowering, fruiting, wildlife-attracting, and other useful shrubs. A small sampling: blueberry, rose, hazelnut, butterfly bush, bamboo, serviceberry, the nitrogen-fixing *Elaeagnus* species and Siberian pea shrub, and dozens of others. The broad palette of available shrubs allows the gardener's inclinations to surface, as shrubs can be chosen to emphasize food, crafts, ornamentals, birds, insects, native plants, exotics, or just raw biodiversity.

Shrubs come in all sizes, from dwarf blueberries to nearly tree-sized hazelnuts, and thus can be plugged into edges, openings, and niches of many forms. Shade-tolerant varieties can lurk beneath the trees, sun-loving types in the sunny spaces between.

4. THE HERB LAYER. Here "herb" is used in the broad botanical sense to mean nonwoody vegetation: vegetables, flowers, culinary herbs, cover crops, as well as mulch producers and other soil building plants. Emphasis is on perennials, but we won't rule out choice annuals and self-seeding species. Again, shade-lovers can peek out from beneath taller plants, while sun-worshiping species need the open spaces. At the edges, a forest garden can also hold more-traditional garden beds of plants dependent on full sun.

5. THE GROUND COVER LAYER. These are low, ground-hugging plants—preferably varieties that offer food or habitat—that snuggle into edges and the spaces between shrubs and herbs. Sample species include strawberries, nasturtium, clover, creeping thyme, ajuga, and the many prostrate varieties of flowers such as phlox and verbena. They play a critical role in weed prevention, occupying ground that would otherwise succumb to invaders.

6. THE VINE LAYER. This layer is for climbing plants that will twine up trunks and branches, filling the unused regions of the all-important third dimension with food and habitat. Here are food plants such as kiwifruit, grapes, hops, passionflower, and vining berries; and those for wildlife such as honeysuckle and trumpet-flower. These can include climbing annuals such as squash, cucumbers, and melons. Some of the perennial vines can be invasive or strangling, hence they should be used sparingly and cautiously.

7. THE ROOT LAYER. The soil gives us yet another layer for the forest garden; the third dimension goes both up *and* down. Most of the plants for the root layer should be shallow rooted, such as garlic and onions, or easy-to-dig types such as potatoes and Jerusalem artichokes. Deep-rooted varieties such as carrots don't work well because the digging they require will disturb other plants. I do sprinkle a few seeds of daikon (Asian radish) in open spots, since the long roots can often be pulled with one mighty tug rather than dug, and if I don't harvest them, the blossoms attract beneficial bugs and the fat roots add humus as they rot.

Designing the Forest Garden

The forest garden design process largely follows the sequence laid out in chapter 3: observation, visioning, planning, development, and implementation. As well, extra focus on a few points will be helpful:

- In an exposed site, wind barriers (fences and hedges) will greatly speed the establishment of the other plants.
- Trees and woody plants should go in first, since these take the longest to mature and define the shape of the garden. Remember to design for the full size of trees—it's easy to place spindly seedlings too close together, leading to overcrowding and dense shade when they mature. Leave room for sunlight to penetrate between full-grown trees, rather than creating a closed tall-tree layer. The more northerly the garden,

the weaker the sun will be, so more space will be needed between trees.

- Early on, include plenty of nitrogen-fixing and other soil-building plants. The dense plantings of the forest garden will demand lots of nutrients during their youth, so the soil must be in great shape. The fertile, organic-rich soil built by nutrient-accumulating plants will accelerate growth and speed succession along.
- Buying the plants for a forest garden all at once

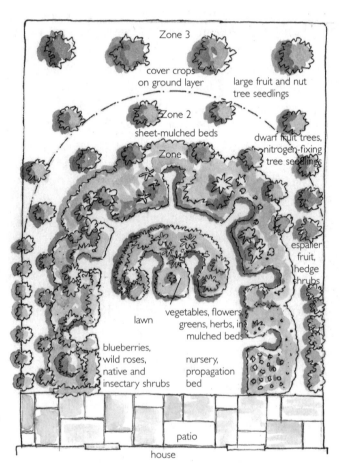

A freshly planted evolving ecological garden, about 40 feet by 50 feet. A nursery and propagation bed lies conveniently close to the house for regular care. Temporary, well-composted beds line the lawn in Zone 1 for fast, early food and flower production. Young trees and shrubs—as many as can be afforded—begin to fill the more distant Zones 2 and 3. Zone 2 is deeply sheet-mulched to quickly build soil, while the less-urgently needed Zone 3 is cover-cropped for long-term soil restoration.

can get expensive, so those with a limited budget should consider setting aside a small area as a nursery for seed-starting, rooting cuttings, and general plant propagation. It's best to place the nursery in Zone 1, so you can keep close watch on the tender youngsters. Here, you can start perennials for the herb, root, and ground cover layers from seed en masse; propagate cuttings for trees, shrubs, and herbs; divide established plants to yield numerous progeny; and create a swelling population of plants to colonize the new garden. You can nurture these for a year or two and then move them to their permanent homes. Those with the expertise can graft tree varieties too. A nursery is invaluable for furnishing huge number of plants very cheaply.

• The open spaces between trees and shrubs can at first be filled with annual vegetables, flowers, nitrogen-fixing cover crops such as clover, and nursery stock. As the upper layers grow and the nursery plants become ready to transplant, these beds will shrink.

For a design example, let's look at the typical case of a homeowner wanting to take out a lawn and install a more ecologically sound forest garden. We'll select a U-shaped design, which provides a private, warm, and sheltered space in the center (see the illustration on page 169). Ideally the U would open toward the south for maximum sunshine.

This design will emphasize food—three dimensions of fruit, berries, vegetables, and herbs, with a minor emphasis on flowers. We want plenty of vegetables and flowers in the lower layers for the first few years, but we know that as time goes by, the upper layers will be the principal providers. With these goals in mind, we can begin the design.

First, map the area for the new garden, and sketch in any existing foliage that will be saved. Then draw in the new plantings. The sunny, open area in the center of the U can be kept as lawn or converted to flower and vegetable beds. Many parents opt to preserve an expanse of lawn for chil-

dren to play in, but once the forest fills in, I guarantee that the kids will abandon the open grass for the more enchanting shrubbery, a perfect place for hideaways and forts. The lawn can be kept just big enough for a little sunbathing.

For a windbreak and privacy screen, we'll create an edge of hedge and wall plants: espaliered or cordoned fruit trees, berry bushes, shrub willows, roses, dogwoods, elderberries, and useful native shrubs.

Then sketch in the tree layers. Tall trees are best placed to the north to reduce the shade cast on

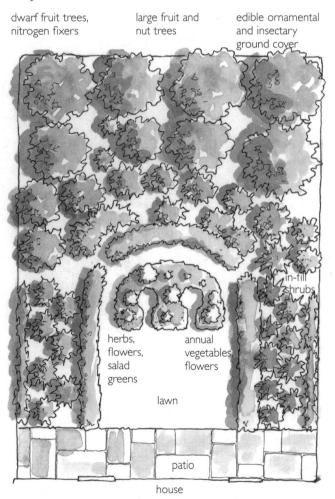

After five to ten years, the garden has filled in. Since the perennial shrubs and trees are now producing abundantly, the temporary keyhole beds have shrunk to narrow, edge beds. A ground cover of edible, flowering, and insectary herbs and shrubs fills in the gaps between and below major trees.

Table 10-1.

PLANTS FOR THE FOREST GARDEN

I have omitted the herb layer from this table, as there are thousands of suitable species and many of them are listed elsewhere in this book.

Common name	Botanical name	N-fixer	Wildlife value	Insectary	Edible
Tall-Tree Layer					
Acacia	Acacia spp.	•		•	
Algoroba	Prosopis dulcis, P. juliflora	•			
American chestnut	Castanea dentata				•
Apple	Malus sylvestris			•	•
Asian pear	Pyrus serotina				•
Black locust	Robinia pseudoacacia	•		•	
Black walnut	Juglans nigra				•
Buartnut	Juglans x bisbyi				•
Bur oak	Quercus macrocarpa		•		
Butternut	Juglans cinerea				•
Cherry	Prunus cerasus, P. avium		•	•	•
Chinese chestnut	Castanea mollisima				•
European pear	Pyrus communis				•
Heartnut	Juglans ailantifolia cordiformis				•
Hickory	Carya spp.				•
Honey locust	Gleditsia triacanthos		•	•	
Mesquite	Prosopis spp.	•		•	
Peach	Prunus persica				•
Pecan	Carya illinoensis				•
Piñon pine	Pinus cembroides				•
Plum	Prunus domestica				•
Stone pine	Pinus pinea				•
Tagasaste	Chaemocytisus palmensis	•			
White oak	Quercus alba		•		
Low-Tree Layer					
Almond	Prunus amygdalus				•
Apple, dwarf or semi-dwarf	Malus pumila				•
Apricot	Prunus armeniaca				•
Bamboo	Phylostachys spp., Fargesia spp.			•	
Crabapple	Malus spp.		•	•	•
Cornelian cherry dogwood	Cornus mas		•		•
Fig	Ficus carica				•
Filbert/hazel	Corylus spp.		•		•
Golden-chain tree	Laburnum spp.	•			
Hawthorn	Crataegus spp.		•		•
Jujube	Ziziphus jujuba				•
Loquat	Eriobotrya japonica				•
Mayhaw	Crataegus opaca				•
Medlar	Mespilus germanica				•
Mountain ash	Sorbus spp.		•		•
Mulberry	Morus spp.		•		•
Osage orange	Maclura pomifera		•		
Pawpaw	Asimina trilobata				•

Common name	Botanical name	N-fixer	Wildlife value	Insectary	Edible
Peach, dwarf or semi-dwarf	*Prunus persica*				•
Pecan	*Carya illinoensis*				•
Persimmon	*Diospyros* spp.				•
Pomegranate	*Punica* spp.				•
Quince	*Cydonia oblongata*			•	•
Silk tree	*Albizia julibrissin*	•			

Shrub Layer

Common name	Botanical name	N-fixer	Wildlife value	Insectary	Edible
American cranberry	*Viburnum trilobum*		•		
Aronia (chokeberry)	*Aronia melanocarpa*		•		•
Autumn olive	*Elaeagnus umbellata*	•	•		•
Blackberry	*Rubus* spp.		•		•
Blueberry	*Vaccinium* spp.		•		•
Buffaloberry	*Shepardia argentea*	•	•		
Currant	*Ribes* spp.		•		•
Elderberry	*Sambucus* spp.		•		•
False indigo	*Amorpha fruticosa*	•	•		
Gooseberry	*Ribes hirtellum*		•		•
Goumi	*Elaeagnus mulitflora*	•	•		•
Hackberry	*Celtis* spp.		•		
Hansen's bush cherry	*Prunus besseyi*		•	•	•
Highbush cranberry	*Vaccinium macrocarpon*		•		•
Indigo	*Indigofera tinctoria*	•			
Japanese barberry	*Berberis thunbergii*		•		
Jostaberry	*Ribes x Rubus* hybrid		•		•
Nanking cherry	*Prunus tomentosa*		•	•	•
Pineapple guava	*Feijoa sellowiana*				•
Raspberry	*Rubus idaeus*		•		•
Red azarole	*Crataegus azarolus*		•		•
Rugose rose	*Rosa rugosa*		•		•
Russian olive	*Elaeagnus angustifolia*	•	•		•
Sea buckthorn	*Hippophae rhamnoides*	•			•
Serviceberry (saskatoonberry)	*Amelanchier alnifolia*		•		•
Siberian pea shrub	*Caragan arborescens*	•			
Summersweet clethra	*Clethra alnifolia*		•		
Witch hazel	*Hamamelis virginiana*		•		

Vine Layer

Common name	Botanical name	N-fixer	Wildlife value	Insectary	Edible
Clematis	*Clematis* spp.			•	•
Cucumber	*Cucumis sativus*				•
Grape	*Vitis vinifera*				•
Honeysuckle	*Lonicera* spp.		•	•	
Hops	*Humulus lupulus*		•	•	•
Jasmine	*Jasminum* spp.		•		
Kiwifruit	*Actinidia deliciosa*				•
Melon	*Cucumis melo*				•
Nasturtium	*Tropaeolum majus*			•	•
Passionfruit	*Passiflora* spp.			•	•
Pea	*Pisum sativum*				•
Scarlet runner bean	*Phaseolus coccineus*				•
Squash	*Cucurbita* spp.				•

Common name	Botanical name	N-fixer	Wildlife value	Insectary	Edible
Ground Cover Layer					
Ajuga	*Ajuga reptans*			•	
Bearberry (kinnickinnick)	*Arctostaphylos uva-ursi*		•		•
Clover	*Trifolium* spp.	•		•	
Creeping phlox	*Phlox stolonifera*			•	
Creeping thyme	*Thymus praecox, T. vulgaris*			•	
Lingonberry	*Vaccinium vitis-idaea*				•
Nepalese raspberry	*Rubus nepalensis*				•
Protrate verbena	*Verbena peruviana, V. tenera*			•	
Stonecrop	*Sedum* spp.			•	
Strawberry	*Fragaria* spp.			•	•
Sweet violet	*Viola odorata*				•
Thrift	*Phlox subulata*			•	
Trailing bellflower	*Campanula poscharskyana*			•	•
Wild ginger	*Asarum canadense*				•
Root Layer					
Camas	*Camassia quamash*			•	•
Garlic	*Allium sativa*				•
Garlic chives	*Allium tuberosum*				•
Groundnut	*Apios americana*	•			•
Hardy ginger	*Zingiber mioga*				•
Horseradish	*Armoraciaa rusticana*				•
Jerusalem artichoke	*Helianthus tuberosus*		•	•	•
Mashua	*Tropaeolum tuberosum*			•	•
Mountain yam	*Dioscorea batata*				•
Oca	*Oxalis tuberosa*				•
Peanut	*Arachis hypogaea*	•			•
Potato	*Solanum tuberosum*				•
Ramson	*Allium ursinum*				•

other plantings, but wide spacing will also allow ample sunlight to fall between trees. The spacing reflects the mature size of the tree. Since this is a fair-sized suburban property, we have room for some full-sized trees: apple, pear, walnut, plum, and cherry. We want some nitrogen fixers, so we'll add black locust and golden-chain tree. In the low-tree layer are dwarf and semi-dwarf fruit trees plus, under the taller trees, naturally small persimmons, pawpaws, and mulberries. In this example, no tall trees are close to the house, which will allow ample light for the Zone 1 understory.

The shrub and lower layers require some thought, since we want to have constant food production while the upper layers mature. To give the owners lots of Zone 1 and 2 vegetables and herbs until the trees begin to bear, we'll design some keyhole beds near the house: temporary ones under the low trees, and permanent beds in the open center. One of the short-term beds is reserved for plant propagation. This arrangement means that the low trees near the house won't be underplanted with perennials as densely—yet—as those farther away.

Three factors interact to mold the design of the more distant parts of this forest garden. One is the zone effect: The farther-off places—Zones 2 and 3—won't be visited as often as the nearer, so they can't demand as much care. A second factor is that of time: The young plantings will start small and need one or more years to mature. And the third is budget: Many gardeners won't want to spend the large sum necessary to plant the entire yard densely all at once, and this far-off zone is the best place to plant sparsely until more stock is ready. So we need to develop a planting strategy that reflects these constraints. This less-maintained zone will sport only a few small specimens at first, thus it is prone to weed invasion and neglect while the woody plants mature and the low layers fill in.

My recommendation is this: In Zone 2, mulch heavily between the young trees and shrubs, and plant the herb, root, and ground cover layers as time, nursery stock, and money become available. Renew the mulch once or twice a year to build the soil quickly and smother weeds. To try to cultivate and plant this large area would probably be biting off too large a chunk at once. Remember, the wisest strategy is to get Zone 1 established first and then expand outward. With the above approach, the shrubs, trees, and soil of Zone 2 will be ready when Zone 1 is up and running.

The farthest reaches of this yard elicit yet another approach. It's doubtful we can conjure up enough mulch to cover the entire forest garden, and since the full-sized trees and large shrubs of Zone 3 will take longest to mature, soil-building isn't as urgent a task. Once the trees and major shrubs are in place in this more distant zone, I'd advise planting a soil-building, habitat-providing cover crop mix. This will keep weeds at bay and boost fertility until we're ready to plant the lower layers. One choice for a cover crop is clover and annual rye mixed with beneficial-insect attracting herbs such as yarrow, dill, and fennel, and maybe a little subsoil-loosening daikon thrown in. This lush mix need be mowed only once or twice a year, so it needs very little maintenance while it boosts fertility. Cover crops are a good strategy for less-visited parts of a garden.

Thus, we have created three zones in this forest garden: an intensively cultivated Zone 1, a well-mulched but lightly planted (for now) Zone 2, and a long-term set of soil-building cover crops beneath the young shrubs and trees of Zone 3. Of course, the lucky gardener with sufficient money and access to labor and materials might, if confident enough in the design scheme, just joyously install the whole design at once, with dense plantings and mulch in place of the cover crops.

Guilding the Food Forest

Let's look at the possibilities for guilds that will connect the pieces of our food forest design. Creating guilds based on the major fruit trees is fairly straightforward; we can plug in many elements from the apple-tree guild described in chapter 9. This means placing grass- and rodent-suppressing bulbs near the tree trunk, insect-attracting and soil-building plants in the herb and shrub layers, and fitting in more food-providing plants and other useful species.

Remember, though, that this guild doesn't stand in isolation—it's nestled among other trees and large shrubs, so the pattern of planting is tugged and shaped by the neighboring vegetation. One lone guilded tree could be surrounded by concentric circles of its companion plants, but not in the forest garden, with its numerous trees. Concentric rings of mulch plants and others beneath the tree's drip-line is no longer the right pattern now that other shrubs and trees are close by. Instead, mulch plants, insect-attractors, and other guild members—depending on their need for light—should be tucked into openings between neighboring trees and shrubs, nestled into pockets under the branches, or lined alongside paths to allow access for picking and pruning. Plants that suppress weeds—bulbs and some of the thick mulch plants—can form, instead of a circle under one tree, a natural boundary around a whole cluster of trees and shrubs, or can define the outline of a clearing or a sunny edge.

In addition to fruit-tree guilds, we can also design a walnut-tree guild for this garden. Remember, though, that walnuts are allelopaths, whose mildly toxic root secretions will stunt the growth of many other plants. This is where the use of buffer plants, described earlier, is essential. The lofty walnut, together with its guild of hackberries, currants, and solanaceous annuals such as peppers and tomatoes, will go at the north end of the yard. Then we can insert buffering black locusts, mulberries, and Russian olives between the walnut and any fruit trees.

The semi-dwarf fruit trees closer to the house can also be guilded, but we'll underplant these trees with smaller shrubs and fewer of them, since the central trees aren't very large and we want plenty of light and edge for the Zone 1 herb, root, and ground cover layers. Good candidates for these guilds are nitrogen-fixing small shrubs such as buffaloberry, ceanothus, and indigo; weed-suppressing and mulch plants including comfrey, borage, and nasturtium, and any of the wealth of smaller insectary plants.

A guild next to the house will have a different composition than one farther away. Guilds very near the house should emphasize plants for food, medicine, and other human use, with less flora for wildlife, mulch production, and the like. Our own labor can substitute for the natural mulching, weed-prevention, and other guild functions that we give up in exchange for having enhanced yields right outside our door. It's no problem to add a bit of compost and squish a few cucumber beetles right off the back porch, but I'd rather nature did those jobs 75 feet away in Zone 3.

To install the forest garden, first eliminate most of the grass, preferably without toxic herbicides. This means stripping the sod by hand and composting it, or power-tilling the sod at intervals a few weeks apart to kill emerging grass remnants, throwing a giant sheet mulch party to smother the lawn, or a combination of all three. This is the best time to amend and improve the soil with lime, organic matter, and long-term fertilizers, because much of the yard will soon be covered in perennials, which makes digging-in fertilizer less easy. As mentioned, the center of the ∪-shaped garden can be left in grass for a play and relaxation space.

Next plant the trees. The back one-third of the yard (Zone 3) should then be planted with the cover crops and green manures mentioned above. Zone 2 and much of Zone 1 now receives a soil-building layer of deep sheet-mulch, with some of the closest Zone 1 beds getting a topping of rich compost to get them ready for immediate use. Keep the mulch back from the tree trunks to discourage bark-gnawing rodents.

Finally, plant shrubs and other perennial plants, bulbs and other members of the root layer, and ground covers right into the sheet mulch (for a review of creating and planting sheet mulch, check back to chapter 4).

HOW THE FOOD FOREST EVOLVES

Besides bringing food and blossom nearly all year, the many rhythms and cycles of a forest garden can fascinate and inform. In a garden full of annuals or even in a single-layer perennial garden, most plants follow a simple yearly cycle: growth in spring, dieback in fall, and renewal—or replanting—the next spring. But in a forest garden, the life spans of many of the occupants are measured not in one year but in decades or more. Thus, the garden's character will constantly change over its entire existence. Besides the regular annual cycle of all flora, the trees, shrubs, and perennials have different life spans and growth rates, and varying responses to the seasons and to each other. Complex natural rhythms play off one another, interlocking and contrasting in varied syncopation.

Even the seasonal cycles are more complex than in a conventional garden. In a staggered sequence of green that ripples from the garden floor to the canopy, each layer of the garden shares light and nutrients with the others. Each spring, the lower layers of a forest garden are the first to leaf out and drink in the early sunlight, just as in a natural woodland. Next, the shrubs put on their green covering, followed in a few weeks by the trees overhead. Many of the plants also reach peak size at different times of the season, further sharing resources. This cooperative aspect of the forest garden is balanced, however, with a little competition. The plants, particularly in the lower layer, do a little jostling of each other, spreading and shrinking as they compete for light, water, and nutrients. The gardener also affects these cycles, with trowel, pruners, and harvest basket.

These rhythms and diversity are augmented by the movement of wild plants into the forest—both so-called weeds and unusual natives—and the gardener, after observing the newcomer, can vote on whether it should stay or go. Birds, insects, snakes, lizards, and small mammals will also find safe harbor here, further adding to the complexity and interest. Watching and learning these varied rhythms provides the best possible introduction to ecology and the natural world. Yet we can do a little intelligent tinkering here too, favoring a useful or attractive species here, encouraging a nascent guild there.

The evolution of the forest garden over the years—not just over the seasons—offers its own benefits. Though the beauty and value of a mature landscape can't be denied, we're not just idly passing time until those tiny seedlings and baby shrubs grow up. Each phase of the garden carries a new set of rewards. When the garden is young, and the scattering of freshly planted trees is at the "twig farm" stage, the sunny spaces between seedlings can be filled with annual and perennial vegetables and flowers. In a year or three, the shrubs and berry bushes will begin to show their true colors and fruit, and for the next five to ten years, before the trees cast much shade, they will be at peak form. Meanwhile, the open ground for annual beds will slowly shrink, soil fertility will grow from the thickening leaf litter, and niches for wildlife will compound by the minute.

After three or four years, the fruit trees will begin to bear, and the backbone of the garden will be apparent. By the fifth year, as trees and shrubs fill out, the herb and ground layers will thin in the reduced light, and herbs, flowers, and vegetables can migrate to the edges and deliberate clearings. In spots, flowering and fruiting vines will tie the upper layers together. The gardener won't need to import much fertilizer and mulch any more, as the forest, through the rain of leaves and the upward tug of deep-soil nutrients through roots, will be just about self-sufficient. In ten years, the trees will approach their full height, and the canopy will begin to close. The garden will take on the serenity and majesty of maturity, but will continue to fill out for another ten or twenty years. By then, much of the original herb layer will have been renewed with new plantings, and some shrubs and small trees will have reached the end of their lives. The substitutes will continue the evolution of this garden. Even at maturity, the garden continues to change gracefully.

The changes in the evolving forest garden are mainly these:

- from most plants being in full sun in the early years to only the upper layers, clearings, and edges receiving all-day sunshine;
- from drought-prone and vulnerable to the vicissitudes of weather and neglect to evenly moist, self-regulating, and filled with mild microclimates;
- from windy and exposed to calm and sheltered;
- from most of the flower and food production, habitat, mulch, and biomass being created by the lower layers to these being produced mainly by the shrub and tree layers;
- from needing imports of mulch and fertilizer to generating abundant fertility and soil via leaf fall and deep-rooted nutrient collection.

Earlier, I've sung the virtues of extending the garden upward into the third dimension. The forest garden reaches yet further, into the fourth dimension of time. The long unfolding of this growing garden brings new opportunities and benefits into reach.

Chapter 11

Pop Goes the Garden

I**N THE PREVIOUS TEN CHAPTERS**, I lay out a tool kit for assembling an ecologically sound garden. Here I'll quickly review where we've been and describe what happens when theory meets practice: how real ecological gardens work, what the limitations are, and what to expect as the garden matures. For those who like the big picture, I'll also discuss some of the underlying principles that make ecological gardens tick—why connections, not just pieces, are so important, and suggest some directions for further exploration.

At the heart of any garden or landscape, at the base of the ecological pyramid, is soil. Create healthy soil and the rest of the job gets much simpler. Because we use techniques such as composting, deep mulches, cover crops, and nutrient-storing plants, the ecological gardener's soil teems with worms and beneficial microorganisms that shunt fertility to plant roots. This rich, humusy earth can support a broad array of soil life, which in turn will nurture diverse plant species and the wide spectrum of helpful insects, birds, and other animals that come to share in the bounty.

Healthy soil ensures that the second element of a self-sustaining garden, water, is in abundance. Deep, spongy humus will hold every drop of rain and irrigation water, better and more cheaply than any other medium. Deep mulches slow evaporation. To weather long droughts, we can also store water in ponds and tanks that are filled by rain, recycled through greywater systems, or, less sustainably, piped from a well or municipal source. All this means that the natural condition of this garden is abundantly moist.

Soil and water are the behind-the-scenes elements that make the garden work. A third element, on center stage, is the vegetation. Chosen to play many roles, the useful and beautiful species have here been selected from native plants, naturalized varieties, noninvasive exotics, indigenous and foreign rare species needing preservation, heirloom crops, and cuttings from neighbors' and friends' yards—in short, from as many sources as are available and ethical. Each plant serves at least two functions—oh, perhaps a handful of them just look pretty; we're human, after all—and in combination they offer benefits to both people and the rest of nature.

Finally, by choice and by serendipity, the garden extends a home to many animals. In the right circumstances, rabbits, chickens, ducks, or even a pot-bellied mini-pig may be at work here, tilling and manuring soil, converting weeds and waste to fertilizer, and connecting us to a more-than-human nature. But even without domestic animals, an ecological garden swarms with niches for pollinators, pest controllers, and scavengers that work the blossoms, nibble the ample foliage and wild berries, or search for prey. The garden is alive with buzzing, fluttering, soaring, scampering allies.

Soil, water, plants, and animals are the four dynamic components of the ecological garden. To this list I might add a fifth, the designers and occupants, who will interact with and shape all the others. The garden also contains a sixth, static element: the structures. Though inert, greenhouses and other buildings, fences, trellises, compost piles, paths, and gates shape the flows that move through the garden.

But as I've said before, these are just pieces. The beauty and effectiveness of the ecological garden is in how the parts are connected. It is the flows between objects, not the objects themselves, that define a natural, sustainable environment.

This garden combines many strategies to create a dense web of connectedness. Stacking functions is one method we use to ensure that everything is linked to one or more other elements. Here, elements serve multiple functions. A Maximilian sunflower hedge at one edge of the garden, for example, provides an impenetrable weed barrier, edible shoots, late fall color, seeds for birds, and plenty of mulch material. These uses tie the sunflower to many other parts of the garden, and reduce work and imports such as fertilizer.

Also, each function is served by multiple elements. The sunflower hedge reduces cold fall winds, and could be combined with other hedges and trees, a carefully placed greenhouse, a rock

wall, and even an earth berm to form a sheltered place for tender plants or a little sunbathing. Combining several techniques that serve the same purpose provides backups in case one method fails, and often yields unexpected synergies. Look: Now that combination of windbreaks has also blocked noise from the nearby highway and screened the view from the neighbors. Now we have a perfect sanctuary or a hot-tub site.

The garden's pieces are also connected by careful use of the Zone-and-Sector method, which locates each plant or other feature by how often it needs attention, and how it interacts with sun, wind, a view, or other energies from outside the site.

Patterns from nature shape the garden's design. Paths and plantings curl into mounded spirals to save space, bend into keyhole beds for easy reach, and use branch, net, lobe, and other patterns to catch and save energy. The right balance of edge and interior gives both diversity and protected habitat. The garden is stacked in layers to broaden its reach into the third dimension, where it can reap sunlight effectively and also supply many niches for wildlife.

Here, plants harvest and store sunlight, ponds catch water, greywater wetlands capture and use wastes that would otherwise be lost. All these pieces link together to forge a complete and harmonious whole that hums with life. The garden is a net, a sieve, sifting and sorting energy and nutrients from whatever passes through it, and transforming them into flowers, birds, insects, food, and healthy people.

The diversity of this landscape makes it flexible and resilient. With so many inhabitants, connected by such a multitude of interactions, there are many pathways, loops, and possibilities. Cycles ebb and flow with changes in the environment, adapting to new conditions. Too many aphids in one corner are met with a sudden surge of ladybugs that have lain semi-dormant amid yarrow and

Ecological gardens are constantly evolving.

fennel, waiting for such a feast. A heavy load of fallen fruit, rotting because the owners are on vacation, is pounced upon hungrily by birds, insects, and soil life, to be reincarnated as soil and more life before the owners return, unaware of the janitorial frenzy that's gone on in their absence. Small miracles like these are commonplace here.

Ecological gardens are constantly evolving, and the process of their evolution—not just the final product—is fascinating to watch. It's exhilarating to see sterile soil enrich and heal each year, to watch new birds or insects find a home, to taste the first lingonberry, grape, or heirloom apple. Each year brings new treats and is an endpoint in itself, rather than some stage to be impatiently hurried through.

CHOOSING THE RIGHT PIECES

Providing the right pieces and getting important cycles going is most of the work in creating an ecological garden. And once again, by "pieces" I don't mean simple objects—trees, shrubs, fences—but pieces that *do* things: soil builders, sunlight harvesters, and the like. So here I'll summarize much of what is spread over the pages of this book by listing the functions (the roles for plants, and ways to harvest and store resources) and relationships (the nutrient cycles and other important interactions) that make up a successful ecological garden. Some of this section will be simple recap, but I'll also present some ideas in new or larger contexts. With these elements in the right places, the garden is almost guaranteed to coalesce into a mini-ecosystem.

Building Fertility

Catching and holding resources is the key to a sustainable garden (or society, for that matter). All plants harvest carbon and minerals, and if left to compost in place, will add them to the soil. Some plants are better at this than others, though. Particularly in the young landscape or in gardens that are harvested regularly, fertility-building plants are critical to create and maintain healthy

soil, since they channel nutrients to impoverished earth, and replenish what is lost in the harvest basket. Fertility builders can make up as much as half of a young garden. These plants, many of whom we met in chapter 6, can be divided into three groups (species are listed in the appendix):

NITROGEN FIXERS. Nitrogen is often the limiting nutrient in a garden, thus N-fixing plants like legumes and the many others listed in the appendix will slash the need for fertilizer, and at the same time pour more organic matter into the soil than fertilizer ever could. This is perhaps the most important class of plant to have in a young garden. In poor soils, having 25 percent N-fixing plants to begin with is not too many. They can be culled as the garden matures. Remember to use nitrogen-fixing trees and shrubs too, not just perennial and annual herbs.

NUTRIENT ACCUMULATORS. These deep-rooted plants mine minerals from the subsoil, ferrying nutrients into the garden where they can be swept into the intermeshing cycles of matter and energy by other plants, microbes, and animals.

MULCH PLANTS. All plants add mulch to the soil at leaf fall, but some excel at this. Plants with large leaves and dense canopies that can tolerate heavy pruning are the best choice. Initially, most mulch will come from the herb layer, but as the garden matures, trees and shrubs will take over much of this role.

Including Life's Other Kingdoms

Though plants are the central feature of a garden, to truly thrive a backyard ecosystem must extend its connections into the rest of nature. These links draw energy and nutrients into the garden in ways that the flora and the gardener can't, and create more complex and resilient cycles. When a bird flies into the garden, it often carries new seeds from elsewhere that will broaden diversity or fill an unused niche. Also it will likely plop a small offering of manure that it harvested from outside the garden. To some this may just be bird poop, but from the ecological viewpoint it's a useful input that the gardener didn't have to work for. Each visitor to the garden shuttles in energy and nutrients garnered from elsewhere. Plus, every arriving bird, insect, or other animal creates new links in the food web, reaping unused resources, providing food for others, and adding to the dynamic balancing act that is an ecosystem.

To attract beneficial visitors and encourage them to stay, we need plant varieties that forge partnerships with the other kingdoms of life. Here are some classes of vegetation that will do this.

INSECTARY PLANTS. Familiar by now, these are species that offer nectar or pollen, attract prey species (such as aphids and caterpillars), or furnish homes for insects. They should include native plants to attract indigenous beneficial bugs, but exotics as well, since a huge proportion of the insects around us are imports that have become naturalized, and need non-native hosts. A wide variety of insectaries should be included so they'll bloom and otherwise work their magic over a long period. This way pollinators and pest fighters will always be ready to buzz in when needed.

WILDLIFE ATTRACTORS. Herbs, shrubs, and trees that offer food and shelter for birds, mammals, reptiles, and amphibians will bring layers of diversity to the garden and reduce pest problems. Again, variety is important. Choose plants of different heights, both woody and soft-tissued ones, having diverse fruit, flowers, leaves, and twigs to support the many types of feeding styles, with dense and open foliage, and a selection that offers food at all seasons.

FEED AND FORAGE SPECIES. I've shown how small animals such as chickens, ducks, rabbits, and others can make us less dependent on imports such as fertilizer, and do useful work in the course of their normal activities. So why not further close the loop and give our animal helpers their own feed and forage from plants that provide seeds, nuts, pods, fruit, fodder, and browse?

PLANTS FOR PEOPLE.
All gardens need to offer something for humans, thus we also tailor the flora to suit ourselves by including plants for food, income, crafts, fiber, medicine, building supplies, nursery stock, seed-saving, and just plain beauty.

Harvesting and Recycling Resources

An ecological garden is like a net, sieving and holding whatever resources (minerals, organic matter, sunlight, water, and organisms) flow through it. And just as important, these landscapes are consummate recyclers, shuttling each bit of matter and energy from soil to plant to animal and back again, over and over until every last bit of benefit has been extracted. This careful stewardship of all resources is one key to a sustainable garden. So we employ an array of techniques to grab and recycle as many of the resources entering the garden as possible. The best of these methods are passive, needing no work from the gardener beyond setting them up, after which they pull in resources and cycle them in the garden, day in, day out. That's a simple way to build abundance. I have identified a number of strategies for resource recycling.

HARVESTING WATER. Digging swales and channels to catch runoff, adding humus to soil, using deep mulches and dense plantings, and capturing roof-top rain in tanks and ponds are all good methods to catch and hold most of the water needed to keep the garden growing. This will reduce the demand on wells and other high-input, less-renewable water sources.

CATCHING NUTRIENTS. A greywater system will net minerals and organic matter that would otherwise be lost down the sewer. Humus-rich soil will prevent that precious matter from leaching away in rains. Composting and mulching (as opposed to leaving trimmings at the curb for pickup) will keep fertility on the site. Neighbors will often happily part with their own yard waste (silly them!), a great free source of organic matter. And the plants themselves will pull nutrients out of rain, and harvest dust and wind-blown debris.

GARDENING IN LAYERS. The immense leafy area of a multistoried garden that mixes trees, shrubs, and low plants will capture sunlight and turn it into life far more efficiently than a one-layer landscape. These multiple layers will also slow moisture loss from evaporation, and perhaps even harvest fog to boost total precipitation. The 3-D garden will also attract many more birds and beneficial insects to its varied habitat, with all the bonuses they offer.

USING SECTORS. By locating plants, buildings, paths, windbreaks, and other elements in the right relationship to seasonal sun and wind patterns, views, fire and wildlife corridors, and other energies coming from off the site, we can harvest these forces' benefits and reduce their draining effects.

ADDING ANIMALS. Animals are often overlooked as garden elements. But they have many roles. They will eat whatever is in excess and turn it into work, more animals, and manure. We can choose which of these multiple gifts we want. Techniques for drawing animals into the garden can be as simple as hanging a bird feeder where we want soil scratched and manure dropped, or as complex as incorporating many-specied plantings that provide nutritious chicken forage and raising poultry for eggs and meat in chicken tractors.

Animals will chow down on surplus and unusable fruit and foliage, prepping it via their digestive tracts so the decomposers can easily pump it back into the garden ecosystem. They are the consumers that bind producer plants and decomposer soil life together.

Building Interconnections

In the rich interconnectedness of an ecosystem, small failures are shrugged off. The loss of a few plants or an outbreak of disease isn't the setback it would be in an orderly row-crop garden. That's because those connections and redundancy turn the garden ecosystem into a resilient net. Sever a few threads and the whole remains. And in a living net, the breaks are quickly repaired by the shifting, breeding, swarming surge of life. It is this webwork, more than any other factor, that distinguishes the ecological garden from the more conventional, vulnerable forms. So creating these connections, deep, multiple, and strong, is a chief goal of the ecological gardener. Here are some strategies for forging this webwork.

DESIGNING WITH ZONES. The first links to build are the ones that tie the gardener to the elements of the landscape. A garden that is not well connected to a gardener will speedily revert to vacant-lot wilderness. The Zone system forges links whose length— the distance between the element and the house—depends on how often the element needs attention. The busiest connections are the shortest, which saves time and ensures that fussy or oft-used plants don't suffer from neglect. And best of all, using zones means living in the center of a garden.

OFFERING NICHES FOR THE GARDENER'S ALLIES. The vast majority of wildlife, whether bug, microbe, or vertebrates, are helpful or harmless to the garden. And in general, the more varieties of species, the less chance that any one will get out of control. I've described plants that attract wildlife. Other niche-enhancers include birdhouses and feeders, rockeries for helpful lizards and snakes, brush piles for insects and birds, and ponds to offer homes for fish and amphibians and drinking spots for other animals.

ENHANCING SURVIVAL AND GROWTH WITH NURSE PLANTS. Nurse, scaffold, and chaperone plants will help ensure that young or tender species will become established. They will also boost their protégé's growth rate far beyond what a young plant could achieve alone. Providing nutrient accumulation, shelter from wind and fierce sun, natural mulch, and often harboring beneficial insects and wildlife, nurse plants and others mediate critical connections between young transplants and the forces that can kill or aid them. Helper plants are one of the biggest factors that propel a garden toward behaving like an ecosystem. Use them liberally.

COMMUNITY-BUILDING VIA GUILDS. Guilds, or plant communities that mimic those in nature while providing for people, let plants and animals pick up much of the gardener's work. A stand-alone fruit tree, for example, must be watered, fertilized, and sprayed, and its pollination chances and disease- and pest-resistance are at the whim of the elements. But if we design a guild that connects the tree to plants and animals that will do these tasks, not only are the gardener and the tree happier, but the rich, multilayered webwork of the guild will harvest more resources, sculpt new niches, and boost biodiversity.

STACKING FUNCTIONS. Designing each element to have multiple functions—a nurse plant, for example, that provides shade and nitrogen to its young charge, nectar to hummingbirds, berries for wildlife, and fast-growing mulch—builds a dense network of connections. Each role played by a plant or other garden element connects it to something else. As this web grows thicker and more interlinked, the garden becomes easier to maintain because most of the tasks are done by the garden itself, and if one organism fails, another is there to pick up the slack. Also, a deeply interwoven landscape begins to act as a single being, with its own character and novelties. This make the ecological garden a fascinating place.

GROWING BY CHUNKING.
Imposing an arbitrary, large, and untested pattern on a landscape—all at once—is a recipe for disaster. This often results in unsuitable plantings, disconnected elements that don't work well together,

and constant rescue efforts. Instead, start small and close to the house, find out what works, get one area growing successfully, and then repeat this pattern (with appropriate variations for new sites). In time, these many small patches of fertility and thriving plants will link up, bonding into a resilient, healthy whole. Ecological designers call this approach "growing by chunking."

THE GARDEN GETS POPPING

For me, there is one time in the maturing of an ecological garden that is particularly exciting. That's when, after an initial period of sluggish plant growth and imperceptible soil improvement, the garden suddenly roars into life, and seethes with greenery, fruit, blossoms, and wildlife. The early establishment phase can take a few years, but then look out! The whole place suddenly "pops" as if some critical mass has been reached. The garden surges into vital action, moving from near-desert to lush jungle in a seeming instant, exploding with living energy. Everyone who practices permaculture and ecological gardening for a few years has seen this amazing transformation. Let me describe one example.

In the first chapter, I introduced Roxanne Swentzell's garden in New Mexico. Remember that when she and her two young children moved in, the place was gravel desert. "At first, everything we planted died," Roxanne had said. "It was just too harsh." The plants would cook in summer, and freeze or dry out in winter. "We'd bring in big old rocks or logs for protection and plant little trees behind them," she recalled. "That helped a little. But we still had to plant a lot of things over and over." They trucked in manure and mulch, and built rock walls to hold heat on cold nights, trying to foster benign microclimates that would enfold tiny pockets of fertility.

On my second visit, permaculture designer Joel Glanzberg, who had helped design and install the garden, arrived to show me around. Explaining their strategy for coaxing plants to survive, he told me, "In the beginning we'd find a sheltered spot, like along a swale. We'd mulch it and put in pioneer species, usually native and exotic nitrogen fixers like New Mexico locust, Russian olive, and Siberian pea shrub." In the shade of these, they planted fruit and nut trees that would eventually soar past the nitrogen-fixing nurse plants to form the canopy. "We'd work on creating a favorable spot, concentrating our resources there, and then grow out from those nuclei," Joel said. "And those nuclei started to link up. Rox figured out quickly that you get little areas under control, and once you're successful there, move on and repeat the pattern." This strategy, duplicating small successes rather than trying to do everything at once—growing by chunking—pares down the chance of failure by building on past successes.

The strategies worked. In about the fifth year, life began to take hold and gain momentum. The soil was rich enough, the shade amply dense, the leaf litter so abundant, the roots sufficiently deep, for the pieces to coalesce into a whole. The system "popped." Plants that had struggled for several years suddenly were detonating, growing several feet in a season. The soil stayed moist through month-long droughts. Fruit burst through the thick foliage. Bushel basket and pruning saw replaced shovel and sprinkler as the most useful tools. Birds filled the new forest with song. And a nearly closed canopy of greenery now cast cool shade that offered refuge from the intense New Mexico sun, and kept the soil from burning to dry powder. A completely different energy now suffused the place. Someone with a mystical bent would say that a spirit had come to inhabit the land and give it life.

As Roxanne described the garden's beginnings, I watched honeybees fly from a hive near the back door to a thick carpet of flowers ringing a small pond. Roxanne clipped more branches from a luxuriant Russian olive. "Our biggest problems now are too much shade and too much water," she said. "And I can't even throw a peach pit into the bushes, because next year there'll be a peach tree growing there." Yet only a few years back the place had been barren. Outside the fence, the ground was still naked gravel and the air blistering hot, while just inside, the temperature was ten degrees cooler. In winter, frosts were fewer and nighttime lows less severe. The garden's design had changed the merciless high-desert climate into something sweet and benign. That's a significant feat.

I looked over the surrounding bare, eroded hills and imagined the Southwest covered in a rich food forest such as this one. Each house could be a nucleus for an expanding net of green canopy and deep soil, eventually linking into a continuous carpet of lush, abundant nature.

The phenomenon I was seeing, the "pop" of a young ecological garden into a self-sustaining ecosystem, is well recognized. It's happened for the Bullock brothers, for Penny Livingston, for Roxanne, for Jerome Osentowski. It's happening for me right now. Carolyn and I began improving our own Zones 1 and 2 here in Oregon five years ago, and suddenly, this year and last, once-struggling trees are shooting skyward, wildflowers we've never seen are blossoming everywhere, and, since I'm tied to my desk until I finish writing this book, I must abandon all hope of keeping the wildly flourishing growth under control. Three years ago, the ground outside my study window was hard clay that baked to pavement in summer, broken only by a few tufts of grass that were burnt brown by the fourth of July. After deep mulching and dense planting, that soil is black and full of worms, deeper this year than last. I won't need to water until six weeks into the dry season. The once-baked ground is shaded by fruit trees, a wealth of shrubs, and bush-sized perennial flowers interspersed with salad greens, herbs, and strawberries.

Someone with a mystical bent would say that a spirit had come to inhabit the land and give it life.

In the wilder, untended parts of our yard, where three or four stunted weed and grass species once labored to survive, a dozen or more wildflowers and native grasses now grow tall and thick—and I didn't plant them. Without looking very hard, I've counted over fifteen bee and beneficial wasp species, innumerable beetles, and four different lizards. Birds that had once only visited briefly, such as western tanagers, have now taken up residence. And I know next year will be even better.

It's useful to ask two questions here: What's happening when a garden pops? And, how do we make it happen quickly?

In just a few years, Flowering Tree Permaculture Institute grew from sun-baked, barren desert into a lush oasis that hums with life.

The Garden as an Organism

First, what's happening? For one thing, an ecological garden moves rapidly through the pioneer phase—where it's full of fast-growing, low plants with limited habitat for other species, rather like conventional gardens—into a more mature, many-layered, high-biomass, high-diversity, closed-loop ecosystem.

Many of the techniques described in this book are designed to accelerate this natural process of succession and to make the connections among organisms tight, many-layered, and efficient. Deep mulches, for example, quickly boost the amount of energy and food available for soil life. Thousands of species of soil organisms arrive with this mulch, drift in on air currents and raindrops, or are present but dormant. In the welcoming habitat, they spring to life. This rapidly enlarges the decomposer component in the all-important producer-consumer-decomposer cycle.

As I've said before, in most gardens, the decomposers are few and weak, only able to cycle and release low levels of nutrients. This poverty constricts the vigor and number of the producers (plants) and consumers (birds, insects, and you) that depend on the decomposers to provide raw materials for growth. Ramping up the activity of the decomposers by adding plenty of organic matter unchains the once-stunted plant and animal life. The vigorously cycling soil life pumps out an enormous surplus of nutrients, throwing off food and energy in wild abundance and in many forms, so that more plants and animals, both in terms of diversity and sheer numbers, can thrive. Deep mulch also generates humus, which becomes a capacious reservoir for minerals like calcium, potassium, and others essential for plant growth.

Think of the whole garden as an organism. Deep mulching the area around a house, combined with dense planting, creates an expanding circle of vigorous life and fertility. The densely interconnected soil, plant, and animal life are now surging with nutrients, water, pollen, chemical messages, and other "information flows." As the gardener gradually expands this intensely planted area farther from the house, the area of thick interconnections expands, nutrient and energy flows link

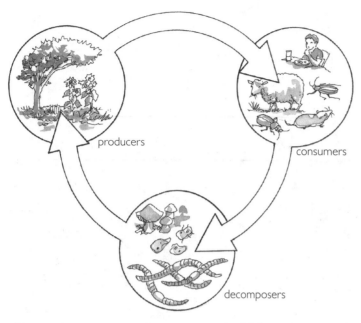

The producer-consumer-decomposer cycle. All three elements of this cycle are equally important. In most yards, the decomposers (worms, bacteria, fungi, and other soil creatures) are neglected, which starves the producers (plants), and in turn, the consumers (animals), of resources. If each link flourishes, the others grow stronger too.

up and fatten, new niches appear, and more species can thrive in this vibrant place. The living interconnectivity of the garden is so boosted that it becomes a fibrous knot of life, virtually impossible to wound, invade, or otherwise destabilize.

This resilience exists for many reasons. Having so many species from all of life's kingdoms provides a huge assortment of food types and habitat. This means each inhabitant of the garden has several places to feed instead of a single "all-eggs-in-one-basket" food supply that might fail. And with so many habitats present, every inhabitant has a good chance of finding the right microclimate, soil type, branch height, or other quality needed to survive. This high biodiversity—lots of species—means that if one species dies out, many others that play similar roles stand nearby to plug into the gap and keep the community functioning.

This garden is hard to damage. A new species may appear from the wild or the nursery, but rarely will it become invasive. The odds are high that it will find fertile soil and the right conditions to grow. But with so many other species present—potential competitors—it's not likely to find enough unused food or space to become a pest. If it spreads too fast, it becomes a delicious and abundant food source for one of the thousands of species of insects, soil fungi, or other consumers that will keep it in check. Remember how muskrats at the Bullocks' bog were knocked back by the arriving otters? Be assured that this wasn't an isolated case. The brothers had a similar problem with slugs, too, until ducks moved in and munched the slimy invaders down to manageable numbers. This will happen in any balanced ecosystem.

Also, this kind of garden fills in quickly because nearly any potential resource that enters it will be grabbed by some waiting organism. That translates into fast growth and dense interconnections. Here's why. In conventional gardening, with expanses of bare soil and little variety, fertilizer can leach out of uninhabited ground, precious water evaporates, sunlight falls on empty space, and with many links missing in the producer-consumer-decomposer webwork, many resources—from dead branches to dried leaves to old corn cobs in the compost—go unused because the creatures capable of recycling and using them are missing.

But in a diverse garden, nothing goes to waste. Something is always there to use it. Any potential food or habitat source is seized upon hungrily by one of the zillion species present, and incorporated into the ever-building structure of the garden. It's another example of the "rich get richer" phenomenon, more formally called the law of increasing returns. Once an ample framework for harvesting wealth is built—in this case, wealth being sunlight, food, and incoming species, the framework being fertile soil and a multistoried assemblage of plants—the garden keeps getting richer and more diverse. The ever-enlarging wheel of life just gets better and better at harvesting and using nutrients and the constant stream of free energy from the sun, which powers yet further growth and interconnection.

Also, the design itself makes sure that little goes to waste. Using greywater means that nutrients that would otherwise go down the drain are captured and stingily held by the soil, then fed to plants and recycled in the garden. Designing with zones ensures that the places that need the most care are the closest to hand, making it easy to notice the little bare spot that needs mulching, the drooping ground cover crying out for water, or the slugs perforating the lettuce. Taking sectors into account effectively uses free energy such as sunlight and damps down the battle against wind or fire, freeing our time for more productive work. Using insectary and wildlife plants extends the garden's reach beyond the plant kingdom into the realms of microbes, insects, and other animals. This lets us bring oft-overlooked allies and energy into the garden, filling it with busy workers while we sip lemonade in a hammock.

Another reason for the "popping" phenomenon is that we've mimicked natural plant communities. This takes advantage of a few billion years of groundwork done by evolution. A plant community's species coevolved over eons and so are familiar partners. They know what to do with each other. The interconnections and flows of nutrients, chemical signals, and pollen, as well as the niches for the beneficial supporting cast of soil life, have already been worked out. This is why the guild approach is so much more successful than just planting blocks of a single species. Like a great sports team, the members have rehearsed their moves so many times that when we bring them together, they blend into a smoothly performing ensemble and get to work. Ecologist Stuart Pimm,

who has studied natural communities, described this process in an interview with author Kevin Kelly. Pimm said that in these communities, "The players have played many times. They know what the sequence is. Evolution not only evolves the functioning community, it finetunes the assembly process of the gathering until the community practically falls together." So putting together the members of an existing plant community fattens the chance of a successful and rapid meshing, and shrinks the possible niches for invaders such as pest species.

In a garden this full of life, seething with complex food webs and a rich supply of nutrients, plenty of opportunities exist for successful, mutually beneficial links to form and thicken. That makes the system pop. Now let's look at how we can speed up the process to accelerate our arrival at that delightful popping stage.

Where to Begin?

I've described the process of designing the garden, and given lots of techniques to use. But ecological gardening is a new field crammed with fresh information, so I wouldn't be surprised if you are looking at your design sketches, nicely drawn according to zones and sectors and full of multifunctional plants, and asking, "Yes, but what do I do *first?*" Sure, begin at your doorstep, but begin doing what? What are the very first things to do that will help a garden become an ecosystem?

The title of an excellent book by Grace Gershuny gives the answer: *Start with the Soil.* Not only is the soil the base of the ecological pyramid and thus the logical place to begin, but very shortly the soil will be stuffed with perennial plants and thus be much harder to work on. Bringing the soil to rich, loamy fertility will accelerate and invigorate all that succeeds it. So the first step is to create a small bed of rich soil near the front or back door, or other close-in site (how to choose the exact spot for this bed is explained in a few paragraphs).

Think of this luxuriantly fertile region as the

heart of Zone 1, the place that will support the first set of dense plantings and will probably be heavily harvested. So this soil needs to be immensely fertile. This will be the initial nucleus of high fertility and diversity, to later be linked up with others, just as Joel Glanzberg described.

To get the garden going, we want to build this startup bed's soil rapidly. If there's a source of compost available, then the fastest method to boost fertility in a small space is to remove unwanted vegetation from this bed, and scratch in an inch or two of compost. Also add other necessary amendments such as lime, phosphate, and potassium (a soil test will show what's needed). If no compost is handy, then sheet mulching is the method I prefer.

As I mentioned in chapter 4, I consider adding compost to be a short-term method, an emergency technique to quickly bring soil to decent fertility so that a patch of ground can be pushed into production fast. But to build soil that is truly surging with life, I like sheet mulching—composting in place—because it encourages multiple generations of soil life (ecological succession in the soil), fills the garden bed with the rich excretions of decomposer organisms instead of wasting them beneath the compost pile, and leaves the soil creatures undisturbed. Besides, it's less work than building a compost pile in one place and then transporting and working-in full carts of the finished product. The downside is that the sheet-mulched bed won't

ECOLOGICAL COMPROMISES, OR YOU CAN'T MAKE AN OMELET . . .

In a perfect, environmentally optimized world, we'd never power-till, all of our mulch supplies would come from nearby—ideally from our own property—and we'd find renewable sources of soil amendments instead of mined, exhaustible products such as rock phosphate and greensand. But it's not a perfect world, and I'm not going to be so dogmatic as to demand we create and use our gardens using only completely sustainable techniques. When it's time to get our hands dirty, idealism runs into the brick wall of practicality. I'd much rather see gardeners consume some nonrenewable resources to create eventually self-sustaining gardens than have them sit paralyzed by the fear of committing an environmentally incorrect act.

We do what we're comfortable with. David Holmgren, the co-originator of permaculture's concepts, says, to the horror of purists, that he doesn't oppose a one-time use of herbicide to prepare land for tree planting, considering the energy used and destruction caused by the alternative: bringing in machines to clear the site year after year until the trees are established. And otherwise-organic gardener Doug Clayton now applies the insecticide Imidan once a year to his fruit trees. He believes a single dose of this effective pesticide is far less harmful than what he once used: almost-weekly sprayings of organically acceptable yet very toxic pyrethrums and rotenone.

If renting a power-tiller once, or buying peat moss from fossilized north-Canada sphagnum beds, or bulldozing to grade a site, or some other method eschewed by the idealist is what it takes to get your backyard ecosystem up and running, then do it. Especially in the establishment phase, when we're working hard to restore abused land and heal broken cycles, we should be forgiving.

Use techniques that work for you. I've seen permaculture sites that mix conventional raised beds full of annual plants with semi-wild forest gardens. The raised beds are efficient to harvest, plus it's easy to see what's going on. In a forest garden, plants occasionally get lost in the diversity. Mixing and matching an assortment of techniques is fine.

One rule of thumb for making these sorts of choices is to think long term. Using nonrenewable resources to create a landscape is justified if in the long run, that landscape will conserve or provide more resources than it took to build it. Using a less-than-natural technique that produces homegrown food and reduces the pressure on wild land is preferable to giving up in exhaustion. Overall, doing an imperfect something is better than doing a perfect nothing.

reach maximum fertility for a year or two. But it still can and should be planted immediately by using soil pockets or a thin top-dressing of good soil.

How big should this first bed be? That depends on how much compost or sheet-mulch material—and labor—is available. A typical wheelbarrow, powered by a non-Herculean human, can hold 1 to 3 cubic feet of compost, enough to cover 10 to 30 square feet of ground 1 inch deep. That's not much—it will take a lot of wheelbarrow loads to do a single garden bed. And as I explained in chapter 4, one pickup load of mulch material will cover about 50 square feet. Also, remember to cover a small area well rather than a large area thinly.

Where exactly to locate these precious first garden beds? Here's where knowing a little about microclimates comes in handy. Joel Glanzberg talked about placing the first plantings along swales, where water would collect and linger, and where potential shelter from wind and sun already existed. In high-mountain Colorado, Jerome Osentowski built rock terraces that held heat in his frost-prone garden. And near cool, foggy San Francisco, Penny Livingston planted a peach tree amid a set of small ponds, where stored heat from the water as well as reflected light would speed growth. Finding (or creating) and using benign microclimates will boost the odds of success and accelerate plant growth, speeding the arrival of that happy day of system-pop.

Which microclimates to choose depends on the overall environment and climate. What's benign in the desert—a moist, shady, not well-drained site, for example—would be disastrous in a damp northern climate, where a sunny, fairly dry spot is far better. In general, look for sites that have no wild swings of temperature, moisture, or sunlight. Whatever the local climate extremes are in the region—brutally high or low temperatures, sogginess or drought, leaf-crisping sun or months of kill-me-now gray skies—find a place that will counter or mitigate those extremes. Desirable in almost any location is lack of wind, so locate the heart of Zone 1 in the still shelter of a house, earth berm, wall, or planted windbreak.

If favorable microclimates don't exist, as they didn't for Roxanne Swentzell, then make them. Pile up rocks or logs, or build a wall for a windbreak. Dig a swale for wind protection and added moisture. Create a raised bed to improve drainage, or a sunken one in dry climates to catch infrequent rain. Prune a tree to let in light. Find and create good microclimates to give the garden the edge that it needs for a successful start.

ASSEMBLING THE GARDEN REVISITED

How hard is it to click together all the pieces of an ecological garden? It might sound daunting. On previous pages I've told stories of wild chiles that need particular nurse-plants and hot-sauce–tolerant birds to thrive, and saguaro cacti that depend on mesquites and white-winged doves for survival. If nature's assembly rules are that specific and complex, what are the chances that a humble gardener can collect all the right elements to make a landscape pop? What are the odds that we will have the species and conditions necessary to create a smoothly functioning set of plant communities?

Very good odds, it turns out. Nature is very forgiving and resilient, as both its continued survival in the face of human damage, and ecology research prove. A number of ecologists have looked into the assembly of natural communities, and what they've found is encouraging and useful for ecological gardeners.

Two of these scientists are Jim Drake and Stuart Pimm, at the University of Tennessee. Drake and Pimm studied how communities of organisms form. They added fifteen to forty species of bacteria, algae, and microscopic animals (a blend of producers, consumers, and decomposers) one at a time, in many different combinations and sequences, to tanks full of nutrient broth. They were surprised to find how often this random mixing resulted in a stable ecosystem. Instead of dying in what could have been an unsuitable home, the microbes connected with each other, building food webs, multiplying, and preying on each other in a well-linked ecosystem. Pimm remarked that after making these random groupings, they watched the organisms assemble toward a network that was much more structured than expected from such a haphazard collection.

Drake and Pimm also performed computer simulations to support their findings. They programmed a computer with 125 software "species" and, after creating an initial stable community of three electronic organisms in the machine, added new species one at a time. At first, each invading species made the grouping fluctuate in population and often bumped out other species in waves of extinction, but eventually the communities settled down, clicked into place, and became impervious to new invaders. This showed that simply adding random species together could create invasion-proof communities of interacting members.

In both sets of experiments, many species would survive for a while and then die off. They didn't wind up as part of the final community. But they turned out to be important ingredients of a successful, stable ensemble. If these species were dropped from the assembly process, the community ended up with a different final composition; it took an alternative path. These short-term species played the same role as nurse plants, performing some useful job along the way, but weren't part of the end product.

These experiments confirm what many permaculture gardeners have learned: We don't know exactly how the assembly of successful guilds and ecosystems works, but if we begin with a wide array of plant types, nature will usually sort out something that clicks. A skimpy selection takes a lot more babying, and often never "pops" at all.

These experiments, as well as the experiences of the ecological gardeners cited in this book, hint that assembling a backyard ecosystem is not as difficult as one might think. Nature adheres to a deep order. It is almost as if living beings "want" to come together into coherent communities. Given half a chance, plants and animals will self-organize into a connected whole. Ecological gardeners take heart: We don't have to master every detail of guild design, or include every single native bacterium, beetle, and plant species of a community to get a garden to "pop." Nature will often supply the missing pieces, click together the right connections, and link up the important cycles. A holistic garden wants to happen; we just need to supply a reasonable selection of pieces and arrange them in a usable order. Nature will choose the ones that work.

I'm not saying creating an ecological garden will take no work. Building soil, nurturing an array of useful plants to maturity, and awaiting the arrival of beneficial insects, birds, and other wildlife will take labor and time. And transforming a viewpoint from a static bits-and-pieces orientation to one based on the interconnectedness of nature may be the biggest hurdle. But that initial investment will pay off handsomely. You'll hardly even remember it as you lie in your hammock, overwhelmed by the choice of fruit, hypnotized by the array of scents wafting your way, and comfortable in the knowledge that your landscape is allowing some bit of farmland to go free.

This book can only be an introduction to an enormous subject, one that could easily consume a lifetime of study, observation, and puttering among the plants. The bibliography offers further resources that go into more depth. The best way to learn, however, is simply to take a good look at the natural world, roll up your sleeves, and begin to create a garden that will provide for both you and the many other beings with whom we live.

APPENDIX

A Sampling of Useful Plants

Thousands of useful plant species exist, thus the plants listed in the following tables represent only small sample of what is available. I've chosen these species because they are relatively common, of exceptional usefulness, and not too difficult to grow.

Sources for this information include the *Plants for a Future Database* (www.pfaf.org); Tilth, *The Future is Abundant* (Tilth, 1982); and Christopher Brickell, *The American Horticultural Society Encyclopedia of Garden Plants* (Macmillan, 1990).

KEY TO APPENDIX TABLES

USDA Zone

Refers to the USDA Hardiness Zone system, representing the lowest temperature that the plant will normally survive, as follows:

Zone	Minimum Temp (°F)
2	-50 to -40°
3	-40 to -30°
4	-30 to -20°
5	-20 to -10°
6	-10 to 0°
7	0 to 10°
8	10 to 20°
9	20 to 30°

Type

Tr Tree (a woody perennial with a single erect stem and a substantial leaf canopy)

Sh Shrub (a woody perennial with multiple stems arising from the base)

Cl Climber (a vining or trailing plant with a flexible stem)

E Evergreen (retaining foliage year-round)

D Deciduous (losing its foliage in winter)

HP Herbaceous perennial (a nonwoody plant that grows for several to many years)

HB Herbaceous biennial (a nonwoody plant that sets seed and dies in its second year)

A Annual

B Perennial

Light

○ Prefers full sun

● Prefers shade

◐ Tolerates partial shade

Edible Part or Use

Bark	Bark
Fr	Fruit
Fl	Flower
Lf	Leaf
Med	Medicinal
Oil	Seed or sap used for oil
Root	Root
Sap	Sap
Seas	Used as seasoning or spice
Sd	Seed
Sht	Shoot
Tea	Tea
Y	Young

Animal Use

Chk	Poultry forage
For	Forage, browse, or other animal feed
Hab	Provides habitat
Hum	Attracts hummingbirds
Ins	Attracts beneficial insects

Other Use

Biomass	Plant produces large quantities of biomass
Bskt	Stem, branches, or root used for basketry
Dye	Some or all of plant used to prepare dye
Fiber	Leaf, stem, flower parts, or root used in paper, cordage, or other fiber product
Fragrance	Has exceptional fragrance, may be used as perfume base
Gourd	Fruit used as gourd
Hr	Hedgerow species
N-fixer	Nitrogen-fixing species
Nutr	Nutrient-accumulator species
Poles	Stem or branches used for poles and support stakes
Polish	Used as furniture polish
Repellent	Used as insect repellent
Soap	Leaves, sap, fruit or other part used as soap
Soil stab	Used for soil stabilization
Wbr	Windbreak species
Wood	Woody parts used for lumber, fire wood, or craft wood

TALL TREES, 50 FEET AND LARGER

Common name	Botanical name	Hardy to USDA Zone	Type	Light	Edible part or use	Animal use	Other uses	Comments
Beech	Fagus spp.	5	D Tr	○◑	Sd, YLf, Med	Hab, For	Wbr, Hr	
Black locust	Robinia pseudoacacia	3	D Tr	○	Fl, Sd	Ins, Hab, Chk, For	Wbr, Hr, Wood	N-fixer
Black walnut	Juglans nigra	4	D Tr	○	Sd, Med	Hab, For	Wbr, Wood	Allelopathic; other species also useful
Chinese chestnut	Castanea mollissima	4	D Tr	○	Sd, Med	Ins, Hab, Chk, For	Wbr, Hr, Wood, Soil stab	
Honey locust	Gleditsia triacanthos	3	D Tr	○	Seedpod	Ins, Hab, Chk, For	Soil stab	
Limber pine	Pinus flexilis	3	E Tr	○	Sd	Hab, For	Wbr, Hr, Wood	
Madrone	Arbutus menziesii	7	E Tr	○◑	Fr	Ins, Hab, For	Wood	
Oak	Quercus spp.	4	E Tr	○	Sd	Hab, Chk, For	Wbr, Hr, Wood	White oaks have least tannin in acorn
Pignut hickory	Carya glabra	4	D Tr	○◑	Sd, Sap	Hab, For	Hr, Wood	
Piñon pine	Pinus cembroides	4	E Tr	○	Sd	Hab, For	Wbr, Hr, Wood	
Ponderosa pine	Pinus ponderosa	4	E Tr	○	Sd	Hab, For	Wbr, Hr, Dye, Wood	
Shagbark hickory	Carya ovata	4	D Tr	○	Sd, Sap	Hab, Chk, For	Wood, Soil stab	
Shellbark hickory	Carya laciniosa	6	D Tr	○◑	Sd, Sap	Ins, Hab, Chk, For	Wood	
Sour cherry	Prunus cerasus	3	D Tr	○	Fr, Tea	Ins, Hab, For	Wbr, Hr	
Stone pine	Pinus pinea	4	E Tr	○	Sd	Hab, For	Wbr, Hr, Wood	Many other species have edible seeds
Sugar maple	Acer saccharum	3	D Tr	○◑	Sap	Ins, Hab, For	Wood	Many other species good for maple syrup
Sweet chestnut	Castanea sativa	5	D Tr	○	Sd, Med	Ins, Hab, Chk, For	Wbr, Hr, Wood	
Tree of heaven	Ailanthus altissima	7	D Tr	○		Ins, Hab	Wbr, Hr, Soil stab	Tolerates pollution
Yellow buckeye	Aesculus flava	3	D Tr	○◑	Sd, Sap	Ins, Hab, For	Wood, Soap	

SHRUBS AND SMALL TREES, 3–50 FEET TALL

Common name	Botanical name	Hardy to USDA Zone	Type	Light	Edible part or use	Animal use	Other uses	Comments
Alder	Alnus spp.	3	D Tr	○	Med	Ins, Hab	Wbr, Hr, Dye, Wood	
Almond	Prunus dulcis	3	D Tr	○	Sd	Ins, Hab, For	Wbr, Hr	
American hornbeam	Carpinus caroliniana	5	D Tr	◑	Sd	Hab, For	Wbr, Hr, Dye	
American persimmon	Diospyros virginiana	5	D Tr	◑	Fr	Hab, For	Hr	
Amur Maackia	Maackia amurensis	4	D Sh	○	YLf	Ins	Hr, N-fixer	
Angelica tree	Aralia chinensis	7	D Sh	◑	Sht			
Apple	Malus sylvestris	3	D Tr	○	Fr	Ins, Hab, For		
Apricot	Prunus armeniaca	4	D Tr	○	Fr	Ins, Hab, For	Hr	
Autumn olive	Elaeagnus umbellata	3	D Tr	○	Fr	Ins, Hab, Chk, For	Wbr, Hr, N-fixer	
Azarole	Crataegus azarolus	5	D Tr	◑	Fr	Ins, Hab, Chk, For	Wbr, Hr	
Bamboo	Bambusa textilis	7	E Sh	○	Sht	Hab, For	Wbr, Hr, Poles, Fiber	
Bamboo	Pseudosasa japonica	5	E Sh	◑	Sht, Med	Hab, For	Wbr, Hr, Poles, Fiber	
Barberry	Berberis vulgaris	3	D Sh	◑	Fr, Tea	Hab, For	Wbr, Hr, Fiber	
Bay tree	Laurus nobilis	8	E Tr	○			Wbr, Hr	
Bitter orange	Poncirus trifoliata	5	E Tr	○	Fr, Med	Hab	Wbr, Hr	
Bittersweet	Celastrus orbiculatus	4	D Tr	◑	YLf, Med	Hab, For	Wbr, Hr	Leaves should be cooked
Black currant	Ribes nigrum	5	D Sh	●	Fr	Ins, Hab, Chk, For	Hr	
Black elderberry	Sambucus nigra	5	D Sh	◑	Fr, Fl, Med	Ins, Hab, Chk, For	Wbr, Hr, Dye	Leaves toxic
Black hawthorn	Crataegus douglasii	5	D Tr	○	Fr	Ins, Hab, Chk, For	Wbr, Hr	Many other species have edible fruits
Black mulberry	Morus nigra	3	D Tr	○	Fr	Chk, Hab, For		Also M. australis, M. mongolica, M. rubra, & M. serrata
Black raspberry	Rubus occidentalis	4	D Sh	●	Fr, Tea	Ins, Hab, Chk, For	Hr	
Blue elderberry	Sambucus caerulea	5	D Sh	◑	Fr, Fl, Med	Ins, Hab, Chk, For	Wbr, Hr, Dye	Leaves toxic
Blue false indigo	Baptisia australis	5	D Sh	○		Ins, Hab, N-fixer	Wbr, Hr	
Blueberry	Vaccinium corymbosum	2	D Sh	◑	Fr	Ins, Hab, For	Hr	Acid soil
Bottlebrush	Callistemon citrinus	8	E Sh	○	Tea	Ins	Wbr, Hr	C. sieberi & C. viridiflorus can also be used
Box	Buxus sempervirens	5	E Sh	◑	Med		Wbr, Hr	
Boxthorn	Lycium barbarum	6	E Sh	○	Fr, Sht, Med	Hab	Wbr, Hr	
Buffaloberry	Shepherdia argentea	2	D Sh	○	Fr	Ins, Hab, Chk, For	Wbr, Hr, Dye, N-fixer	Drought resistant
Bush clover	Lespedeza thunbergii	5	D Sh	○		Ins	N-fixer	
Butterfly bush	Buddleia davidii	5	D Sh	○		Ins		
Cabbage palm	Cordyline australis	8	E Tr	○	Sht, Root		Wbr, Hr, Dye	
California coffeeberry	Rhamnus californica	7	D Tr	◑	Fr, Med	Ins, Hab, Chk, For	Wbr, Hr, Fiber	
Cascara	Rhamnus purshiana	6	D Tr	○	Med	Ins, Hab	Wbr, Hr	
Cherry plum	Prunus cerasifera	4	D Tr	○	Fr	Ins, Hab, For	Wbr, Hr	
Chinese dogwood	Cornus kousa	5	D Tr	◑	Fr, YLf	Hab, For	Hr	

Common name	Latin name	No.	Form	Symbol	Food/Use	Ins/Hab	Wbr/Hr	Notes
Chinese privet	Ligustrum lucidum	7	E Sh	○○	Med		Wbr, Hr	
Cinquefoil	Potentilla fruticosa	5	D Sh	●○	Tea		Wbr, Hr, Dye	
Cornelian cherry	Cornus mas	5	D Tr	○	Fr		Wbr, Hr, Soil stab	
Coyote brush	Baccharis pilularis	8	E Sh	○		Ins, Hab	Wbr, Hr, Soil stab	
Cranberry	Viburnum trilobum	2	E Sh	○○	Fr	Ins, Hab, For	Hr	Acid soil
Curry plant	Helichrysum italicum	8	E Sh	○	Spice		Wbr, Hr	
Damson	Prunus insititia	5	D Tr	○	Fr, Med	Ins, Hab, For	Wbr, Hr	
Date plum	Diospyros lotus	5	D Tr	○●	Fr	Hab, For	Hr	
Devil's club	Oplopanax horridus	4	D Sh	●	Sht, Med	Hab		
Elaeagnus	Elaeagnus x. ebbingei	6	E Sh	●○	Fr	Ins, Hab, Chk, For	Wbr, Hr, N-fixer	
English laurel	Prunus laurocerasus	6	E Tr	○○	Fr	Ins, Hab, For	Wbr, Hr	
Escallonia	Escallonia spp.	9	E Sh	○		Hum, Ins	Wbr, Hr	
Fig	Ficus carica	7	D Tr	○	Fr	Hab, Chk, For	Hr	
Fuchsia	Fuchsia magellanica	6	D Sh	●●	Med	Hum	Wbr, Hr	Flowers toxic
Fuji cherry	Prunus incisa	6	D Tr	○	Fr	Ins, Hab, For	Wbr, Hr	
Giant reed	Arundo donax	6	Grass	○	Root, Med		Bskt, Wbr, Hr, Soil stab	
Golden currant	Ribes aureum	4	D Sh	○○	Fr, Fl, Lf	Ins, Hab, For	Hr	
Golden-chain tree	Laburnum anagyroides	5	D Tr	○○			Fragrance, N-fixer	Tolerates air pollution
Gooseberry	Ribes uva-crispa	5	D Sh	○○	Fr	Ins, Hab, Chk, For	Hr	
Goumi	Elaeagnus multiflora	6	D Tr	○	Fr	Ins, Hab, Chk, For	Wbr, Hr, N-fixer	
Hackberry	Celtis spp.	4	E Sh	○	Fr, Sd	Hab, Chk, For	Wbr, Hr, Dye	
Hazelnut	Corylus spp.	4	D Tr	○○	Sd, Oil	Hab, For	Wbr, Hr, Bskt	
Heavenly bamboo	Nandina domestica	6	D Sh	○○	Sht	Hab	Wbr, Hr, Poles, Fiber	
Himalayan blackberry	Rubus discolor	5	D Cl	○○	Fr	Ins, Hab, Chk, For	Hr	Many species are useful
Hooker's willow	Salix hookeriana	6	D Tr	○○	Med	Hab	Wbr, Hr	
Hyssop	Hyssopus officinalis	3	E Sh	○	Tea, Med	Ins	Wbr, Hr	
Iigeri tree	Idesia polycarpa	5	D Tr	○	Fr			
Indian cherry	Rhamnus caroliniana	6	D Tr	○○	Fr	Ins, Hab, Chk, For	Hr	
Japanese quince	Chaenomeles speciosa	5	D Tr	○○	Root, Med	Ins, Hab, For	Wbr, Hr	
Japanese raisin tree	Hovenia dulcis	6	D Tr	○	Fr	Hab	Hr	
Jujube	Ziziphus zizyphus	6	D Tr	○	Fr	Hab	Hr	
Juneberry	Amelanchier spp.	4	D Sh	○	Fr	Ins, Hab, Chk, For	Wbr, Hr	
Kentucky coffee tree	Gymnocladus dioica	4	D Tr	○	Sd pod	Hab, For	Hr, Soap, N-fixer	
Kerria	Kerria japonica	4	D Sh	○●	YLf		Wbr, Hr	Drought tolerant
Laurel cherry	Prunus caroliniana	7	E Tr	●●	Fr	Ins, Hab, For	Wbr, Hr	
Lavender	Lavandula spp.	5	E Sh	○	Med	Ins	Hr	
Lemonade berry	Rhus integrifolia	3	D Sh	○○	Fr, Fl	Ins, Hab, For	Wbr, Hr	
Lilac	Syringa vulgaris	5	D Sh	○	Med	Ins, Hab	Wbr, Hr, Dye	
Maidenhair tree	Ginkgo biloba	2	E Tr	○	Sd, Med		Hr	
Mallow	Hibiscus syriacus	5	D Sh	○○	Lf, Fl, Oil, Tea	Ins, Hab	Wbr, Hr, Fiber	
Manzanita	Arctostaphyllos manzanita	7	E Sh	○○	Fr	Ins, Hab, Chk, For	Wbr, Hr, Dye	
Mazzard cherry	Prunus avium	5	D Tr	○	Fr	Ins, Hab, For	Hr	
Medlar	Mespilus germanica	6	D Tr	○	Fr	Hab		
Mexican orange	Choisya ternata	7	D Tr	○			Wbr, Hr	

Common name	Botanical name	USDA Hardy to Zone	Type	Light	Edible parts or use	Animal use	Other uses	Comments
Mock orange	Philadelphus coronarius	5	D Sh	○		Ins, Hab	Wbr, Hr	Also useful P. delavayi, P. pubescens, P. purpurocens, & P. x. virginalis
Mountain ash	Sorbus spp.	5	D Tr	○	Fr	For	Wbr, Hr	
Mountain pepper	Drimys lanceolata	8	E Sh	○●	Fr (spice), Med		Wbr, Hr	
Myrtle	Myrtus communis	8	E Tr	○●	Med		Wbr, Hr	
Nanking cherry	Prunus tomentosa	5	D Sh	○	Fr	Ins, Hab, For	Wbr, Hr	
New Zealand flax	Phormium tenax	8	E Sh	○			Wbr, Hr, Bskt, Fiber, Dye	
Oceanspray	Holodiscus discolor	5	D Sh	○●	Fr	Hab	Hr, Wood	
Olive	Olea europaea	8	E Tr	○	Fr, Oil	Hab	Dye, Soil stab	
Osage orange	Maclura pommifera	5	D Tr	○		Hab	Wbr, Hr, Dye	
Oso berry	Oemleria cerasiformis	6	D Sh	○●	Fr	Hab, For	Hr	
Pawpaw	Asimina triloba	6	D Tr	○●	Fr	Hab, Chk, For	Dye, Fiber	
Peach/Nectarine	Prunus persica	6	D Tr	○	Fr	Ins, Hab, For	Hr	
Persimmon	Diospyros kaki	8	D Tr	○●	Fr	Hab, For	Hr	
Pineapple guava	Feijoa sellowiana	8	E Tr	○	Fr, Fl	Ins, Chk, For	Hr	
Plum	Prunus domestica	3	D Tr	○	Fr	Ins, Hab, For	Wbr, Hr	
Portuguese laurel	Prunus lusitanica	6	E Tr	●		Ins, Hab, For	Wbr, Hr	
Purple osier	Salix purpurea	5	D Sh	○	Med	Hab	Wbr, Hr, Bskt	
Red currant	Ribes rubrum	5	D Sh	○●	Fr	Ins, Hab, Chk, For	Hr	
Red raspberry	Rubus idaeus	3	D Sh	○●	Fr	Ins, Hab, Chk, For	Hr	
Redbud	Cercis canadensis	5	D Tr	○●	Fl	Ins, Hab	Hr	
Rose	Rosa spp.	2	D Sh	○●	Fr	Ins, Hab, For	Wbr, Hr	Hybrids and cultivars are less useful
Rosemary	Rosmarinus officinale	7	E Sh	○	Seas	Ins	Ins, Hr	
Russian olive	Elaeagnus angustifolia	2	D Sh	○	Fr	Ins, Hab, Chk, For	Wbr, Hr, N-fixer	
Salt bush	Atriplex canescens	7	E Sh	○	Lf, Sd		Wbr, Hr	
Sassafras	Sassafras albidum	5	D Tr	○●	Lf, Bark, Fr	Hab	Dye	
Scotch heather	Calluna vulgaris	4	E Sh	○	Tea, Med	Ins	Wbr, Hr, Bskt, Dye	Acid soil
Sea buckthorn	Hippophae rhamnoides	3	D Sh	○	Fr, Med	Hab, For	Wbr, Hr, Dye, N-fixer	
Siberian pea shrub	Caragana arborescens	3	E Sh	○	Sd	Ins, Chk, For	Wbr, Hr, Dye, Soil stab, N-fixer	
Silk tree or mimosa	Albizzia julibrisin	6	D Tr	○●	Lf	Ins, Hab	Hr, N-fixer	
Silverberry	Elaeagnus commutata	2	D Sh	○	Fr	Ins, Hab, Chk, For	Wbr, Hr, Fiber, N-fixer	

Common name	Scientific name		Type					Notes
Sloe	*Prunus spinosa*	4	D Tr	○	Fr, Med	Ins, Hab, For	Wbr, Hr, Dye	
Spanish broom	*Spartium junceum*	8	D Sh	○	Med	Ins, Hab	Wbr, Hr, Fiber, Dye, N-fixer	
Spotted laurel	*Aucuba japonica*	7	E Sh	●			Wbr, Hr	
Staghorn sumac	*Rhus typhina*	3	D Sh	○	Fr	Hab	Wbr, Hr, Dye, Soil stab	Also *R. copallina* & *R. glabra*
Strawberry tree	*Arbutus unedo*	7	E Tr	○	Fr	Ins, Hab, For	Wbr, Hr	
Summersweet	*Clethra alnofolia*	4	D Sh	○●	Lf	Hab, For	Hr	Acid soil
Tamarisk	*Tamarix gallica*	5	D Tr	○	Med	Hab	Wbr, Hr	Also *T. africana, T. parviflora, & T. ramosissima*
Tree mallow	*Lavatera arborea*	8	D Sh	○●	Lf	Ins	Fiber	
Tupelo	*Nyssa sylvatica*	3	D Tr	○	Fr	Ins, Hab		
Wax currant	*Ribes cereum*	3	D Sh	○●	Fr	Ins, Hab, Chk, For	Hr, Dye	Alkaline soil
White mulberry	*Morus alba*	3	D Tr	○	Fr, YLf	Chk, Hab, For	Wbr, Hr, Dye, Fiber	
Winter's bark	*Drimys winteri*	8	E Sh	○●	Bark, Med	Hab	Hr	
Witch hazel	*Hamamelis virginiana*	5	D Sh	●	Sd, Med	Hab	Hr	
Yucca	*Yucca spp.*	4	E Sh	○	Fr	Ins, Hab	Hr	

HERBACEOUS PLANTS

Common name	Botanical name	Hardy to USDA Zone	Type	Light	Edible part or use	Animal use	Other use	Comments
Alfalfa	Medicago sativa	5	HP	○	Lf, Sd	Ins, Hab, For	N-fixer	
American licorice	Glycyrrhiza lepidota	3	HP	◑	Root, Med		N-fixer	Less sweet than G. lepidota; invasive
Anise hyssop	Agastache foeniculum	8	HP	○	Lf, Tea	Ins		
Asparagus	Asparagus officinalis	4	HP	○	Stem			
Balsamroot	Balsamorhiza hookeri	5	HP	○	Fl, Sd, Root	Ins		
Breadroot	Psoralea esculenta	7	HP	○	Root		N-fixer, Soil stab	Also P. hypogaea
Bugle	Ajuga reptans	6	HP	◑	Lf	Ins		
Bulrush	Scirpus spp.	4	HP	◑	Lf, Sd, Root, Med	Hab	Fiber	
Bunchberry	Cornus canadensis	2	HP	●	Fr	For		
Camas	Camassia quamash	3	HP	◑	Root	Ins		
Cardoon	Cynara cardunculus	5	HB	○	Fr	Ins		Self-seeds
Cattail	Typha angustifolia	3	HP	◑	Fl, Lf, Sht, Root	Hab, For	Fiber, Soil stab	Bog plant
Cattail	Typha latifolia	3	HP	◑	Fl, Lf, Sht, Root	Hab	Fiber	Bog plant
Chamomile	Chamaemelum nobile	4	HP	○	Tea	Ins	Dye	
Chicory	Cichorium intybus	3	HP	○	Fl, Lf, Root	Ins	Nutr	
Chinese artichoke	Stachys affinis	5	HP	○	Lf, Root			
Chives	Allium schoenoprasum	5	HP	◑	Fl, Lf, Root	Ins	Nutr	
Collards	Brassica oleracea viridis	6	HP	◑	Fl, Lf	Hab		
Columbine	Aquilegia vulgaris	4	HP	○	Fl, Tea	Ins		
Comfrey	Symphytum officinale	5	HP	◑	Lf, Med	Ins, Chk	Nutr, Biomass	
Common milkweed	Asclepias cornuti	3	HP	○	Fl, Lf	Ins	Dye, Fiber	
Creeping thyme	Thymus serpyllum	5	E Sh	◑	Lf, Tea, Med	Ins	Repellent	Also T. vulgaris
Dandelion	Taraxacum officinale	5	HP	◑	Fl, Lf, Root	Ins	Nutr	
Daylily	Hemerocallis fulva	4	HP	◑	Fl, Lf, Root	Hum	Fiber	
Egyptian onion	Allium cepa proliferum	5	HP	○	Fl, Lf, Root		Nutr, Dye, Repellent	
European licorice	Glycyrrhiza glabra	7	HP	◑	Root, Med		N-fixer	
Fairy thimble	Campanula cochleariifolia	6	HP	◑	Fl, Lf	Ins, For		
Fennel	Foeniculum vulgare	5	HP	◑	Lf, Sd, Root	Ins, Hab, Chk	Nutr	
French sorrel	Rumex scutatus	6	HP	◑	Lf		Dye	Also R. acetosa
Garlic	Allium sativum	5	HP	○	Fl, Lf, Root		Nutr	
Garlic chives	Allium tuberosum	5	HP	◑	Fl, Lf, Root		Nutr	
Garlic cress	Peltaria alliacea	6	HP	◑	Fl, Lf			
Ginseng	Panax ginseng	6	HP	●	Root, Med			
Globe artichoke	Cynara scolymus	6	HP	○	Fl, Lf	Ins		
Goldenberry	Physalis peruviana	8	HP	○	Fr			
Good King Henry	Chenopodium bonus-henricus	5	HP	◑	Fl, Lf, Med	Ins	Nutr, Dye	

Common name	Botanical name	#	Type	Sun	Parts	Wildlife	Function	Notes
Greek oregano	Origanum vulgare hirtum	5	HP	○○	Lf, Seas	Ins		
Groundnut	Apios americana	3	HP	◐○	Sd, Root	Ins	N-fixer	
Groundplum milkvetch	Astragalus crassicarpus	4	HP	○○	Seedpod	Ins	N-fixer	
Harebell	Campanula persicifolia	3	HP	◐○	Fl, Lf, Root	Ins, For		
Indian water lotus	Nelumbo nucifera	5	HP	○	Fl, Lf, Root	Ins, Hab		Water plant
Jerusalem artichoke	Helianthus tuberosus	4	HP	○○	Root	Hab	Hr, Biomass	
Kale, curly	Brassica oleracea sabellica	6	HP	○○	Fl, Lf	Hab		
Kale, perennial	Brassica oleracea ramosa	6	HP	○○	Fl, Lf	Hab		
King's spear	Asphodeline lutea	7	HP	○○	Fl, Lf, Root	Ins		
Lupine	Lupinus spp.	5	HP	○	Sd, Med	Ins	N-fixer	
Maca or Peruvian ginseng	Lepidium meyenii	6	HP	○○	Root, Med	Ins		
Maximilian sunflower	Helianthus maximilianii	4	HP	○	Root, Sht	Ins		
Mexican tarragon	Tagetes lucida	9	HP	○	Tea	Ins	Dye, Repellent	Grown as annual
Mitsuba	Cryptotaenia japonica	5	HP	●◐	Lf	Ins		
Musk mallow	Malva moschata	3	HP	○○	Fl, Lf, Sd	Ins	Fiber	
Nasturtium	Tropaeolum minus	9	HP	○	Fl, Lf, Sd		Repellent	Grown as annual
Nine-star perennial broccoli	Brassica oleracea botrytis aparagoides	6	HP	○○	Fl, Lf	Ins		
Oca	Oxalis tuberosa	7	HP	○○	Fl, Lf, Root			Can be grown as annual
Painted milkvetch	Astragalus pictus-filifolius	5	HP	○	Root	Ins	N-fixer	
Peppermint	Mentha × piperita vulgaris	3	HP	●◐	Lf, Tea	Ins		
Perennial buckwheat	Fagopyrum dibotrys	5	HP	○○	Lf, Sd	Ins, Hab, Chk		
Pig nut	Bunium bulbo-castanum	5	E Sh	○○	Lf, Root	Ins		
Pink purslane	Claytonia sibirica	3	HP	●◐	Lf	Ins, For		
Pleurisy root	Asclepias tuberosa	3	HP	○	Fl, Lf	Ins	Fiber	
Pokeweed	Phytolacca americana	4	HP	○	Lf, Med	Hab	Dye	Leaves toxic unless cooked and rinsed well
Potato	Solanum tuberosum	8	HP	○	Root		Biomass	Grown as annual
Reed	Phragmites australis	5	HP	○○	Lf, Root	Hab	Dye, Fiber, Bskt	Bog plant
Rhubarb	Rheum rhabarbarum	3	HP	○○	Stem		Dye	Leaves are toxic
Russian sage	Perovskia atriplicifolia	6	HP	○○	Lf	Ins, Hum	Wbr, Hr	
Salad burnet	Sanguisorba minor	5	HP	○○	Lf		Soil stab	
Sarsaparilla	Aralia nudicaulis	4	HP	○○	Fr, Lf	Ins		
Scorzonera	Scorzonera hispanica	6	HP	○○	Fl, Lf, Root			
Seakale	Crambe maritima	5	HP	○○	Fl, Lf			
Showy milkweed	Asclepias speciosa	2	HP	○	Fl, Lf	Ins	Dye, Fiber	

HERBACEOUS PLANTS

Common name	Botanical name	Hardy to USDA Zone	Type	Light	Edible part or use	Animal use	Other use	Comments
Spearmint	Mentha spicata	3	HP	◑●	Lf, Tea	Ins		
Stinging nettle	Urtica dioica	6	HP	○○	Lf	Nutr, Dye,	Fiber, Biomass	
Stonecrop	Sedum spp.	5	HP	○○	Lf, Med	Ins		
Strawberry	Fragaria spp.	3	HP	○○	Fr, Lf,	Ins	Nutr	
Sweet cicely	Myrrhis odorata	5	HP	●◑	Lf, Sd, Root	Ins	Polish	
Sweet flag	Acorus calamus	3	HP	○○	Lf, Root		Fiber	
Sweet vetch	Hedysarum boreale	3	HP	○	Root	Ins	N-fixer	
Sweet violet	Viola odorata	5	HP	○○	Fl, Lf	Ins		
Tarragon	Artemisia dracunculus	6	HP	●◑	Lf (seas)	Ins		
Thrift	Phlox subulata	4	HP	○○		Ins	Ground cover	
Trailing bellflower	Campanula poscharskyana	3	HP	○○	Fl, Lf	Ins, For		
Tuberous water lily	Nymphaea tuberosa	5	HP	○	Root, Sd			Water plant
Turkish rocket	Bunias orientalis	7	HP	○○	Fl, Lf	Ins		
Wapato	Sagittaria latifolia	6	HP	○○	Root			Also *S. sagittifolia*
Water chestnut	Trapa natans	5	HP	○	Sd			Water plant
Watercress	Nasturtium officinale	6	HP	●○	Lf, Sd	Ins	Nutr	Water plant
Welsh onion	Allium fistulosum	6	HP	○	Fl, Lf, Root		Nutr, Repellent	
Wild ginger	Asarum caudatum	2	HP	○	Seas			
Winter savory	Satureia montana	6	E Sh	○	Lf	Ins		
Yacon	Polymnia edulis	8	HP	○○	Root			Can be grown as annual
Yampah	Perideridia gairdneri	7	HP	○○	Lf, Root			
Yarrow	Achillea millefolium	2	HP	○	Lf, Tea, Med	Ins	Nutr, Dye	

VINES AND CLIMBING PLANTS

Common Name	Botanical name	Hardy to USDA Zone	Type	Light	Edible part or use	Animal use	Other use	Comments
Akebia	Akebia quinata	5	D Cl	○◐	Fr		Bskt	Also A. trifoliata
Clematis	Clematis spp.	5	D Cl	○◐		Ins		
Cucumber	Cucumis sativus	9	D Cl	○	Fr, Fl	Ins		Grown as annual
Grape	Vitis vinifera	6	D Cl	○	Fr, Lf	Hab, Food	Dye	
Hardy kiwi	Actinidia arguta	4	D Cl	○	Fr			
He Shou Wu	Polygonum multiflorum	7	D Cl	○◐	Fr, Lf, Med		Bskt	
Honeysuckle	Lonicera spp.	4	D Cl	○◐	Fl, Tea	Ins, Hab		
Hops	Humulus lupulus	5	D Cl	○	Fl, Lf, Med	Ins, Hab	Fiber, Dye	
Jasmine	Jasminum officinale	6	D Cl	○◐	Fl	Ins, Hab	Fragrance	Also J. beesianum, J. humile, J. nudiflorum
Kiwi	Actinidia deliciosa	7	D Cl	○	Fr			
Mashua	Tropaeolum tuberosum	8	D Cl	○	Fl, Lf, Root			Can be grown as annual
Maypop	Passiflora incarnata	6	E Cl	○	Fr, Fl, Lf, Med	Ins		Also P. edulis, P. mollisima
Melon	Cucumis melo	9	D Cl	○	Fr, Fl	Ins		Grown as annual
Mountain yam	Dioscorea batatas	4	D Cl	○◐	Rt			
Nasturtium	Tropaeolum majis	9	A/P Cl	○	Fl, Lf	Ins, Hab		Grown as annual
Passionflower	Passiflora caerulea	7	E Cl	○	Fr, Fl	Ins		
Pea	Pisum sativum	Annual	A Cl	○	Fr, Fl	Ins	N-fixer	
Perennial pea	Lathyrus latifolius	6	D Cl	○◐	YLf	Ins	N-fixer	
Sarsaparilla	Smilax aspera	8	E Cl	○◐	Sht, Root, Med		Wbr, Hr, dye	
Scarlet runner bean	Phaseolus coccineus	9	D Cl	○	Fr, Fl	Ins	N-fixer	Grown as annual
Squash	Cucurbita spp.	9	D Cl	○	Fr, Fl	Ins	Gourd	Grown as annual
Wisteria	Wisteria floribunda	6	D Cl	○		Ins	Bskt, N-fixer	

GLOSSARY

allelopaths Plants that secrete a toxic substance that suppresses competing plants.

biodiversity The variety of organisms present, considered from many levels: cultivar, species, genus, family, and on up to include all five kingdoms, as well as the diversity of habitats and ecosystems.

buffer plants Plants placed between guilds or between allelopathic species. They should be compatible with the trees in each guild, and should have a positive effect on one or both of the guilds to be linked.

chaperone plants Species that protect seedlings from harm until the juveniles are ready for life on their own.

companion planting Placing two or more plant species in a way that at least one species benefits the other(s) by deterring pests, attracting pollinators, and so on.

compost The rich, humusy end-product of decomposition, made by piling surplus organic matter into a mound or bin, and letting it rot.

cover crops Crops planted specifically to build soil, reduce erosion, and smother weeds.

drip line The invisible boundary under a tree's outermost leaves.

edge effect The increase in diversity that occurs where two systems meet, creating conditions favorable to inhabitants of both sides of the edge as well as new conditions at the edge itself that support new inhabitants (as when a rever flows into the sea, or a pond meets its shore).

forest garden A multistoried, food- and habitat-producing landscape that acts like a natural woodland.

greywater The household water from sink, shower, and laundry drains.

guild A harmoniously interwoven group of plants and animals, often centered around one major species, that benefits humans while creating habitat.

hardscaping The term designers use for wood, stone, concrete, and other constructed elements such as walls, sheds, paths, fences, and the like.

humus A fairly stable, complex group of nutrient-storing molecules created by microbes and other forces of decomposition by the conversion of organic matter.

interplanting Combining plant varieties in ways that avoid competition for light, space, or nutrients, and that often discourage pests.

microclimate gardening Arranging plants in a manner that will take advantage of variations in microclimate (such as placing a frost-tender plant against a warm, south-facing wall) or in ways that will create favorable microclimates (such as using a tree to shade a house from hot sun).

mineralization The process of converting organic carbon-containing compounds into inorganic plant food.

monopodial Forming shoots from a central axis, refers here to bamboo species often called running (and thus potentially invasive).

narcissistic Plants that thrive on the leaf litter of members of their own family, such as the Solanaceae.

niche The role or function within an ecosystem played by a particular organism. Think of a niche as a profession, and habitat as the workspace for performing the job.

nitrogen fixers Plants that host symbiotic microorganisms in nodules among their roots that "fix" nitrogen gas from the air by combining it with carbon to make amino acids and related molecules. Includes most members of the legume family plus certain other species.

nurse plants Species that create shelter and other favorable conditions in which more delicate plants can get a start.

parasitoids Small wasps and flies that lay their eggs inside other insects or insect eggs.

permaculture A set of techniques and principles for designing sustainable human settlements.

pioneer plants Certain fast-growing annual grasses, herbs, and flowers that are the first flora to arrive after a disturbance.

plant communities Groupings of trees, shrubs, and nonwoody plants that naturally occur together and seem to be connected as a whole.

pollinators Beneficial insects that transport pollen for fruit and seed set.

polycultures Dynamic, self-organizing plant communities composed of several to many species.

predator insects Beneficial insects that consume pest insect species.

primary decomposers Invertebrates, bacteria, algae, fungi, and actinomycetes that are the first to consume organic matter.

scaffold plants Species whose physical presence lets young or otherwise-vulnerable plants get established.

secondary decomposers Mold mites, springtails, certain beetles, and other organisms that feed on the primary decomposers.

sector Areas where outside energies such as wind, sun, fire, and so forth enter a site. These energies can be mitigated, captured, or otherwise influenced by placement of elements in the design.

sheet mulching Composting in place to eradicate weeds and build soil without the need for herbicides or tilling.

standing biomass The part of an ecosystem that is permanent, such as branches and large roots, as opposed to seasonal, such as fruit or deciduous leaves.

succession Change in composition of organisms in an ecosystem, often progressing from pioneer species to shrubs to trees.

swale A shallow trench laid out dead level along the land's contours to allow water to enter the soil.

sympodial Forming main shoots from secondary ones; refers here to "clumping" bamboo species, which are usually not invasive.

tertiary decomposers Soil organisms that feed on the secondary (and some primary) decomposers.

tilth The loose, crumbly structure of microbially rich soil, created by certain soil bacteria that secrete gums, waxes, and gels that hold tiny particles of earth together.

weeds A highly subjective category of maligned plants that even the United States Department of Agriculture admits are simply "plants that interfere with human activities."

zones A permaculture design method in which elements are placed according to how often they are used or need attention. The more an element is used, the closer to the house it is located.

BIBLIOGRAPHY

Albrecht, William A. *The Albrecht Papers.* Acres USA, 1996. Somewhat quirky collection of papers by a soil scientist with vision.

Alexander, Christopher. *A Pattern Language.* Oxford, 1977. A classic on human-scale design.

Angier, Bradford. *One Acre & Security: How to Live Off the Earth Without Ruining It.* Willow Creek, 2000. A useful and broad-ranging resource for homesteading and small animal care.

Bell, Graham. *The Permaculture Garden.* Thorson's, 1994. A British-oriented introduction to permaculture gardening techniques.

Bennett, Bob. *Raising Rabbits the Modern Way.* Garden Way, 1980. Good introduction to rabbits in the backyard.

Brady, Nyle C. *The Nature and Properties of Soils.* Prentice-Hall, 1996. This major textbook on soils covers the whole subject in depth.

Brickell, Christopher. *American Horticultural Society Encyclopedia of Garden Plants.* Macmillan, 1990. An illustrated guide to most common plants, with thousands of photos.

Brookes, John. *The Book of Garden Design.* MacMillan, 1991. A general guide by a well-known conventional landscape designer.

Buchanan, Rita. *Taylor's Master Guide to Landscaping.* Houghton Mifflin, 2000. A good, comprehensive introduction to landscape design techniques for the homeowner.

Buchmann, Stephen L., and Gary Paul Nabhan. *The Forgotten Pollinators.* Island, 1996. An informative, well-written account of the role of helpful but endangered insects.

Campbell, Stu, and Donna Moore. *The Mulch Book: A Complete Guide for Gardeners.* Storey Books, 1991. A good introduction to mulching.

Capra, Fritjof. *The Web of Life.* Doubleday, 1996. An engaging account of how the new sciences of complexity and self-organization are affecting our understanding of living systems.

Cocannouer, Joseph. *Weeds: Guardians of the Soil.* Devin-Adair, 1950. Describes the role of weeds useful crops and as indicators of fertility, with much historical lore.

Coleman, Eliot. *Four-Season Harvest.* Chelsea Green, 1999. How to extend the growing season to the whole year, even in northern climates.

Creasy, Rosalind. *Organic Gardener's Edible Plants.* Van Patten, 1993. Descriptions of over 130 edible ornamental plants.

———. *The Complete Book of Edible Landscaping.* Sierra Club, 1982. The foundation book that brought vegetables into the front yard.

Dennis, John V. *The Wildlife Gardener.* Knopf, 1985. A good introduction to creating gardens for wildlife habitat.

Douglas, J. Sholto, and Robert Hart. *Forest Farming.* Rodale, 1985. A strong argument for growing trees for food and fodder, with descriptions of many species.

Druse, Ken. *The Natural Habitat Garden.* Potter, 1994. How to create prairie, meadow, woodland, and wetland gardens using native plants.

Facciola, Stephen. *Cornucopia II: A Source Book of Edible Plants.* Kampong, 1998. A comprehensive list and description of edible flora.

Farrelly, David. *The Book of Bamboo.* Sierra Club, 1984. A thoughtful and thorough investigation into the culture, varieties, and uses of bamboo.

Fern, Ken. *Plants for a Future: Edible and Useful Plants for a Healthier World.* Permanent Publications, 1997. Distributed in the United States by Chelsea Green Publishing. A British book covering a wide range of multifunctional plants.

Florea, J. H. *ABC of Poultry Raising: A Complete Guide for the Beginner or Expert.* Dover, 1977. A standard work on small-scale poultry care.

Fukuoka, Masanobu. *The One Straw Revolution.* Rodale, 1978. Nature as a model for agriculture.

Gaddie, Ronald, and Donald Douglas. *Earthworms for Ecology and Profit.* Bookworm, 1977. One of the best books on worm composting and worm beds.

Gershuny, Grace. *Start with the Soil.* Rodale, 1993. A superb handbook on the how and why of creating great soil.

Gessert, Kate Rogers. *The Beautiful Food Garden Encyclopedia of Attractive Food Plants.* Van Nostrand Reinhold, 1983. How to landscape with good-looking vegetables.

Haggard, Ben. *Living Community.* Center for the Study of Community, 1993. The evolution of a premier permaculture site, written by a master designer.

Hart, Robert. *Forest Gardening: Cultivating an Edible Landscape.* Chelsea Green, 1996. A personal account of forest garden design by one of the originators of the field.

Hobhouse, Penelope. *Flower Gardens.* Little, Brown and Co., 1991. A well-illustrated volume by one of the experts on arranging plants by color and form.

Holmes, Roger. *Home Landscaping* (series). Creative Homeowner Press, 1998. A series of books, divided by geographic region of the United States, that covers landscaping basics and lists suitable regional plants.

Howard, Sir Albert. *The Soil and Health.* Rodale, 1976. The relationship between good soil and healthy people by one of the originators of organic farming.

Hunt, Marjorie. *High-Yield Gardening.* Rodale, 1986. A superb guide to extending the growing season, high-density planting, and getting more from the garden.

Jeavons, John. *How to Grow More Vegetables Than You Ever Thought Possible on Less Land Than You Can Imagine.* Ten Speed, 1991. Bio-intensive (and labor-intensive) techniques that boost production; useful, but I've never met anyone who could match its claimed yields.

Jekyll, Gertrude. *Colour Schemes for the Flower Garden.* Ayer, 1983. One of several classic books by Jekyll on garden design.

Kauffman, Stuart. *At Home in the Universe.* Oxford, 1995. Kauffman shows how life inevitably will emerge when there is sufficient complexity.

————. *The Origins of Order.* Oxford, 1994. A dense and scholarly treatment of the ideas expressed in *At Home in the Universe.*

Kelly, Kevin. *Out of Control.* Addison Wesley, 1994. How our new understanding of biology is transforming both ecology and economics.

Kourik, Robert. *Designing and Maintaining Your Edible Landscape—Naturally.* Metamorphic, 1986. A comprehensive, well-researched book with great reference lists and tables.

Kress, Stephen M. *National Audubon Society Bird Garden.* DK, 1995. Designs and plants for gardens that provide food, water, cover, and nesting sites for birds.

Lee, Andy, Pat Foreman, and Patricia L. Foreman. *Chicken Tractor: The Permaculture Guide to Happy Hens and Healthy Soil.* Good Earth, 1998. Using mobile chicken pens, with plenty of information on poultry raising in general.

Ludwig, Art. *Create an Oasis With Greywater: Your Complete Guide to Choosing, Building and Using Greywater Systems.* Oasis Design, 2000. The best practical guide to greywater systems.

Luttmann, Rick, and Gail Luttmann. *Chickens in Your Backyard: A Beginner's Guide.* Rodale, 1976. A good book on small-scale chicken raising for the homeowner.

Mandelbrot, Benoit. *The Fractal Geometry of Nature.* W. H. Freeman & Co, 1983. Key insights into natural patterns by the developer of the fractal concept.

Matson, Tim. *Earth Ponds.* Countryman, 1998. The lore and constructions of earth-dam ponds.

McHarg, Ian. *Design with Nature.* Wiley, 1992. Innovative techniques for appropriate landscape design using map overlays.

McKinley, Michael. *How to Attract Birds.* Ortho Books, 1999. Instructions for attracting specific birds with plants and feeders.

Mollison, Bill, and Reny Slay. *An Introduction to Permaculture.* Tagari, 1991. Concise coverage of permaculture's basic principles.

Mollison, Bill. *Permaculture: A Designers' Manual.* Tagari, 1988. The fat bible on permaculture, worth many re-readings and perusings.

Morrow, Rosemary. *Earth User's Guide to Permaculture.* Simon & Schuster, 2000. An informal introduction to permaculture by an experienced teacher.

Neill, William, and Pat Murphy. *By Nature's Design.* Chronicle, 1993. Stunning photographs and clear explanations of nature's patterns.

O'Neill, R. V. *A Hierarchical View of Ecosystems.* Princeton, 1986. An advanced look at how ecosystems function.

Odum, Eugene P. *Fundamentals of Ecology.* W. B. Saunders, 1971. An early textbook that covers the basics of ecology in depth.

Pacey, Arnold, and Adrian Cullis. *Rainwater Harvesting.* Intermediate Technology, 1996. Many techniques for using rainwater.

Pfeiffer, Ehrenfried. *Weeds and What They Tell.* Bio-Dynamic Farming & Garden Association, 1981. How to use weeds to assess the type and fertility of the local soil.

Reid, Grant W. *Landscape Graphics.* Whitney Library of Design, 1987. Excellent introduction to professional landscape drawing.

Romanowski, Nick. *Farming in Ponds and Dams.* Lothian, 1994. An Australian book on aquaculture and pond construction.

Seidenberg, Charlotte. *The Wildlife Garden.* University of Mississippi, 1995. An introduction to wildlife habitat gardening with examples of garden designs.

Smith, J. Russell. *Tree Crops: A Permanent Agriculture.* Devin-Adair, 1987. One of the inspirations for the permaculture concept, showing how trees are key to sustainable agriculture.

Stein, Sara. *Noah's Garden: Restoring the Ecology of Our Own Back Yards.* Houghton Mifflin, 1995. A well-written and compelling plea for allowing nature back into our yards, full of natural history.

Stevens, Peter S. *Patterns in Nature.* Little, Brown & Co., 1974. A review of the common classes of patterns found in nature.

Stout, Ruth. *The Ruth Stout No-Work Garden Book.* Rodale, 1975. Using deep mulches to reduce labor and improve fertility.

Tekulsky, Mathew. *The Hummingbird Garden.* Crown, 1986. A guide to cultivating plants that attract these flying jewels; one of the best on the subject.

Thompson, D'arcy Wentworth. *On Growth and Form.* Dover, 1992. A magisterial text on how the shapes and patterns in nature are formed; a classic in the field.

Tilth. *The Future Is Abundant.* Tilth, 1982. An early book on sustainable gardening, still worth reading.

Tufts, Craig, and Peter Loewer. The *National Wildlife Federation's Guide to Gardening for Wildlife.* Rodale, 1995. How to provide garden habitat for birds, insects, and nocturnal animals.

United States Department of Agriculture. *Common Weeds of the United States.* Dover, 1971. A good technical guide to 224 species of weeds, with clear drawings. Organized by plant family, so it requires a little botanical knowledge.

Van der Ryn, Sim, and Stuart Cowan. *Ecological Design.* Island, 1995. The essential concepts of ecological design.

Verey, Rosemary. *The Art of Planting.* Little, Brown & Co., 1990. A good coffee-table guide to placing plants by color, texture, and form.

Whitefield, Patrick. *How to Make a Forest Garden.* Permanent Publications, 1997. Distributed in the United States by Chelsea Green. Instructions and ideas for forest gardens, with a British focus but usable in North America.

Yeomans, P. A., and K. A. Yeomans. *Water for Every Farm.* Keyline Designs, 1993. An inspirational view of how to store water in the soil.

Yepson, Roger, ed. *Encyclopedia of Natural Insect and Disease Control.* Rodale, 1984. Natural pest control, with clear drawings and photos for identifying insects.

RESOURCES

MAGAZINES

Permaculture Activist
PO Box 1209, Black Mountain, NC 28711
http://www.permacultureactivist.net/
$19/year, 3 issues plus newsletters.

Permaculture Magazine (England)
http://www.permaculture.co.uk
In the United States, contact Permaculture Activist
(above) for subscription information. $22/year, 4 issues.

PERMACULTURE TEACHING AND CONSULTING ORGANIZATIONS

Culture's Edge
1025 Camp Elliot Rd., Black Mountain, NC 28711
828-669-3937
pcactiv@metalab.unc.edu

Central Rocky Mountain Permaculture Institute
PO Box 631, Basalt, CO 81621
970-927-4158
http://www.crmpi.org/
jerome@crmpi.org

The Farm Ecovillage Training Center
PO Box 90, Summertown, TN 38483-0090
615-954-3574
ecovillage@thefarm.org

Lost Valley Educational Center
81868 Lost Valley Lane, Dexter, OR 97431
541-937-3351
http://www.lostvalley.org
permaculture@lostvalley.org

Occidental Arts and Ecology Center
15290 Coleman Valley Rd., Occidental, CA 95465
707-874-1557
http://www.oaec.org/
oaec@oaec.org

Permaculture Institute of Northern California
PO Box 341, Point Reyes Station, CA 94956
415-663-9090
http://www.permacultureinstitute.com/
pinc@nbn.com

Permaculture Institute of Southern California
1027 Summit Way, Laguna Beach, CA 92651
714-494-1443
DrRoley@aol.com

Permaculture Institute USA
PO Box 3702, Pojoaque, NM 87501
505-455-0270
pci@permaculture-inst.org

PLANT DATABASES ON THE INTERNET

The Ethnobotany Database
http://ars-genome.cornell.edu/Botany/aboutethnobotdb.html
A database developed by James A. Duke and Stephen M. Beckstrom-Sternberg housed at the National Germplasm Resources Laboratory (NGRL). It contains 80,000 records of plants and their uses worldwide.

GRIN Taxonomy
http://www.ars-grin.gov/npgs/tax/
The USDA's Germplasm Resources Information Network database, with brief descriptions of over 34,000 plant species and links to further information. The focus is mostly on useful plants.

Plants for a Future
http://www.pfaf.org
Over 7,000 useful plants are described, with their uses, culture, and much other information in a well-designed searchable Web site. My favorite source of data on useful plants.

USDA PLANTS Database
http://plants.usda.gov/plants/index.html
This database includes names, checklists, automated tools, identification information, species abstracts, and other plant information on a large number of plants grown in the United States.

SEEDS, LIVE PLANTS, AND GARDEN SUPPLIES

Abundant Life Seed Foundation
PO Box 772, Port Townsend, WA 98368
360-385-5660
http://csf.colorado.edu/perma/abundant/
abundant@olypen.com
Nonprofit growers and collectors of nonhybrid seeds. Catalog $2.

Ames' Orchard and Nursery
Rt. 5, Box 194, Fayetteville, AR 72701
501-443-0282
Specializes in disease-resistant apple, pear, grape, raspberry and other trees and small fruits for the South. Catalog for two first-class stamps.

The Banana Tree, Inc.
715 Northampton St., Easton, PA 18042
610-253-9589
http://www.banana-tree.com
faban@enter.net
Thousands of tropical seeds and bulbs.

Bountiful Gardens
Shafer Ranch Rd., Willits, CA 95490-9626
707-459-6410
http://www.bountifulgardens.org/
bountiful@sonic.net
A nonprofit research organization with a wide selection, including many heirloom cultivars.

Burnt Ridge Nursery
432 Burnt Ridge Rd., Onalaska, WA 98570
350-985-2873
http://landru.myhome.net/burntridge/
burntridge@myhome.net
Many nut and fruit trees varieties.

The Cook's Garden
PO Box 5010, Hodges, SC 29653-5010
802-824-3400
http://www.cooksgarden.com/
webmaster@cooksgarden.com
Retail and wholesale seeds with many heirlooms.

Country Wetlands Nursery
PO Box 126, Muskego, WI 53150
414-679-1268
Plants and seeds of wild rice, cattail, and other wetlands species.

DeGiorgi Seed Co.
6011 N St., Omaha, NE 68117-1634
Over 1,500 varieties, including perennials, vegetables, and grasses.

Deep Diversity

Box 190, Gila, NM 88038

http://store.yahoo.com/seedsofchange/
deepdiversity.html/

The brilliant Alan Kapuler's delightful and esoteric seed collection, licensed to Seeds of Change.

Edible Landscaping Nursery

PO Box 77, Afton, VA 22920

804-361-9134

http://www.eat-it.com/

el@cstone.net

A wide selection of fruits, nuts, kiwis, and edible shrubs.

Fedco Trees

PO Box 520, Waterville, ME 04903-0520

207-873-7333

http://www.fedcoseed.com/trees.html/

Hardy tree fruits and nuts, small fruits, and berries as well as ornamentals.

Forestfarm Nursery

990 Tetherow Rd., Williams, OR 97544-9599

541-846-7269

http://www.forestfarm.com/search/help.asp

forestfarm@aonepro.net

This may be the most extensive supply of useful plants in the United States—over 3,000 varieties. Catalog $5 and worth it.

Garden City Seeds

778 Hwy. 93 North Hamilton, MT 59840

406-961-4837

http://www.gardencityseeds.com/

seeds@montana.com

A nonprofit carrying over 500 cultivars and green manures.

Greenmantle Nursery

3010 Ettersburg Rd., Garberville, CA 95542

707-986-7504

Specializes in fruit and nut trees for homesteaders.

Harmony Farm Supply

PO Box 450, Graton, CA 95444

707-823-9125

http://www.harmonyfarm.com/

info@harmonyfarm.com

Seeds, irrigation supplies, fertilizer, and more for farm and garden.

Hidden Springs Nursery

Rt. 14, Box 159, Cookeville, TN 38501

615-268-9889

hblack@sunbelt.net

Unusual fruits, etc., including medlar, autumn olive. Catalog $1.

J. L. Hudson, Seedsman

PO Box 1058, Redwood, CA 94064

Sells open-pollinated varieties from all over the world. A wide array of useful food and medicinal species. Catalog $1.

Native Seeds/SEARCH

525 N. 4th Ave., Tucson AZ 85705-8450

520-327-9123

http://www.nativeseeds.org/

nss@azstarnet.com

Specializes in heirloom varieties from Mexico and the Southwest. Catalog $1.

Natural Gardens

4804 Shell Lane, Knoxville, TN 37918

615-482-6746

Seeds and nursery-propagated plants of wildflowers, especially butterfly- and bird-attracting types.

Nichols Garden Nursery

190 N. Pacific Hwy., Albany, OR 97321-4580

541-928-9280

http://www.gardennursery.com/index.html

info@gardennursery.com

A wide assortment of herbs and vegetables.

Northern Groves Bamboo Nursery

PO Box 1236, Philomath, OR 97370

541-929-7152

http://www.teleport.com/~dbrooks/bamboo.html

bamboogrove@cmug.com

A fine collection of hardy bamboos of all types.

Oikos Tree Crops

PO Box 19425, Kalamazoo, MI 49019-0425

616-624-6233

Edible native fruits, nuts, tubers, and perennials.

Oregon Exotics Rare Fruit Nursery

1055 Messinger Rd., Grants Pass, OR 97527,

541-846-7578

http://www.exoticfruit.com/

Mouth-watering selection of exotic tubers and fruits. Catalog $4.

Ornamental Edibles

3522 Weedlin Court, San Jose, CA 95132

408-946-7333

http://www.ornamentaledibles.com/

Over 400 varieties of gourmet and edible flowers for urban landscapes.

Peace Seeds

2385 S.E. Thompson St., Corvallis, OR 97333

An extensive selection of heirloom varieties and high-nutrition vegetables, maintained by Alan Kapuler. Catalog $3.50

Peaceful Valley Farm Supply

PO Box 2209, Grass Valley, CA 95945

530-272-4769

http://www.groworganic.com

Seeds, irrigation and natural pest-management supplies, and a very educational catalog.

Perennial Vegetable Seed Company

PO Box 508, Belchertown, MA 01007

413-586-9050

http://www.perennialvegetable.com

Seeds for edible perennial plants, including some unusual and hard-to-find varieties.

Permaculture Seed and Plant Exchange

3020 Whiteoak Creek Rd., Burnsville, NC 28714

704-675-5664

An annual catalog that links growers and collectors with buyers.

Plants of the Southwest

Agua Fria Rd., Rt. 5 Box 11A, Santa Fe, NM 87501

800-788-7333 (orders)

http://www.plantsofthesouthwest.com/

Native plants and seeds from the Southwest.

Redwood City Seed Co.

PO Box 351, Redwood City, CA 94064

http://www.batnet.com/rwc-seed/index.html

An early leader in untreated heirloom seeds; specializes in hot peppers. Catalog $1.

Seed Saver's Exchange

RR 3, Box 239, Decorah, Iowa 52101

Not a retail sales company but a place for members to exchange seeds. SSE preserves and grows 5,000 plant varieties.

Seeds of Change

521 Old Santa Fe Trail, #10, Santa Fe, NM 87501

http://store.yahoo.com/seedsofchange/

Open-pollinated, organically grown, non-GMO seeds selected for nutrition, drought tolerance, and genetic diversity.

Shepherd's Garden Seeds

30 Irene St., Torrington, CT 06790

203-482-3638

http://www.shepherdseeds.com/

Large collection of heirloom vegetable, herb, and flower seeds.

Southmeadow Fruit Gardens

PO Box 211, 10603 Cleveland Ave., Baroda, MI 49101

615-422-2411

Choice and unusual fruit-tree varieties for the connoisseur and home gardener.

St. Lawrence Nurseries

325 State Hwy. 345, Potsdam, NY 13575

315-265-6739

http://www.sln.potsdam.ny.us

trees@sln.potsdam.ny.us

Specializes in fruits and nut trees for northern climates, managed organically.

INDEX

marguerite, golden, 108, 127
marigold, 108, 142, 153, 172
mashua, 114
mature gardens, 22–25
  features of, 24–25
  immature ecosystems compared, 23
maypop, 104–105
mealybugs, 127
Mediterranean-climate plants, 86–87
mesquite, 119, 173
microbes, 61–65, 69, 74
microclimates, 52, 87, 114–20, 143, 193
mineralization, 64
minerals
  in compost pile, 69
  cover crops and, 78, 79, 184
  in humus, 63
  in soil, 59, 64–65
  soil amendments, 72
  tilling, effect of, 67
mint, 48, 109, 127
moisture
  in compost pile, 68, 69
  humus, retained by, 63, 82–83, 185
  mulch, retained by, 81–82, 88, 185
  soil, retained by, 67, 81–83
Mollison, Bill, 4–5, 37, 48, 163
monarda, 87
monocultures, 8, 9, 21, 142
mountain ash, 127, 173
Mt. Pleasant, Jane, 148–49
mulberry, 14, 132, 164, 173
mulches, 13, 18, 45, 52, 68. *See also*
    ground covers; sheet mulch
  carbon to nitrogen (C:N) ratios, 65–66
  chicken tractor use, 135–36
  deep, 25, 81–82, 88, 136, 182, 185, 189–90
  materials for, 15, 71–73, 88
  moisture retained by, 81–82, 88, 185

soil temperature, effect on, 88, 117
mulch plants, 7, 107–108, 152, 167, 179, 184
multifunctional plants, 4, 99–120, 182, 187
  examples of, 102–107
  nurses, scaffolds, and chaperones, 117–20
  trees as, 99–102
  types of, 107–11
multipurpose gardens. *See* plant communities
Murphy, Tim, 156–58, 163
muskrats, 17–19
mustard, 76
  garlic, 172
  insects attracted by, 79, 129
  as mulch plant, 107
  in polyculture garden, 145, 147
  red, 111, 114
  roots, 78, 109
myrtle, wax, 164

N
nasturtium, 19, 107, 108, 151–53, 173
native plants, 8–9, 26, 38, 86, 113
  exotics *vs.*, 10–13
  guilds and, 147, 156–62
  North American, 12
Natural Habitat Garden, The (Druse), 8
nematodes, 108, 142
net garden patterns, 51–52
New Mexico, 13, 81, 118–19, 158, 187–88
niches, 18–19, 31, 143, 146, 184, 186
nitrates, 65, 71
nitrogen, 31, 64–66. *See also* carbon to nitrogen (C:N) ratio
  in compost pile, 68
nitrogen-fixing plants, 7, 35, 103, 107, 108, 184
  cover crops, 76–79
  in forest garden, 167, 172, 173, 174, 176–78

in guilds, 148–49, 153, 158, 163, 164
  as nurse plants, 118–19
  in polyculture gardens, 146
nurse plants, 117–20, 186–87
nutrient accumulating plants, 107–108, 117–20, 152–53, 184
nutrients, 22, 185–86
  in compost pile, 69, 70
  cover crops and, 75, 78
  in humus, 63–65
  tilling, effect of, 67–68
nut trees, 12, 19, 26, 38, 162–64, 173

O
oak, 132, 159–62
  Gambel's, 26
  multiple functions of, 99–102
oats, 76, 78, 79, 107
oca, 114
Occidental Arts and Ecology Center, 122
olive
  autumn, 22, 77, 78, 108
  Russian, 77, 108, 118–19, 158, 164, 172
onions, 26, 109, 142, 145
  in forest garden, 172
  perennial, 112, 152
orchard. *See* fruit trees; nut trees
oregano, 48, 49
Oregon, 91, 159–62, 188–89
organic matter, 22, 81–83. *See also* humus
osage orange, 6, 110
Osentowski, Jerome, 35, 171–72, 188, 193

P
Pacific madrone, 161
parasitic insects (parasitoids), 124, 146
parsley, 48, 49, 112
parsnip, 144, 145
partnerships. *See* connectedness

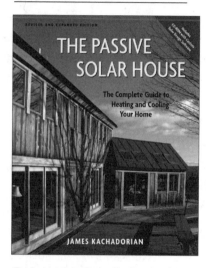

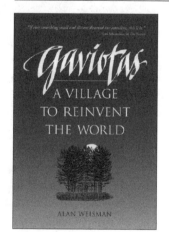

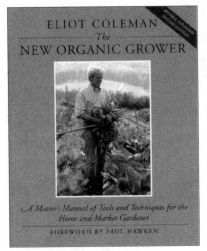